TOMARE!
[STOP!]

You are going the wrong way!

Manga is a completely different
type of reading experience.

To start at the *beginning*, go to the *end!*

That's right! Authentic manga is read the traditional Japanese
way—from right to left. Exactly the *opposite* of how American
books are read. It's easy to follow: Just go to the other end of
the book, and read each page—and each panel—from right side
to left side, ~~starting at the top right. Now you're~~ e experiencing
manga as it was meant to be.

LOVE ROMA

BY MINORU TOYODA

"We have been telling all the people we meet to read this manga!"
—CLAMP, creators of Tsubasa

A fun, romantic comedy, Love Roma is about the simple kind of relationships we all longed for when we were young. It's a story of love at first sight—literally. When Hoshino sees Negishi for the first time, he asks her to be his girlfriend. Shocked, Negishi nevertheless agrees to allow Hoshino to walk her home, while he explains why he is in love with her. Touched, Negishi begins to feel something for this strange young boy from her school.

Ages: 16+

Special extras in each volume! Read them all!

Akira Segami

TRANSLATED BY
Akira Tsubasa

ADAPTED BY
Nunzio DeFilippis & Christina Weir

LETTERED BY
Ryan & Reilly

BALLANTINE BOOKS · NEW YORK

Kagetora *volume 1* is a work of fiction. Names characters, place and incidents are the products of the author's imagination or are used fictitiously. Any resemblance to actual events locales or persons, living or dead, is entirely coincidental.

A Del Rey Books Trade Paperback Edition

Published in the United States by Del Rey Books, an imprint of The Random House Publishing Group, a division of Random House, Inc,. New York.

Del Rey is a registered trademark and the Del Rey colophon is a trademark of Random House, Inc.

Publication rights arranged through Kodansha Ltd.
First published in Japan in 2003 by Kodansha Ltd., Tokyo

Library of Congress Control Number can be obtained from the publisher upon request.

ISBN 0-345-49141-6

Printed in the United States of America

www.delreymanga.com

9 8 7 6 5 4 3

Translator—Akira Tsubasa
Adaptor—Nunzio DeFilippis & Christina Weir
Letterer—Ryan & Reilly Design

A Note from the Author

It got stuck.

Because of my love for historical themes, after many complications, I've decided to write a ninja romantic comedy manga (laugh). I sincerely hope you'll enjoy this series.

Segami

Honorifics

Throughout the Del Rey Manga books, you will find Japanese honorifics left intact in the translations. For those not familiar with how the Japanese use honorifics and, more important, how they differ from American honorifics, we present this brief overview.

Politeness has always been a critical facet of Japanese culture. Ever since the feudal era, when Japan was a highly stratified society, use of honorifics—which can be defined as polite speech that indicates relationship or status—has played an essential role in the Japanese language. When addressing someone in Japanese, an honorific usually takes the form of a suffix attached to one's name (example: "Asuna-san"), or as a title at the end of one's name or in place of the name itself (example: "Negi-sensei," or simply "Sensei!").

Honorifics can be expressions of respect or endearment. In the context of manga and anime, honorifics give insight into the nature of the relationship between characters. Many translations into English leave out these important honorifics, and therefore distort the "feel" of the original Japanese. Because Japanese honorifics contain nuances that English honorifics lack, it is our policy at Del Rey not to translate them. Here, instead, is a guide to some of the honorifics you may encounter in Del Rey Manga.

-san: This is the most common honorific and is equivalent to Mr., Miss, Ms., or Mrs. It is the all-purpose honorific and can be used in any situation where politeness is required.

-sama: This is one level higher than "-san." It is used to confer great respect.

-dono: This comes from the word "tono," which means "lord." It is an even higher level than "-sama" and confers utmost respect.

-kun: This suffix is used at the end of boys' names to express familiarity or endearment. It is also sometimes used by men among friends, or when addressing someone younger or of a lower station.

-chan: This is used to express endearment, mostly toward girls. It is also used for little boys, pets, and even among lovers. It gives a sense of childish cuteness.

Bozu: This is an informal way to refer to a boy, similar to the English term "kid" or "squirt."

Sempai/Senpai: This title suggests that the addressee is one's senior in a group or organization. It is most often used in a school setting, where underclassmen refer to their upperclassmen as "sempai." It can also be used in the workplace, such as when a newer employee addresses an employee who has seniority in the company.

Kohai: This is the opposite of "sempai" and is used toward underclassmen in school or newcomers in the workplace. It connotes that the addressee is of a lower station.

Sensei: Literally meaning "one who has come before," this title is used for teachers, doctors, or masters of any profession or art.

[blank]: Usually forgotten in these lists, but perhaps the most significant difference between Japanese and English. The lack of honorific means that the speaker has permission to address the person in a very intimate way. Usually, only family, spouses, or very close friends have this kind of permission. Known as *yobisute*, it can be gratifying when someone who has earned the intimacy starts to call one by one's name without an honorific. But when that intimacy hasn't been earned, it can also be very insulting.

KAGETORA

カゲトラ

瀬上(せがみ)あきら

1

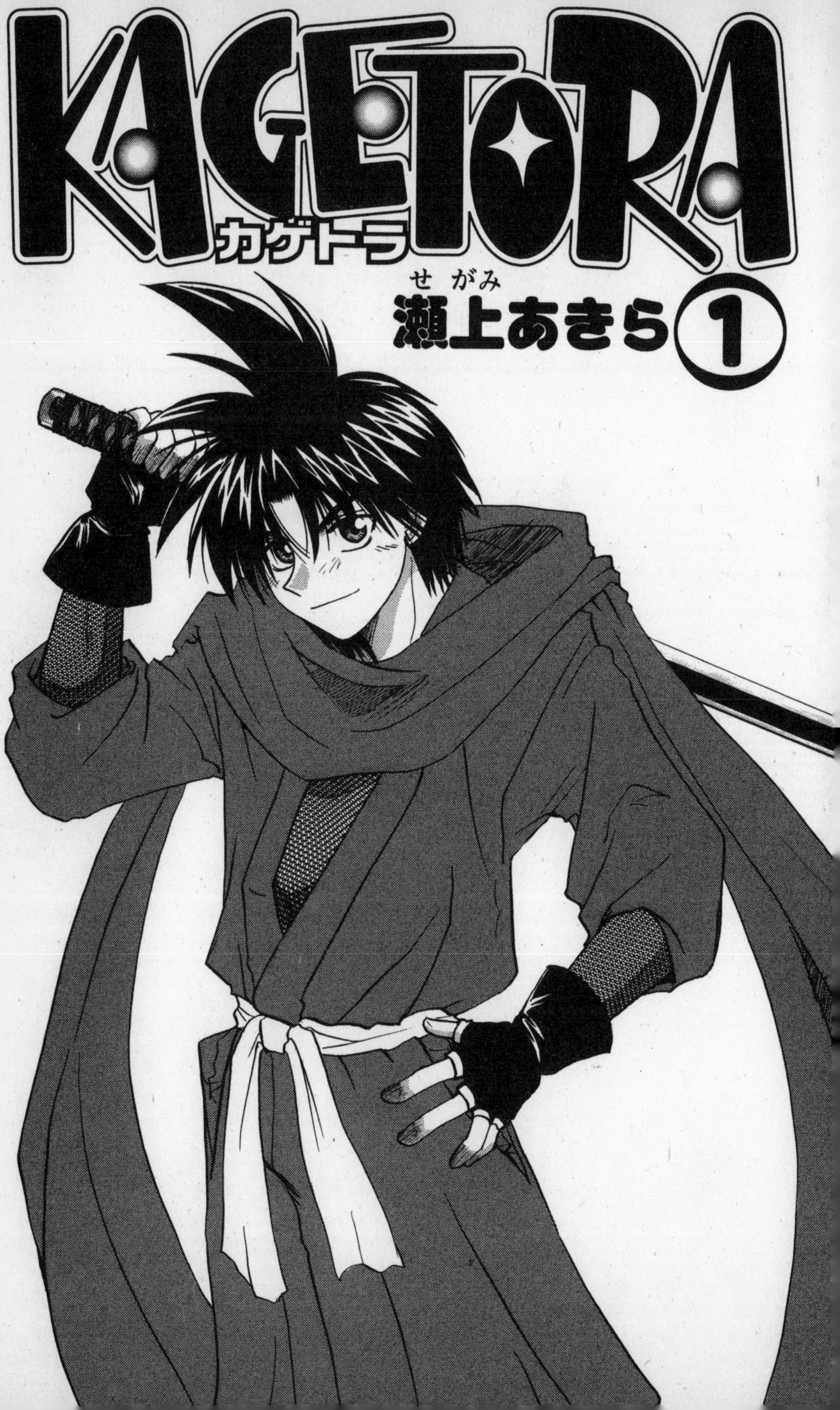

CONTENTS

KAGETORA

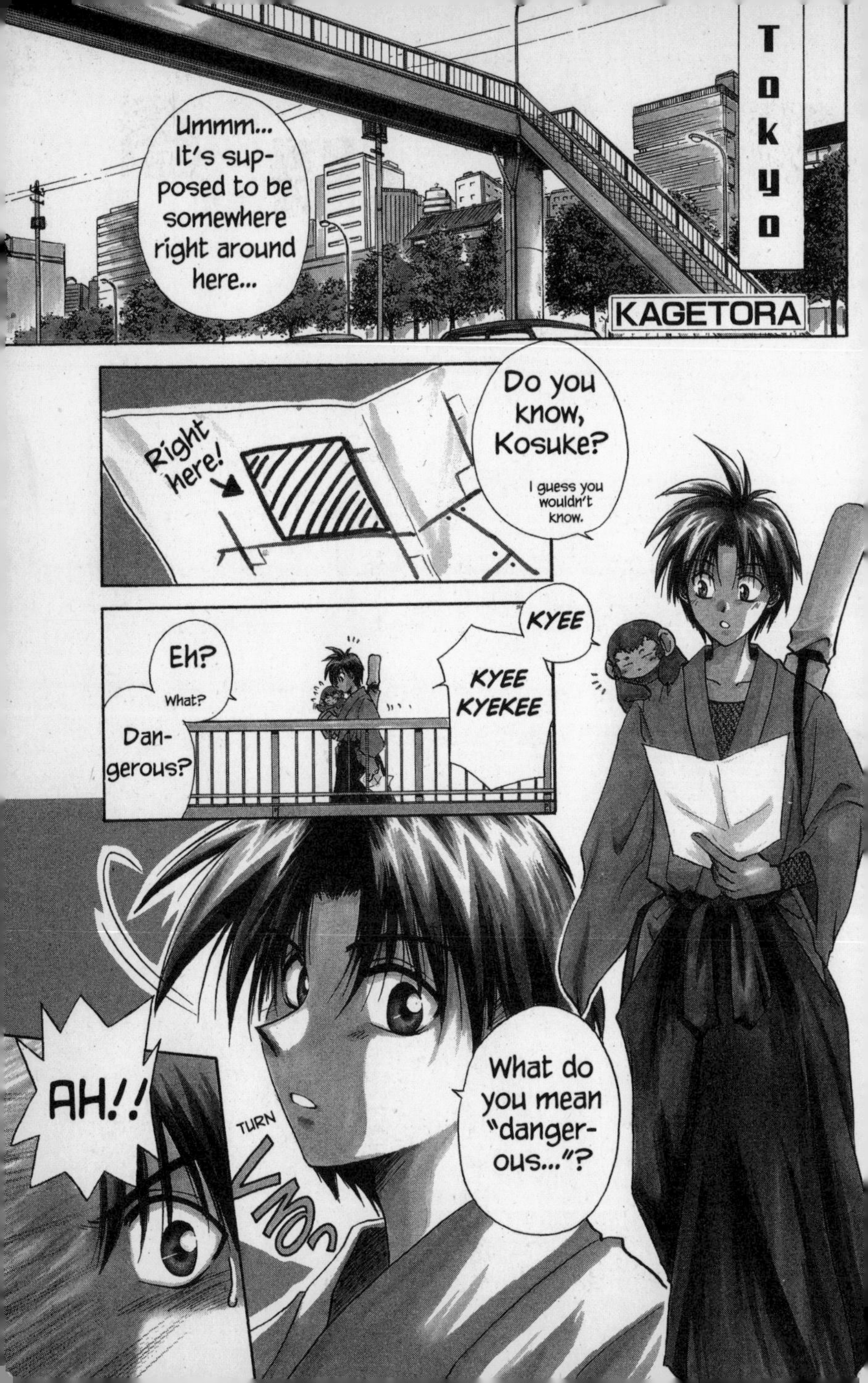

Tokyo
KAGETORA
Ummm... It's supposed to be somewhere right around here...
Do you know, Kosuke?
I guess you wouldn't know.
Right here!
KYEE
KYEE KYEKEE
Eh?
What?
Dangerous?
What do you mean "dangerous..."?
TURN
AH!!

1 Inappropriate Instructor

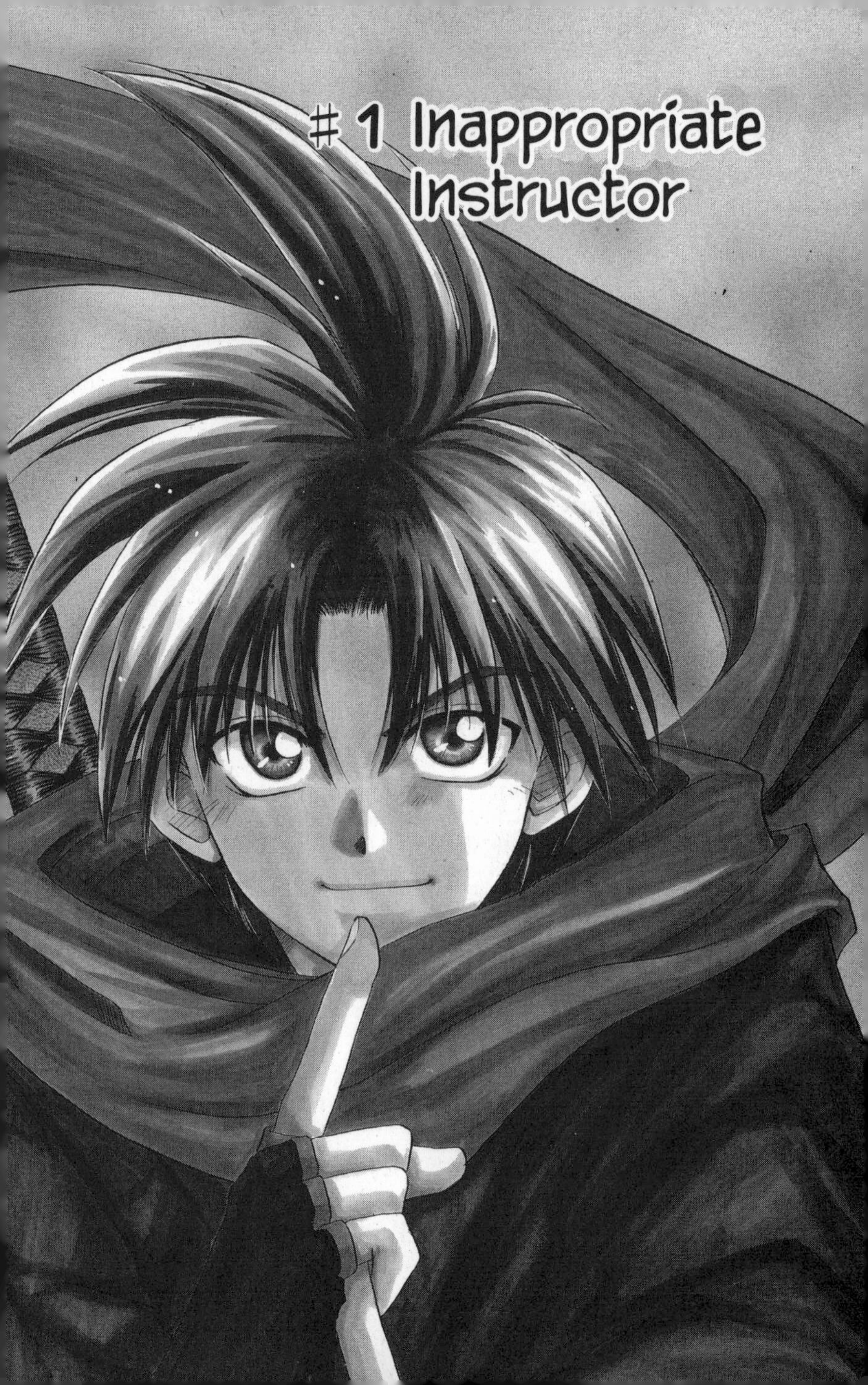

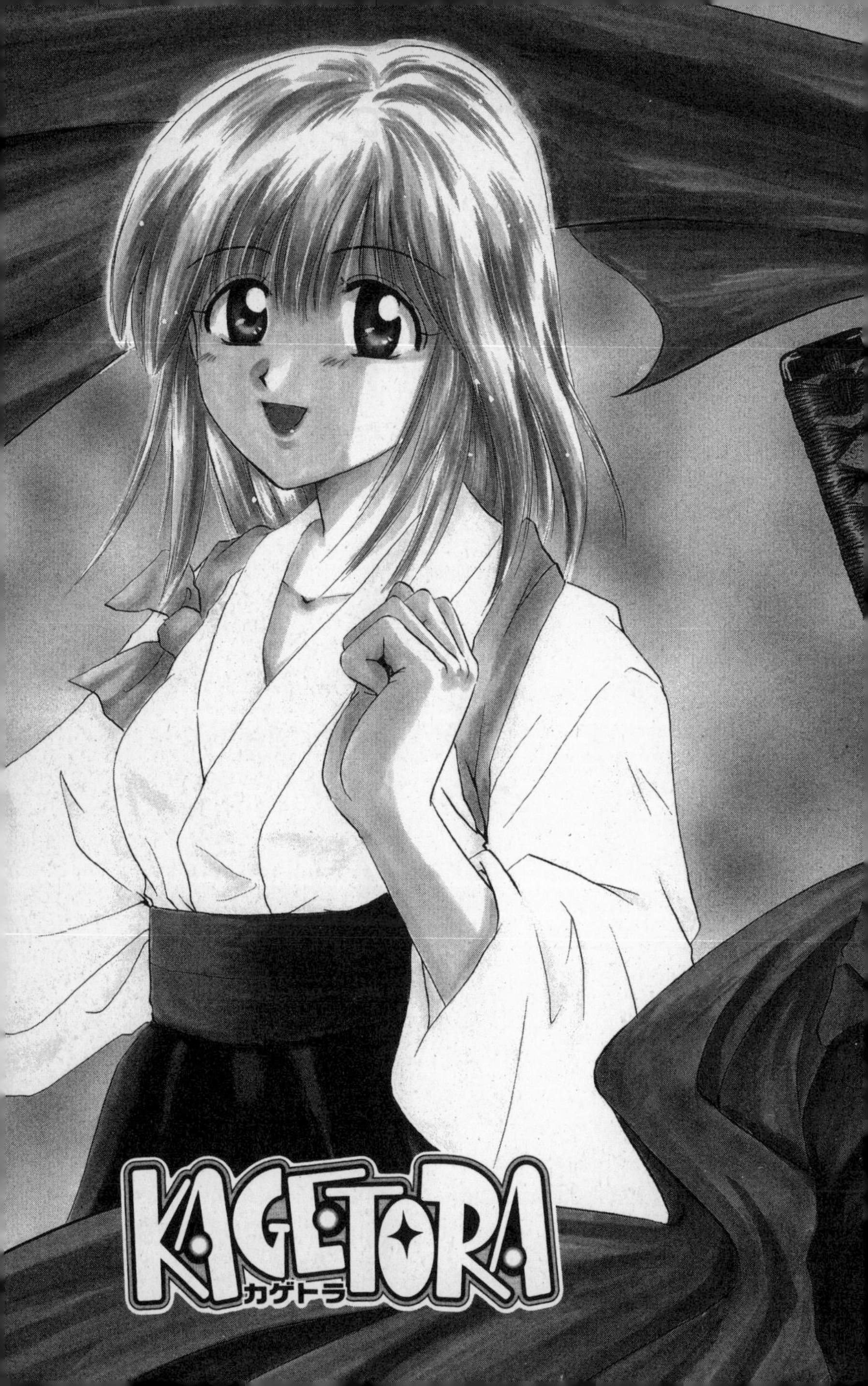
KAGETORA
カゲトラ

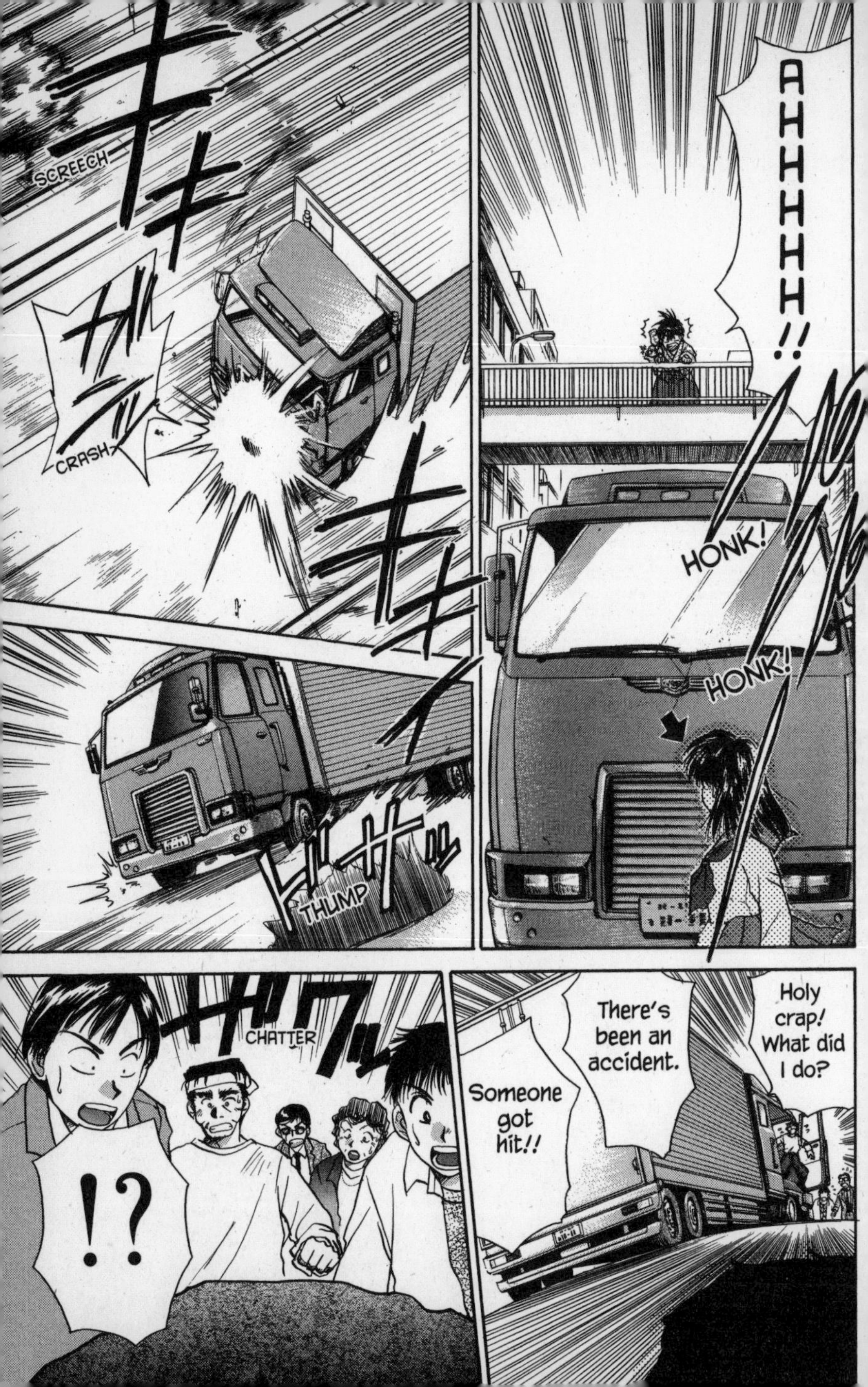
AHHHHH!!
HONK!
HONK!
SCREECH
CRASH
THUMP
Holy crap! What did I do?
There's been an accident.
Someone got hit!!
CHATTER
!?

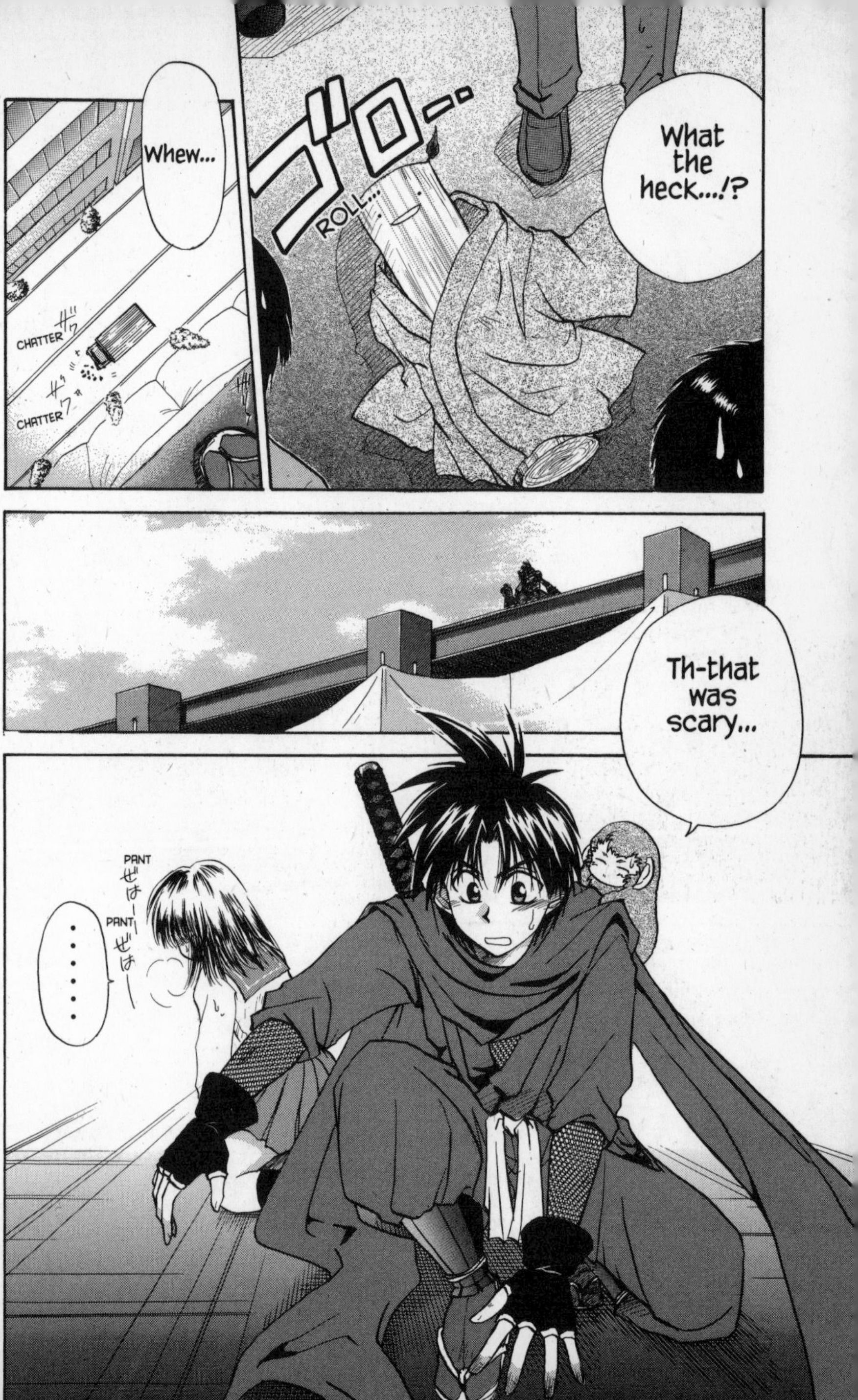
What the heck...!?
ゴロー
ROLL...
Whew...
ザワ
CHATTER
ザワ
CHATTER
Th-that was scary...
PANT
ぜはー
PANT
ぜはー
......

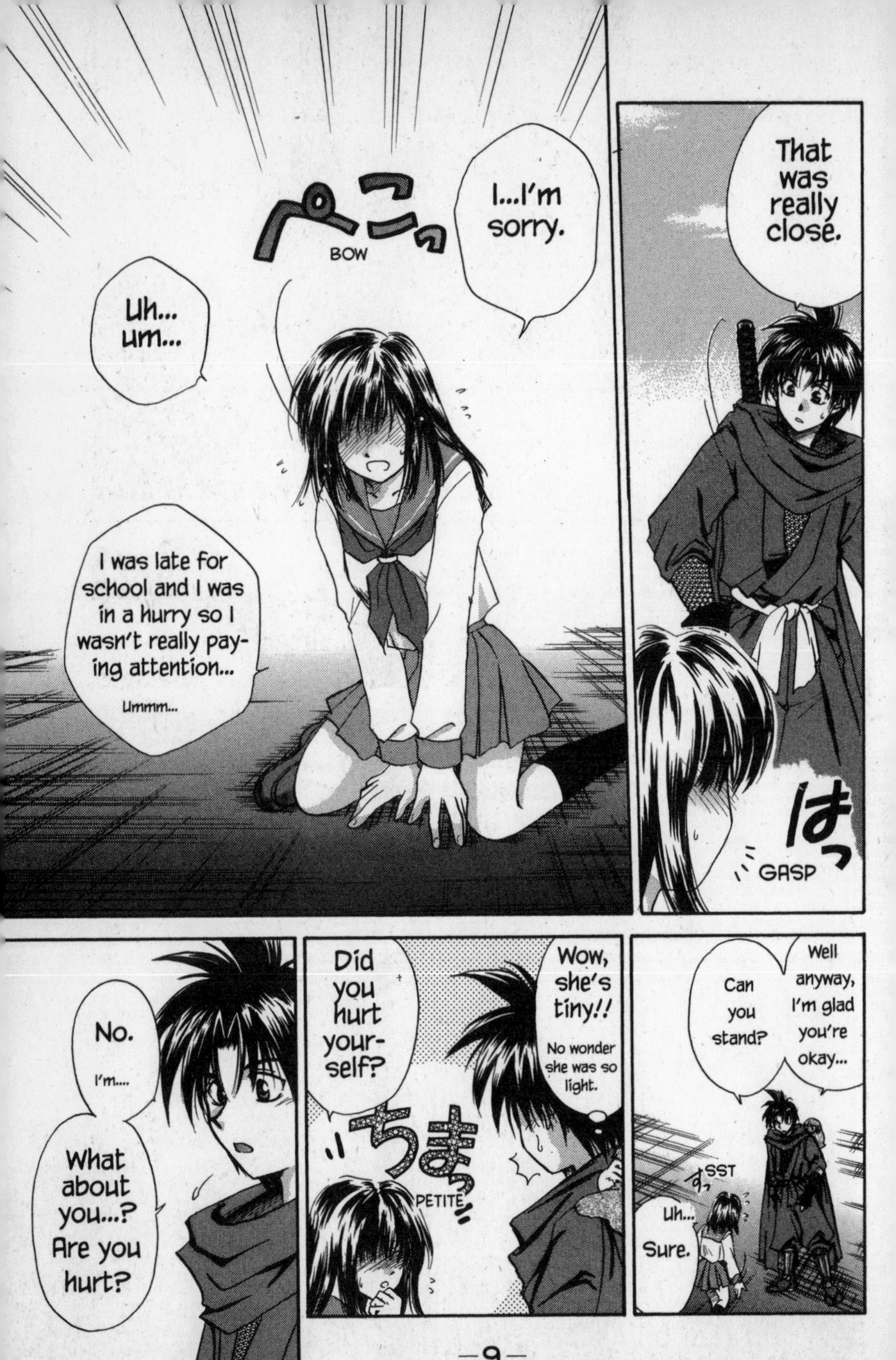
That was really close.
はっ
GASP
I...I'm sorry.
ぺこっ
BOW
Uh... um...
I was late for school and I was in a hurry so I wasn't really paying attention...
Ummm...
Well anyway, I'm glad you're okay...
Can you stand?
すっ
SST
Uh... Sure.
Wow, she's tiny!!
No wonder she was so light.
Did you hurt yourself?
ちまっ
PETITE
No.
I'm....
What about you...? Are you hurt?

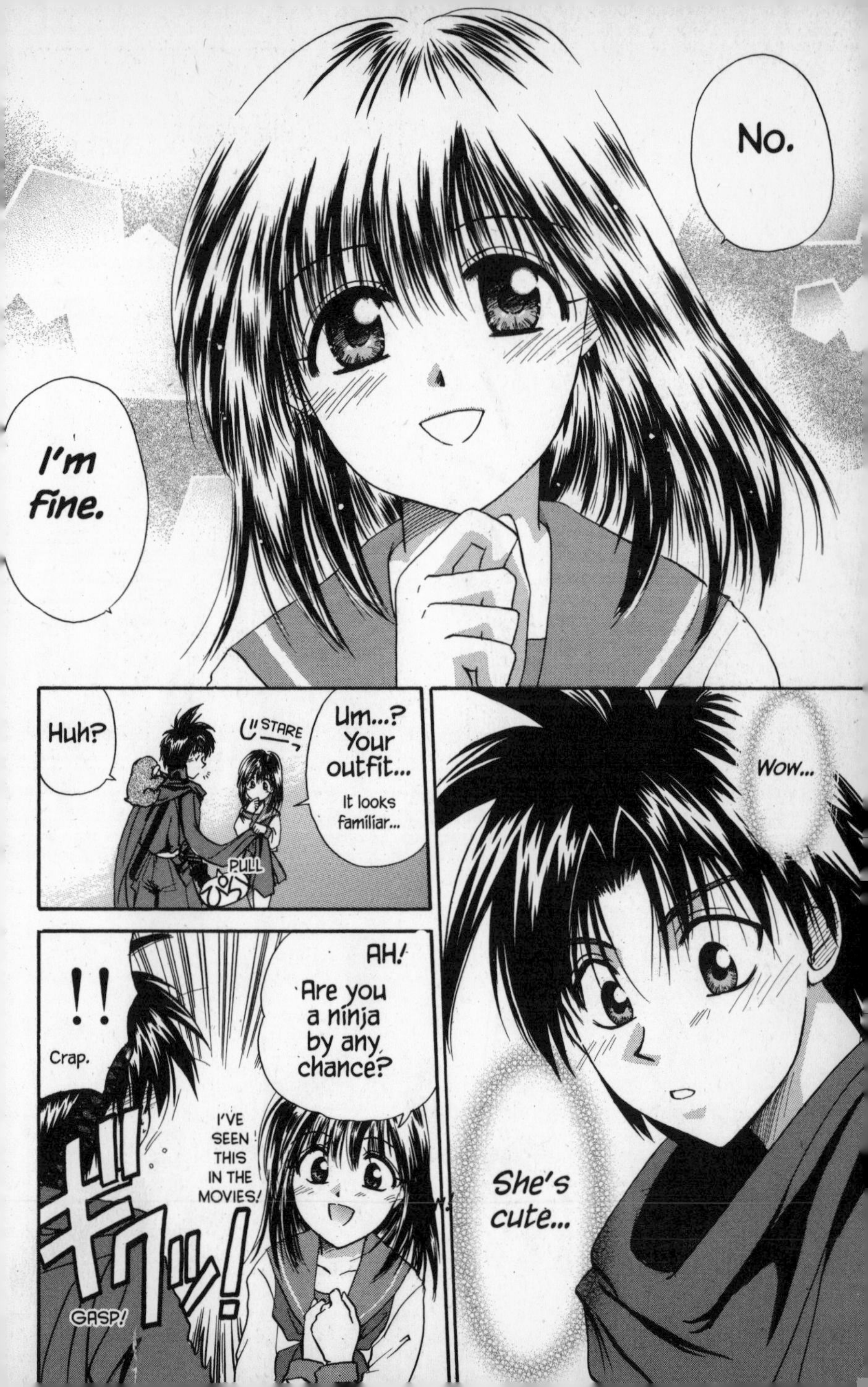
No.
I'm fine.
Wow...
She's cute...
Um...? Your outfit...
It looks familiar...
STARE
PULL
Huh?
AH! Are you a ninja by any chance?
I'VE SEEN THIS IN THE MOVIES!
!!
Crap.
ギクッ!
GASP!

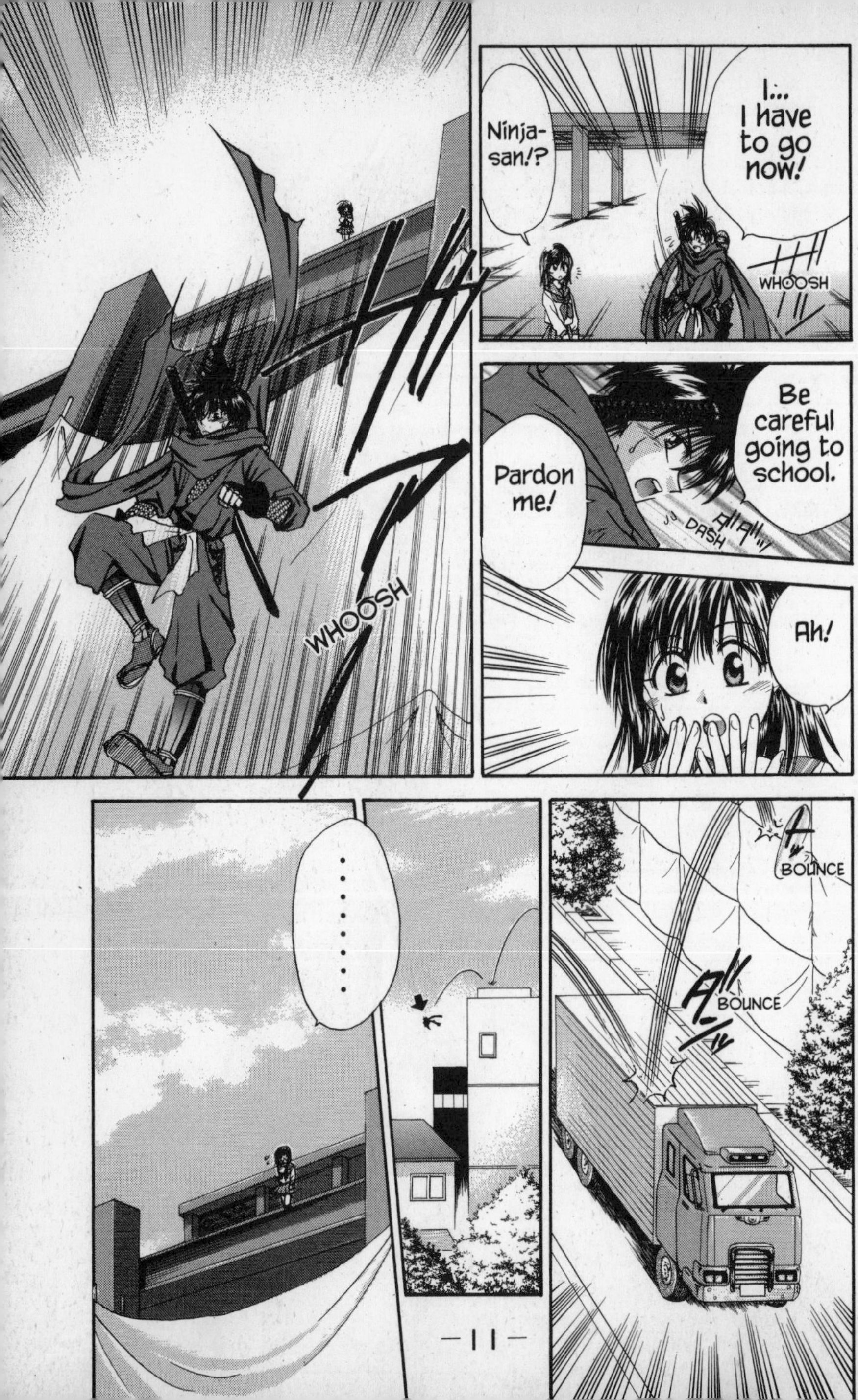
I... I have to go now!
Ninja-san!?
WHOOSH
Be careful going to school.
Pardon me!
DASH
Ah!
WHOOSH
BOUNCE
BOUNCE
......

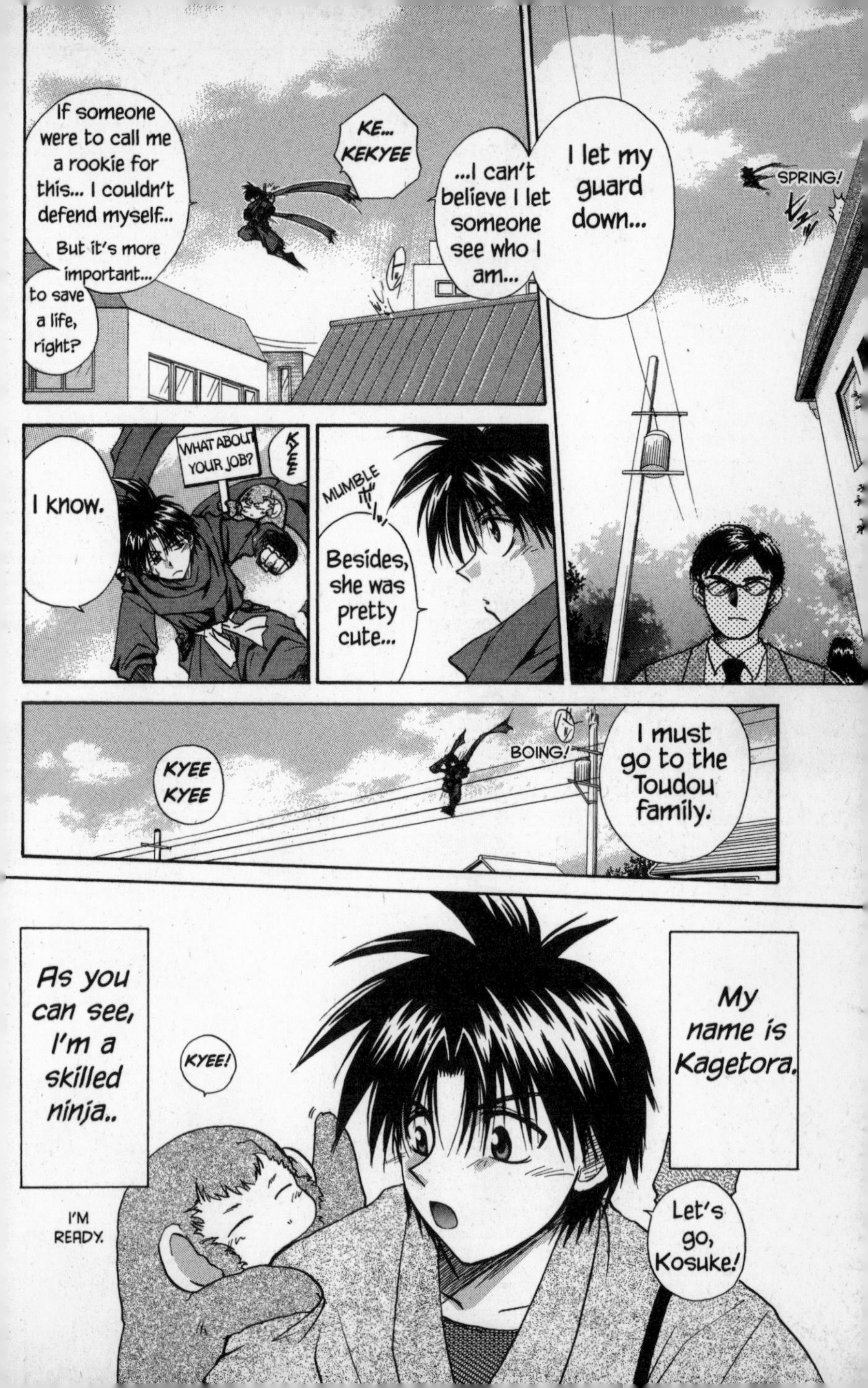
SPRING!
I let my guard down...
...I can't believe I let someone see who I am...
KE... KEKYEE
If someone were to call me a rookie for this... I couldn't defend myself...
But it's more important...
to save a life, right?
MUMBLE
Besides, she was pretty cute...
KYEE
WHAT ABOUT YOUR JOB?
I know.
I must go to the Toudou family.
BOING!
KYEE KYEE
My name is Kagetora.
Let's go, Kosuke!
As you can see, I'm a skilled ninja..
KYEE!
I'M READY.

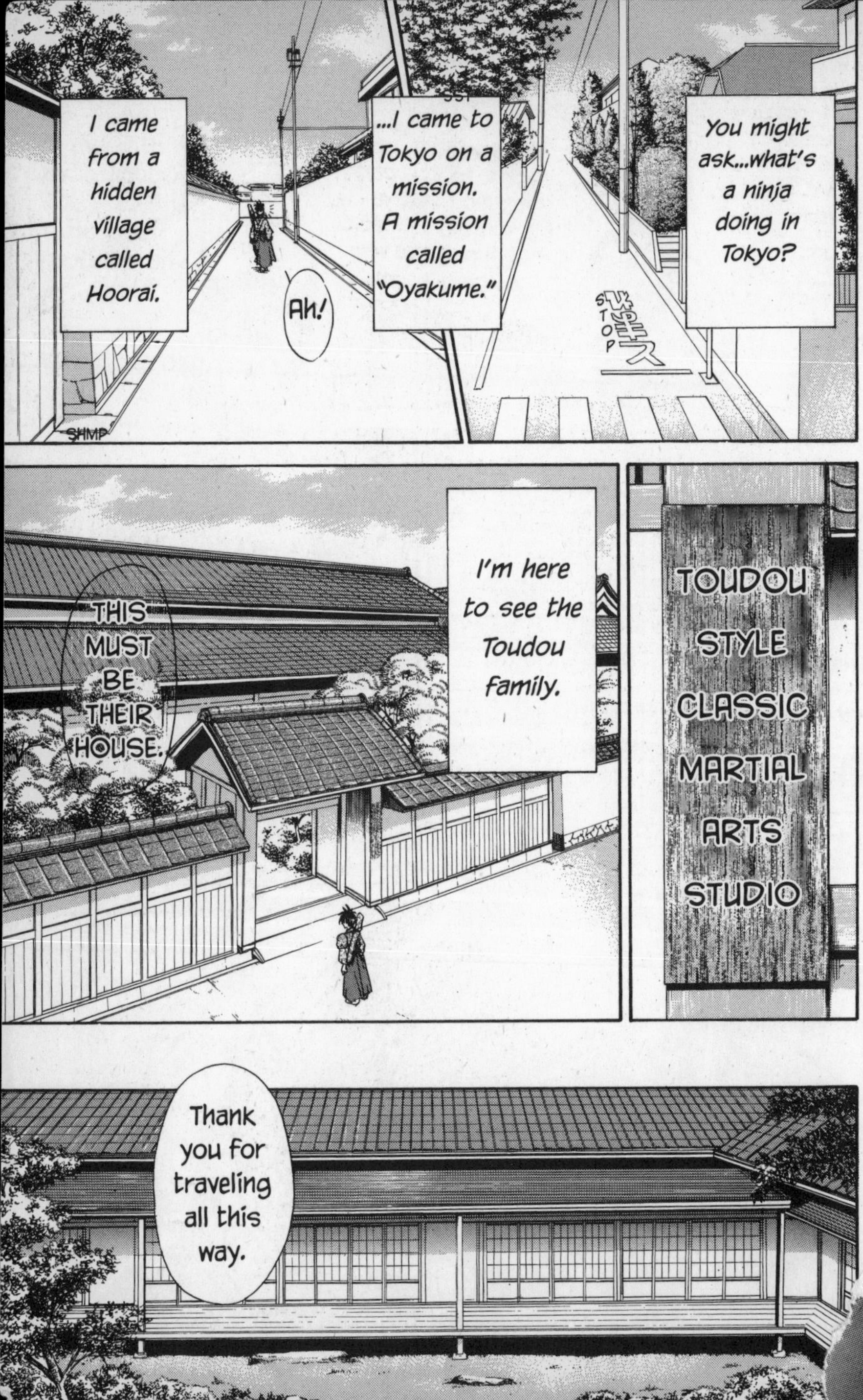
You might ask...what's a ninja doing in Tokyo?
STOP
...I came to Tokyo on a mission. A mission called "Oyakume."
Ah!
I came from a hidden village called Hoorai.
SHMP
TOUDOU STYLE CLASSIC MARTIAL ARTS STUDIO
I'm here to see the Toudou family.
THIS MUST BE THEIR HOUSE.
Thank you for traveling all this way.

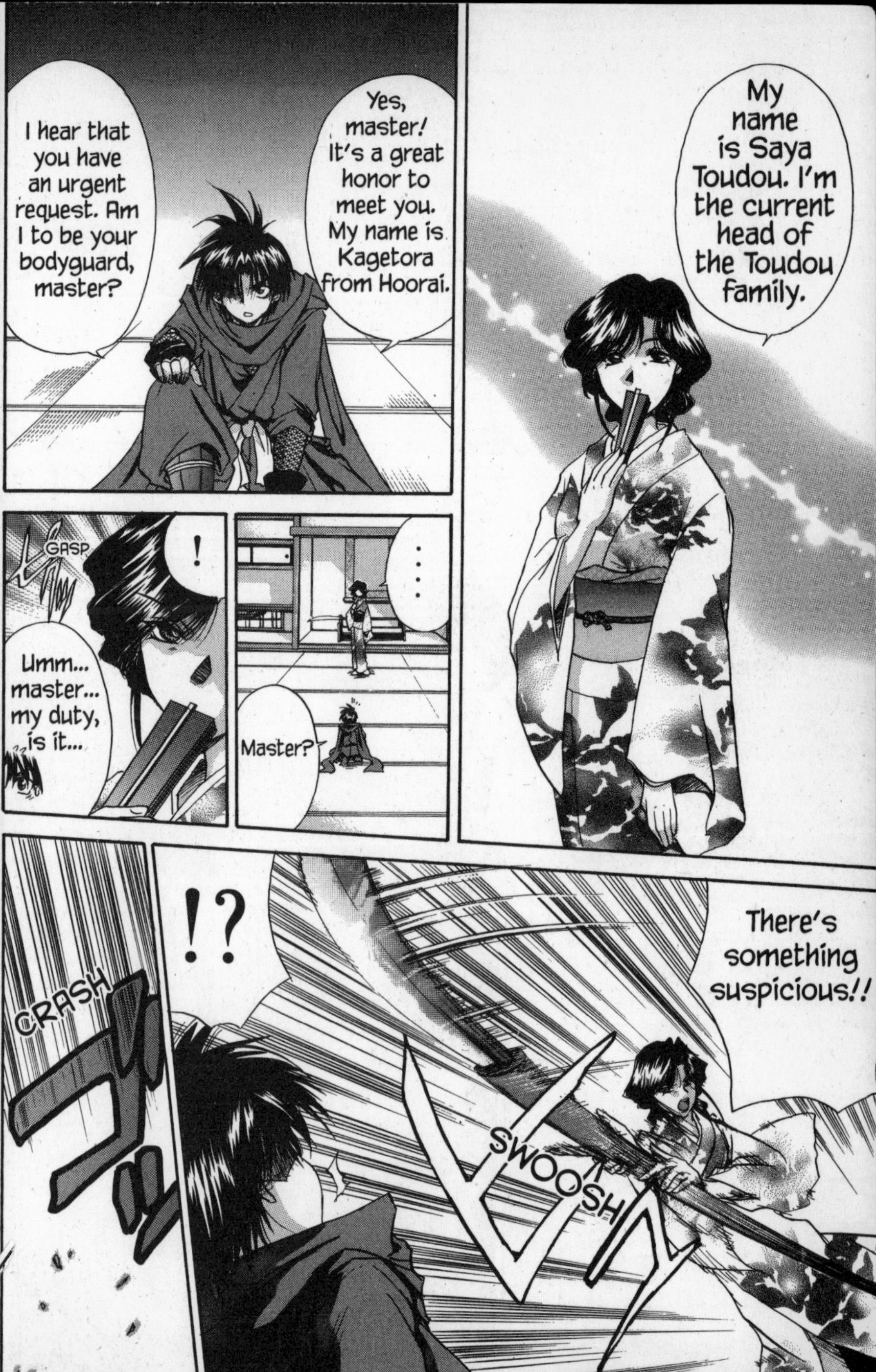
My name is Saya Toudou. I'm the current head of the Toudou family.
Yes, master! It's a great honor to meet you. My name is Kagetora from Hoorai.
I hear that you have an urgent request. Am I to be your bodyguard, master?
....
Master?
GASP
!
Umm... master... my duty, is it...
There's something suspicious!!
SWOOSH
!?
CRASH

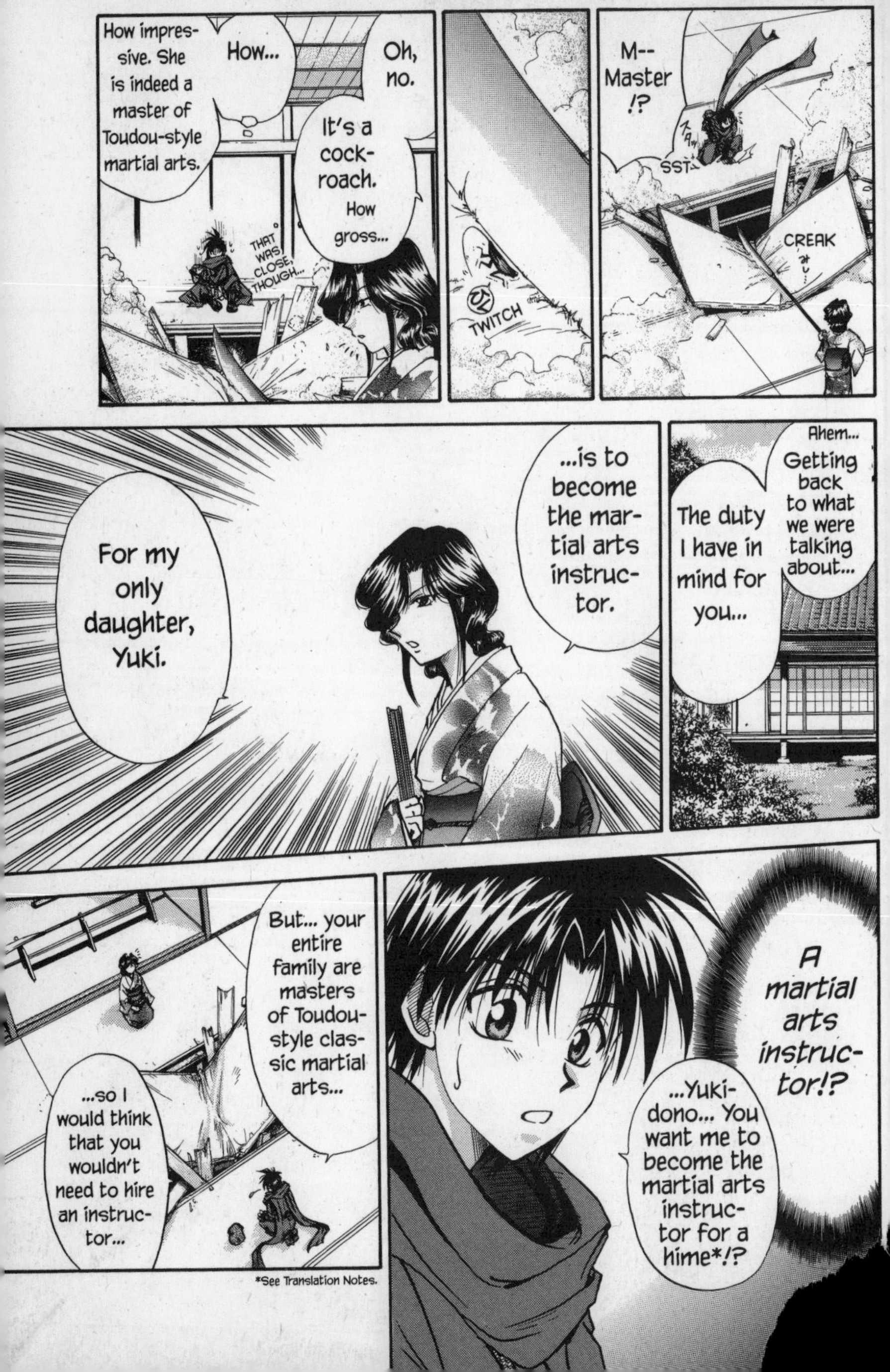
M-- Master !?
SST
CREAK
TWITCH
Oh, no.
It's a cockroach.
How gross...
How...
How impressive. She is indeed a master of Toudou-style martial arts.
THAT WAS CLOSE, THOUGH...
Ahem... Getting back to what we were talking about...
The duty I have in mind for you...
...is to become the martial arts instructor.
For my only daughter, Yuki.
A martial arts instructor!?
...Yuki-dono... You want me to become the martial arts instructor for a hime*!?
But... your entire family are masters of Toudou-style classic martial arts...
...so I would think that you wouldn't need to hire an instructor...

*See Translation Notes.

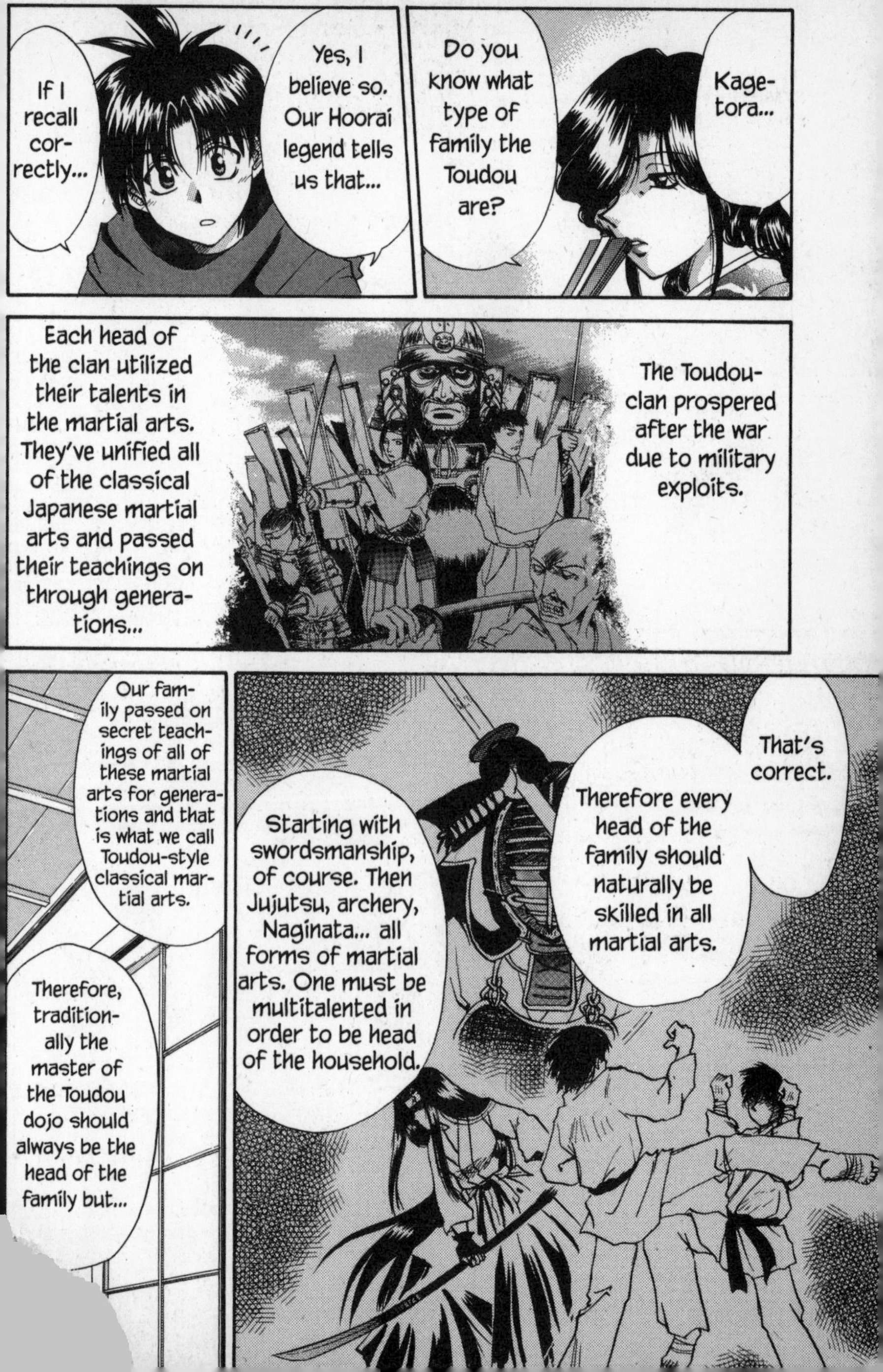
Kagetora...
Do you know what type of family the Toudou are?
Yes, I believe so. Our Hoorai legend tells us that...
If I recall correctly...
The Toudou-clan prospered after the war due to military exploits.
Each head of the clan utilized their talents in the martial arts. They've unified all of the classical Japanese martial arts and passed their teachings on through generations...
That's correct.
Therefore every head of the family should naturally be skilled in all martial arts.
Starting with swordsmanship, of course. Then Jujutsu, archery, Naginata... all forms of martial arts. One must be multitalented in order to be head of the household.
Our family passed on secret teachings of all of these martial arts for generations and that is what we call Toudou-style classical martial arts.
Therefore, traditionally the master of the Toudou dojo should always be the head of the family but...

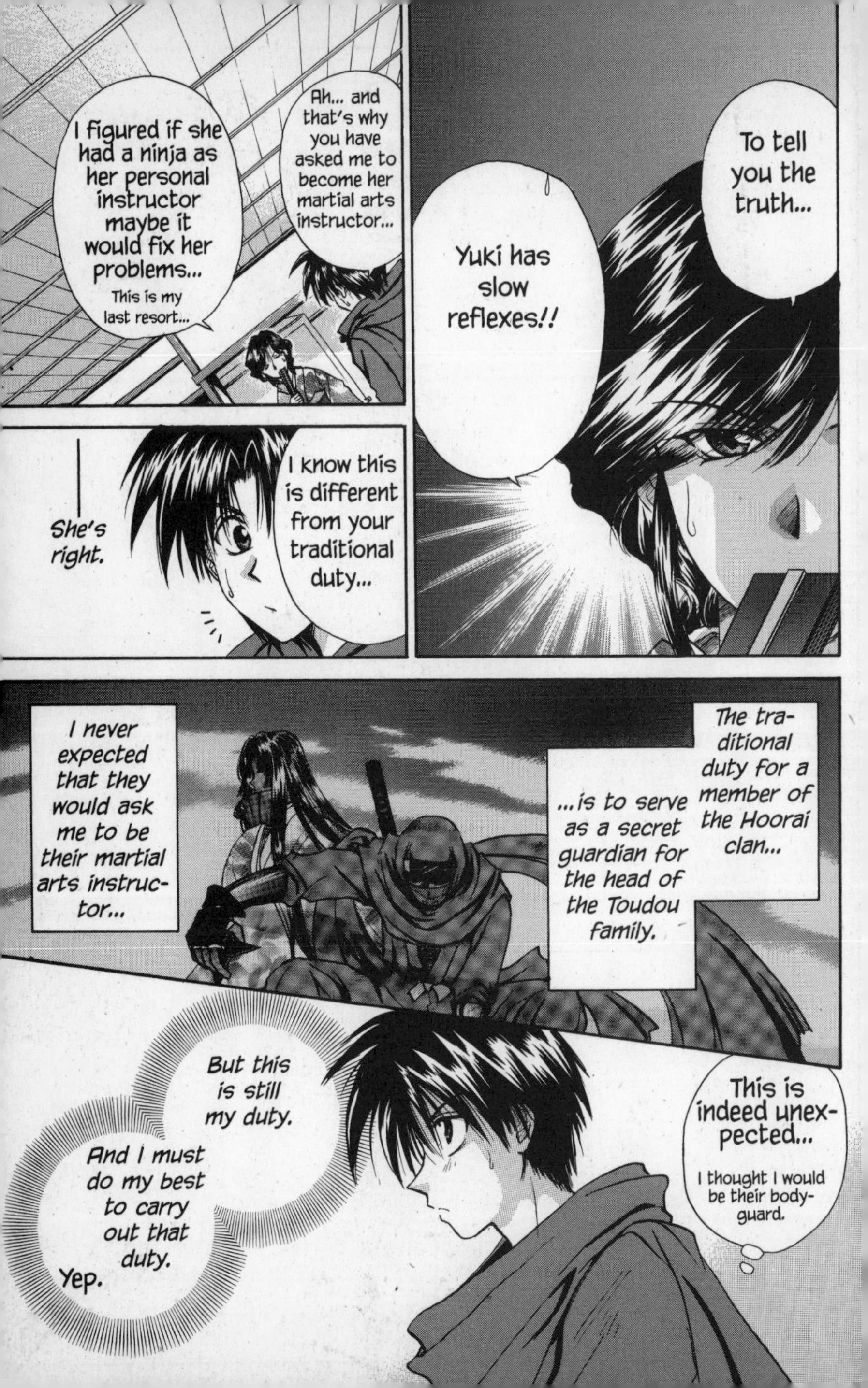
To tell you the truth...
Yuki has slow reflexes!!
Ah... and that's why you have asked me to become her martial arts instructor...
I figured if she had a ninja as her personal instructor maybe it would fix her problems...
This is my last resort...
I know this is different from your traditional duty...
She's right.
The tra-ditional duty for a member of the Hoorai clan...
...is to serve as a secret guardian for the head of the Toudou family.
I never expected that they would ask me to be their martial arts instruc-tor...
This is indeed unex-pected...
I thought I would be their body-guard.
But this is still my duty.
And I must do my best to carry out that duty.
Yep.

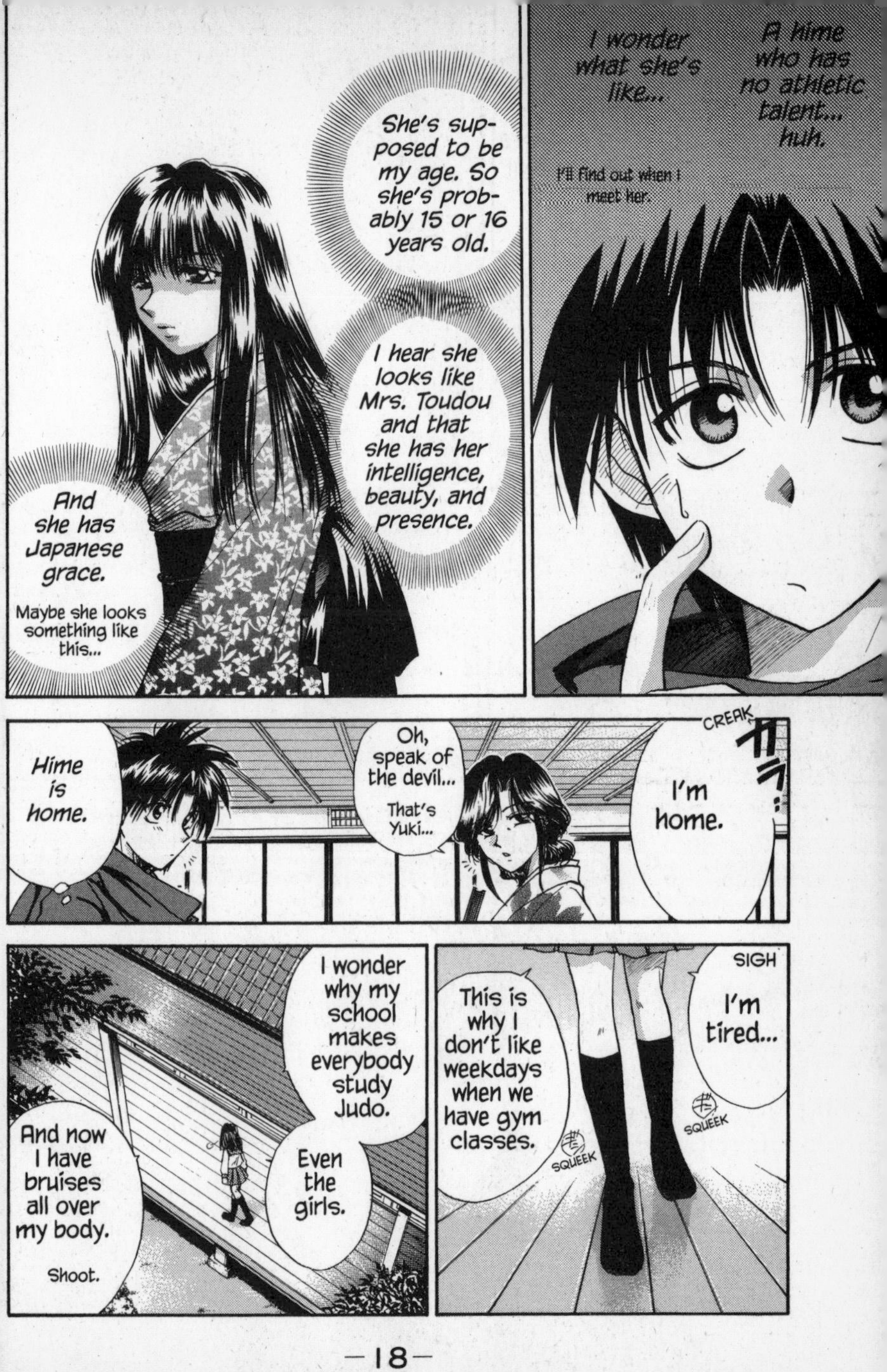
A hime who has no athletic talent... huh.
I wonder what she's like...
I'll find out when I meet her.
She's sup-posed to be my age. So she's prob-ably 15 or 16 years old.
I hear she looks like Mrs. Toudou and that she has her intelligence, beauty, and presence.
And she has Japanese grace.
Maybe she looks something like this...
CREAK
I'm home.
Oh, speak of the devil...
That's Yuki...
Hime is home.
SIGH
I'm tired...
SQUEEK
This is why I don't like weekdays when we have gym classes.
SQUEEK
I wonder why my school makes everybody study Judo.
Even the girls.
And now I have bruises all over my body.
Shoot.

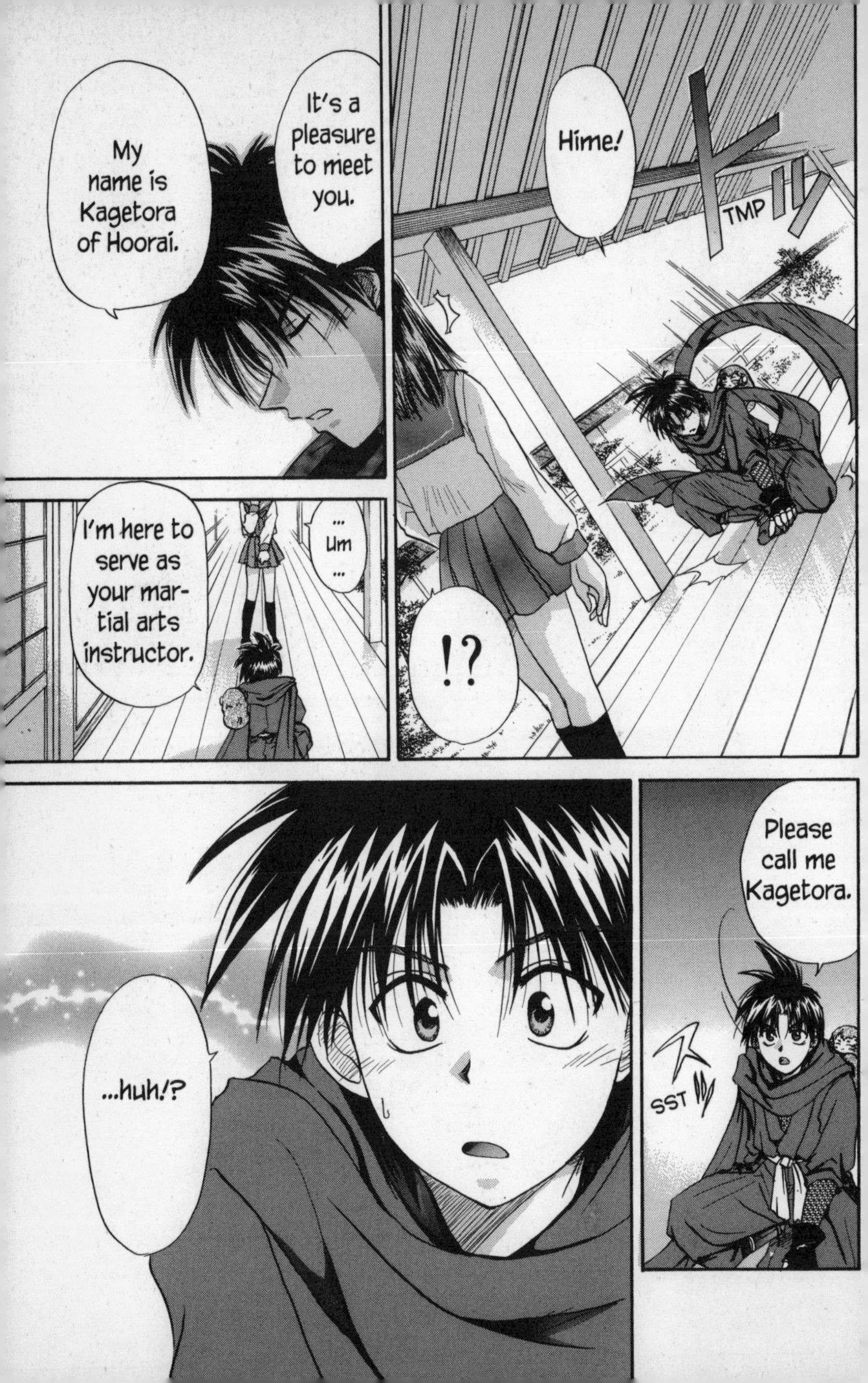
Hime!
TMP
!?
It's a pleasure to meet you.
My name is Kagetora of Hoorai.
... um ...
I'm here to serve as your martial arts instructor.
Please call me Kagetora.
SST
...huh!?

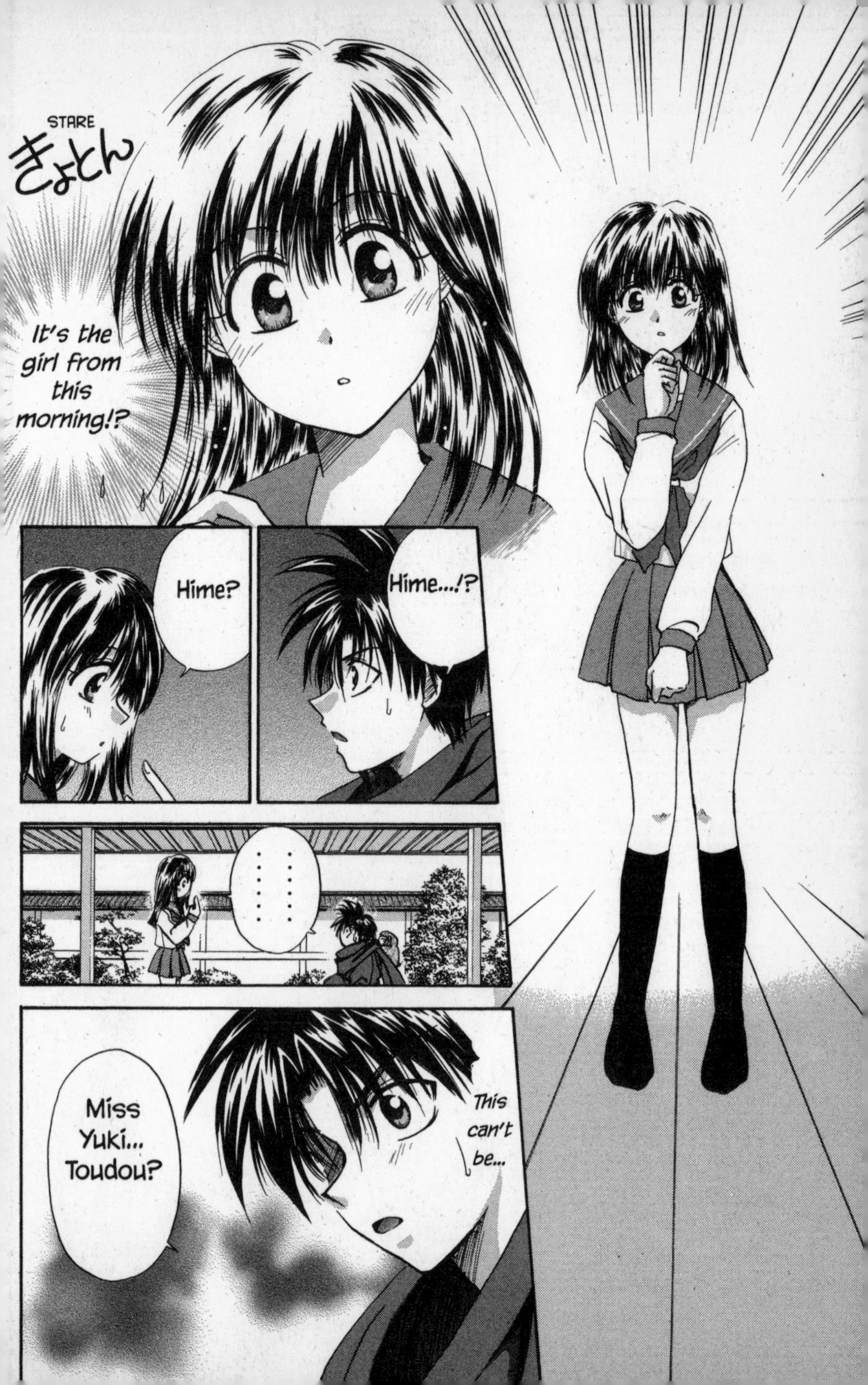
STARE
きょとん
It's the girl from this morning!?
Hime...!?
Hime?
......
This can't be...
Miss Yuki... Toudou?

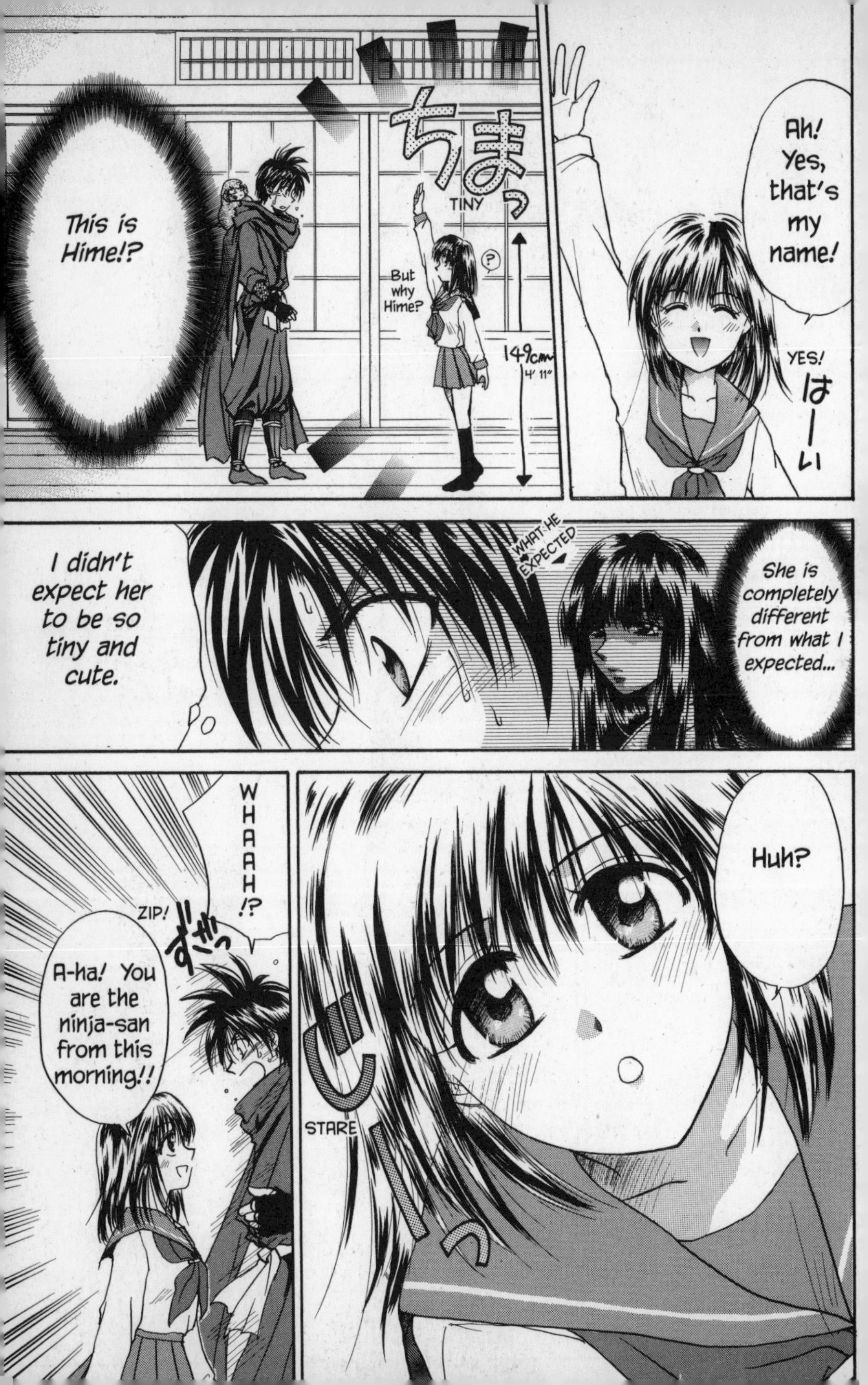
Ah! Yes, that's my name!
YES!
はーい
ちまっ
TINY
But why Hime?
149cm
4' 11"
This is Hime!?
She is completely different from what I expected...
WHAT HE EXPECTED
I didn't expect her to be so tiny and cute.
Huh?
じーっ
STARE
WHAAAH!?
ZIP!
ずざっ
A-ha! You are the ninja-san from this morning!!

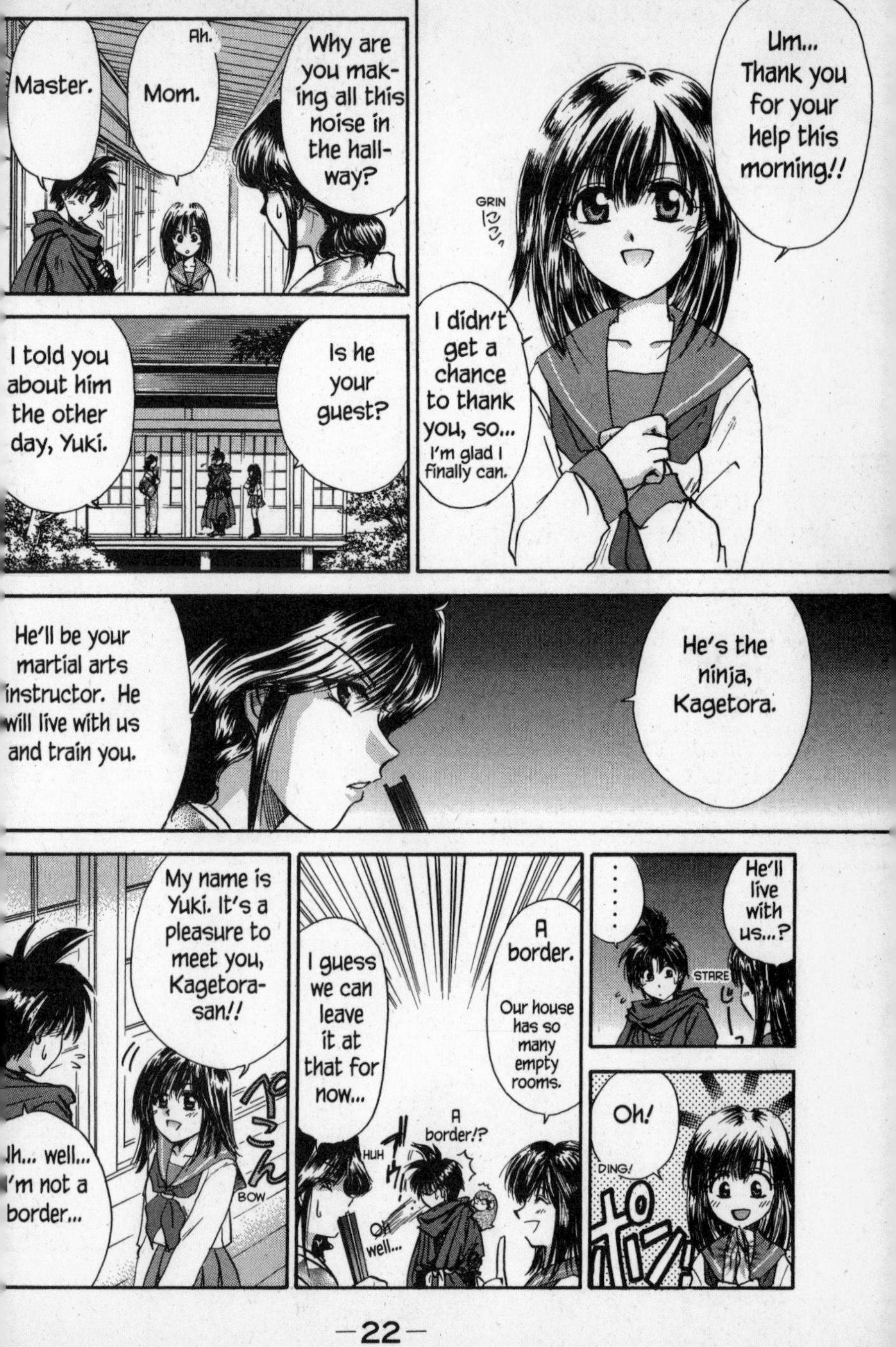
Um... Thank you for your help this morning!!
GRIN
I didn't get a chance to thank you, so... I'm glad I finally can.
Why are you making all this noise in the hallway?
Ah.
Mom.
Master.
Is he your guest?
I told you about him the other day, Yuki.
He's the ninja, Kagetora.
He'll be your martial arts instructor. He will live with us and train you.
He'll live with us...?
STARE
......
Oh!
DING!
A border.
Our house has so many empty rooms.
I guess we can leave it at that for now...
A border!?
HUH
Oh well...
My name is Yuki. It's a pleasure to meet you, Kagetora-san!!
BOW
h... well... 'm not a border...

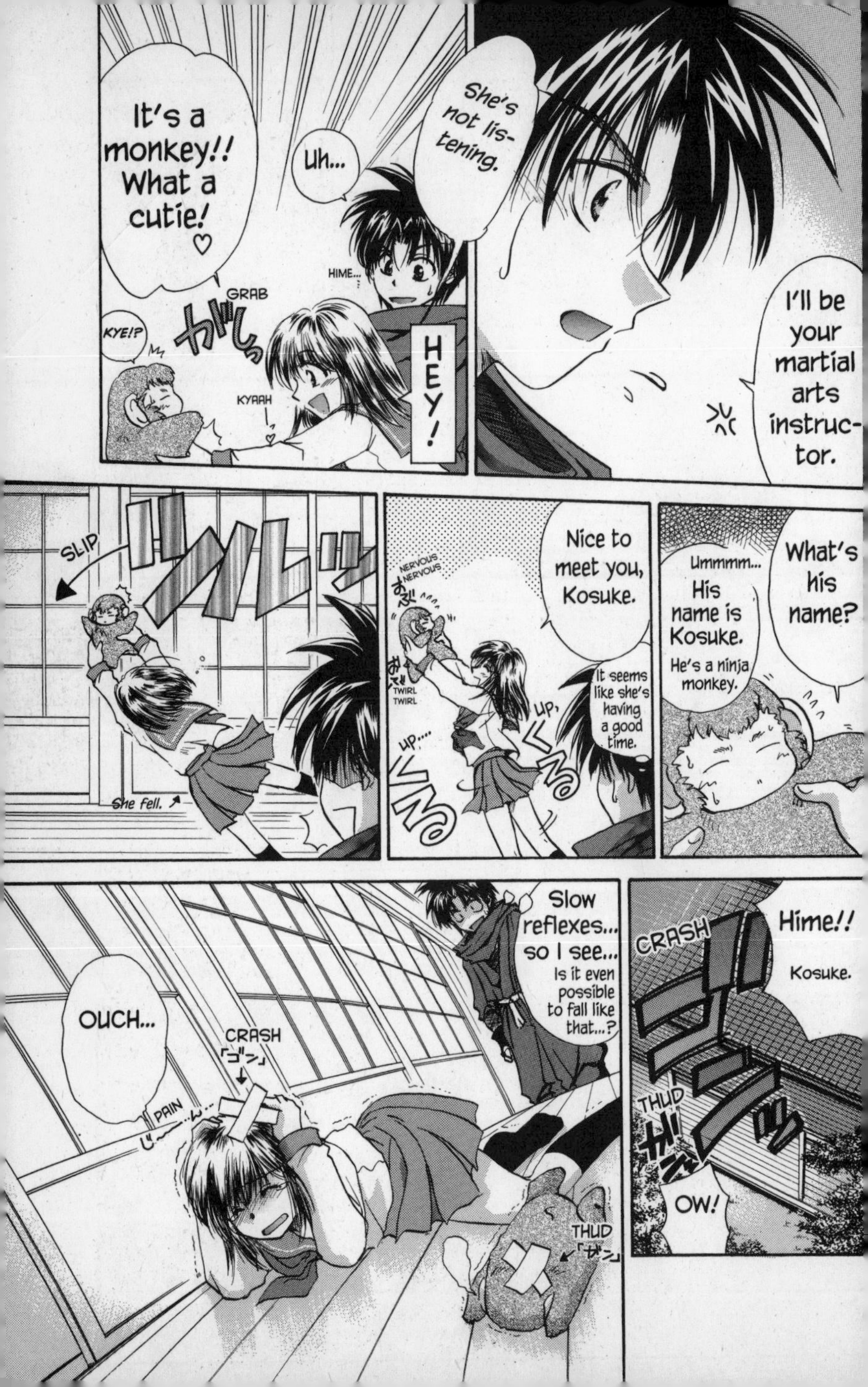
I'll be your martial arts instructor.
She's not lis-tening.
Uh...
It's a monkey!! What a cutie! ♡
HIME...
HEY!
GRAB
KYE!?
KYAAH
What's his name?
Ummmm...
His name is Kosuke.
He's a ninja monkey.
Nice to meet you, Kosuke.
It seems like she's having a good time.
up,
up....
NERVOUS NERVOUS
TWIRL TWIRL
SLIP
She fell.
Hime!!
Kosuke.
CRASH
THUD
OW!
Slow reflexes... so I see...
Is it even possible to fall like that...?
OUCH...
CRASH
「ゴン」
PAIN
THUD
「ガン」

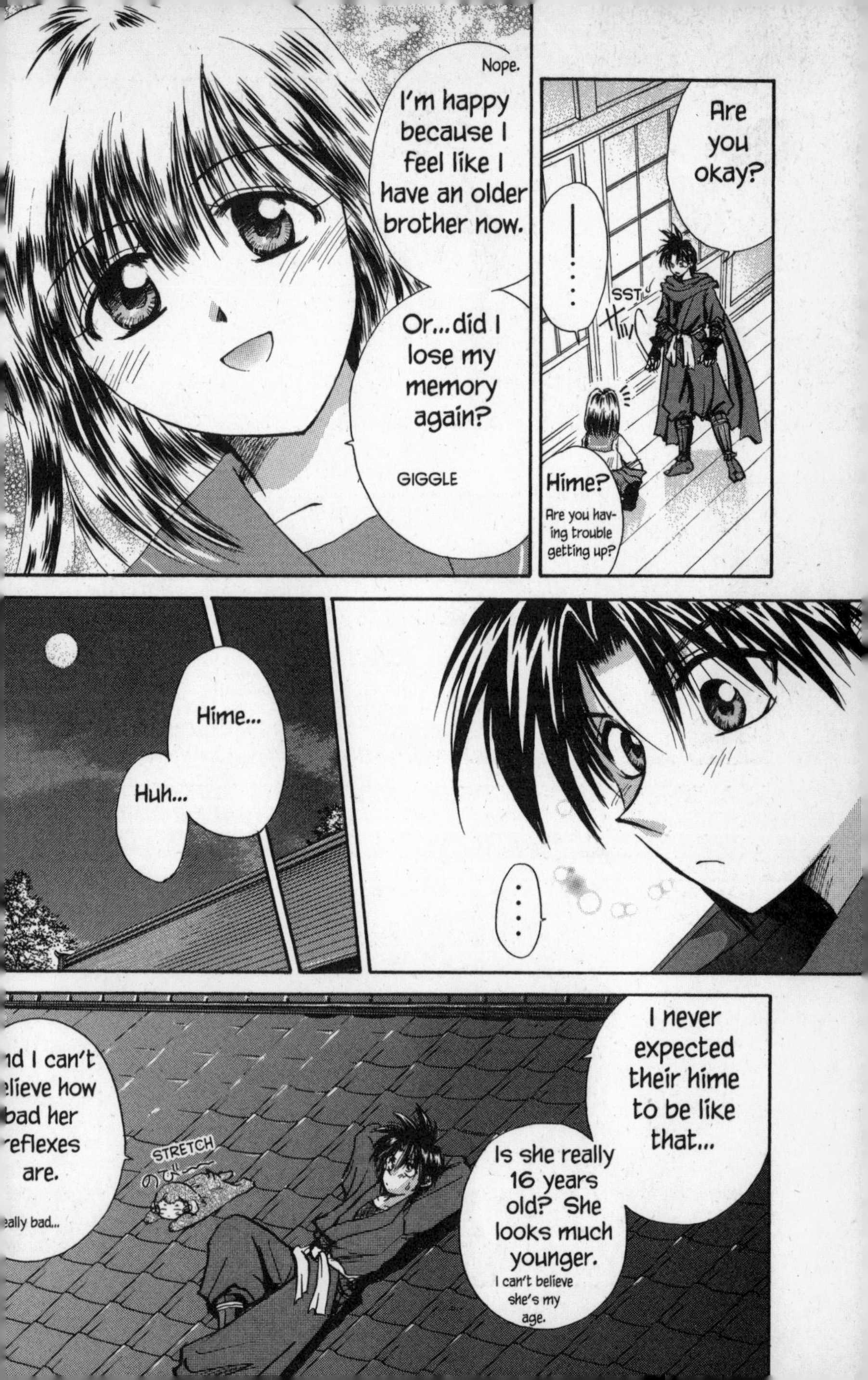
Are you okay?
!....
SST
Hime?
Are you having trouble getting up?
Nope.
I'm happy because I feel like I have an older brother now.
Or...did I lose my memory again?
GIGGLE
....
Hime...
Huh...
I never expected their hime to be like that...
Is she really 16 years old? She looks much younger.
I can't believe she's my age.
nd I can't elieve how bad her reflexes are.
STRETCH
のび
eally bad...

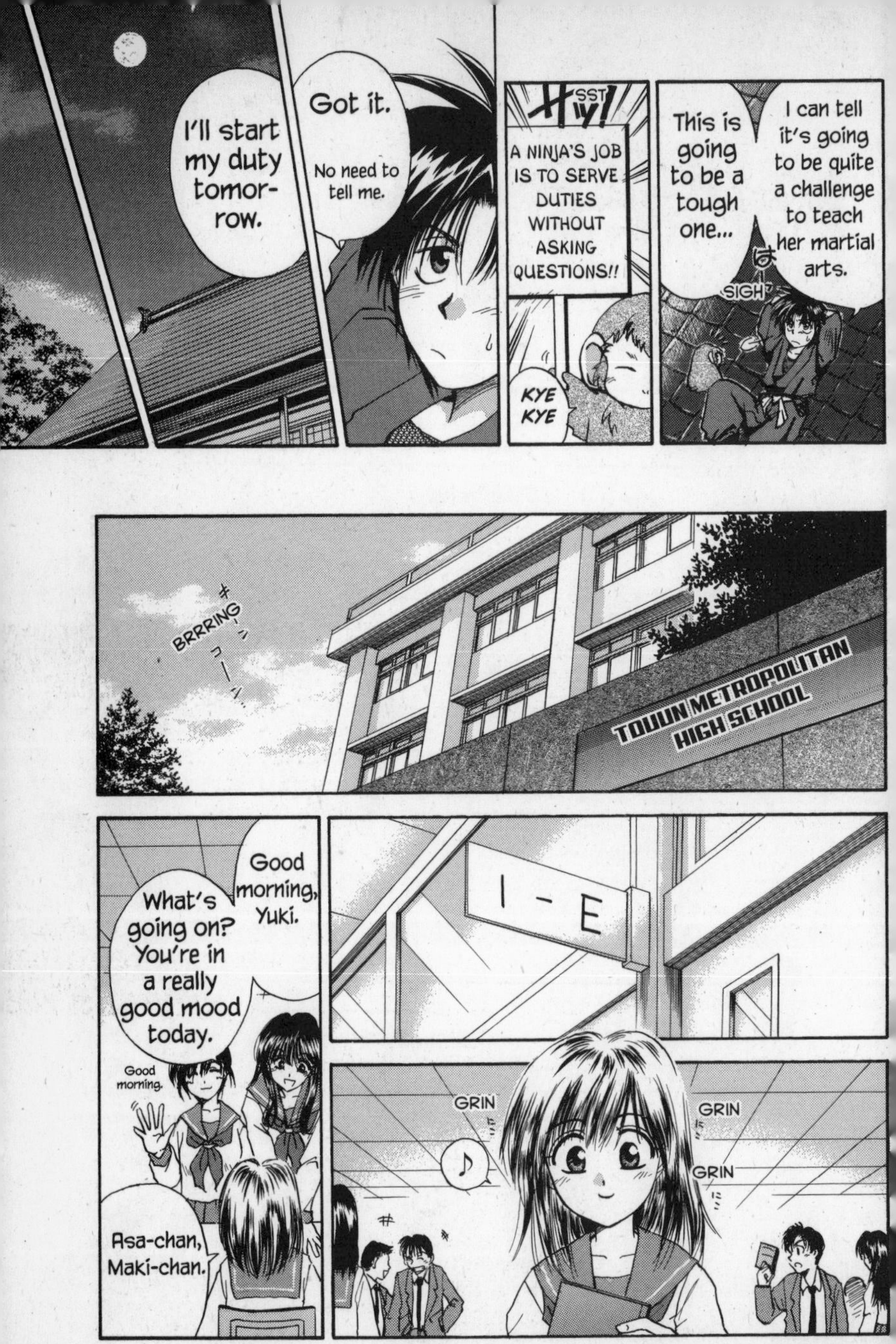
I can tell it's going to be quite a challenge to teach her martial arts.
This is going to be a tough one...
SIGH
SST
A NINJA'S JOB IS TO SERVE DUTIES WITHOUT ASKING QUESTIONS!!
KYE KYE
Got it.
No need to tell me.
I'll start my duty tomorrow.
BRRRING
TOUUN METROPOLITAN HIGH SCHOOL
I - E
GRIN
♪
GRIN
GRIN
Good morning, Yuki.
What's going on? You're in a really good mood today.
Good morning.
Asa-chan, Maki-chan.

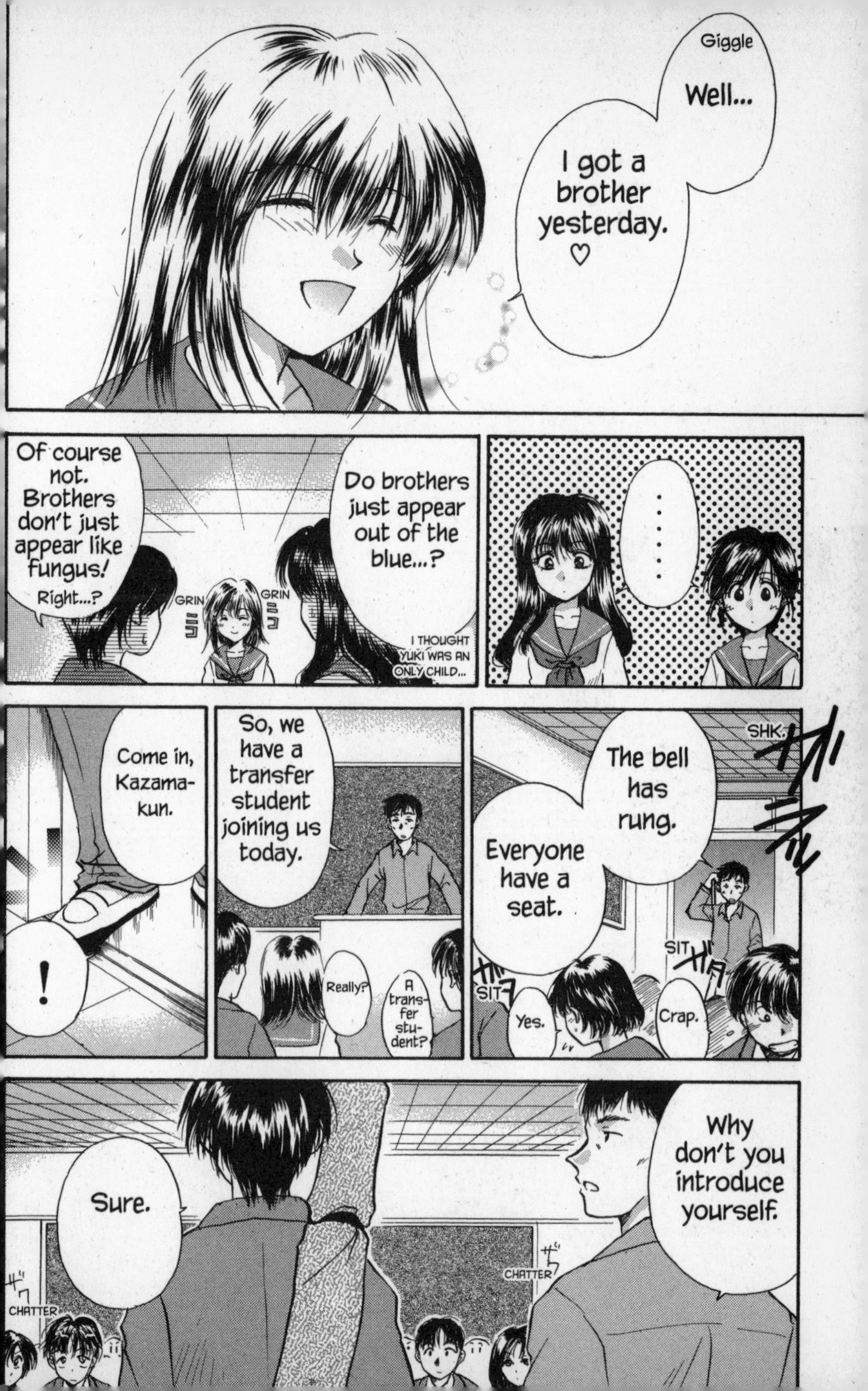
Giggle
Well...
I got a brother yesterday. ♡
......
Do brothers just appear out of the blue...?
I THOUGHT YUKI WAS AN ONLY CHILD...
GRIN
GRIN
Of course not. Brothers don't just appear like fungus!
Right...?
SHK.
The bell has rung.
Everyone have a seat.
SIT
Crap.
Yes.
SIT
So, we have a transfer student joining us today.
A transfer student?
Really?
Come in, Kazama-kun.
!
Why don't you introduce yourself.
CHATTER
Sure.
CHATTER

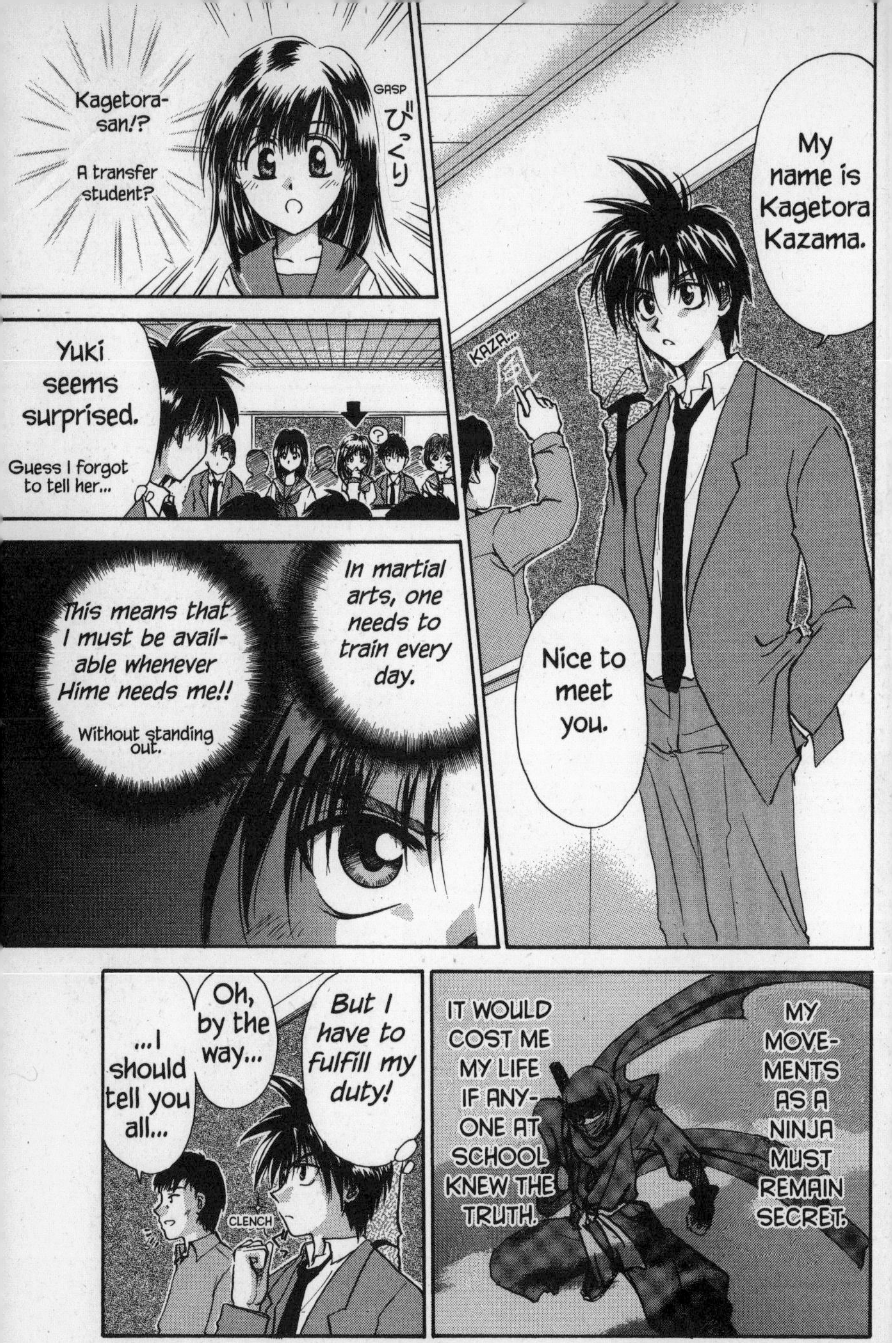
My name is Kagetora Kazama.
KAZA...
Nice to meet you.
GASP
びっくり
Kagetora-san!?
A transfer student?
Yuki seems surprised.
Guess I forgot to tell her...
In martial arts, one needs to train every day.
This means that I must be available whenever Hime needs me!!
Without standing out.
MY MOVEMENTS AS A NINJA MUST REMAIN SECRET.
IT WOULD COST ME MY LIFE IF ANYONE AT SCHOOL KNEW THE TRUTH.
But I have to fulfill my duty!
CLENCH
Oh, by the way...
...I should tell you all...

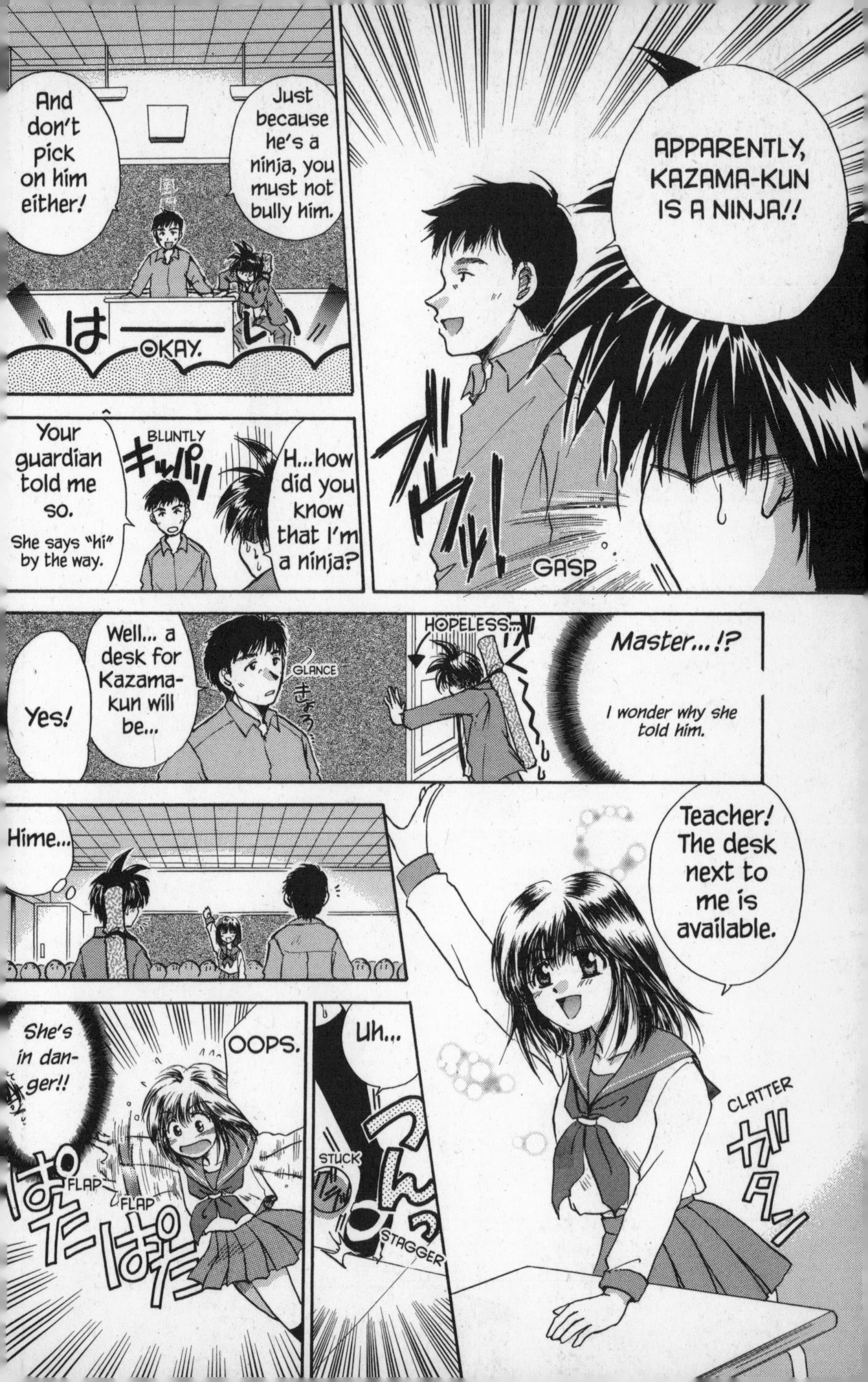
APPARENTLY, KAZAMA-KUN IS A NINJA!!
GASP
Just because he's a ninja, you must not bully him.
And don't pick on him either!
OKAY.
H...how did you know that I'm a ninja?
BLUNTLY
Your guardian told me so.
She says "hi" by the way.
Master...!?
I wonder why she told him.
HOPELESS...
Well... a desk for Kazama-kun will be...
GLANCE
Yes!
Teacher! The desk next to me is available.
CLATTER
Hime...
Uh...
OOPS.
STUCK
STAGGER
She's in danger!!
FLAP
FLAP

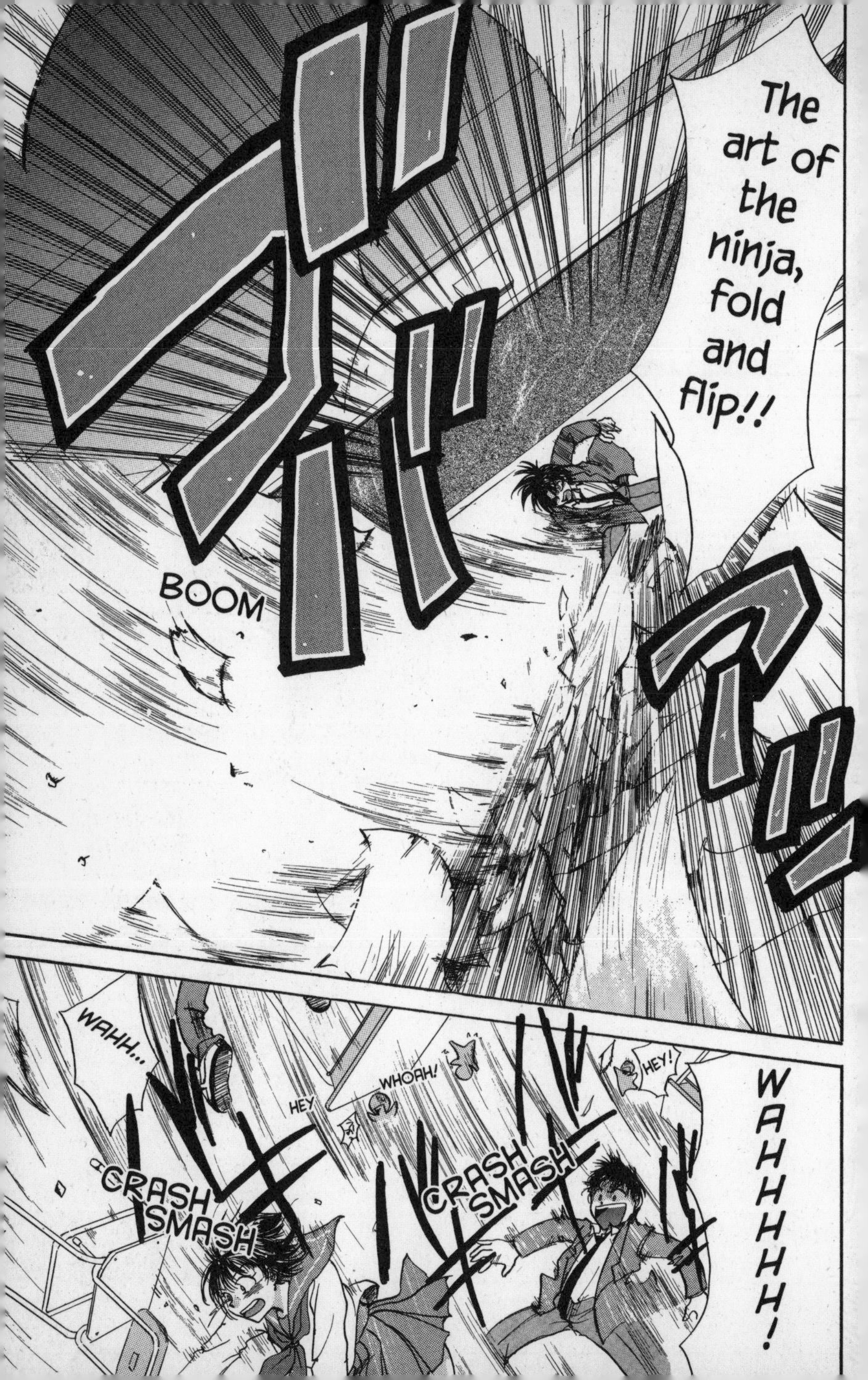
The art of the ninja, fold and flip!!
BOOM
WAHHHHHH!
HEY!
WHOAH!
HEY
CRASH SMASH
WAHH...
CRASH SMASH

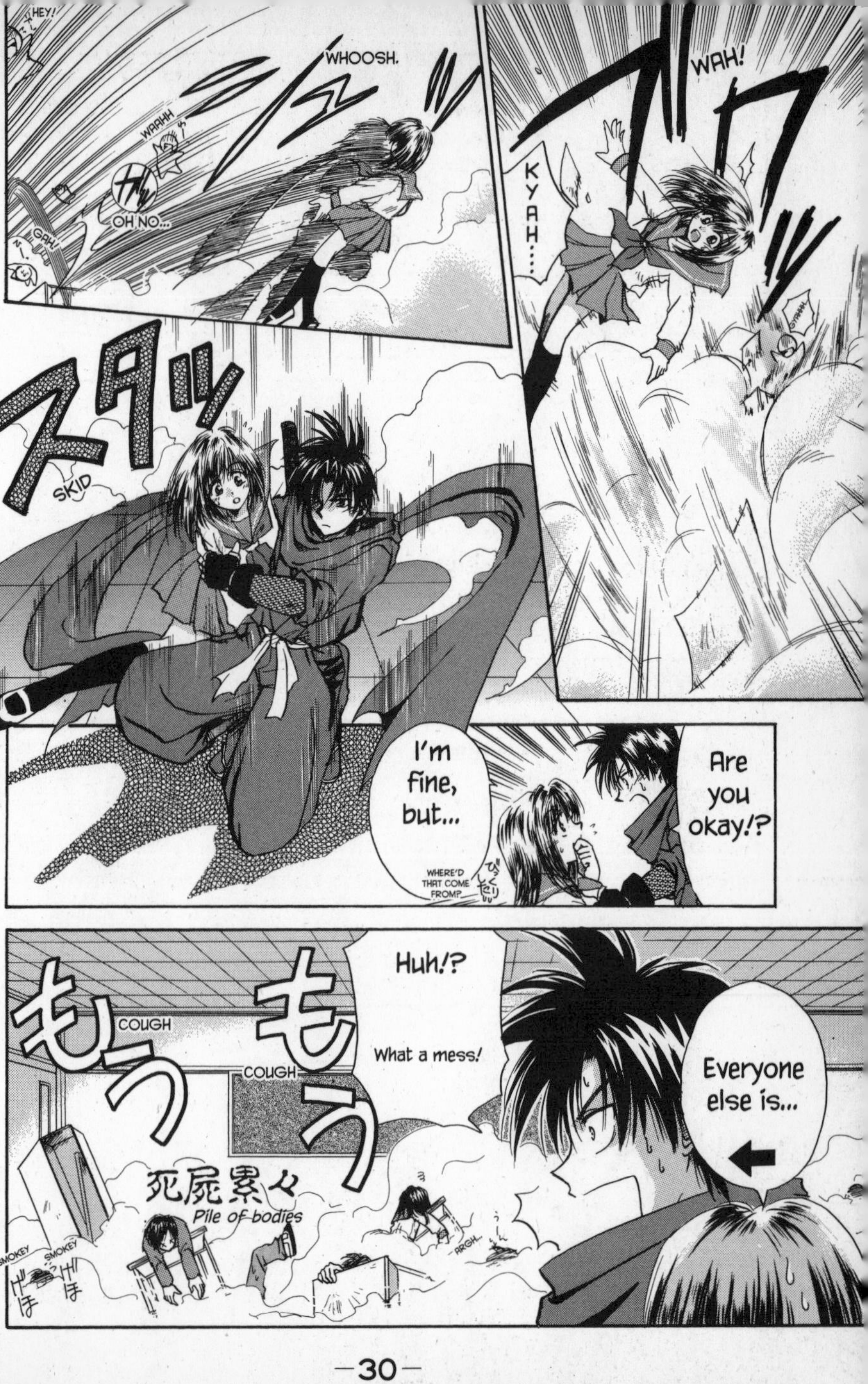

WAH!
KYAH...
WHOOSH.
HEY!
WAAHH
OH NO...
GAH!
スタッ
SKID
Are you okay!?
I'm fine, but...
WHERE'D THAT COME FROM?
Everyone else is...
Huh!?
What a mess!
もう
COUGH
もう
COUGH
死屍累々
Pile of bodies
ARGH...
SMOKEY
SMOKEY

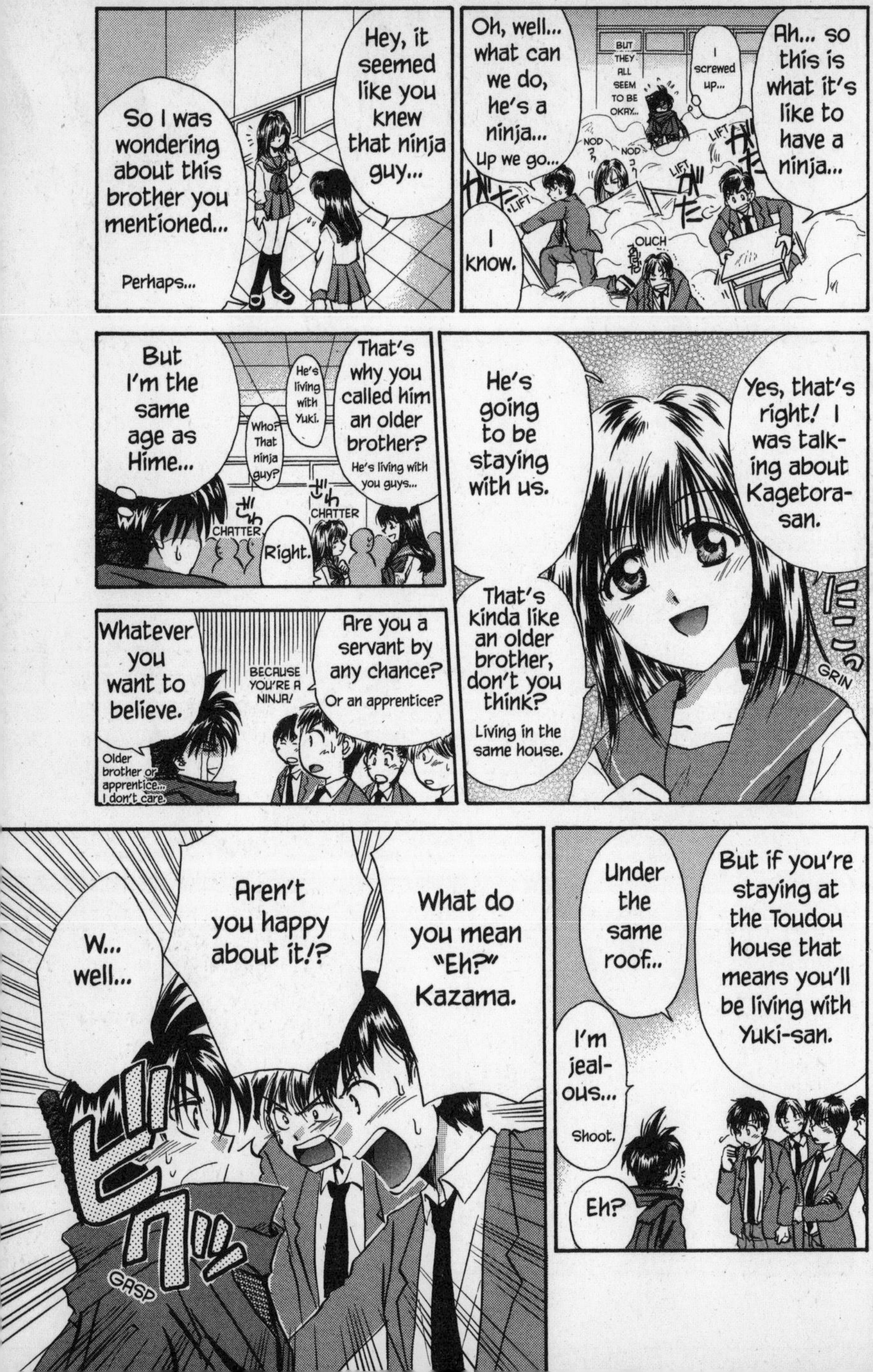
Ah... so this is what it's like to have a ninja...
I screwed up...
BUT THEY ALL SEEM TO BE OKAY...
LIFT
LIFT
NOD
NOD
OUCH
Oh, well... what can we do, he's a ninja... Up we go...
LIFT
I know.
Hey, it seemed like you knew that ninja guy...
So I was wondering about this brother you mentioned...
Perhaps...
Yes, that's right! I was talking about Kagetora-san.
He's going to be staying with us.
GRIN
That's kinda like an older brother, don't you think? Living in the same house.
That's why you called him an older brother? He's living with you guys...
He's living with Yuki.
But I'm the same age as Hime...
Who? That ninja guy?
CHATTER
CHATTER
Right.
Are you a servant by any chance? Or an apprentice?
BECAUSE YOU'RE A NINJA!
Whatever you want to believe.
Older brother or apprentice... I don't care.
But if you're staying at the Toudou house that means you'll be living with Yuki-san.
Under the same roof...
I'm jealous... Shoot.
Eh?
What do you mean "Eh?" Kazama.
Aren't you happy about it!?
W... well...
GASP

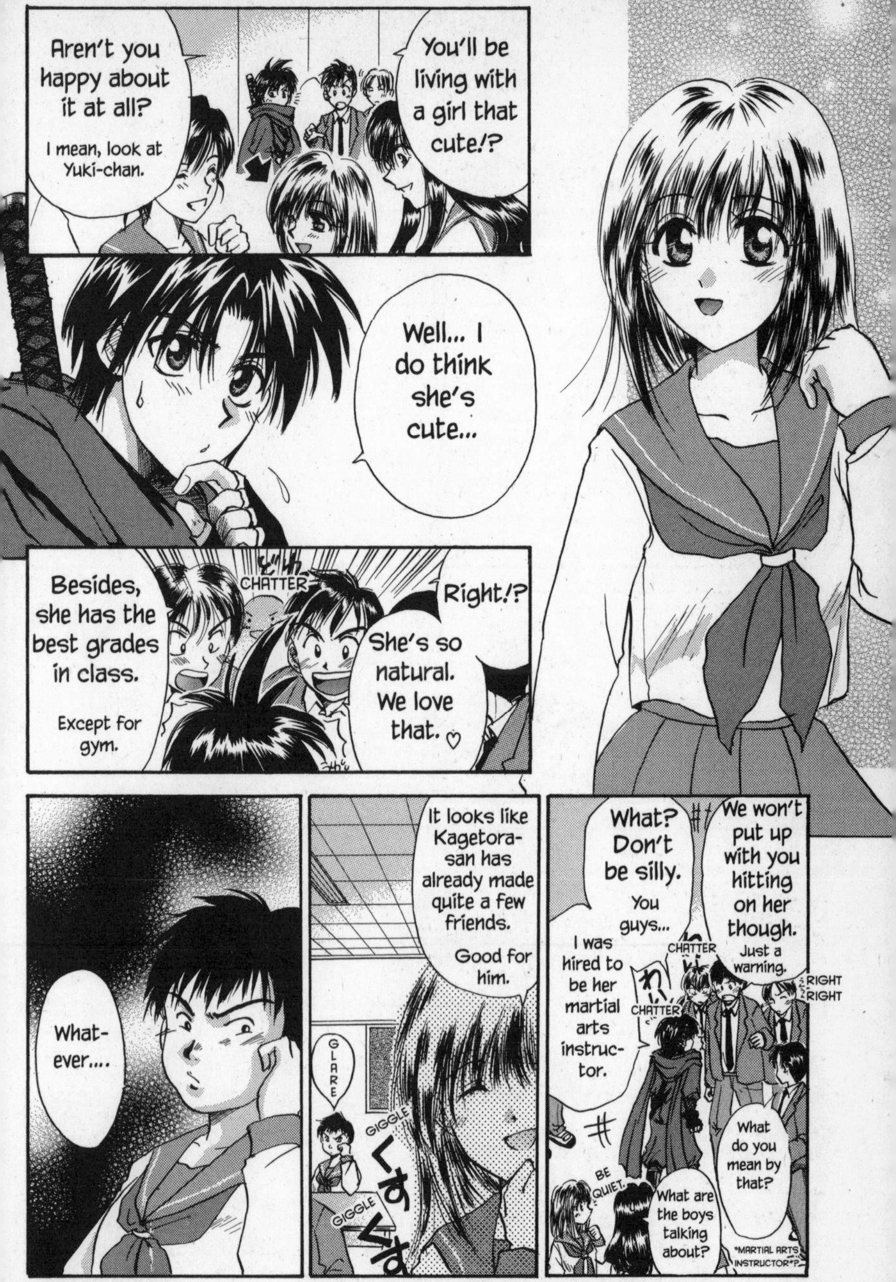
You'll be living with a girl that cute!?
Aren't you happy about it at all?
I mean, look at Yuki-chan.
Well... I do think she's cute...
Right!?
She's so natural. We love that. ♡
CHATTER
Besides, she has the best grades in class.
Except for gym.
We won't put up with you hitting on her though.
Just a warning.
What? Don't be silly.
You guys...
RIGHT RIGHT
CHATTER
CHATTER
I was hired to be her martial arts instructor.
What do you mean by that?
MARTIAL ARTS INSTRUCTOR?
What are the boys talking about?
BE QUIET.
It looks like Kagetora-san has already made quite a few friends.
Good for him.
GLARE
GIGGLE
くすくす
GIGGLE
Whatever....

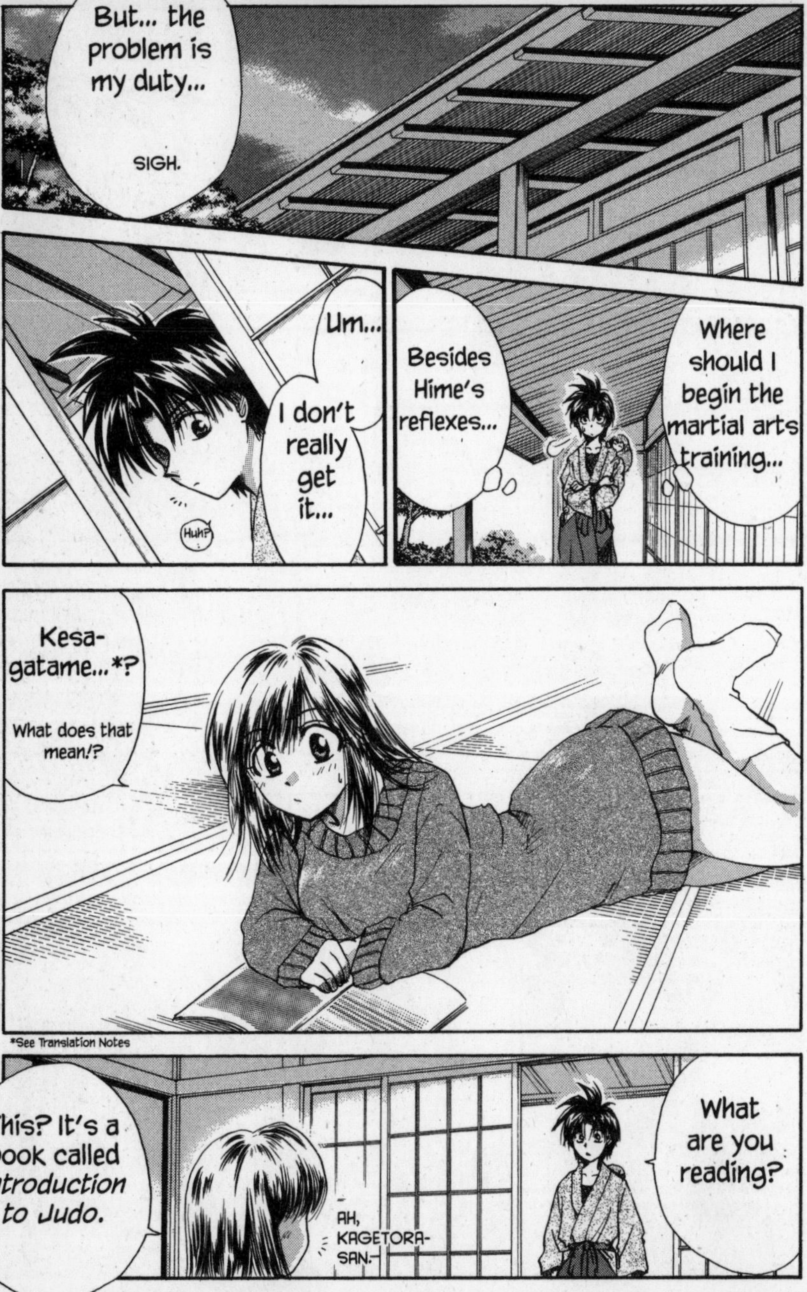
But... the problem is my duty...
SIGH.
Where should I begin the martial arts training...
Besides Hime's reflexes...
Um...
I don't really get it...
Huh?
Kesa-gatame...*?
What does that mean!?
*See Translation Notes
What are you reading?
AH, KAGETORA-SAN.
This? It's a book called *Introduction to Judo*.

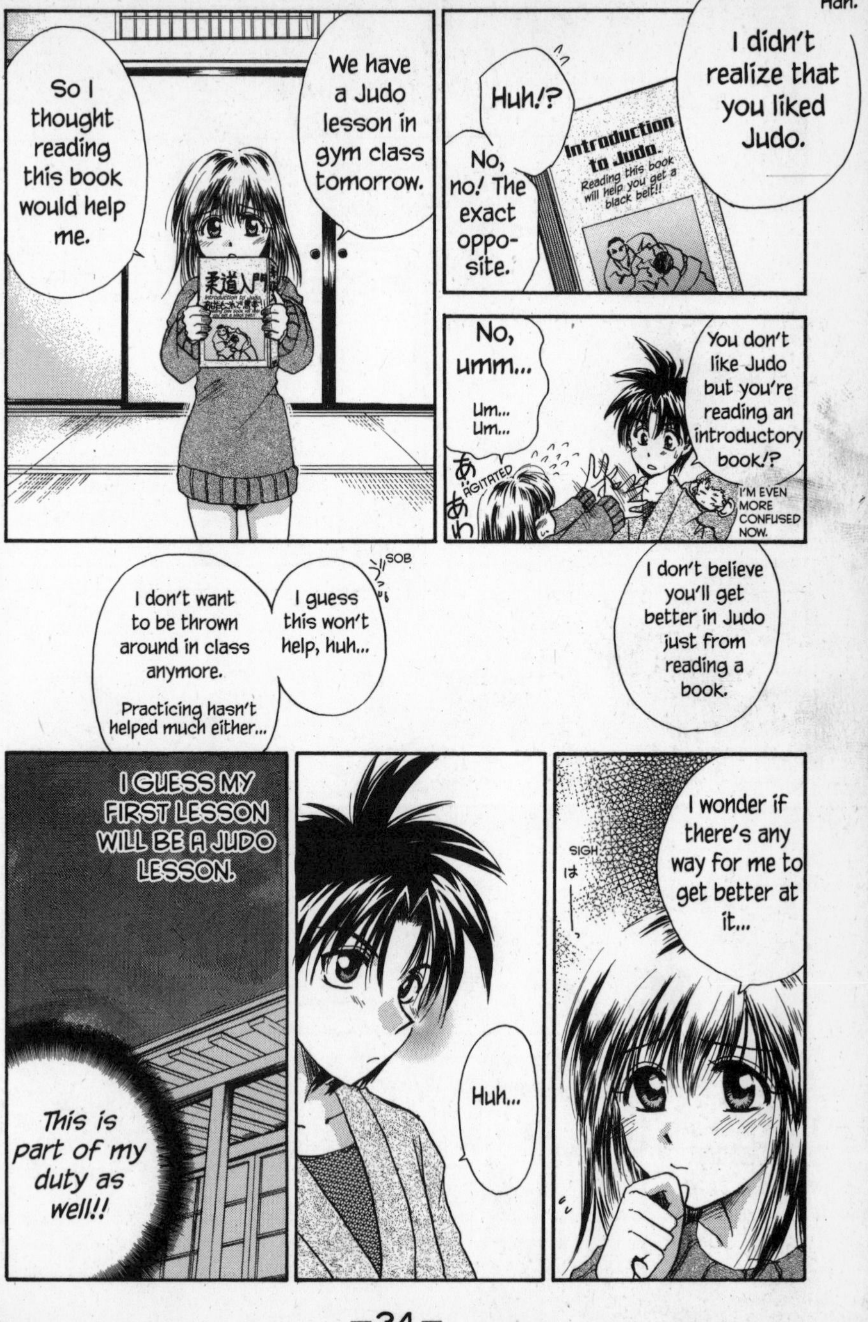
Hah.
I didn't realize that you liked Judo.
Huh!?
No, no! The exact oppo-site.
Introduction to Judo. Reading this book will help you get a black belt!!
You don't like Judo but you're reading an introductory book!?
I'M EVEN MORE CONFUSED NOW.
No, umm...
Um... Um...
AGITATED
We have a Judo lesson in gym class tomorrow.
So I thought reading this book would help me.
Introduction to Judo
I don't believe you'll get better in Judo just from reading a book.
SOB
I guess this won't help, huh...
I don't want to be thrown around in class anymore.
Practicing hasn't helped much either...
I wonder if there's any way for me to get better at it...
SIGH
Huh...
I GUESS MY FIRST LESSON WILL BE A JUDO LESSON.
This is part of my duty as well!!

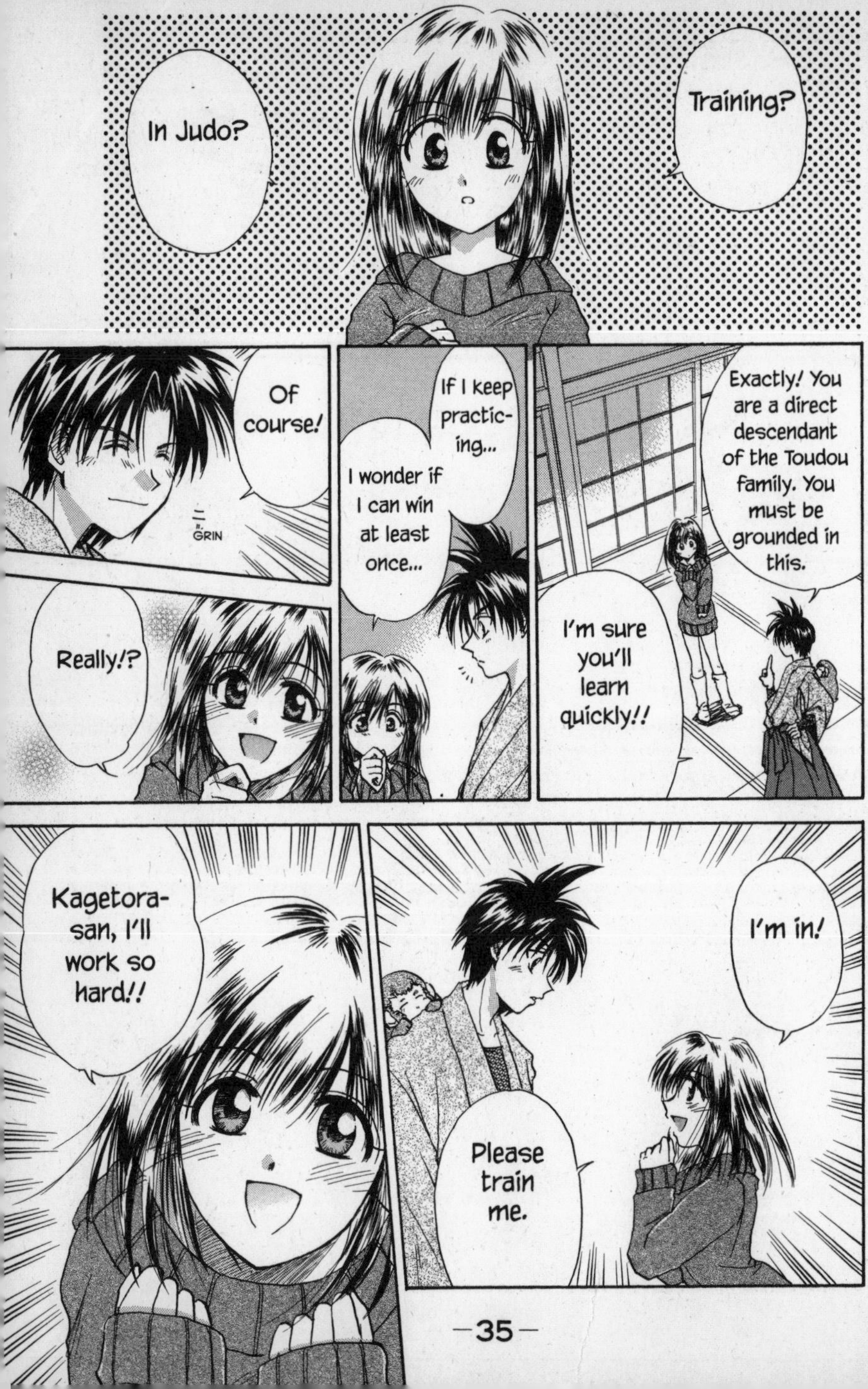
Training?
In Judo?
Exactly! You are a direct descendant of the Toudou family. You must be grounded in this.
I'm sure you'll learn quickly!!
If I keep practic-ing...
I wonder if I can win at least once...
Of course!
GRIN
Really!?
I'm in!
Please train me.
Kagetora-san, I'll work so hard!!

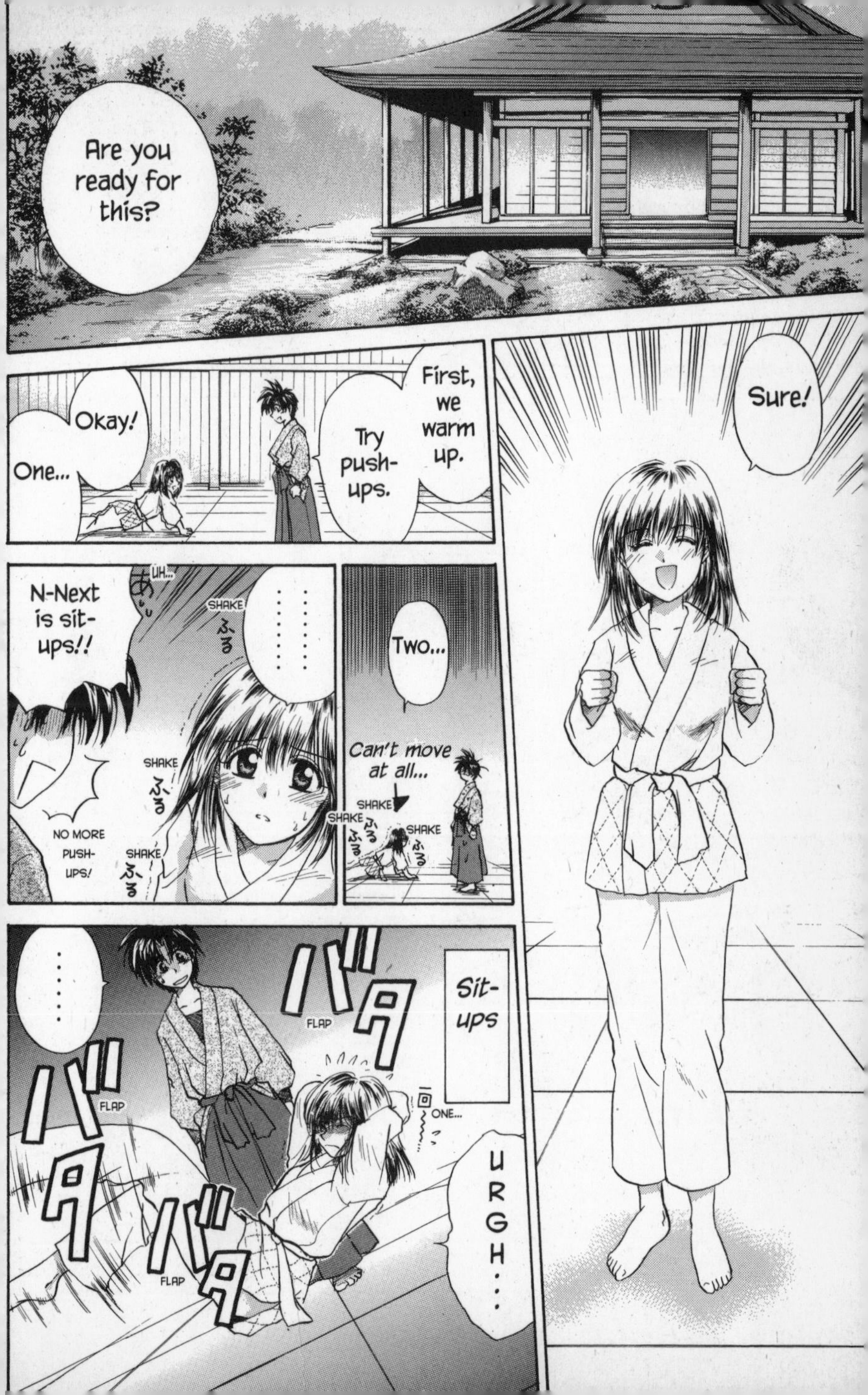

Are you ready for this?
Sure!
First, we warm up.
Try push-ups.
Okay!
One...
Two...
Can't move at all...
SHAKE
SHAKE
SHAKE
......
SHAKE
UH...
N-Next is sit-ups!!
SHAKE
NO MORE PUSH-UPS!
SHAKE
Sit-ups
FLAP
ONE...
URGH...
FLAP
FLAP
......

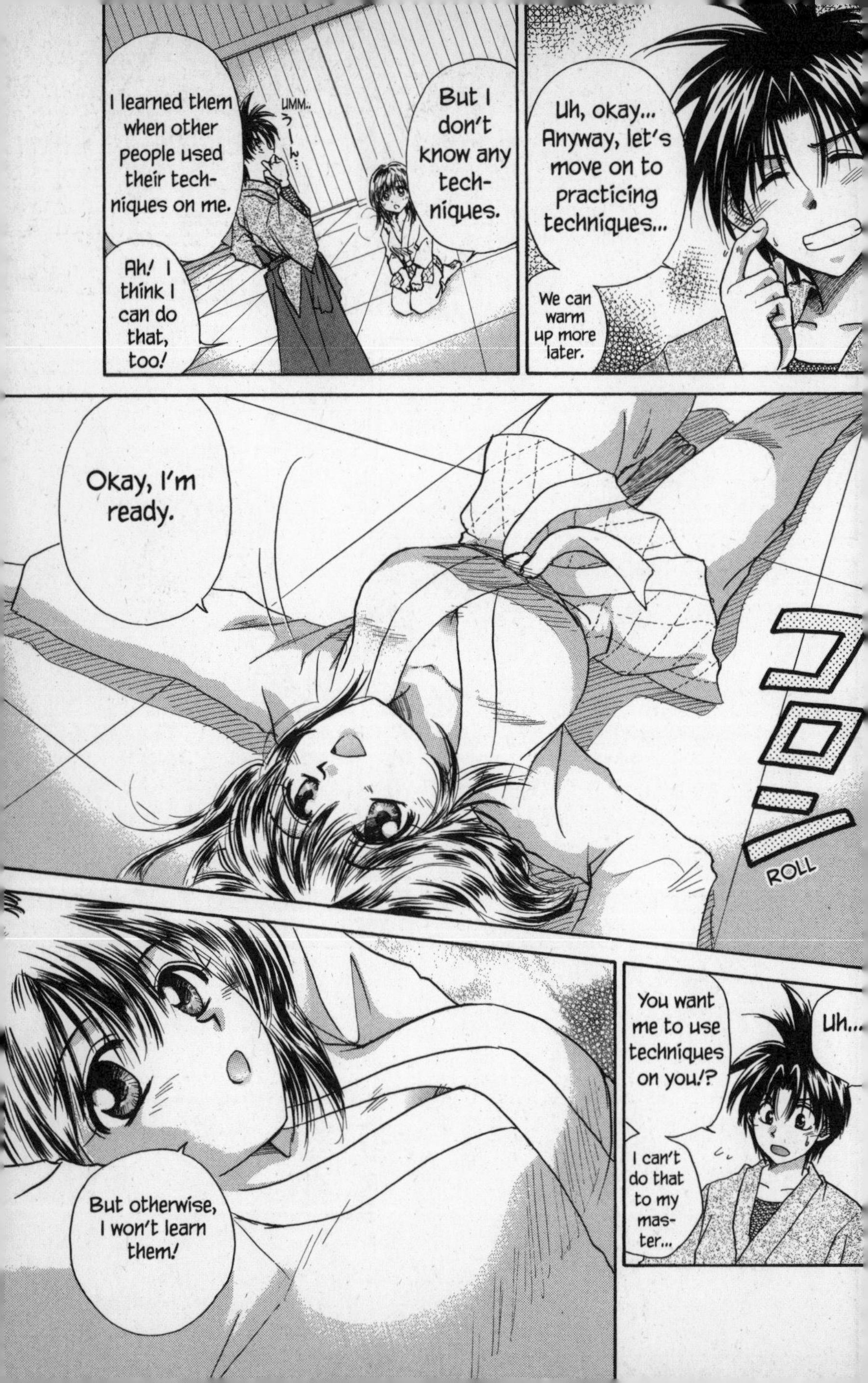
Uh, okay... Anyway, let's move on to practicing techniques...
We can warm up more later.
But I don't know any techniques.
UMM..
うーん…
I learned them when other people used their techniques on me.
Ah! I think I can do that, too!
Okay, I'm ready.
コロン
ROLL
Uh...
You want me to use techniques on you!?
I can't do that to my master...
But otherwise, I won't learn them!

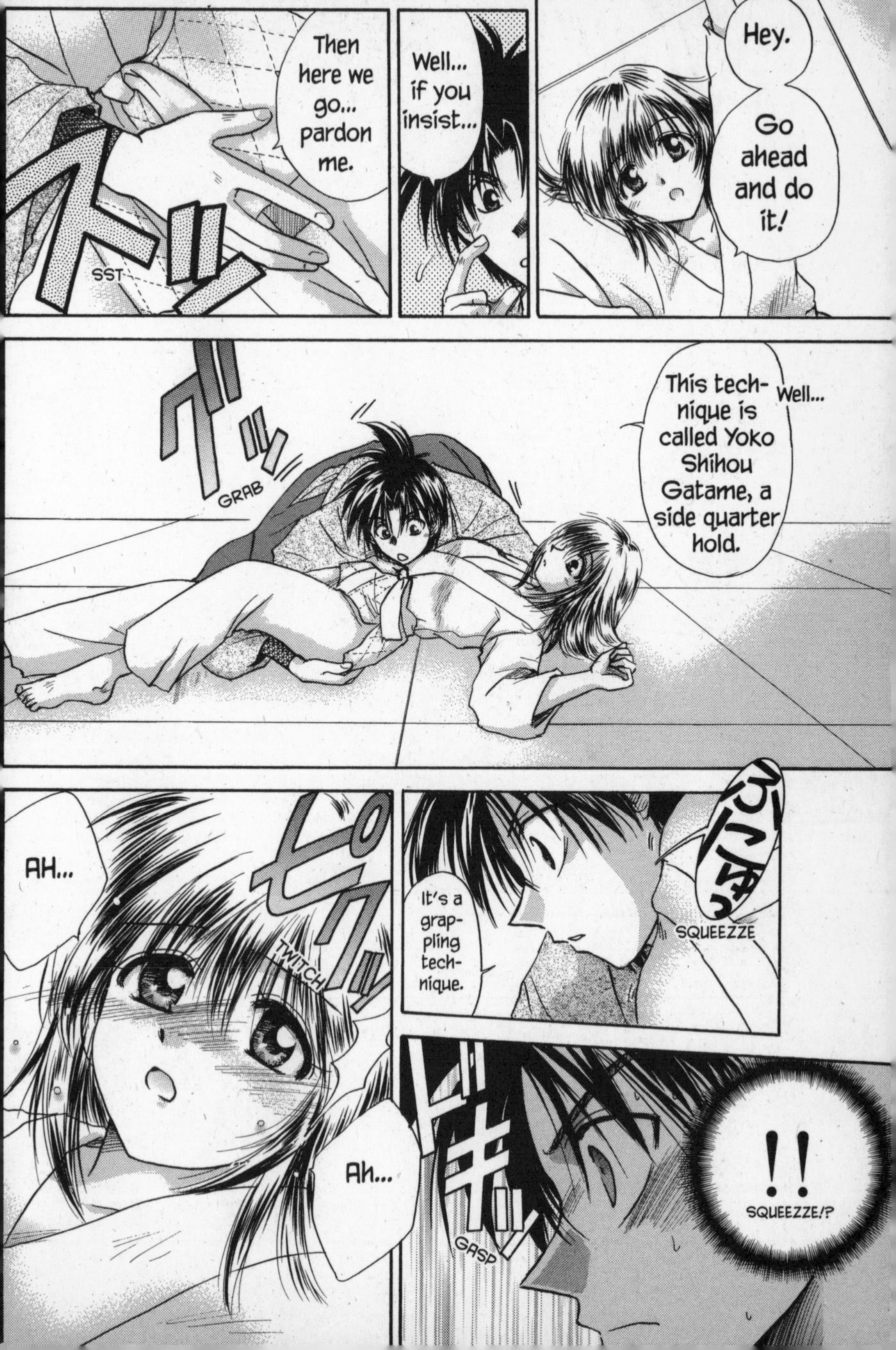
Hey.
Go ahead and do it!
Well... if you insist...
Then here we go... pardon me.
SST
This technique is called Yoko Shihou Gatame, a side quarter hold.
Well...
GRAB
SQUEEZZE
It's a grappling technique.
AH...
TWITCH
Ah...
!!
SQUEEZZE!?
GASP

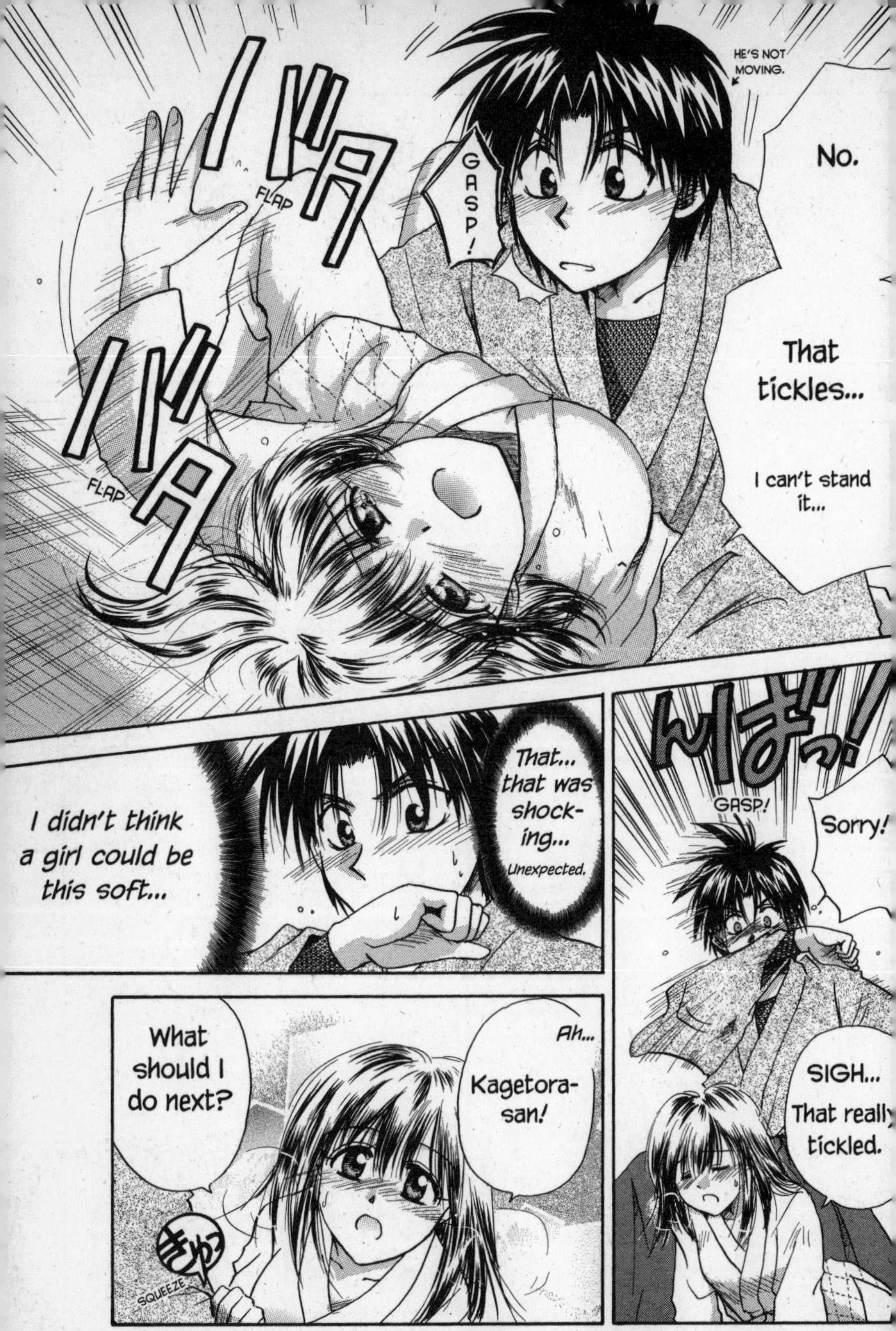
HE'S NOT MOVING.
No.
That tickles...
I can't stand it...
GASP!
パタ
FLAP
パタ
FLAP
んぱっ!
GASP!
Sorry!
SIGH... That really tickled.
That... that was shocking...
Unexpected.
I didn't think a girl could be this soft...
Ah... Kagetora-san!
What should I do next?
きゅっ
SQUEEZE

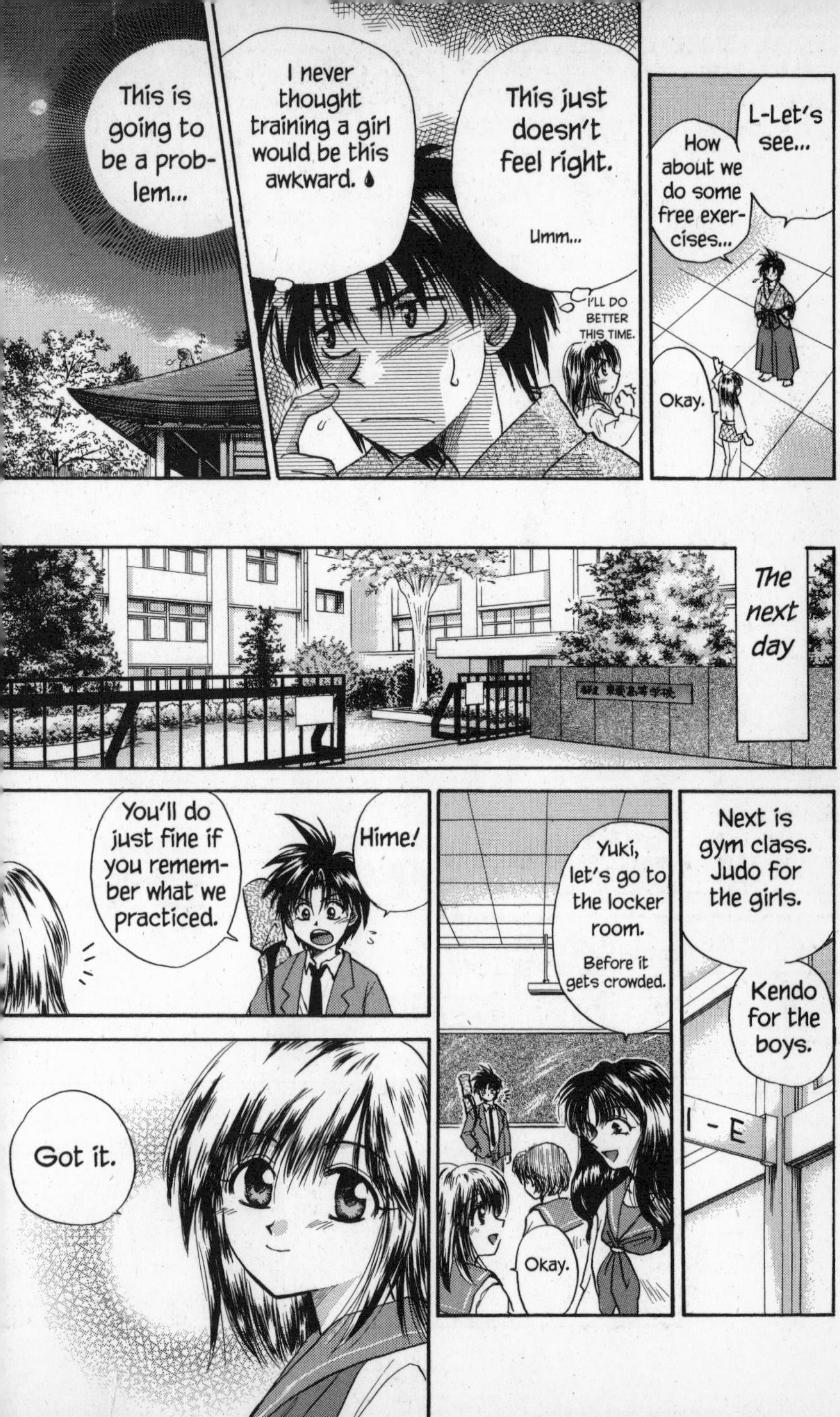
L-Let's see...
How about we do some free exer-cises...
Okay.
This just doesn't feel right.
I never thought training a girl would be this awkward.
Umm...
I'LL DO BETTER THIS TIME.
This is going to be a prob-lem...
The next day
Next is gym class. Judo for the girls.
Kendo for the boys.
I - E
Yuki, let's go to the locker room.
Before it gets crowded.
Okay.
Hime!
You'll do just fine if you remem-ber what we practiced.
Got it.

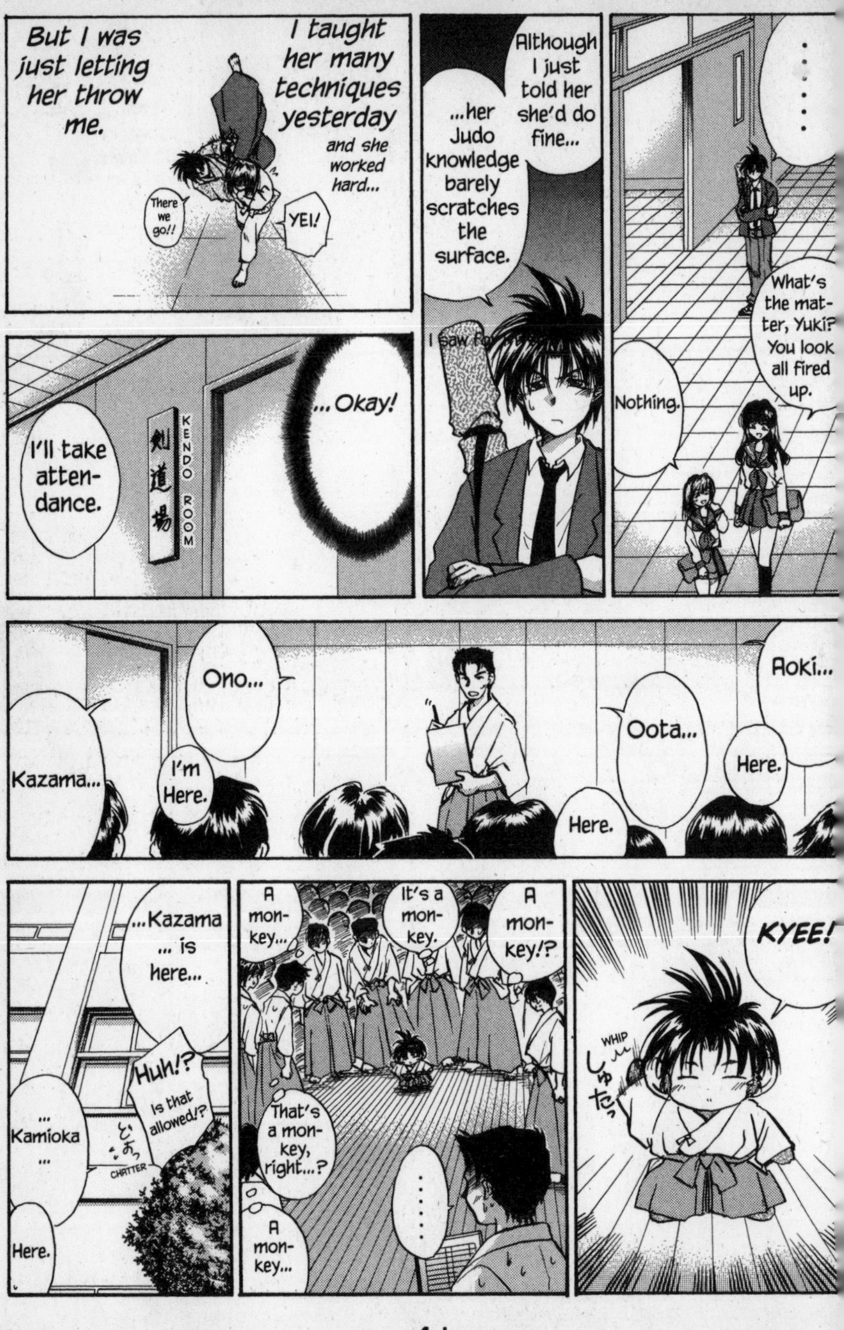
......
What's the matter, Yuki? You look all fired up.
Nothing.
Although I just told her she'd do fine...
...her Judo knowledge barely scratches the surface.
I taught her many techniques yesterday
and she worked hard...
But I was just letting her throw me.
YEI!
There we go!!
...Okay!
剣道場
KENDO ROOM
I'll take attendance.
Aoki...
Here.
Oota...
Here.
Ono...
I'm Here.
Kazama...
KYEE!
WHIP
しゅたっ
A monkey!?
It's a monkey.
A monkey...
......
That's a monkey, right...?
A monkey...
...Kazama ... is here...
Huh!?
Is that allowed!?
とおっ
CHATTER
... Kamioka ...
Here.

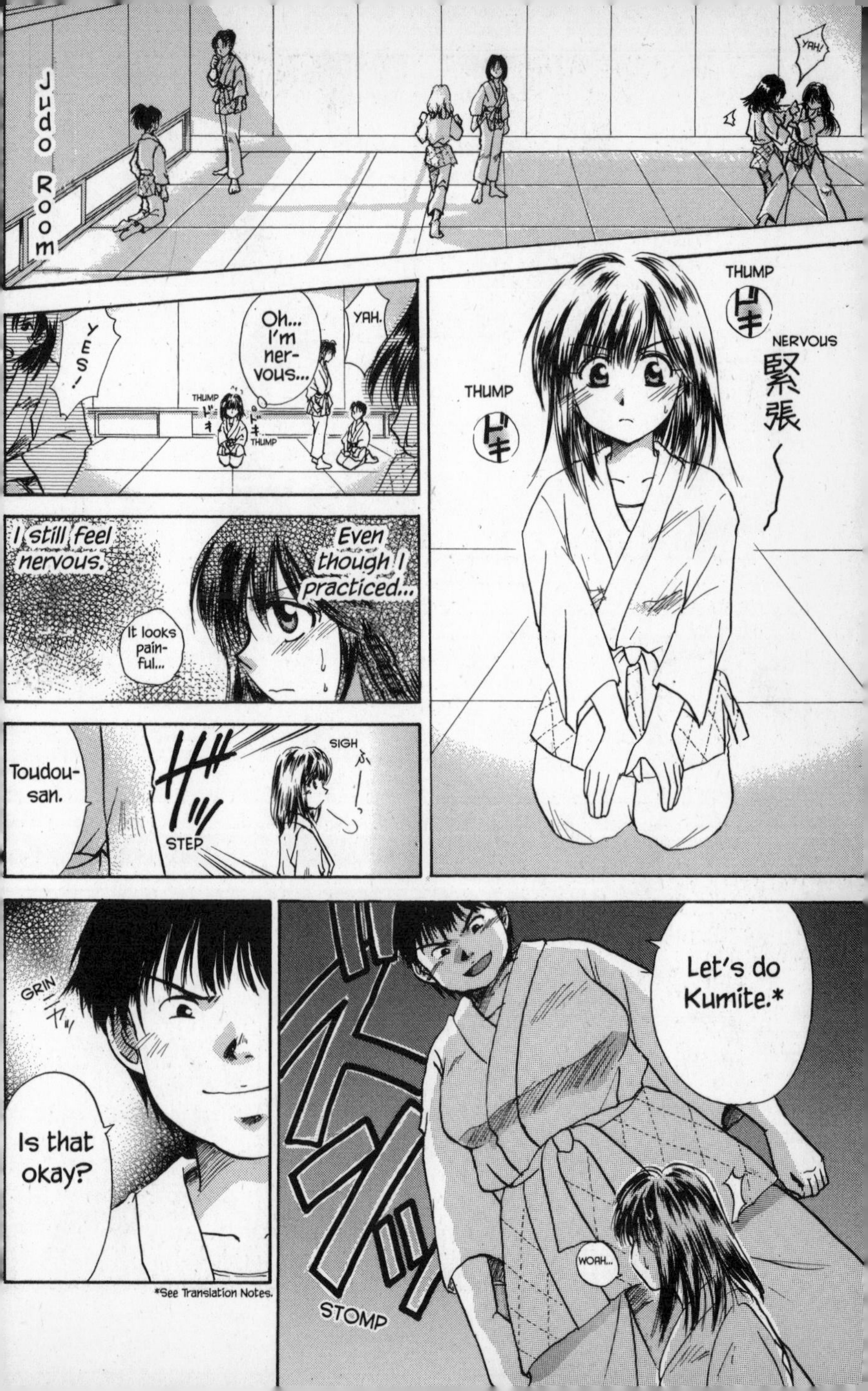
YAH!
Judo Room
THUMP
ドキ
NERVOUS
緊張
THUMP
ドキ
YAH.
Oh... I'm ner-vous...
THUMP
ドキ
ドキ
THUMP
YES!
Even though I practiced...
I still feel nervous.
It looks pain-ful...
SIGH
ふ
STEP
Toudou-san.
Let's do Kumite.*
WOAH...
STOMP
GRIN
Is that okay?

*See Translation Notes.

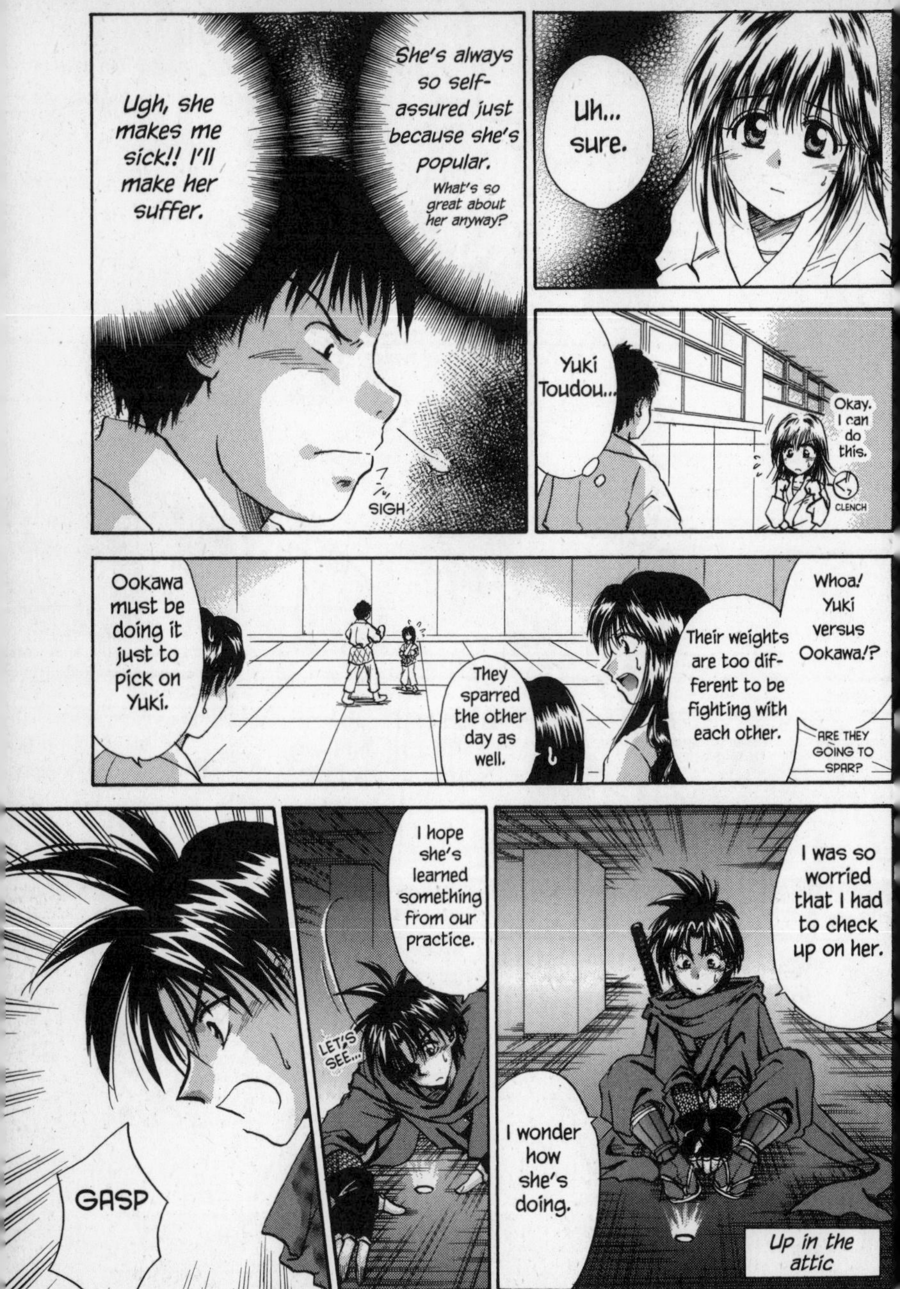
Uh... sure.
Okay. I can do this.
CLENCH
Yuki Toudou...
She's always so self-assured just because she's popular.
What's so great about her anyway?
Ugh, she makes me sick!! I'll make her suffer.
SIGH
Whoa! Yuki versus Ookawa!?
ARE THEY GOING TO SPAR?
Their weights are too different to be fighting with each other.
They sparred the other day as well.
Ookawa must be doing it just to pick on Yuki.
I was so worried that I had to check up on her.
I wonder how she's doing.
Up in the attic
I hope she's learned something from our practice.
LET'S SEE...
GASP

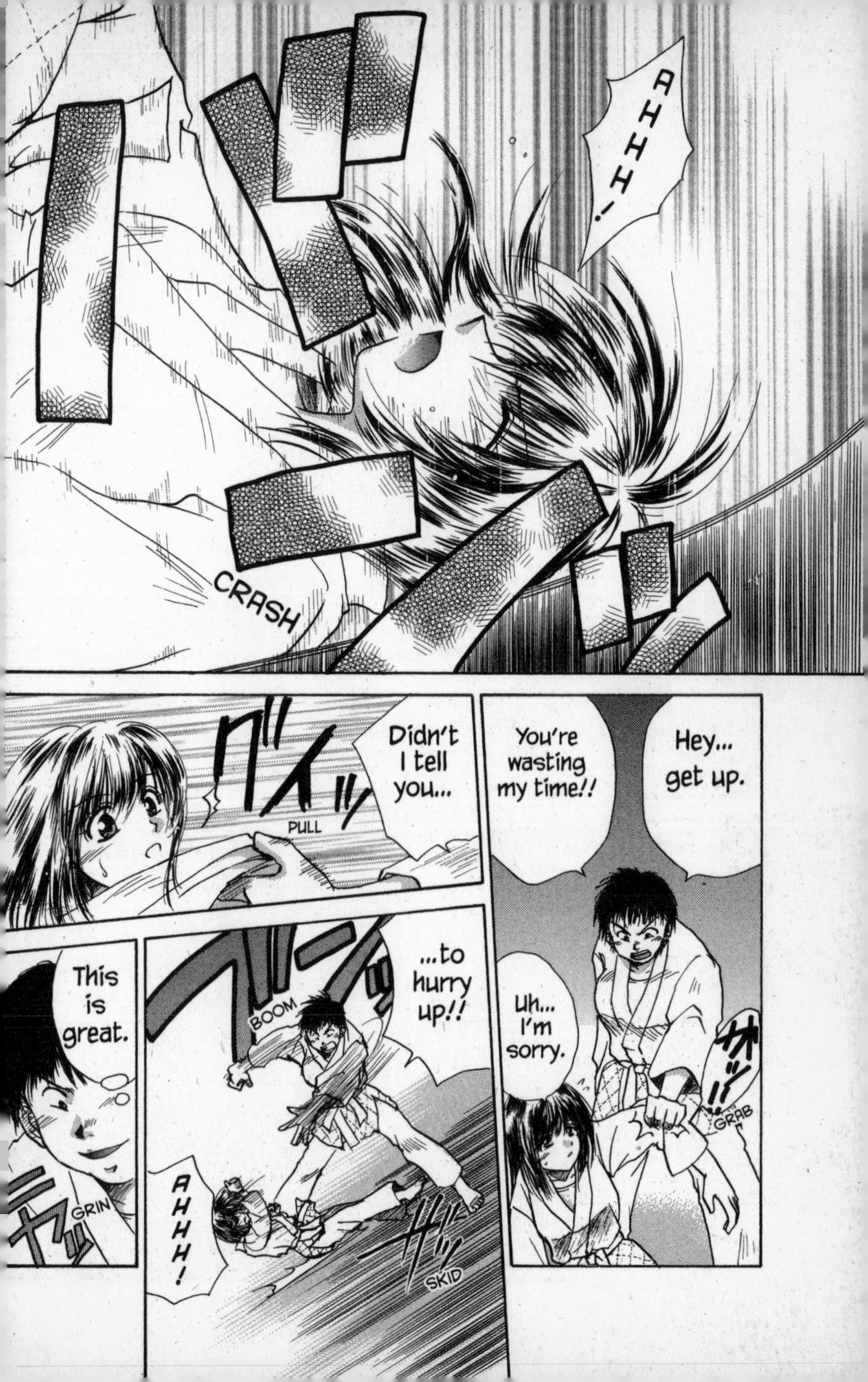
AHHHH!
CRASH
Hey... get up.
You're wasting my time!!
Uh... I'm sorry.
GRAB
Didn't I tell you...
PULL
...to hurry up!!
BOOM
AHHHH!
SKID
This is great.
GRIN

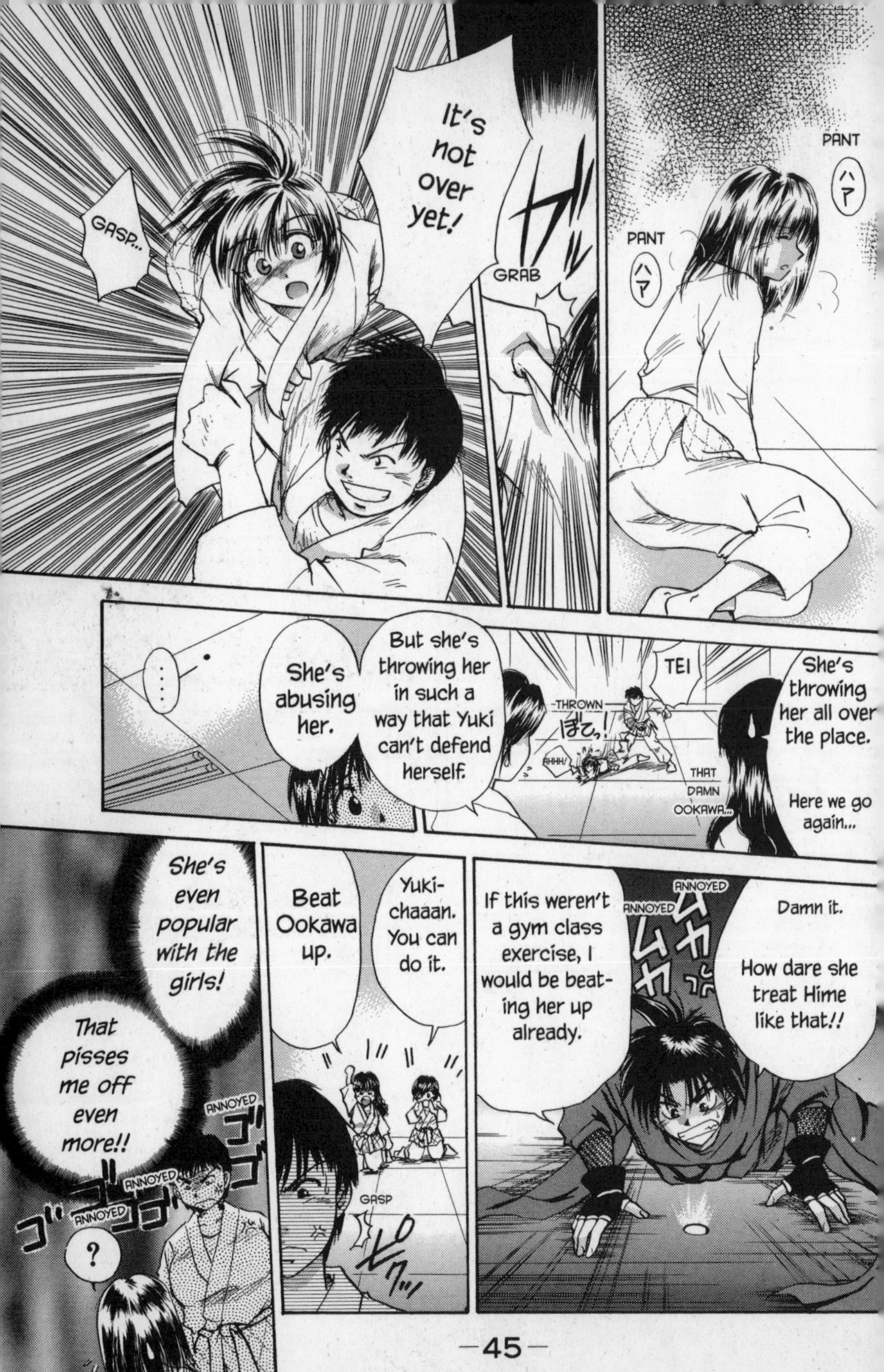
PANT
ハア
PANT
ハア
GRAB
It's not over yet!
GASP...
She's throwing her all over the place.
Here we go again...
THAT DAMN OOKAWA...
TEI
THROWN
ぽてっ!
AHHH!
But she's throwing her in such a way that Yuki can't defend herself.
She's abusing her.
...
Damn it.
How dare she treat Hime like that!!
ANNOYED
ANNOYED
If this weren't a gym class exercise, I would be beat-ing her up already.
Yuki-chaaan. You can do it.
Beat Ookawa up.
GASP
She's even popular with the girls!
That pisses me off even more!!
ANNOYED
ANNOYED
ANNOYED
?

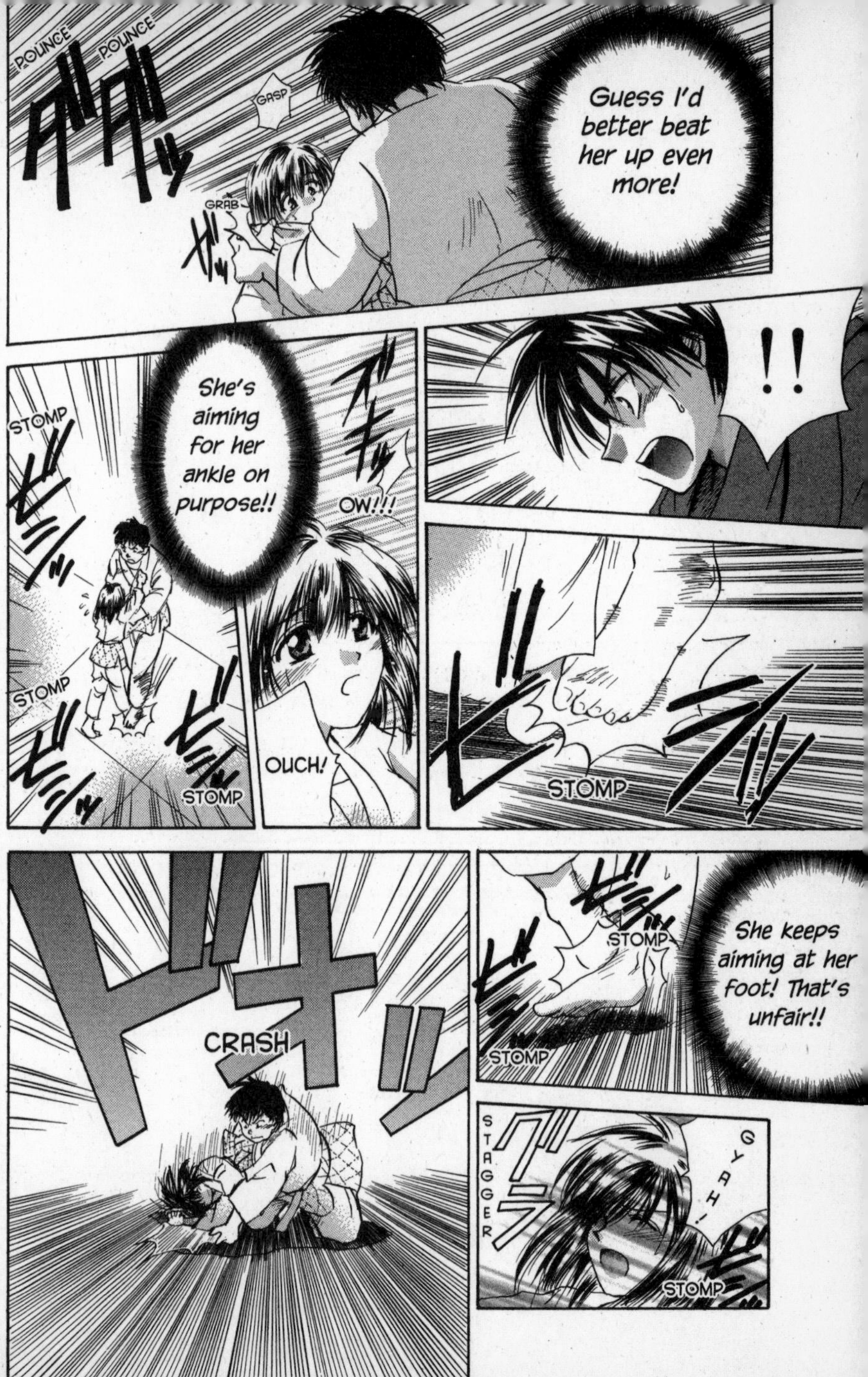
Guess I'd better beat her up even more!
GASP
POUNCE
POUNCE
GRAB
!!
STOMP
She's aiming for her ankle on purpose!!
OW!!!
OUCH!
STOMP
STOMP
STOMP
She keeps aiming at her foot! That's unfair!!
STOMP
STOMP
GYAH!
STOMP
STAGGER
CRASH

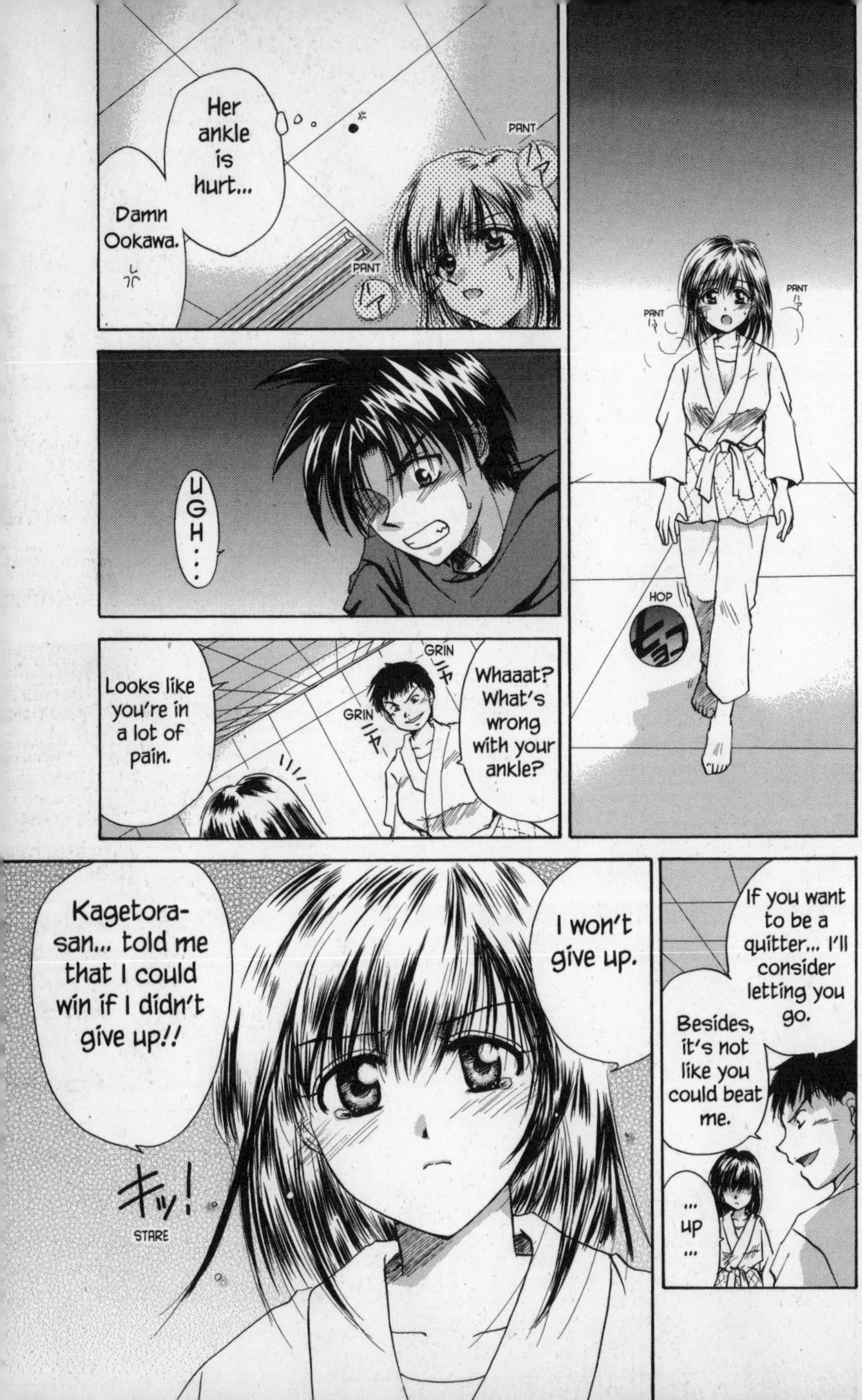

PANT
PANT
HOP
PANT
Her ankle is hurt...
Damn Ookawa.
PANT
UGH...
GRIN
GRIN
Whaaat? What's wrong with your ankle?
Looks like you're in a lot of pain.
If you want to be a quitter... I'll consider letting you go.
Besides, it's not like you could beat me.
... up ...
I won't give up.
Kagetora-san... told me that I could win if I didn't give up!!
キッ!
STARE

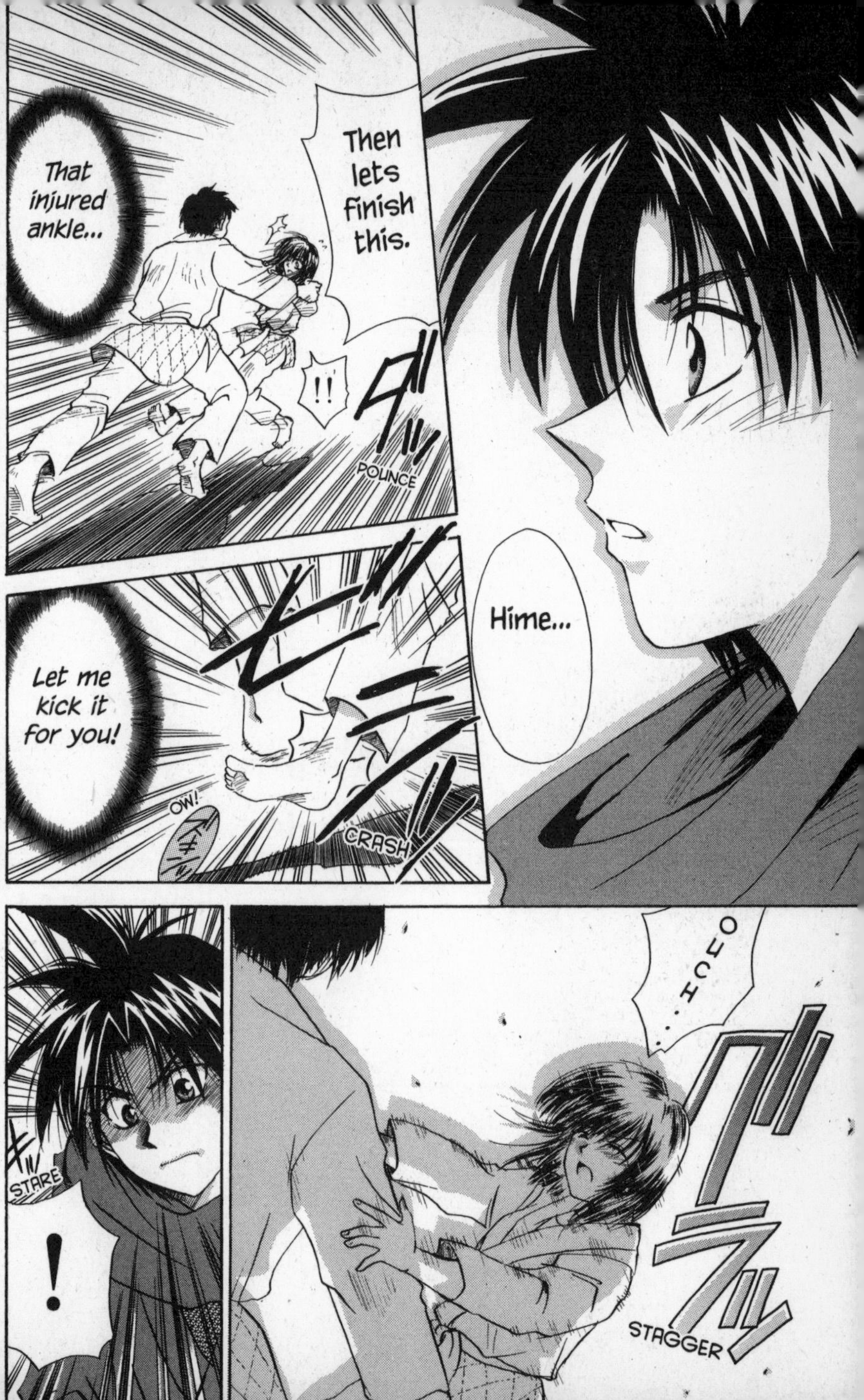
Hime...
Then lets finish this.
That injured ankle...
!!
POUNCE
Let me kick it for you!
CRASH
OW!
OUCH...
STAGGER
STARE
!

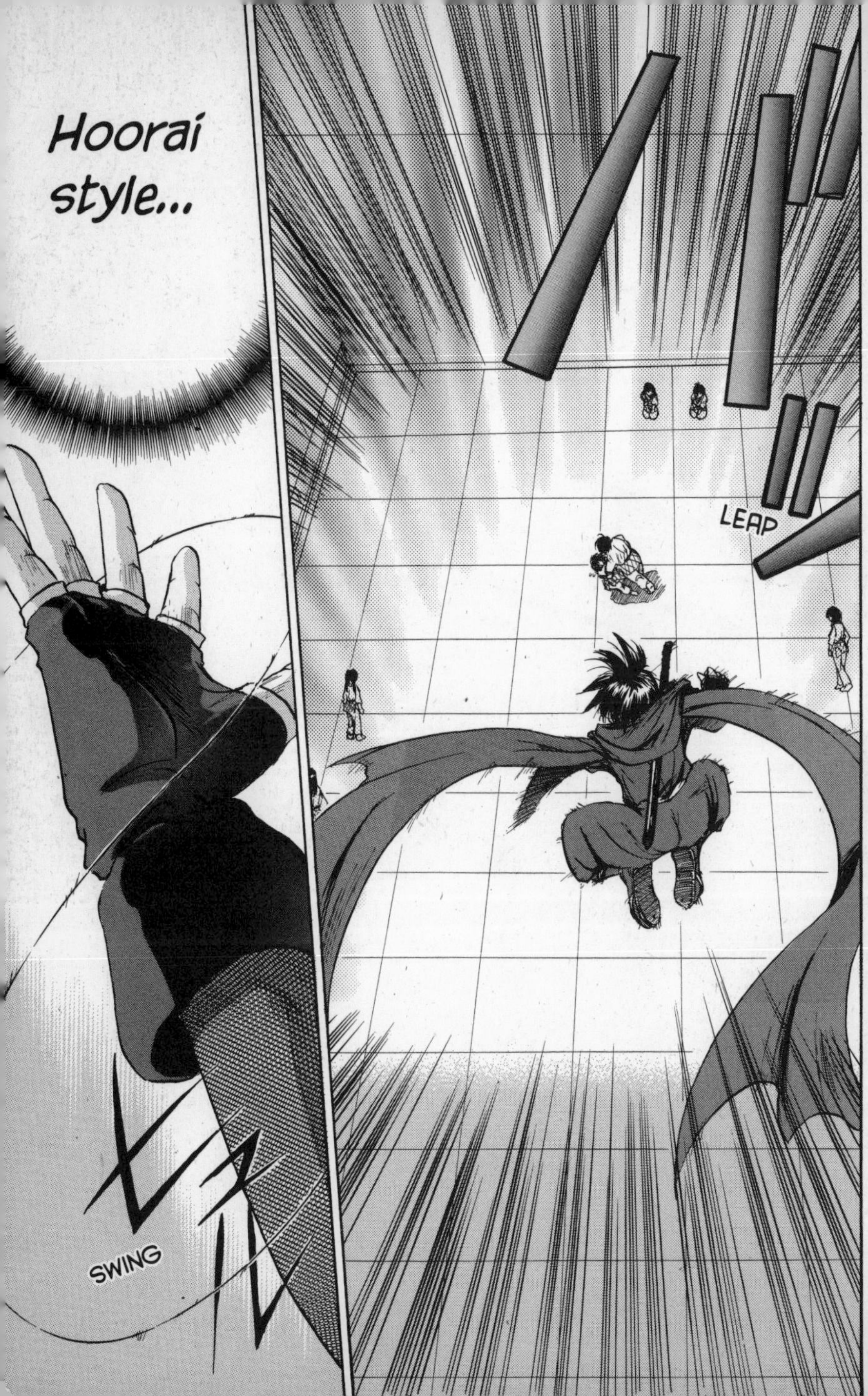
LEAP
Hoorai style...
SWING

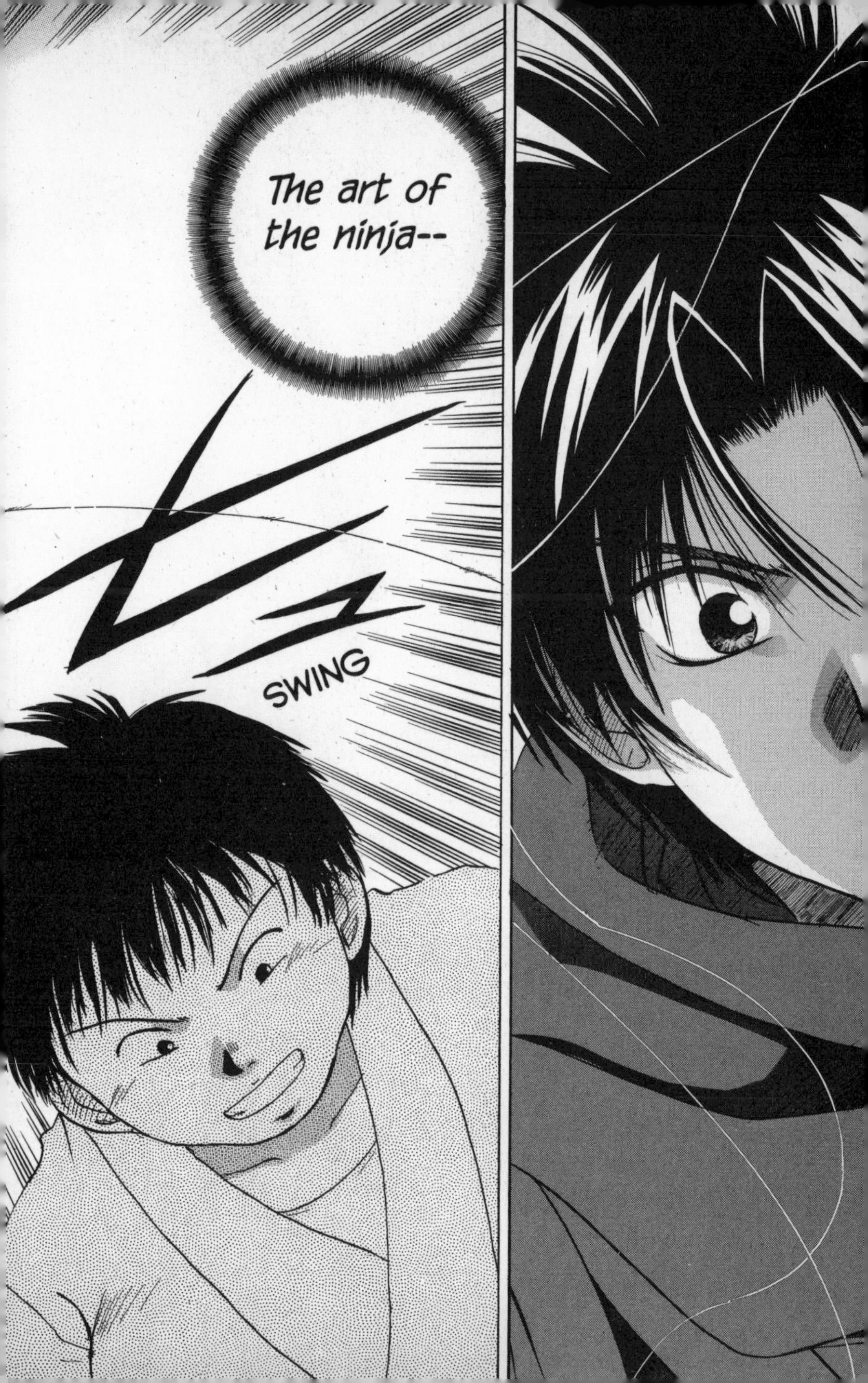
The art of the ninja--
SWING

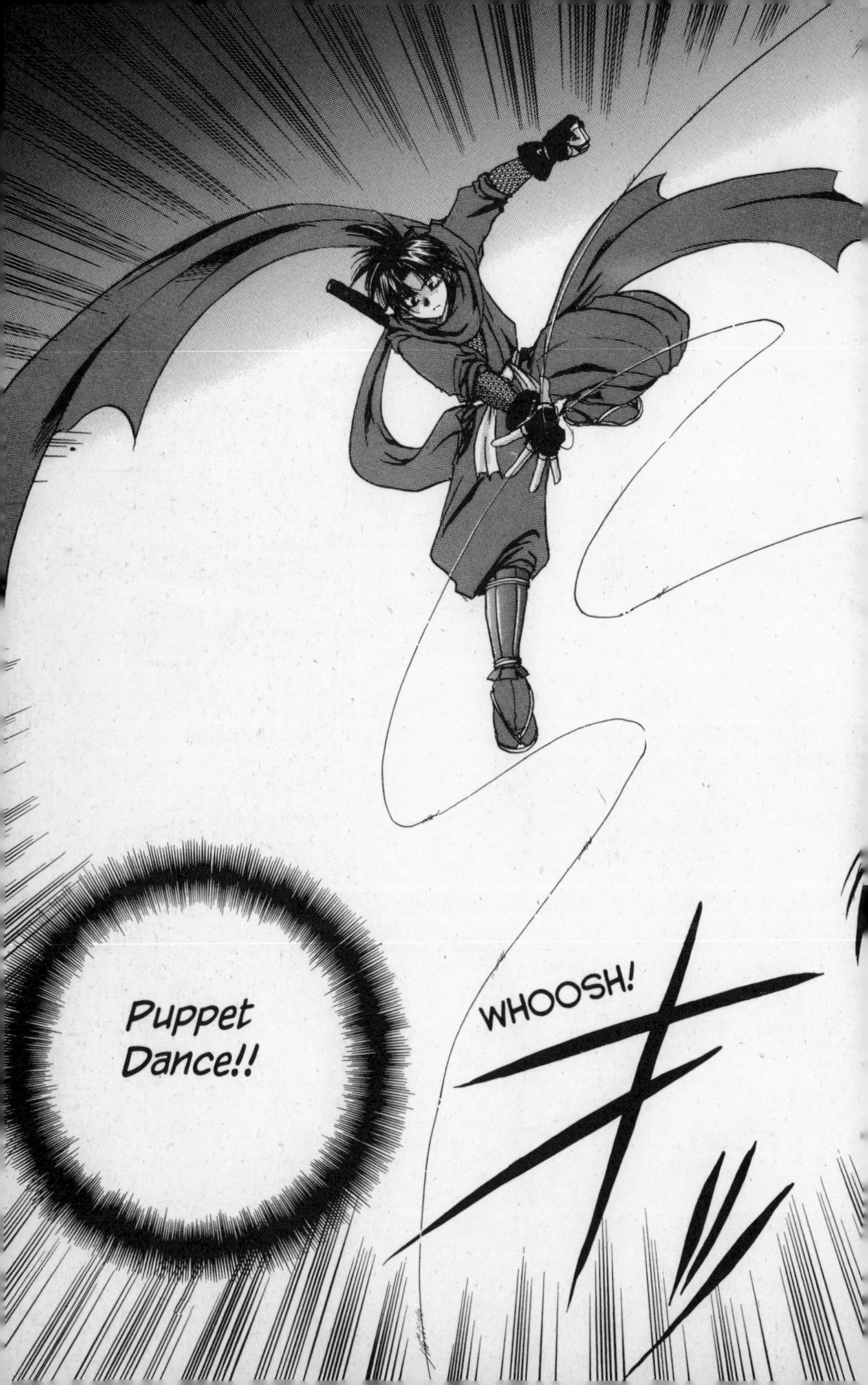
Puppet Dance!!
WHOOSH!

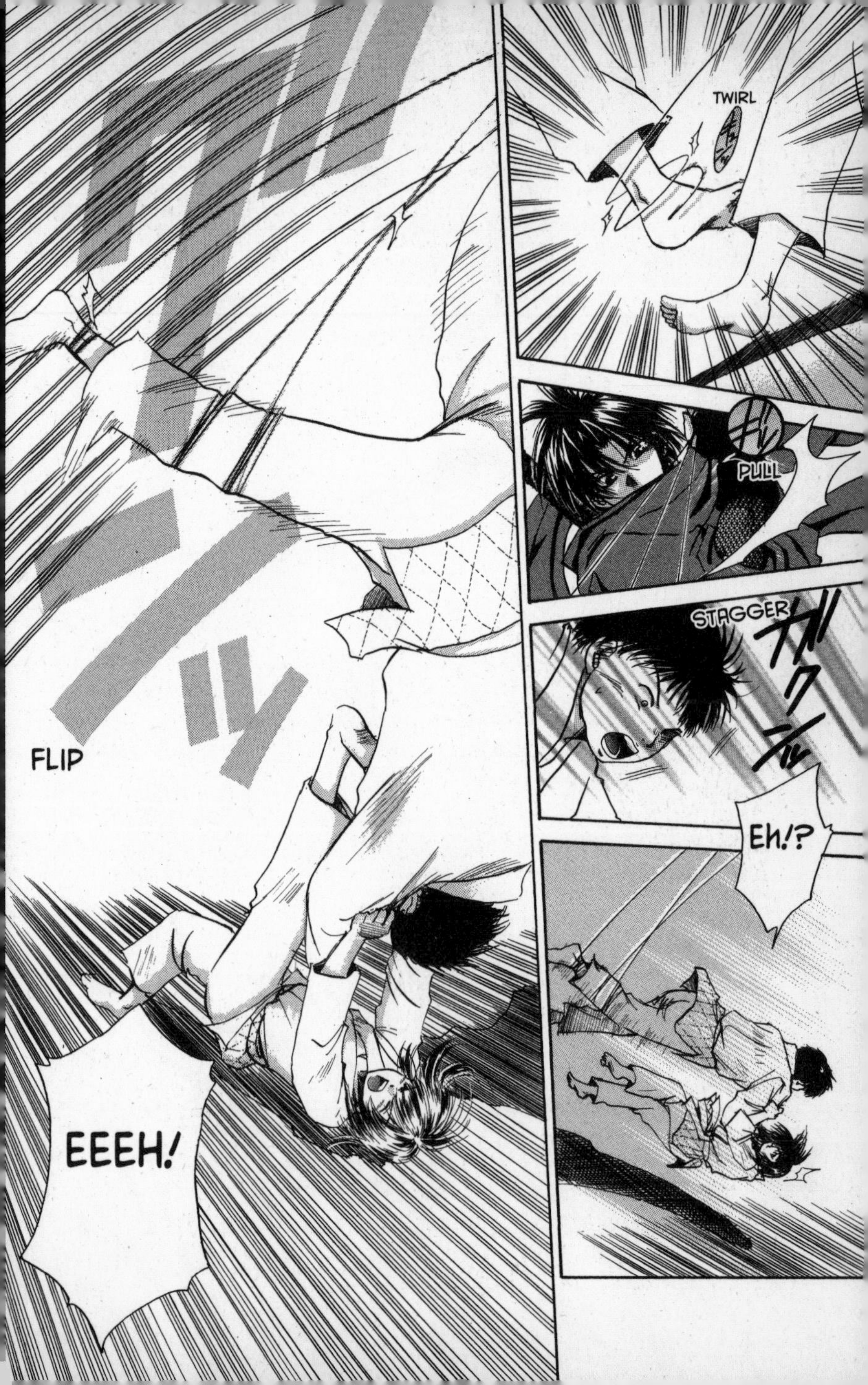
TWIRL
PULL
STAGGER
Eh!?
FLIP
EEEH!

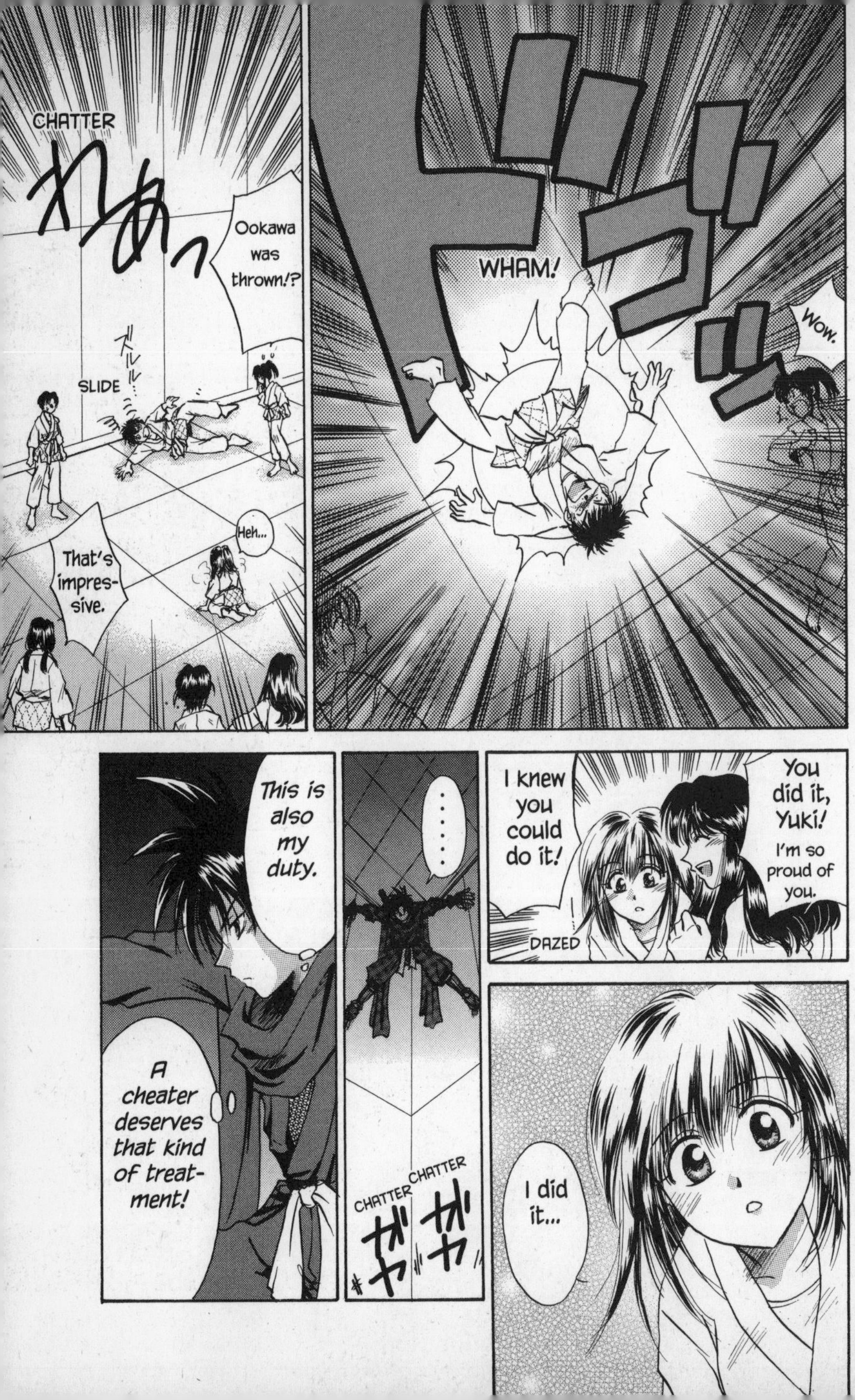
WHAM!
Wow.
CHATTER
わあっ
Ookawa was thrown!?
ズルル…
SLIDE
Heh...
That's impressive.
You did it, Yuki! I'm so proud of you.
I knew you could do it!
DAZED
I did it...
......
CHATTER CHATTER
ガヤガヤ
This is also my duty.
A cheater deserves that kind of treatment!

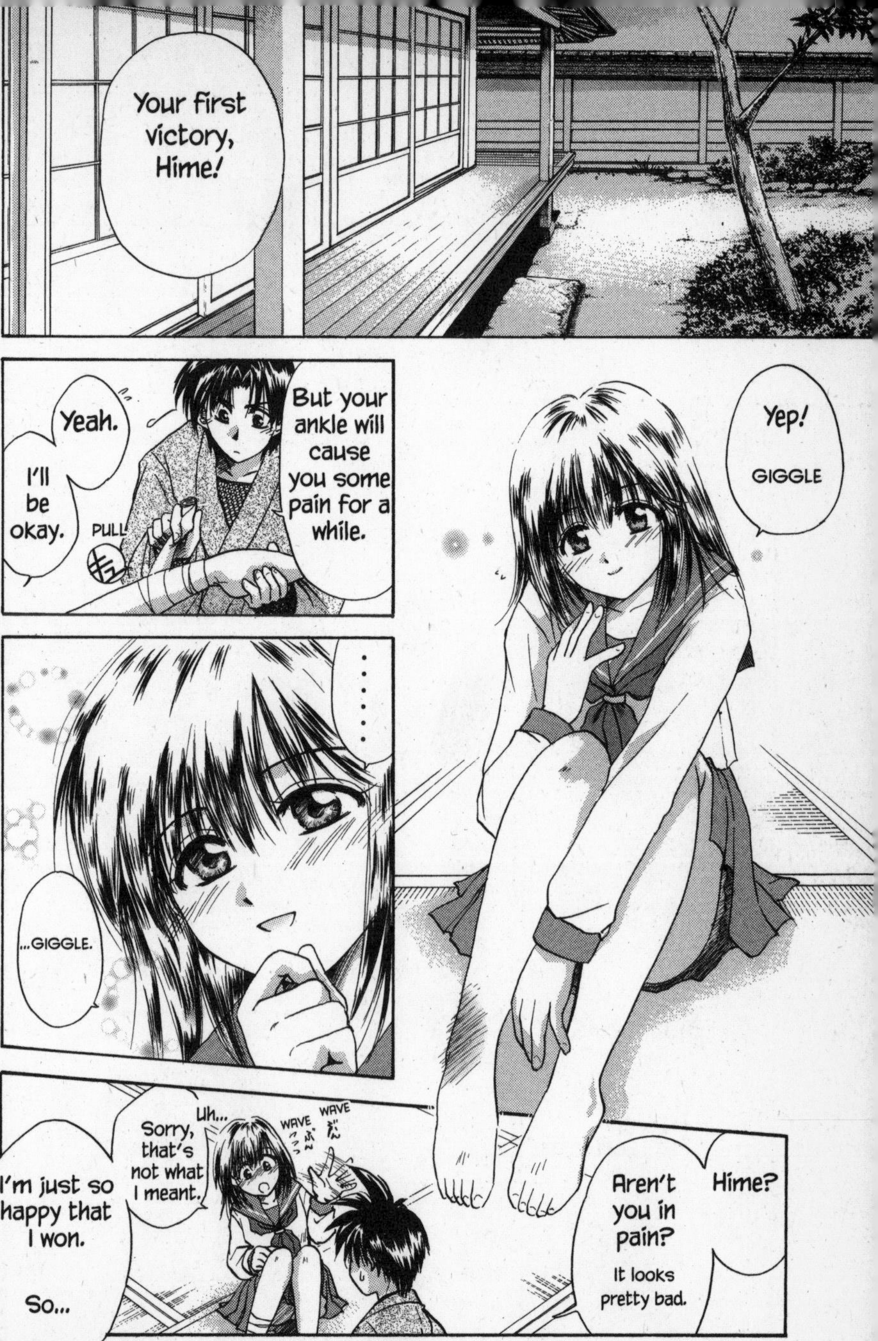
Your first victory, Hime!
Yep!
GIGGLE
But your ankle will cause you some pain for a while.
Yeah.
I'll be okay.
PULL
......
...GIGGLE.
Hime?
Aren't you in pain?
It looks pretty bad.
Uh...
WAVE WAVE
Sorry, that's not what I meant.
I'm just so happy that I won.
So...

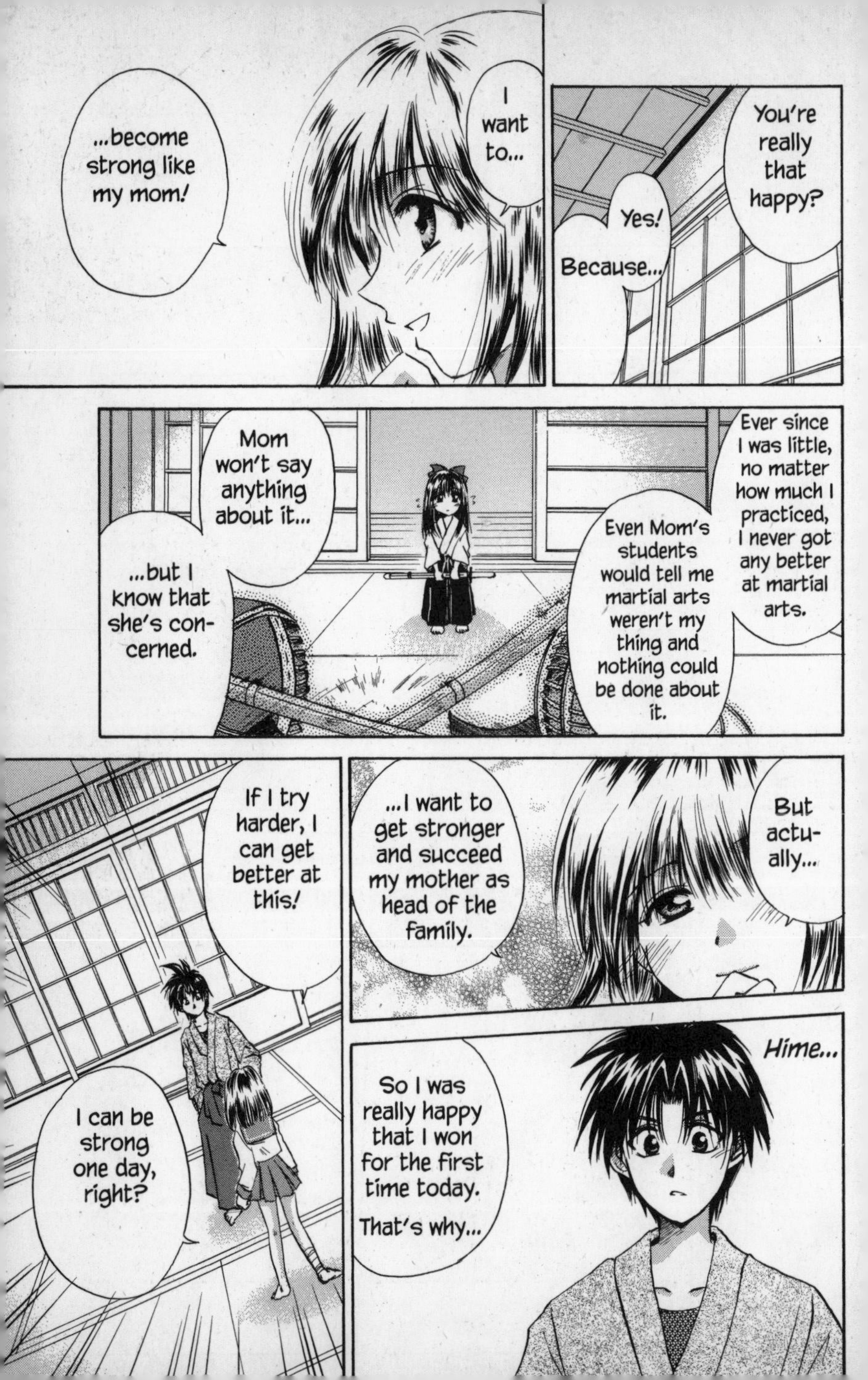
You're really that happy?
Yes!
Because...
I want to...
...become strong like my mom!
Ever since I was little, no matter how much I practiced, I never got any better at martial arts.
Even Mom's students would tell me martial arts weren't my thing and nothing could be done about it.
Mom won't say anything about it...
...but I know that she's concerned.
But actually...
...I want to get stronger and succeed my mother as head of the family.
Hime...
So I was really happy that I won for the first time today.
That's why...
If I try harder, I can get better at this!
I can be strong one day, right?

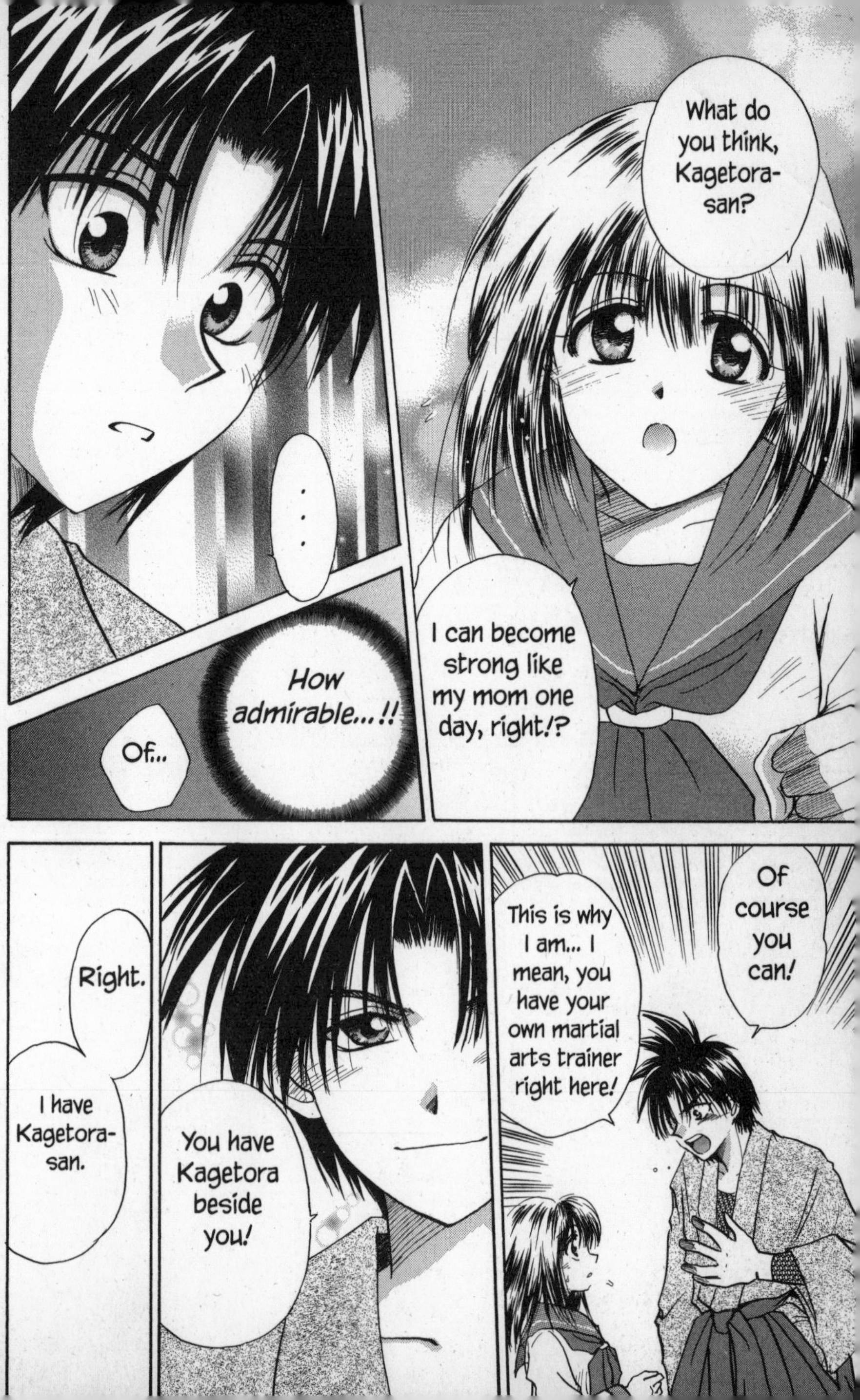
What do you think, Kagetora-san?
I can become strong like my mom one day, right!?
...
How admirable...!!
Of...
Of course you can!
This is why I am... I mean, you have your own martial arts trainer right here!
You have Kagetora beside you!
Right.
I have Kagetora-san.

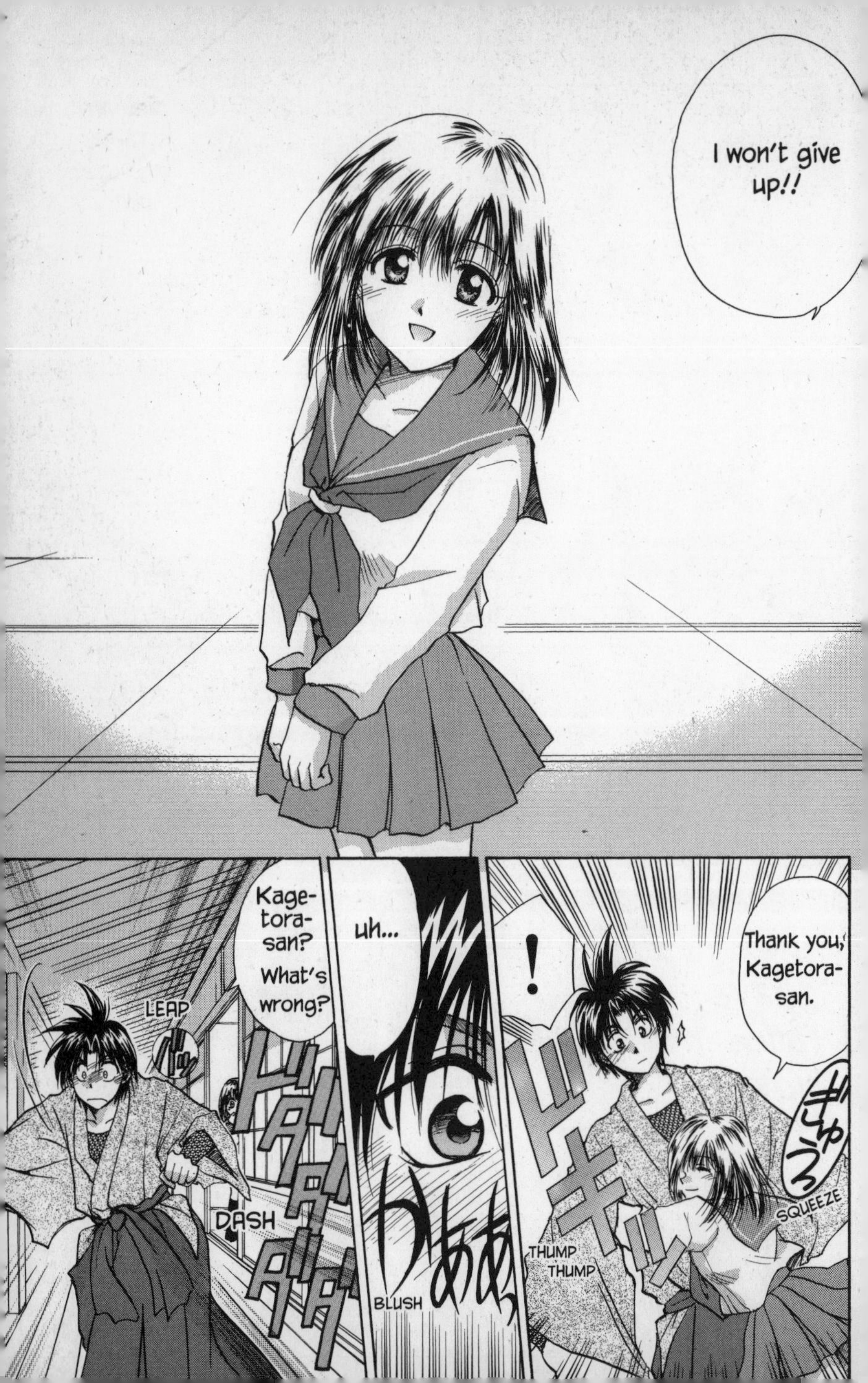
I won't give up!!
Thank you, Kagetora-san.
SQUEEZE
!
THUMP THUMP
uh...
BLUSH
Kagetora-san? What's wrong?
LEAP
DASH

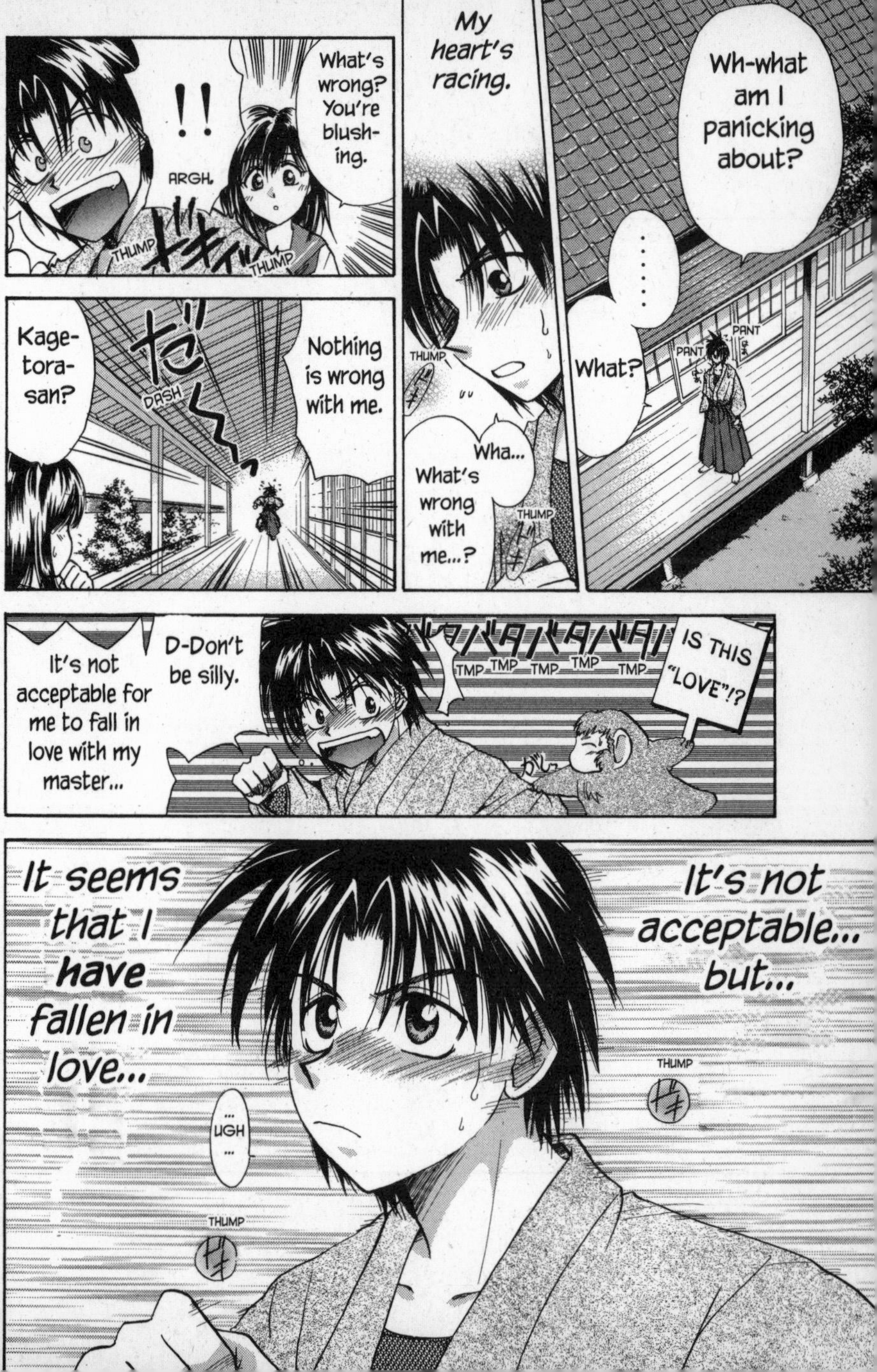
Wh-what am I panicking about?
......
PANT
PANT
What?
My heart's racing.
THUMP
Wha... What's wrong with me...?
THUMP
What's wrong? You're blushing.
!!
ARGH
THUMP
THUMP
Nothing is wrong with me.
DASH
Kage-tora-san?
IS THIS "LOVE"!?
TMP TMP TMP TMP TMP
D-Don't be silly.
It's not acceptable for me to fall in love with my master...
It's not acceptable... but...
It seems that I have fallen in love...
THUMP
...UGH...
THUMP

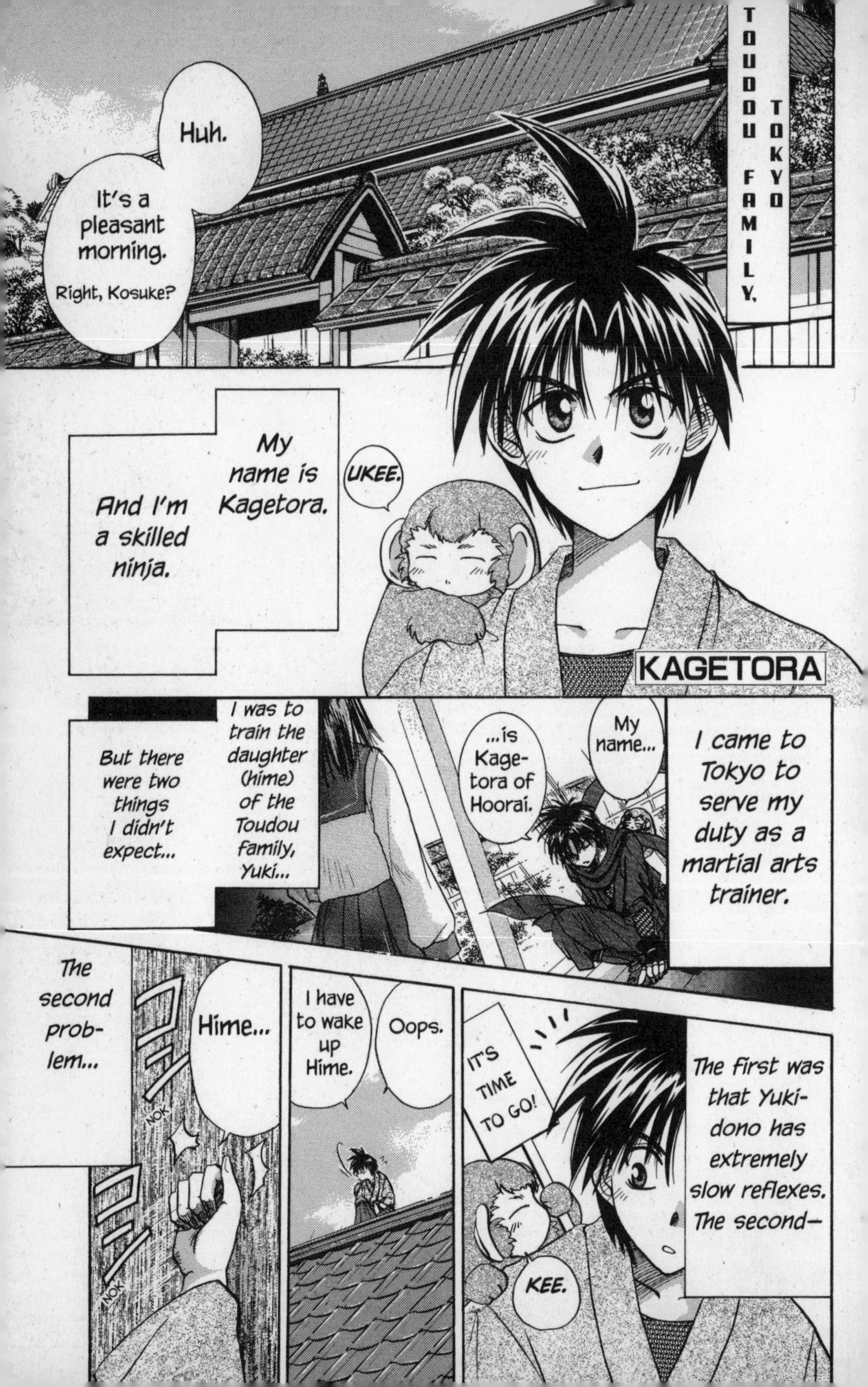
TOUDOU FAMILY, TOKYO
Huh.
It's a pleasant morning.
Right, Kosuke?
My name is Kagetora.
UKEE.
And I'm a skilled ninja.
KAGETORA
I came to Tokyo to serve my duty as a martial arts trainer.
My name...
...is Kagetora of Hoorai.
I was to train the daughter (hime) of the Toudou family, Yuki...
But there were two things I didn't expect...
The first was that Yuki-dono has extremely slow reflexes. The second—
IT'S TIME TO GO!
KEE.
Oops.
I have to wake up Hime.
Hime...
NOK
NOK
The second problem...

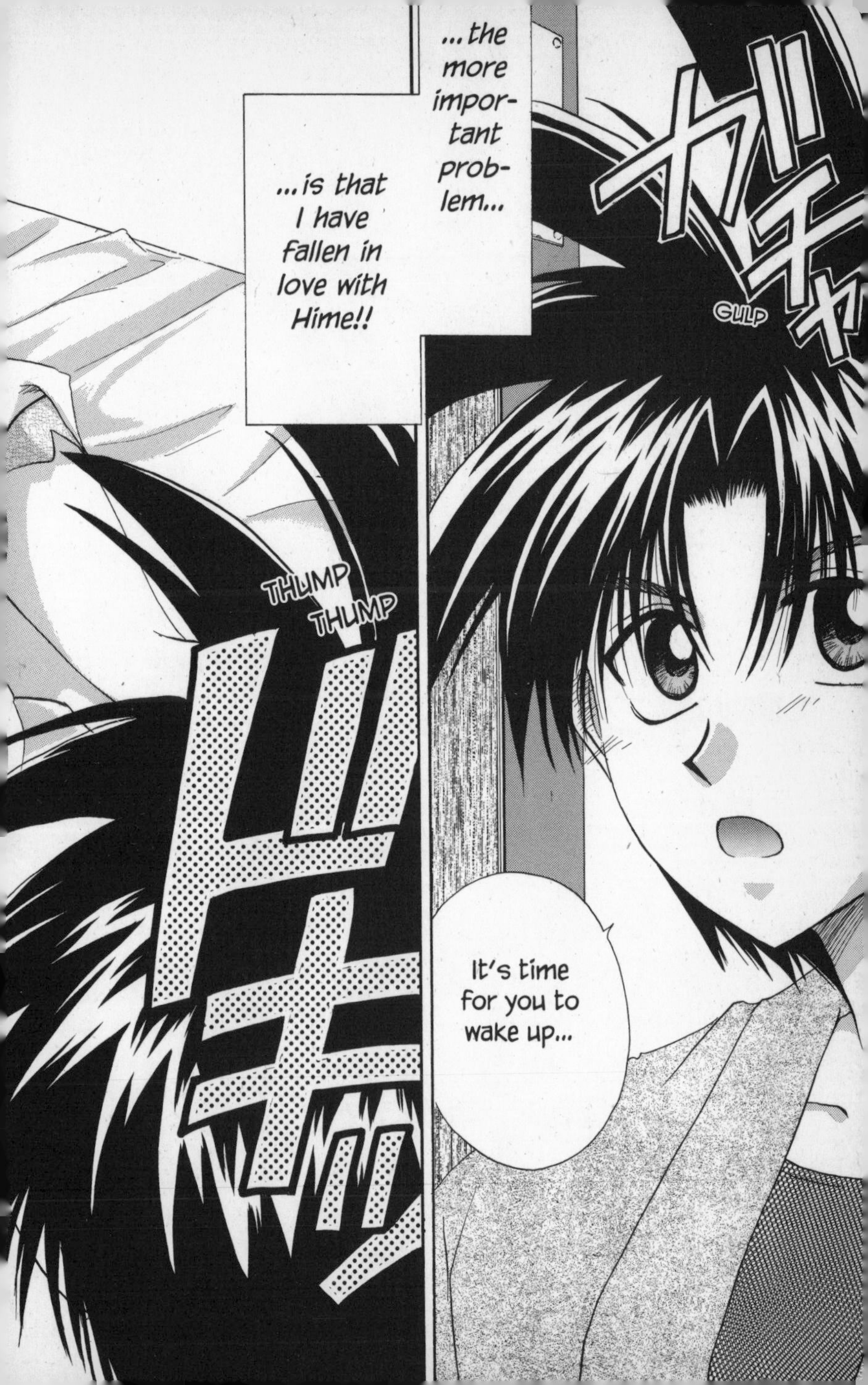
...the more important problem...
...is that I have fallen in love with Hime!!
ガチャ
GULP
It's time for you to wake up...
THUMP THUMP
ドキ

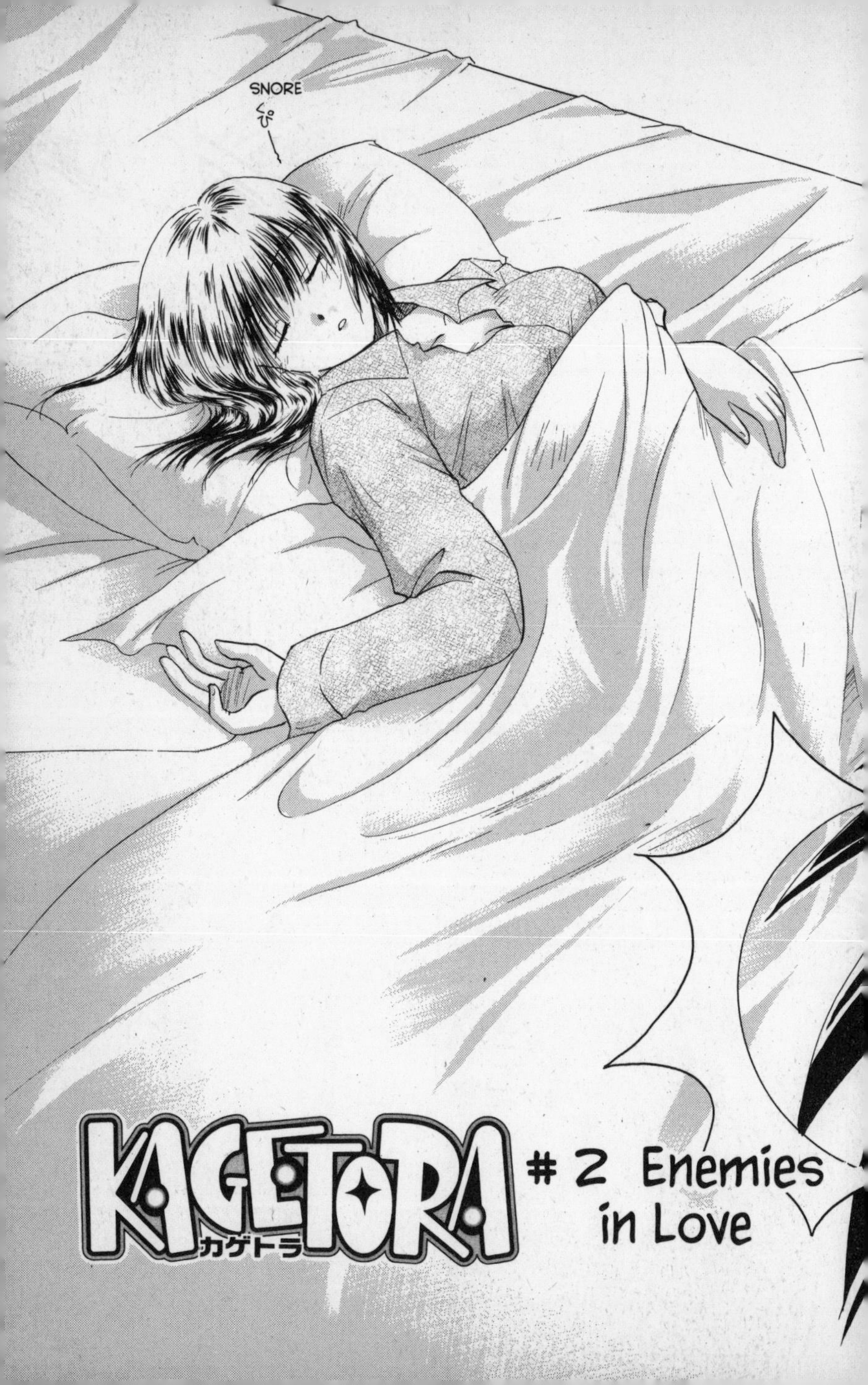
SNORE
くぴー
KAGETORA
カゲトラ
2 Enemies in Love

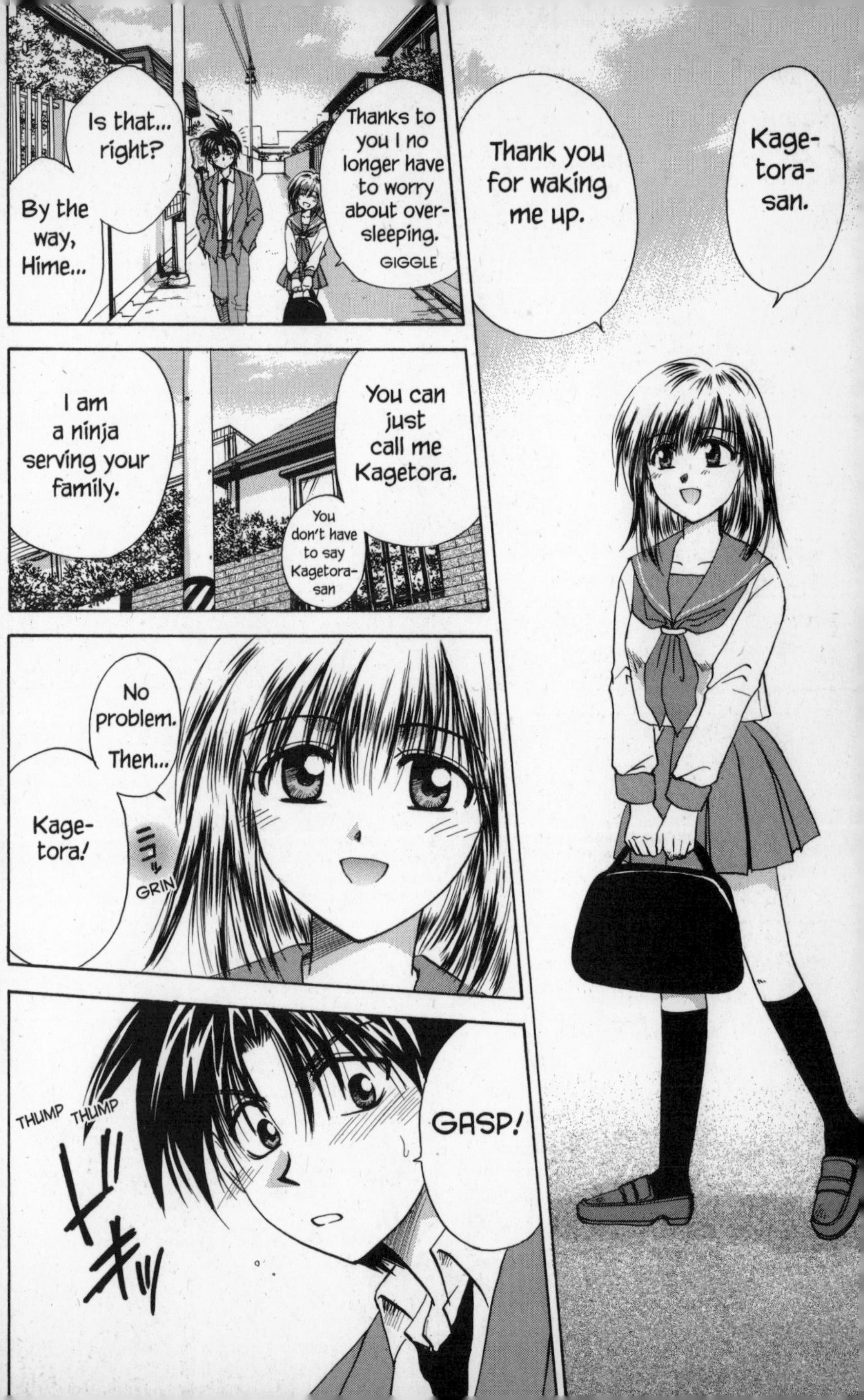
Kage-tora-san.
Thank you for waking me up.
Thanks to you I no longer have to worry about over-sleeping.
GIGGLE
Is that... right?
By the way, Hime...
You can just call me Kagetora.
You don't have to say Kagetora-san
I am a ninja serving your family.
No problem.
Then...
Kage-tora!
GRIN
GASP!
THUMP THUMP

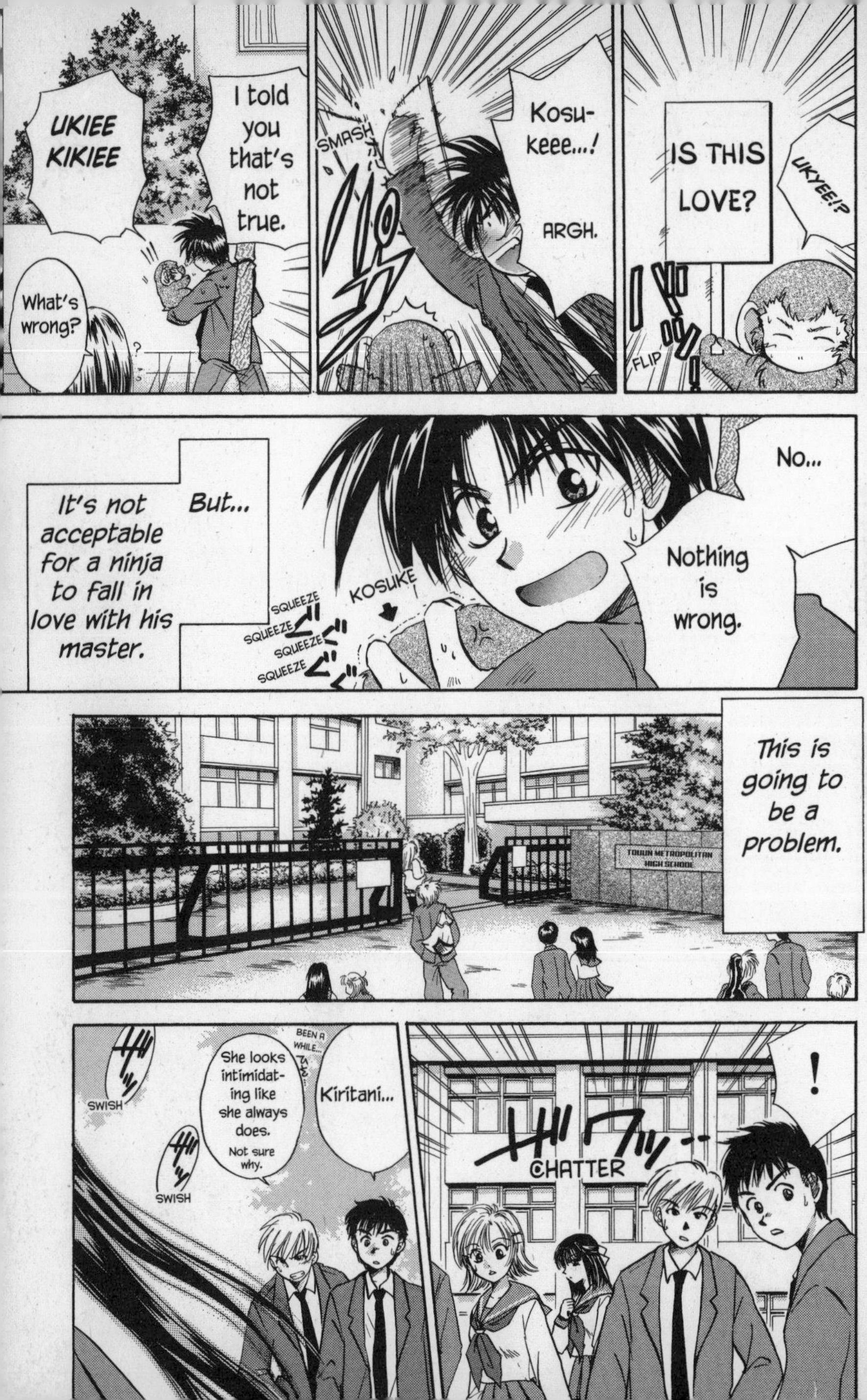
UKYEE!?
IS THIS LOVE?
FLIP
Kosu-keee...!
SMASH
ARGH.
I told you that's not true.
UKIEE KIKIEE
What's wrong?
No...
Nothing is wrong.
KOSUKE
SQUEEZE
SQUEEZE
SQUEEZE
SQUEEZE
But...
It's not acceptable for a ninja to fall in love with his master.
This is going to be a problem.
!
CHATTER
Kiritani...
BEEN A WHILE...
She looks intimidating like she always does.
Not sure why.
SWISH
SWISH

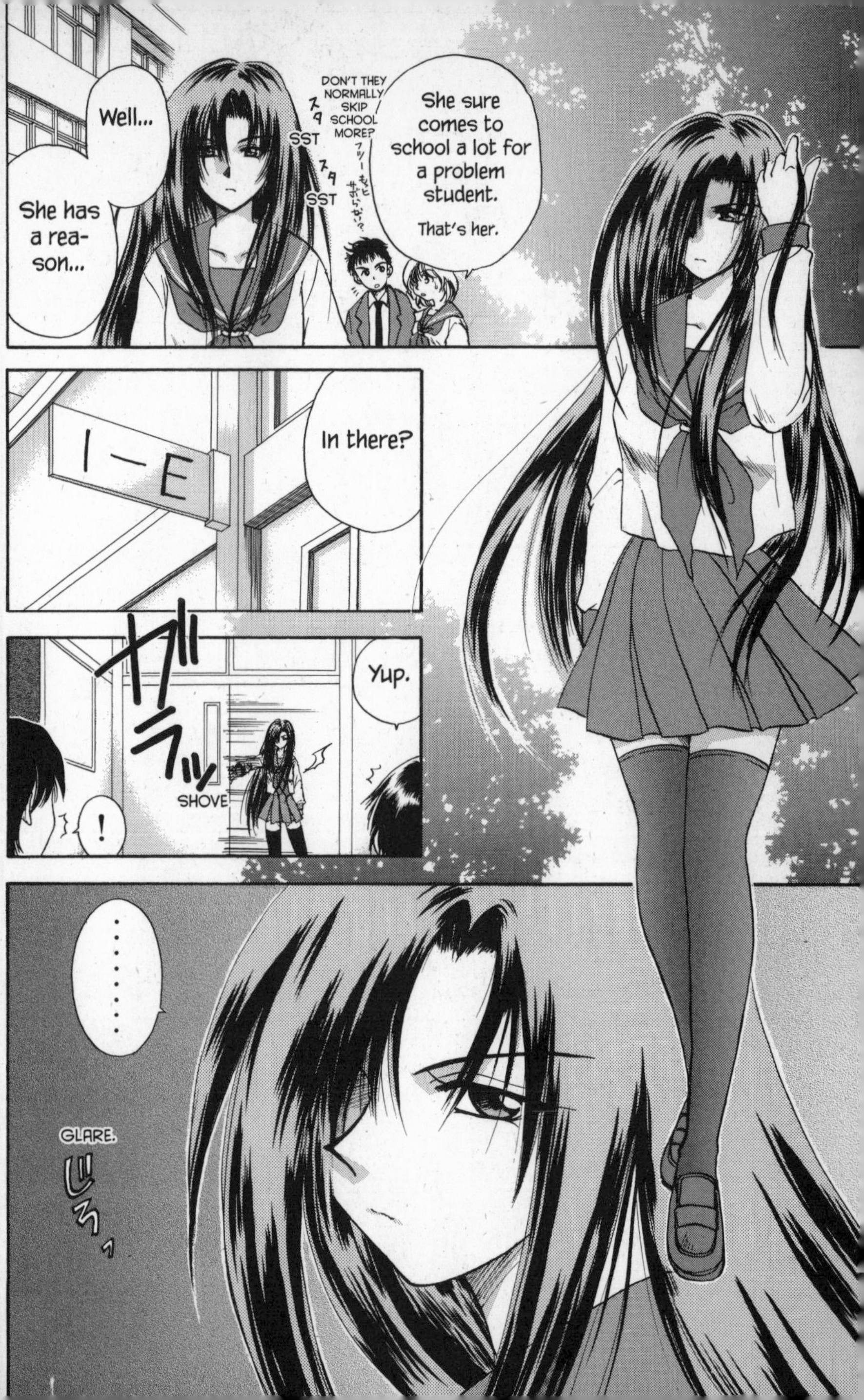
She sure comes to school a lot for a problem student.
That's her.
DON'T THEY NORMALLY SKIP SCHOOL MORE?
SST
SST
Well...
She has a rea-son...
In there?
I-E
Yup.
SHOVE
!
......
GLARE.

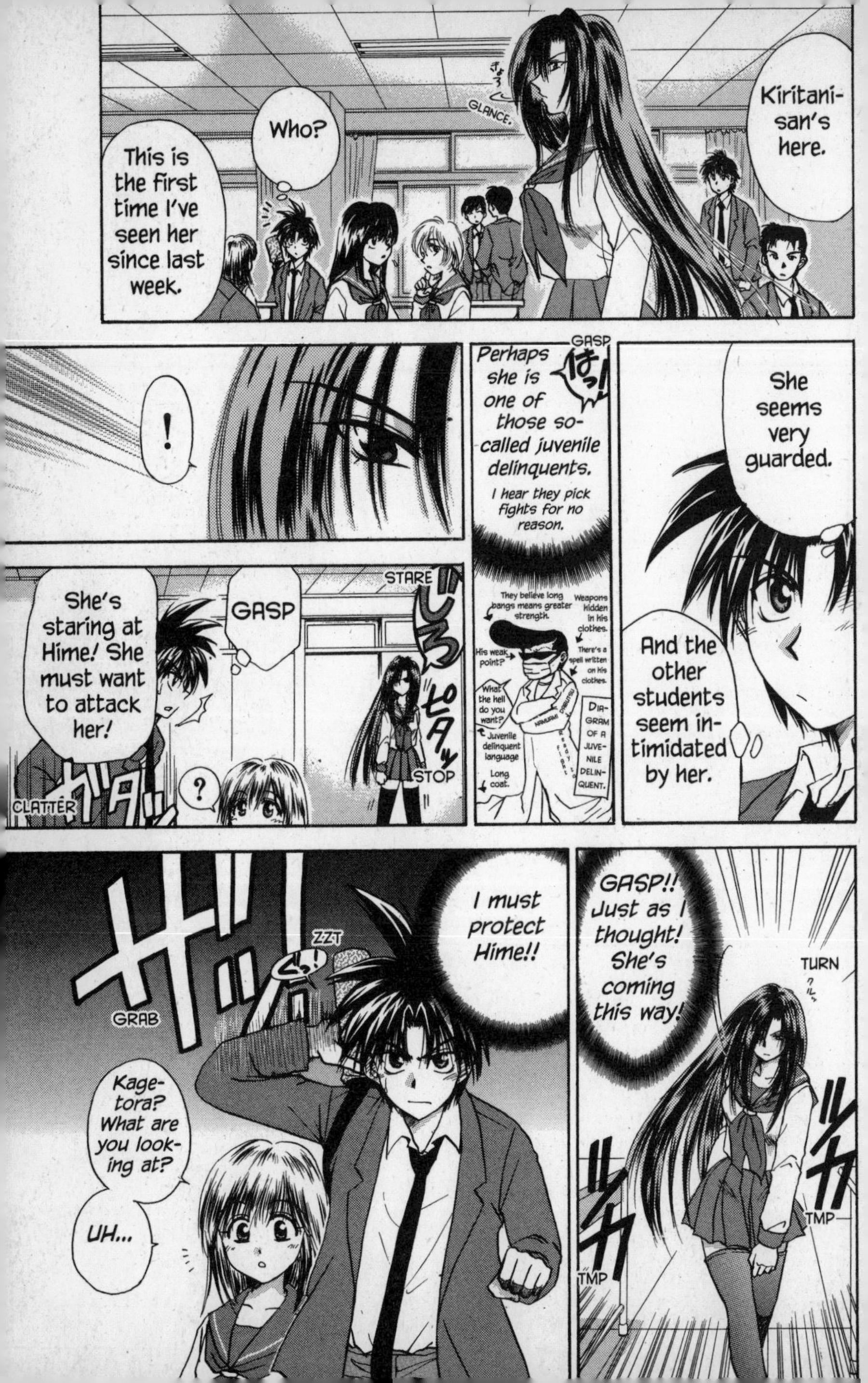
Kiritani-san's here.
GLANCE.
Who?
This is the first time I've seen her since last week.
She seems very guarded.
And the other students seem intimidated by her.
GASP
Perhaps she is one of those so-called juvenile delinquents.
I hear they pick fights for no reason.
!
They believe long bangs means greater strength.
Weapons hidden in his clothes.
His weak point?
There's a spell written on his clothes.
What the hell do you want?
Juvenile delinquent language
Long coat.
DIAGRAM OF A JUVENILE DELINQUENT.
STARE
STOP
GASP
She's staring at Hime! She must want to attack her!
CLATTER
?
GASP!! Just as I thought! She's coming this way!
TURN
TMP
TMP
I must protect Hime!!
ZZT
GRAB
Kage-tora? What are you look-ing at?
UH...

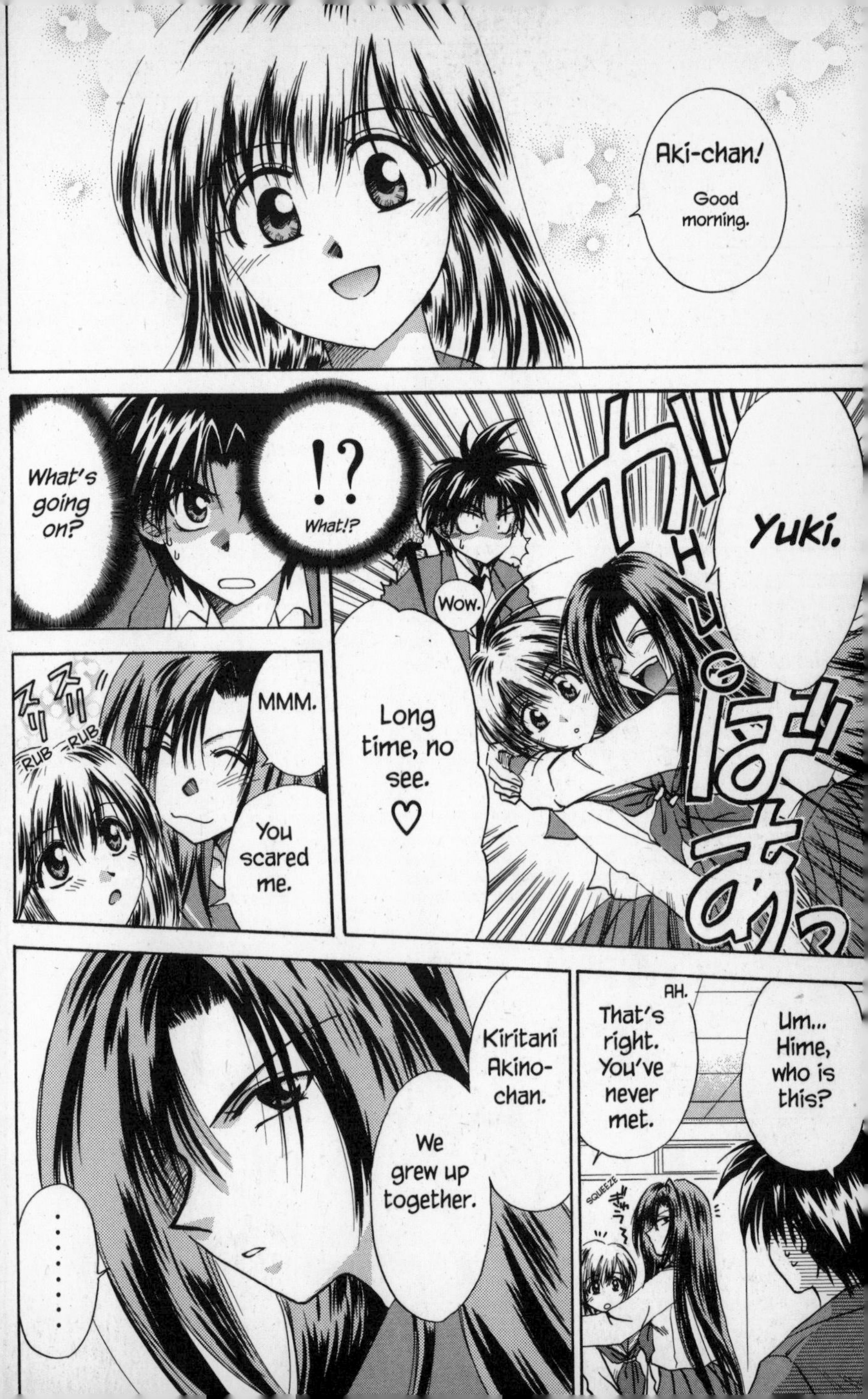
Aki-chan!
Good morning.
Yuki.
HUG
Wow.
Long time, no see. ♡
!?
What!?
What's going on?
MMM.
You scared me.
RUB RUB
Um... Hime, who is this?
AH.
That's right. You've never met.
SQUEEZE
Kiritani Akino-chan.
We grew up together.
......

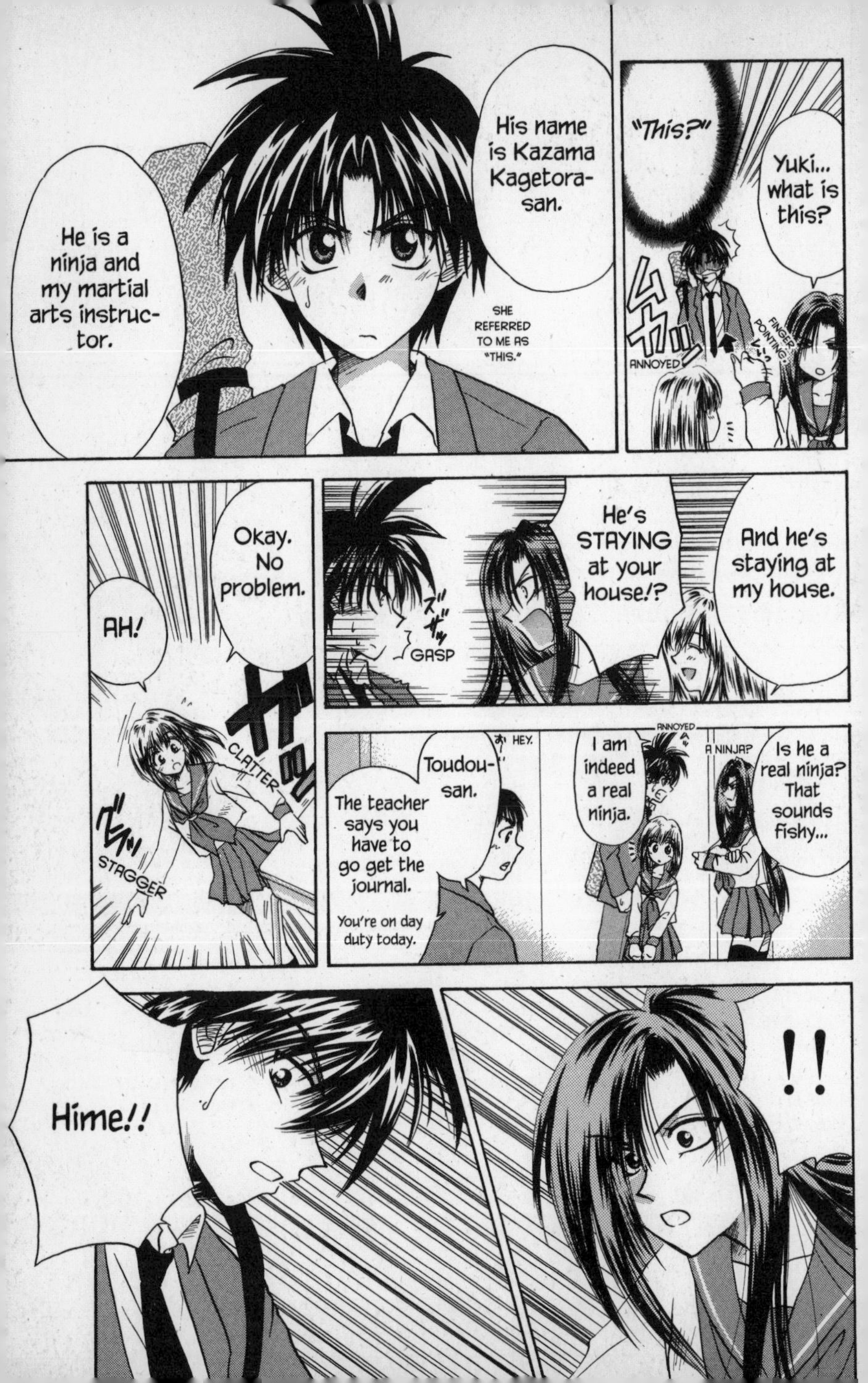
Yuki... what is this?
FINGER POINTING
"This?"
ANNOYED
His name is Kazama Kagetora-san.
SHE REFERRED TO ME AS "THIS."
He is a ninja and my martial arts instructor.
And he's staying at my house.
He's STAYING at your house!?
GASP
Is he a real ninja? That sounds fishy...
A NINJA?
ANNOYED
I am indeed a real ninja.
HEY.
Toudou-san.
The teacher says you have to go get the journal.
You're on day duty today.
Okay. No problem.
AH!
CLATTER
STAGGER
!!
Hime!!

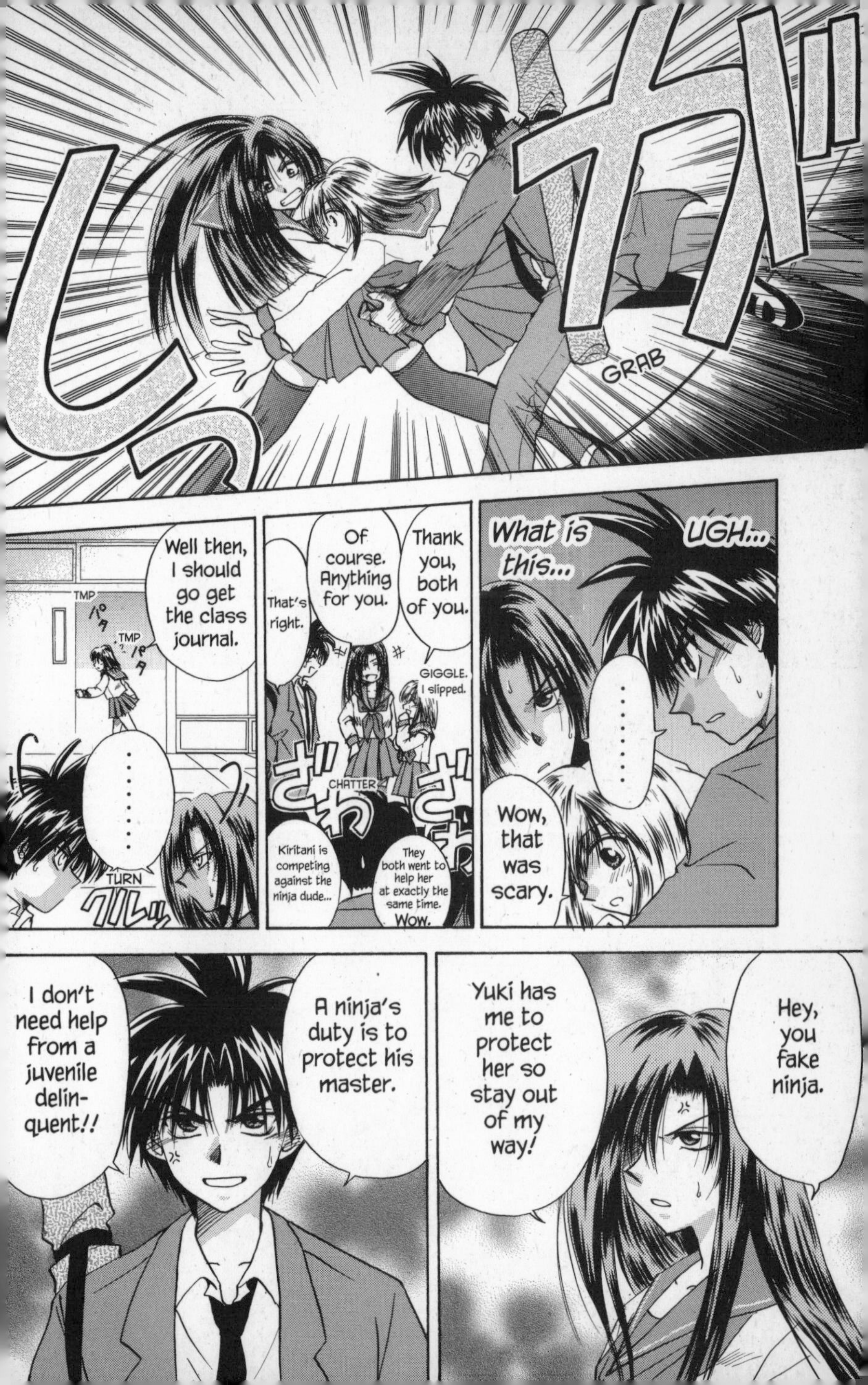
GRAB
UGH...
What is this...
......
Wow, that was scary.
Thank you, both of you.
Of course. Anything for you.
That's right.
GIGGLE. I slipped.
CHATTER
ざわ ざわ
They both went to help her at exactly the same time. Wow.
Kiritani is competing against the ninja dude...
Well then, I should go get the class journal.
TMP パタ
TMP パタ
......
TURN
クルッ
Hey, you fake ninja.
Yuki has me to protect her so stay out of my way!
A ninja's duty is to protect his master.
I don't need help from a juvenile delin-quent!!

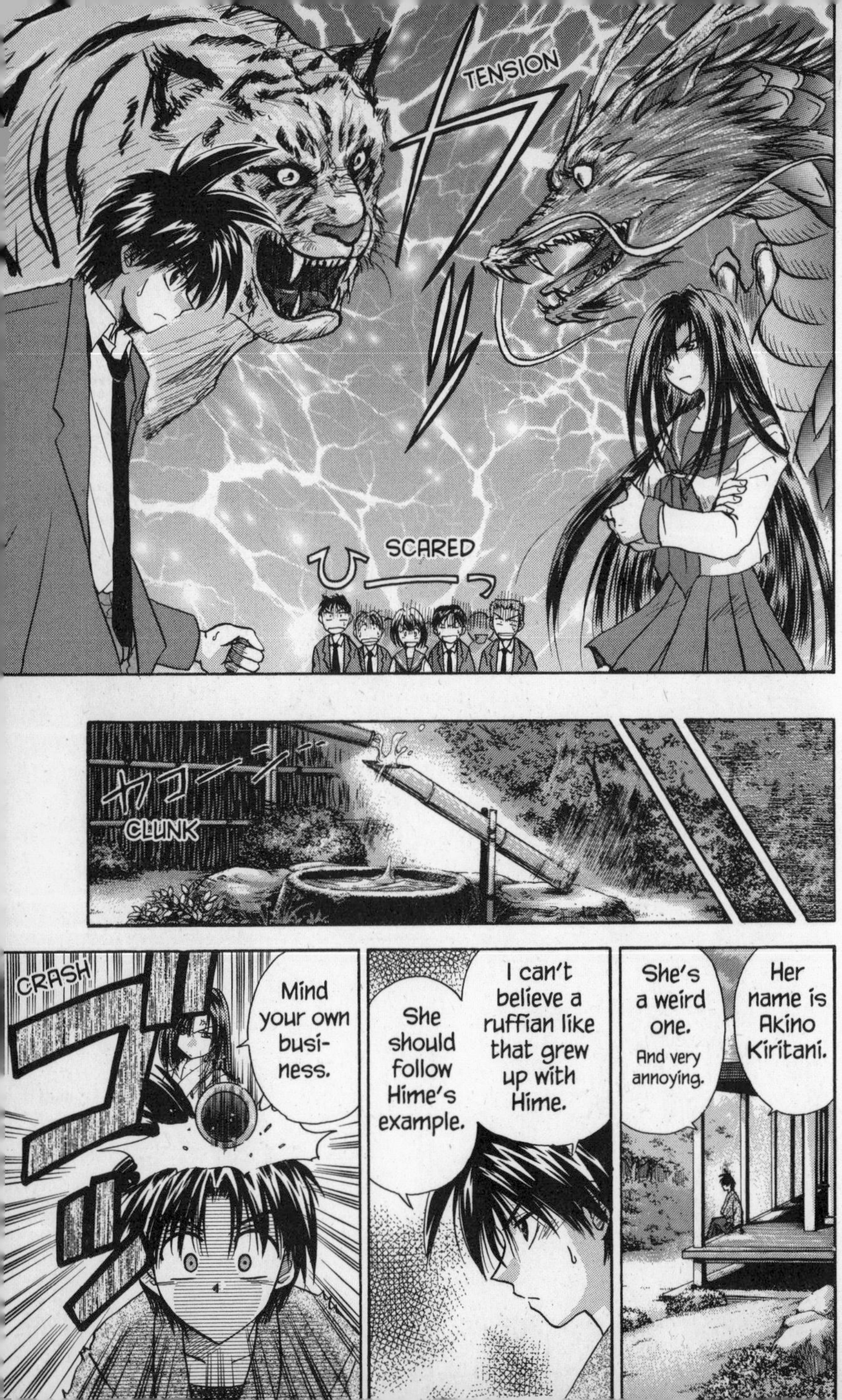
TENSION
SCARED
CLUNK
Her name is Akino Kiritani.
She's a weird one.
And very annoying.
I can't believe a ruffian like that grew up with Hime.
She should follow Hime's example.
CRASH
Mind your own busi-ness.

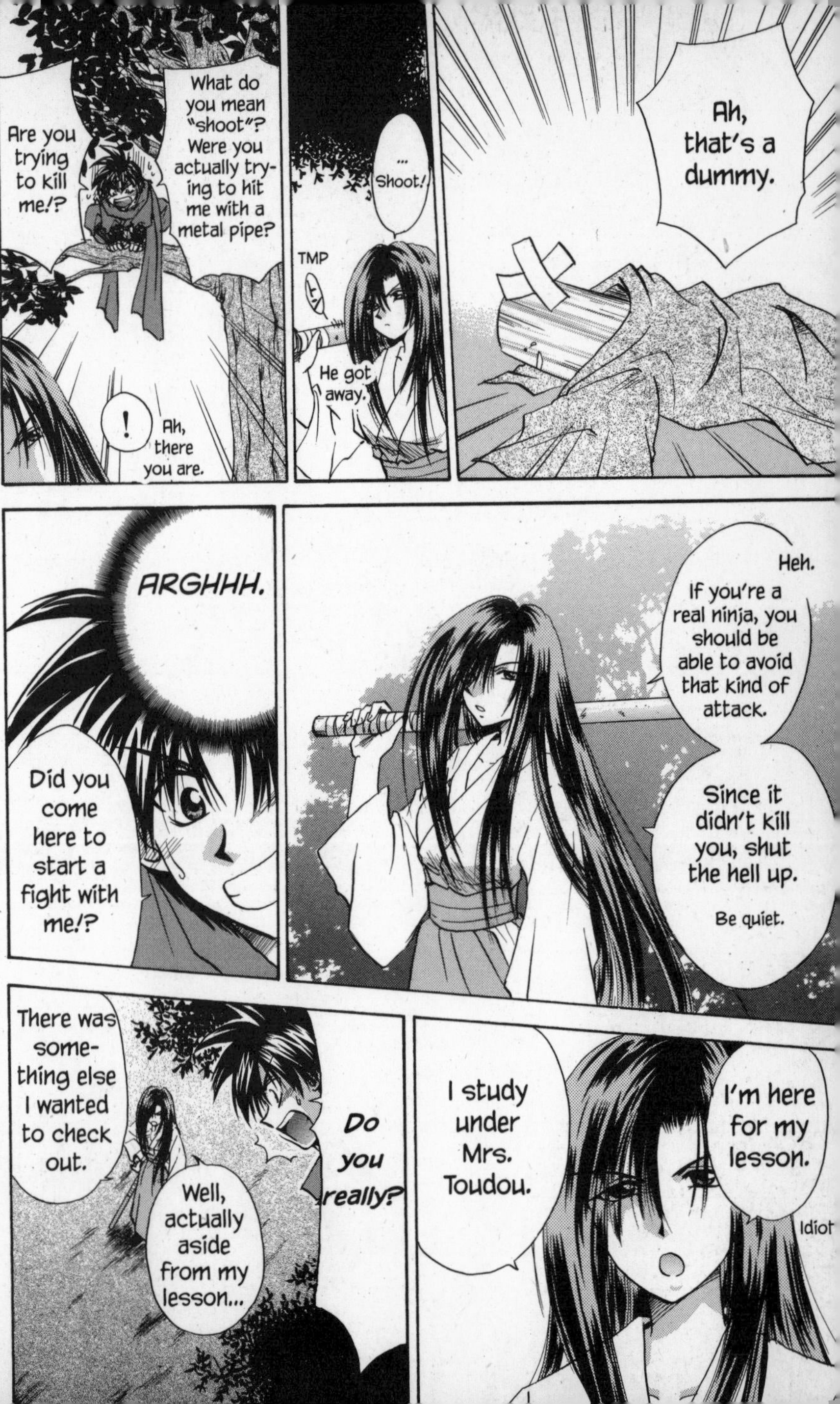
Ah, that's a dummy.
... Shoot!
TMP
He got away.
What do you mean "shoot"? Were you actually trying to hit me with a metal pipe?
Are you trying to kill me!?
!
Ah, there you are.
Heh. If you're a real ninja, you should be able to avoid that kind of attack.
Since it didn't kill you, shut the hell up.
Be quiet.
ARGHHH.
Did you come here to start a fight with me!?
I'm here for my lesson.
Idiot
I study under Mrs. Toudou.
Do you really?
Well, actually aside from my lesson...
There was something else I wanted to check out.

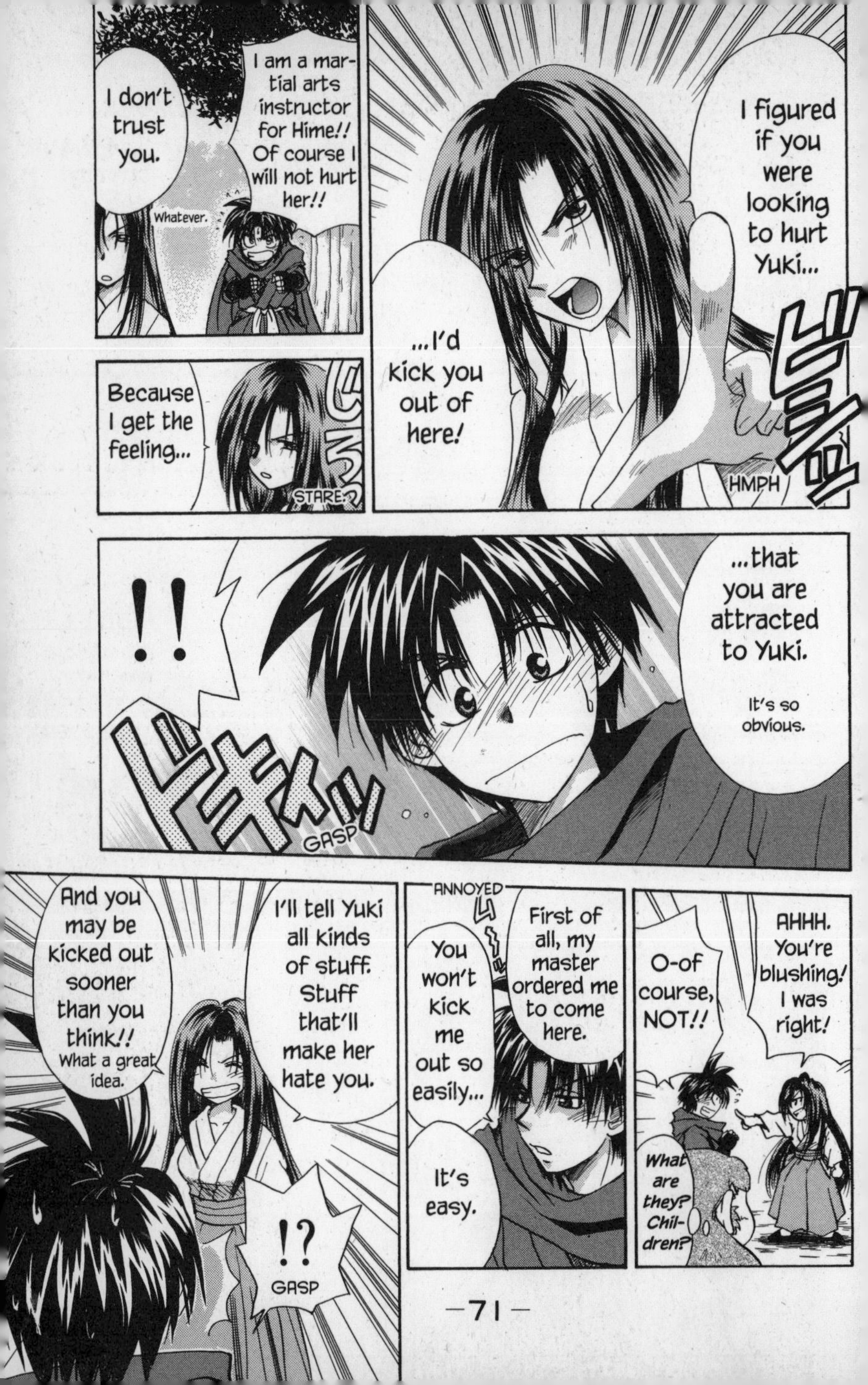
I figured if you were looking to hurt Yuki...
...I'd kick you out of here!
HMPH
I am a martial arts instructor for Hime!! Of course I will not hurt her!!
I don't trust you.
Whatever.
Because I get the feeling...
STARE
...that you are attracted to Yuki.
It's so obvious.
!!
GASP
AHHH. You're blushing! I was right!
O-of course, NOT!!
What are they? Children?
ANNOYED
First of all, my master ordered me to come here.
You won't kick me out so easily...
It's easy.
I'll tell Yuki all kinds of stuff. Stuff that'll make her hate you.
And you may be kicked out sooner than you think!! What a great idea.
!?
GASP

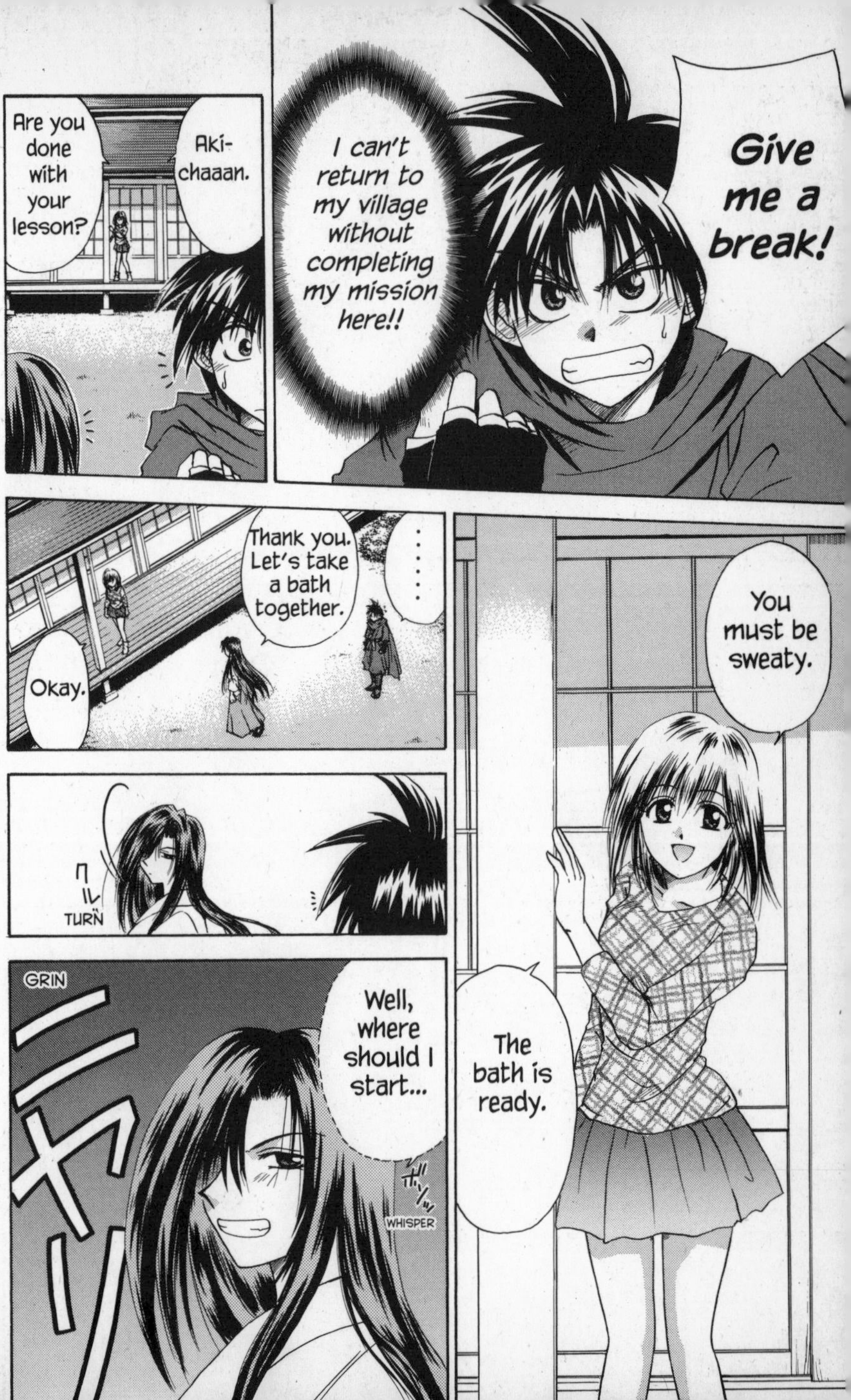
Give me a break!
I can't return to my village without completing my mission here!!
Aki-chaaan.
Are you done with your lesson?
You must be sweaty.
The bath is ready.
......
Thank you. Let's take a bath together.
Okay.
TURN
GRIN
Well, where should I start...
WHISPER

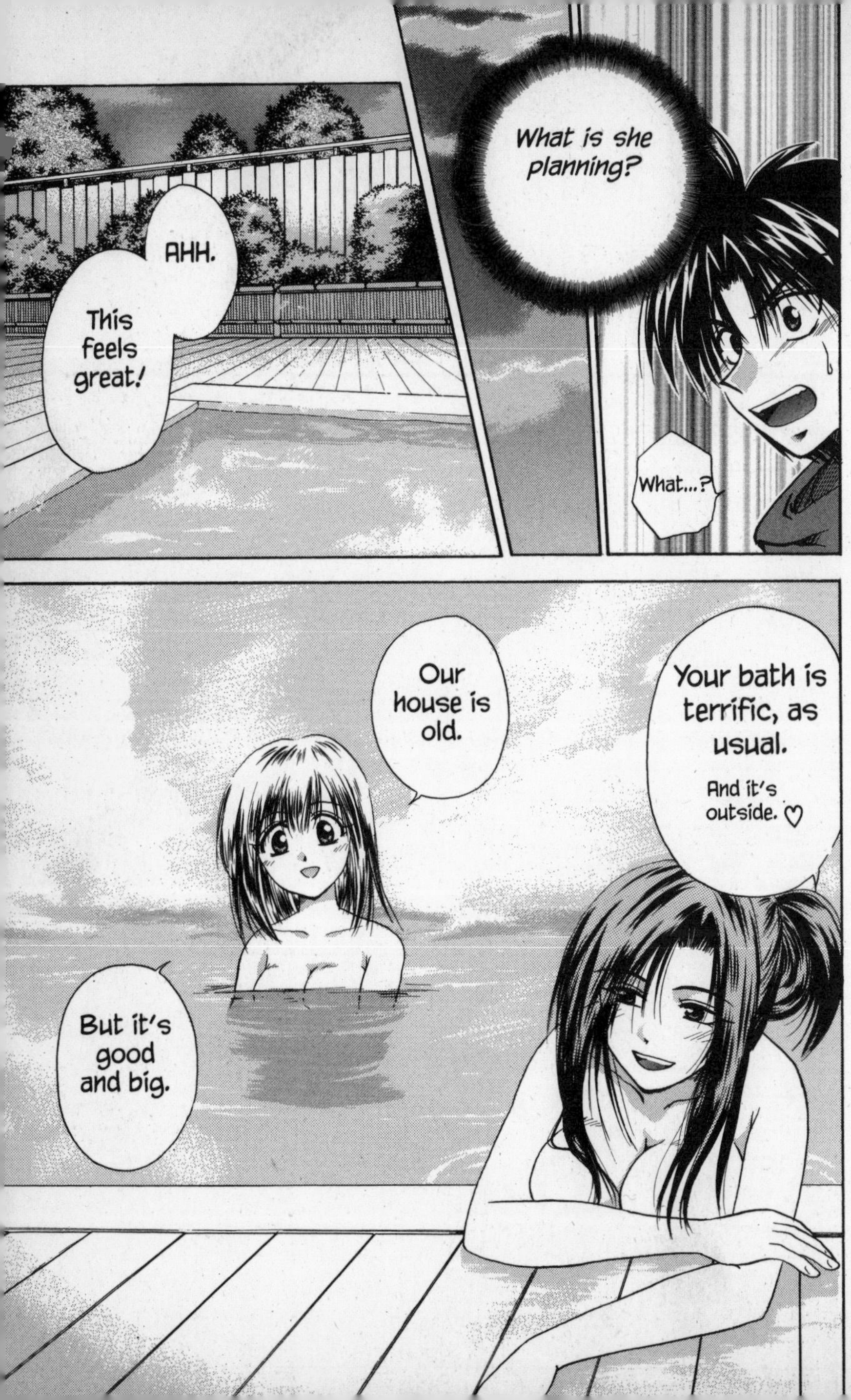
What is she planning?
What...?
AHH.
This feels great!
Your bath is terrific, as usual.
And it's outside. ♡
Our house is old.
But it's good and big.

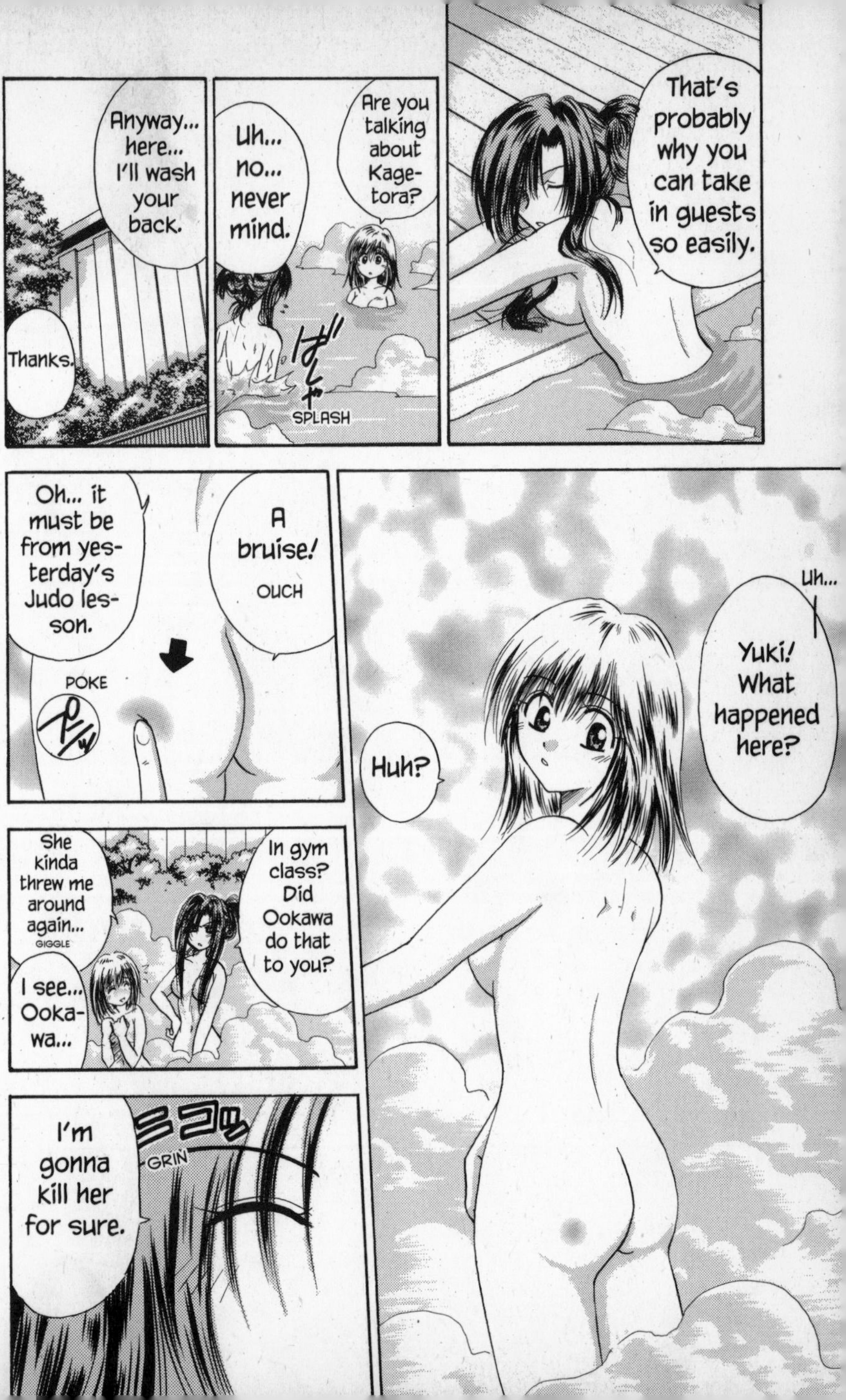
That's probably why you can take in guests so easily.
Are you talking about Kage-tora?
Uh... no... never mind.
SPLASH
Anyway... here... I'll wash your back.
Thanks.
Uh...
Yuki! What happened here?
Huh?
A bruise!
OUCH
Oh... it must be from yesterday's Judo lesson.
POKE
In gym class? Did Ookawa do that to you?
She kinda threw me around again...
GIGGLE
I see... Ooka-wa...
I'm gonna kill her for sure.
GRIN

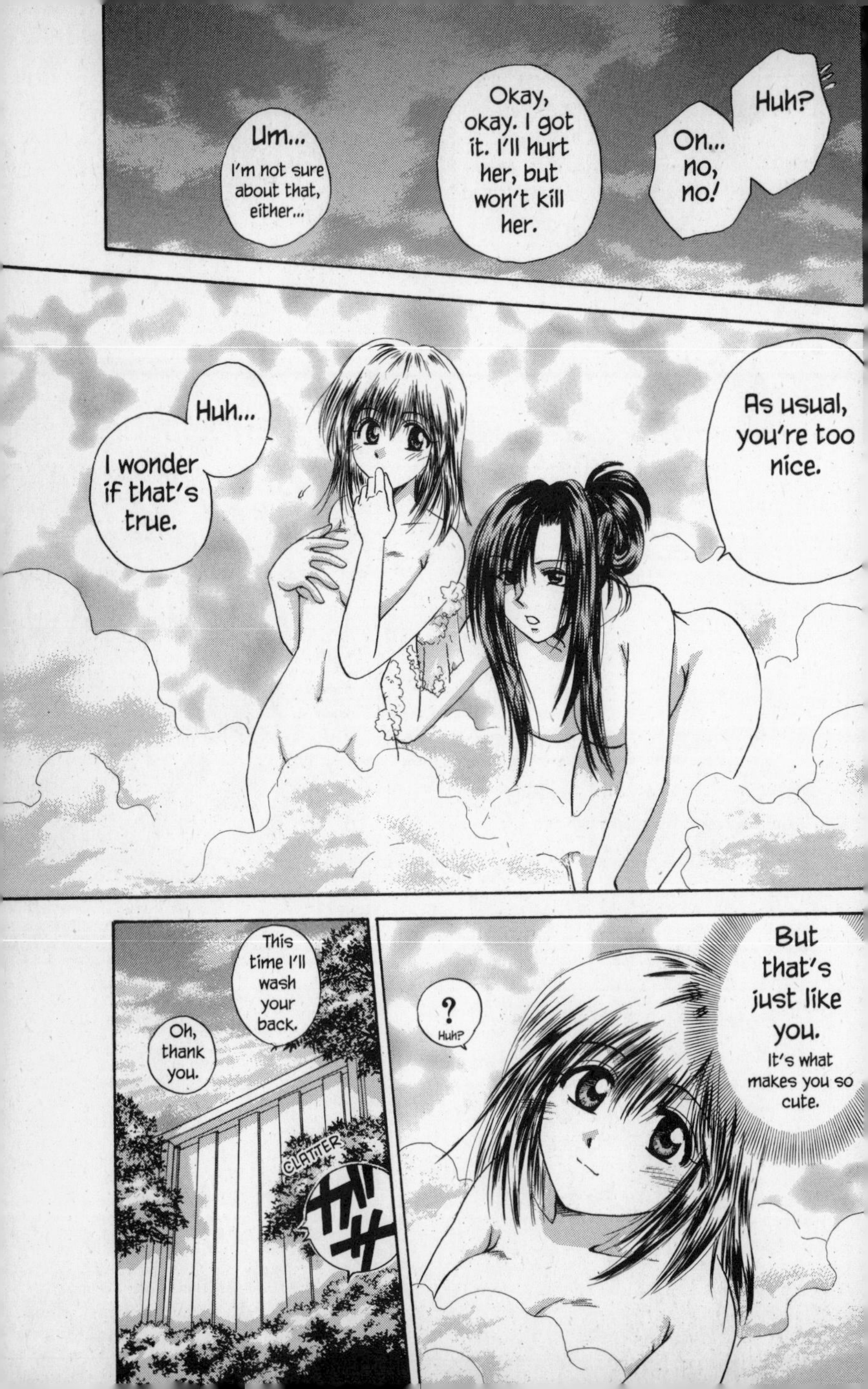
Huh?
On... no, no!
Okay, okay. I got it. I'll hurt her, but won't kill her.
Um... I'm not sure about that, either...
As usual, you're too nice.
Huh... I wonder if that's true.
But that's just like you. It's what makes you so cute.
? Huh?
This time I'll wash your back.
Oh, thank you.
CLATTER

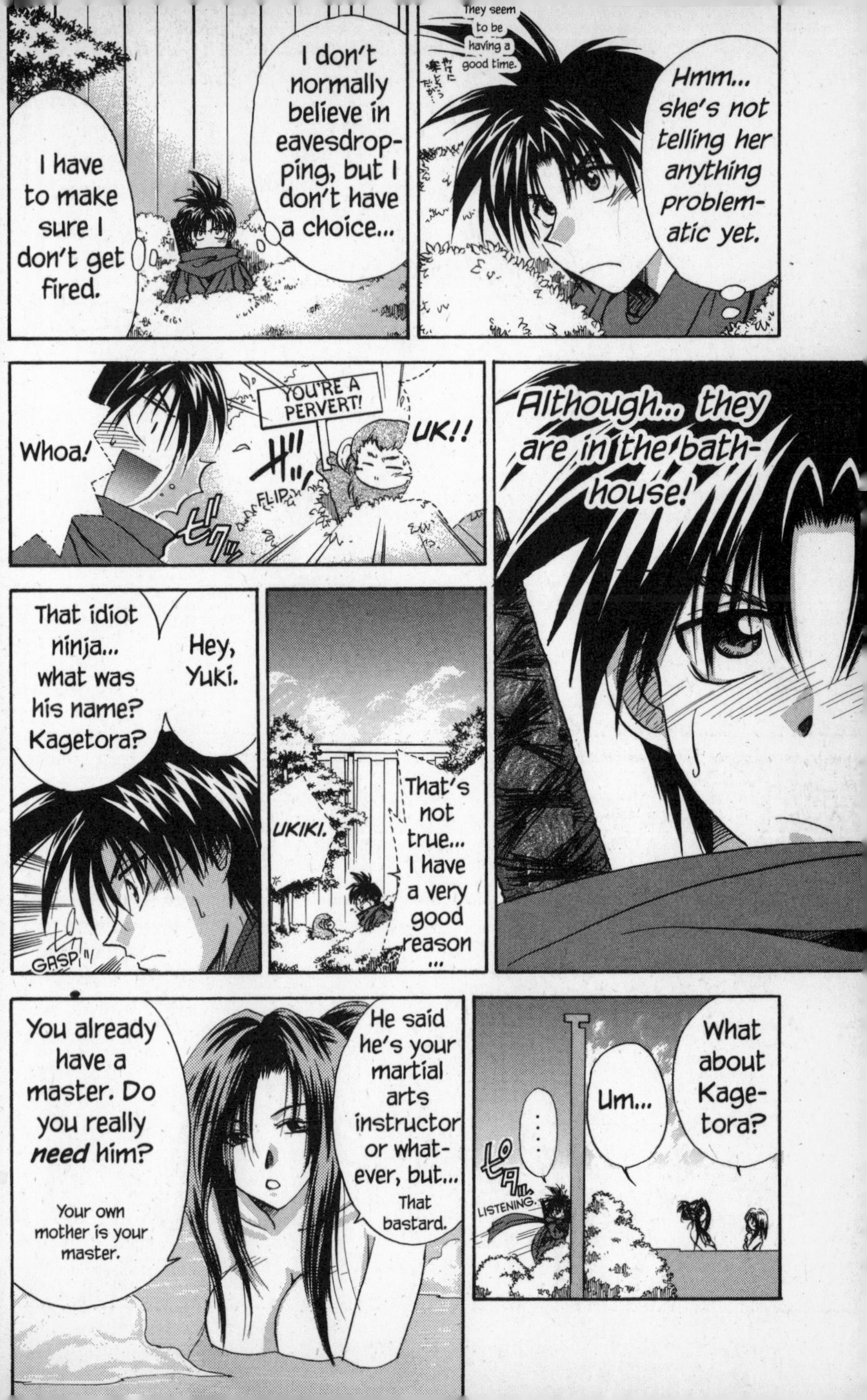
They seem to be having a good time.
Hmm... she's not telling her anything problematic yet.
I don't normally believe in eavesdropping, but I don't have a choice...
I have to make sure I don't get fired.
Although... they are in the bath-house!
UK!!
YOU'RE A PERVERT!
FLIP
Whoa!
That's not true... I have a very good reason ...
UKIKI.
Hey, Yuki.
That idiot ninja... what was his name? Kagetora?
GASP!
What about Kagetora?
Um...
...
LISTENING.
He said he's your martial arts instructor or whatever, but...
That bastard.
You already have a master. Do you really *need* him?
Your own mother is your master.

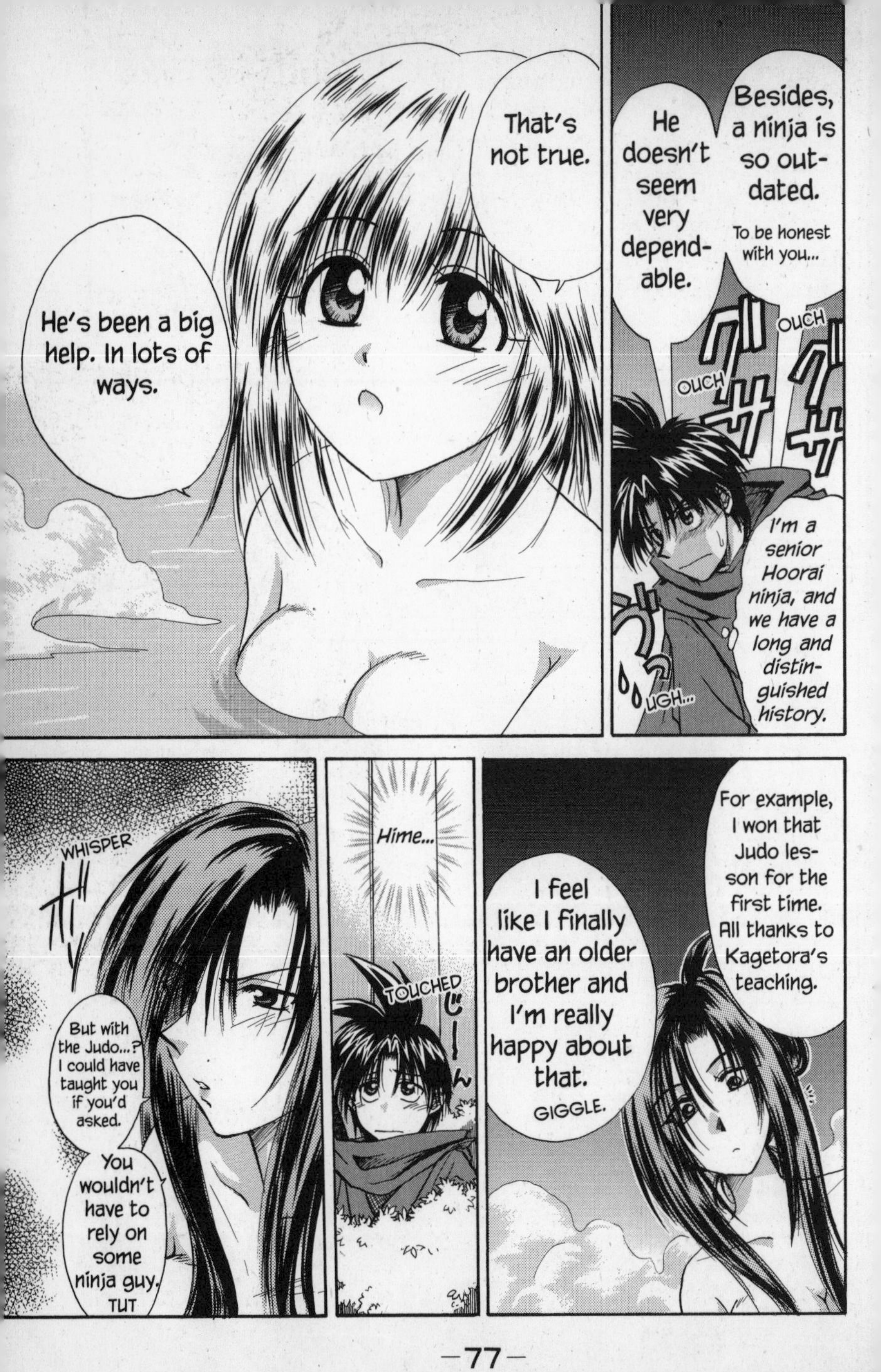
Besides, a ninja is so outdated.
To be honest with you...
He doesn't seem very dependable.
OUCH
OUCH
I'm a senior Hoorai ninja, and we have a long and distinguished history.
UGH...
That's not true.
He's been a big help. In lots of ways.
For example, I won that Judo lesson for the first time. All thanks to Kagetora's teaching.
I feel like I finally have an older brother and I'm really happy about that.
GIGGLE.
Hime...
TOUCHED
WHISPER
But with the Judo...? I could have taught you if you'd asked.
You wouldn't have to rely on some ninja guy.
TUT

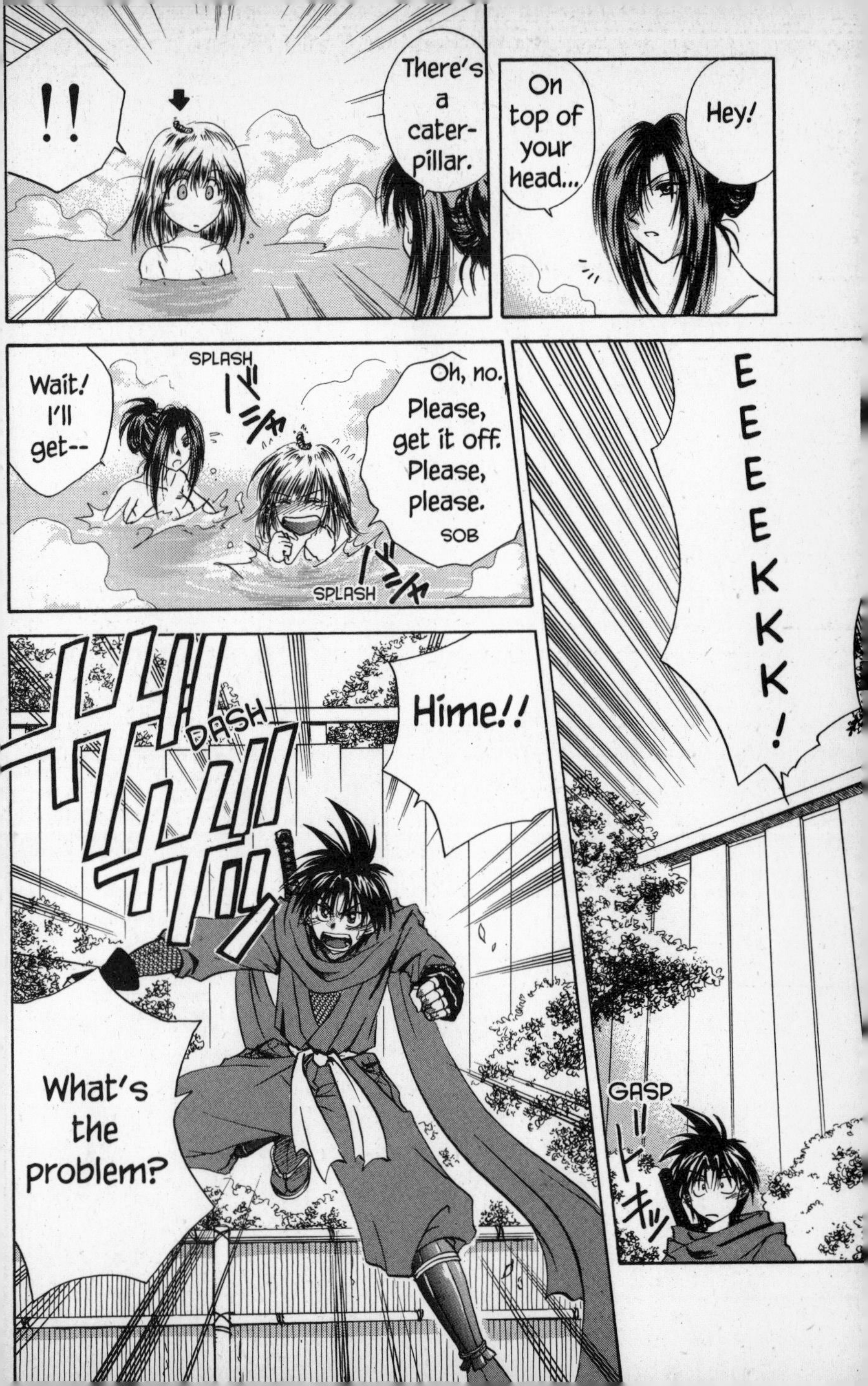
Hey!
On top of your head...
There's a cater-pillar.
!!
EEEEKKK!
Oh, no. Please, get it off. Please, please.
SOB
SPLASH
Wait! I'll get--
SPLASH
Hime!!
DASH
What's the problem?
GASP

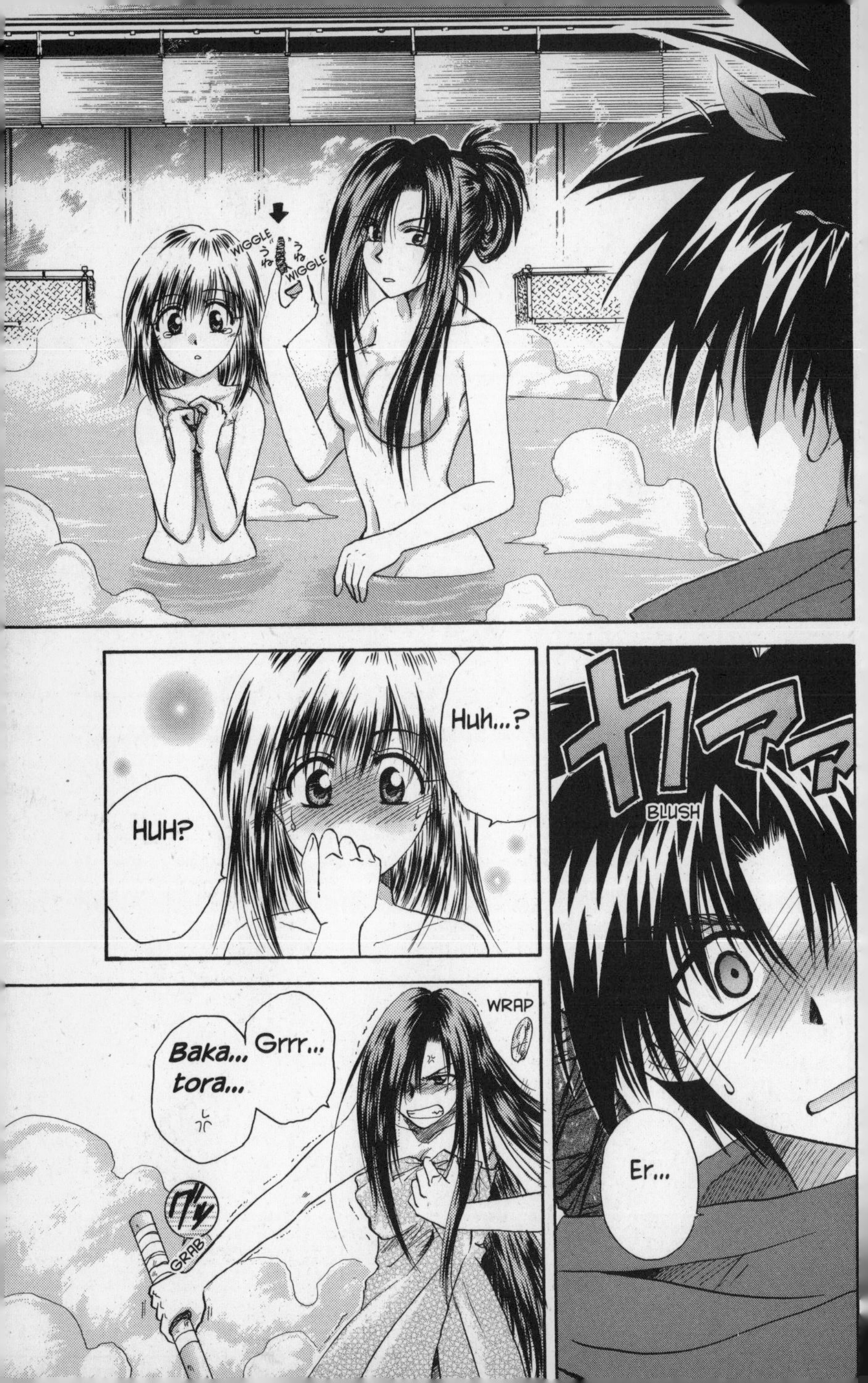
WIGGLE
WIGGLE
BLUSH
Er...
Huh...?
HUH?
Grrr...
Baka... tora...
WRAP
GRAB

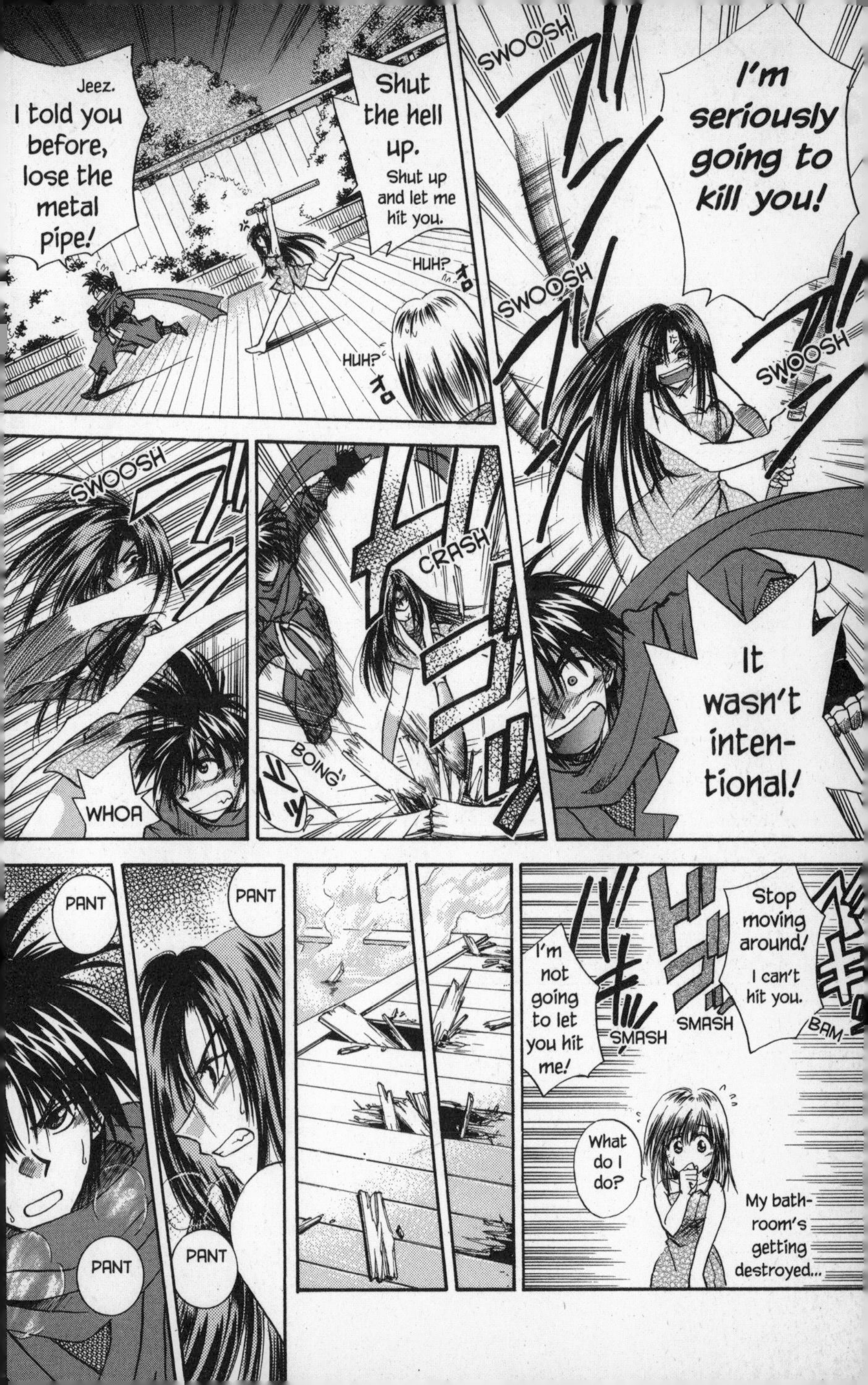
SWOOSH
I'm seriously going to kill you!
SWOOSH
SWOOSH
It wasn't intentional!
Shut the hell up.
Shut up and let me hit you.
Jeez.
I told you before, lose the metal pipe!
HUH?
HUH?
CRASH
BOING
SWOOSH
WHOA
Stop moving around!
I can't hit you.
BAM
SMASH
I'm not going to let you hit me!
SMASH
What do I do?
My bathroom's getting destroyed...
PANT
PANT
PANT
PANT

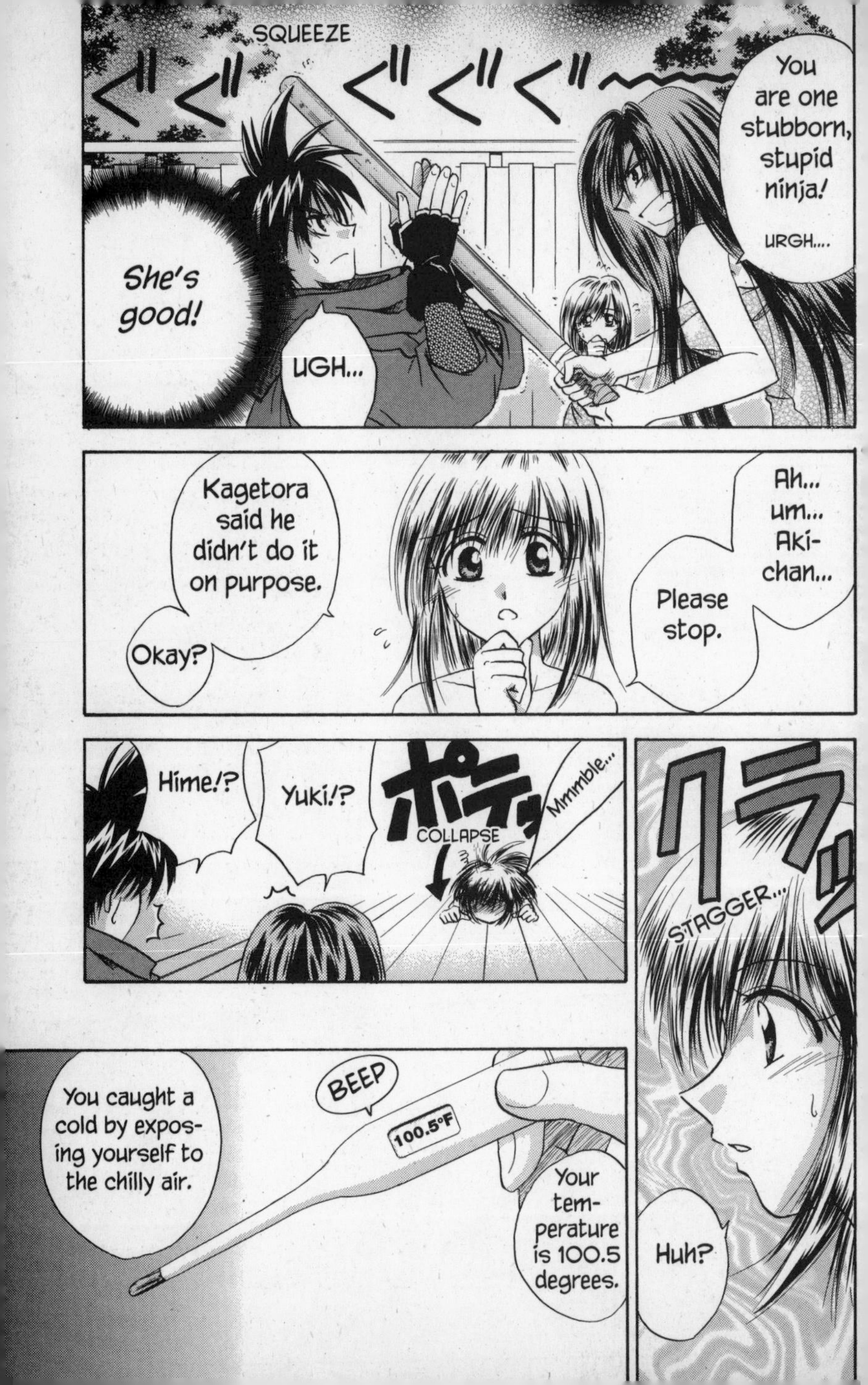
You are one stubborn, stupid ninja!
SQUEEZE
URGH...
She's good!
UGH...
Ah... um... Aki-chan...
Please stop.
Kagetora said he didn't do it on purpose.
Okay?
STAGGER...
Huh?
Mmmble...
COLLAPSE
Yuki!?
Hime!?
Your temperature is 100.5 degrees.
BEEP
100.5°F
You caught a cold by exposing yourself to the chilly air.

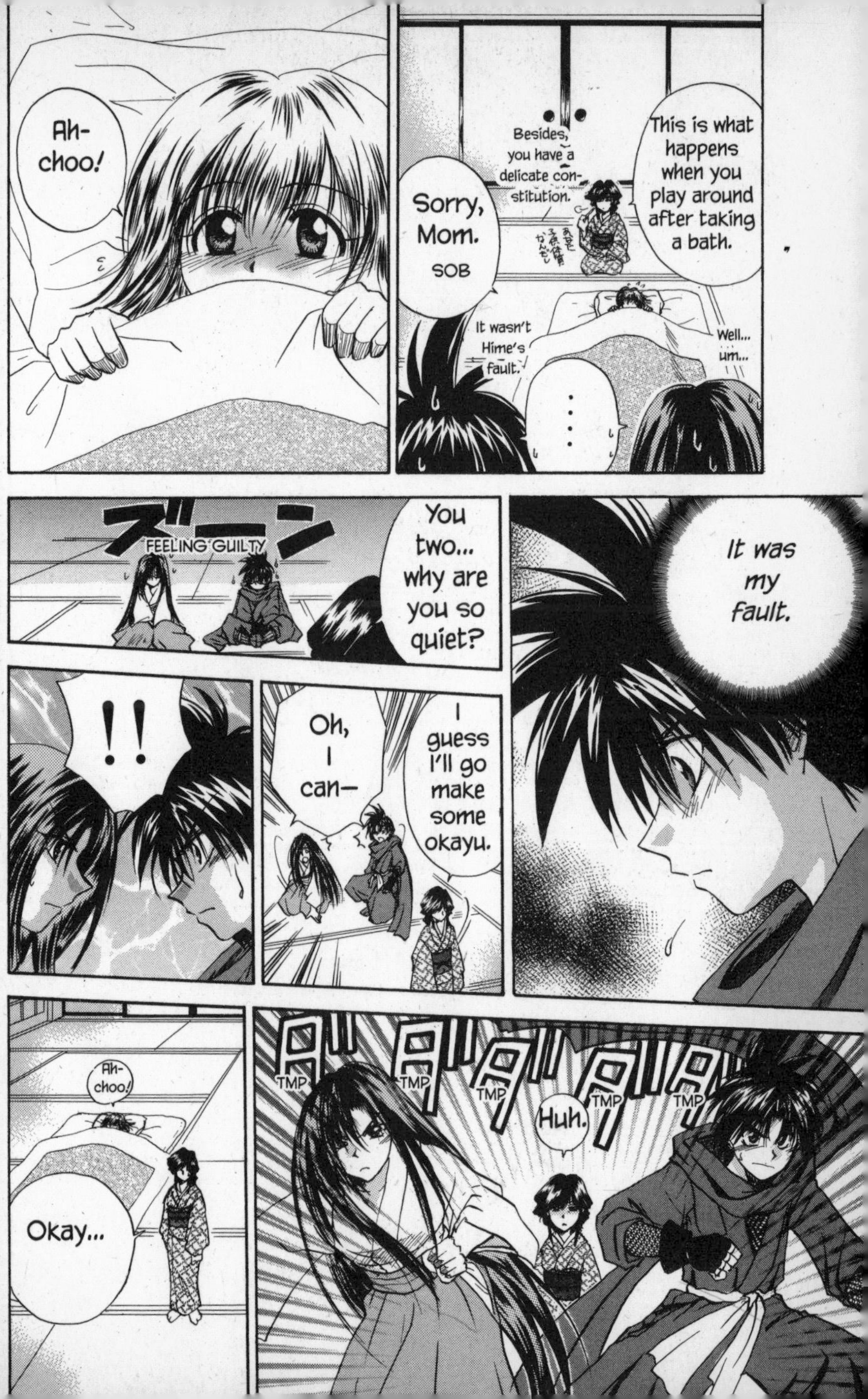

This is what happens when you play around after taking a bath.
Besides, you have a delicate constitution.
Sorry, Mom.
SOB
Well... um...
It wasn't Hime's fault.
....
Ah-choo!
It was my fault.
You two... why are you so quiet?
FEELING GUILTY
I guess I'll go make some okayu.
Oh, I can—
!!
A A A A A A
TMP TMP TMP TMP TMP
Huh.
Ah-choo!
Okay...

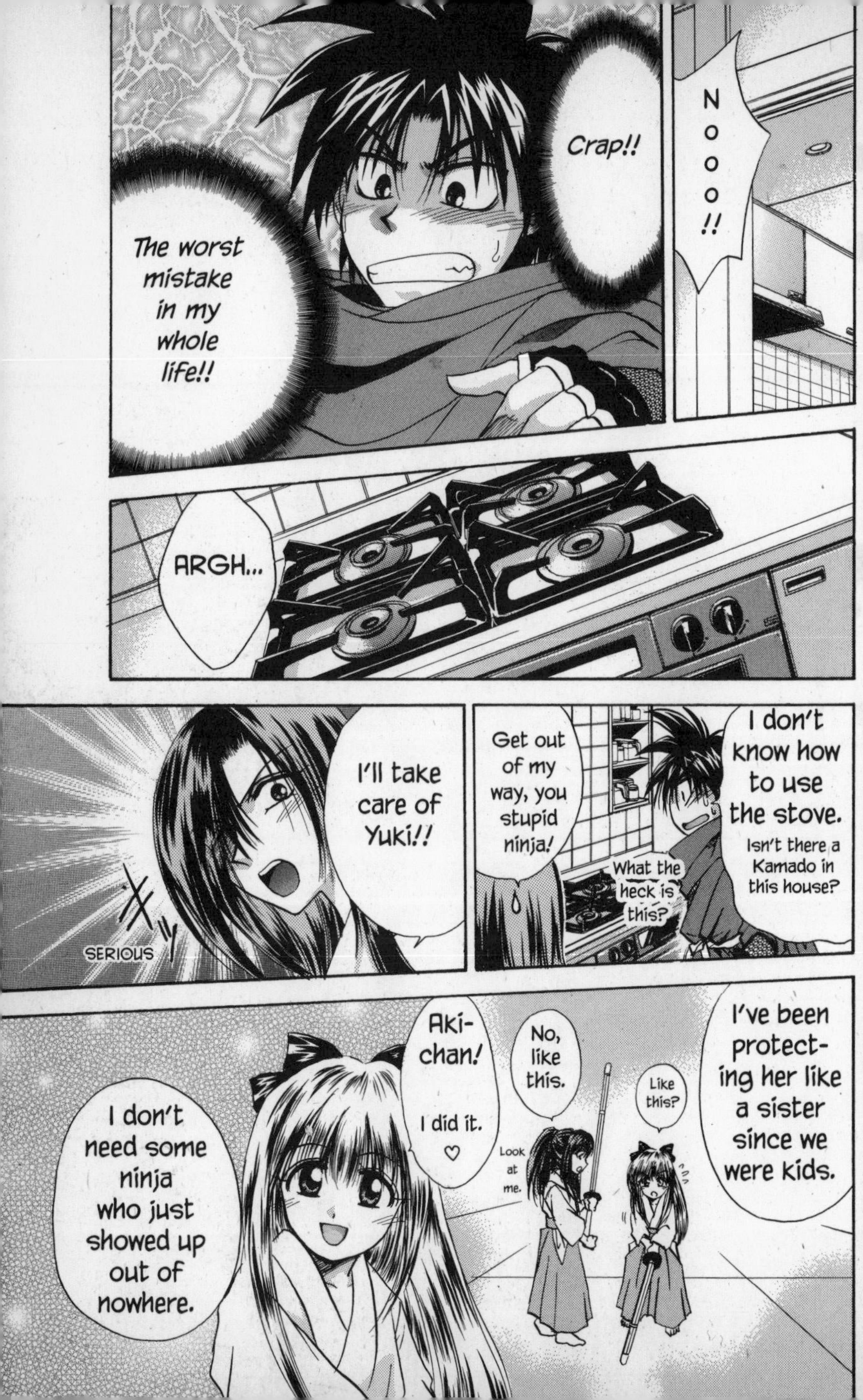
NOOOO!!
Crap!!
The worst mistake in my whole life!!
ARGH...
I don't know how to use the stove.
Isn't there a Kamado in this house?
What the heck is this?
Get out of my way, you stupid ninja!
I'll take care of Yuki!!
SERIOUS
I've been protecting her like a sister since we were kids.
Like this?
No, like this.
Look at me.
Aki-chan!
I did it. ♡
I don't need some ninja who just showed up out of nowhere.

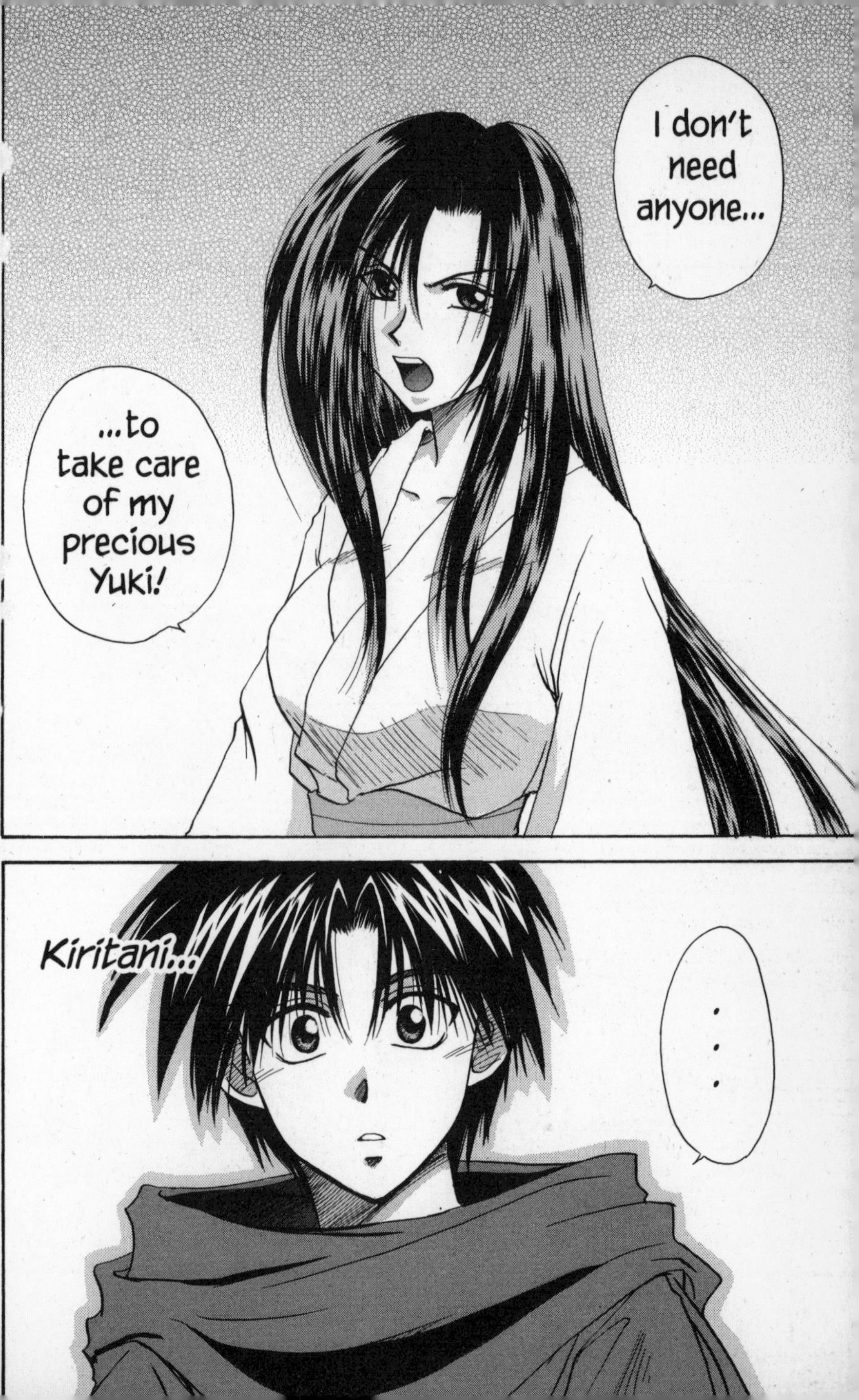
I don't need anyone...
...to take care of my precious Yuki!
Kiritani...
. . .

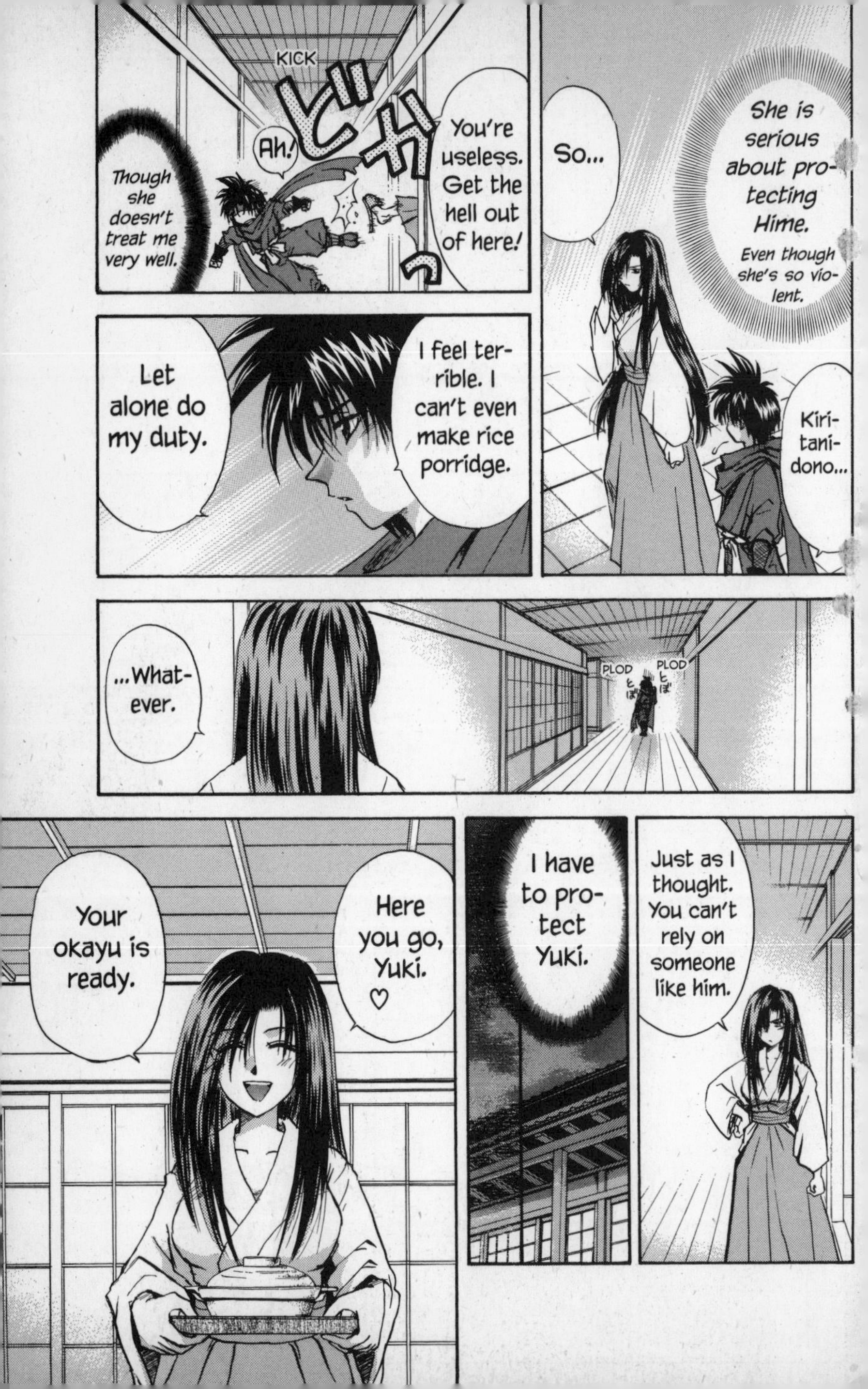
She is serious about pro-tecting Hime.
Even though she's so vio-lent.
So...
Kiri-tani-dono...
KICK
You're useless. Get the hell out of here!
Ah!
Though she doesn't treat me very well.
I feel ter-rible. I can't even make rice porridge.
Let alone do my duty.
PLOD
PLOD
...What-ever.
Just as I thought. You can't rely on someone like him.
I have to pro-tect Yuki.
Here you go, Yuki. ♡
Your okayu is ready.

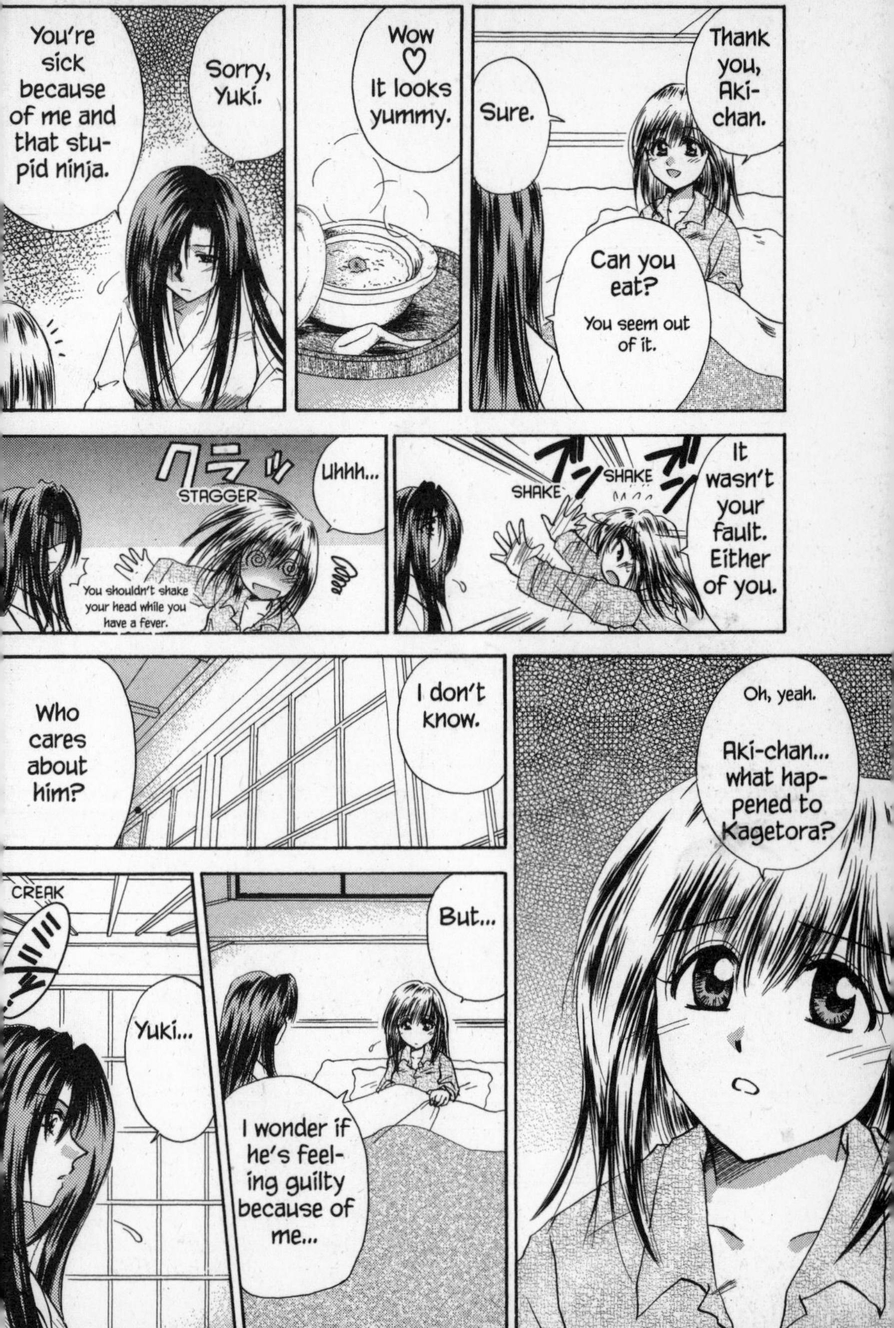
Thank you, Aki-chan.
Sure.
Can you eat?
You seem out of it.
Wow ♡ It looks yummy.
Sorry, Yuki.
You're sick because of me and that stupid ninja.
It wasn't your fault. Either of you.
SHAKE
SHAKE
Uhhh...
STAGGER
You shouldn't shake your head while you have a fever.
Oh, yeah.
Aki-chan... what happened to Kagetora?
I don't know.
Who cares about him?
But...
I wonder if he's feeling guilty because of me...
Yuki...
CREAK

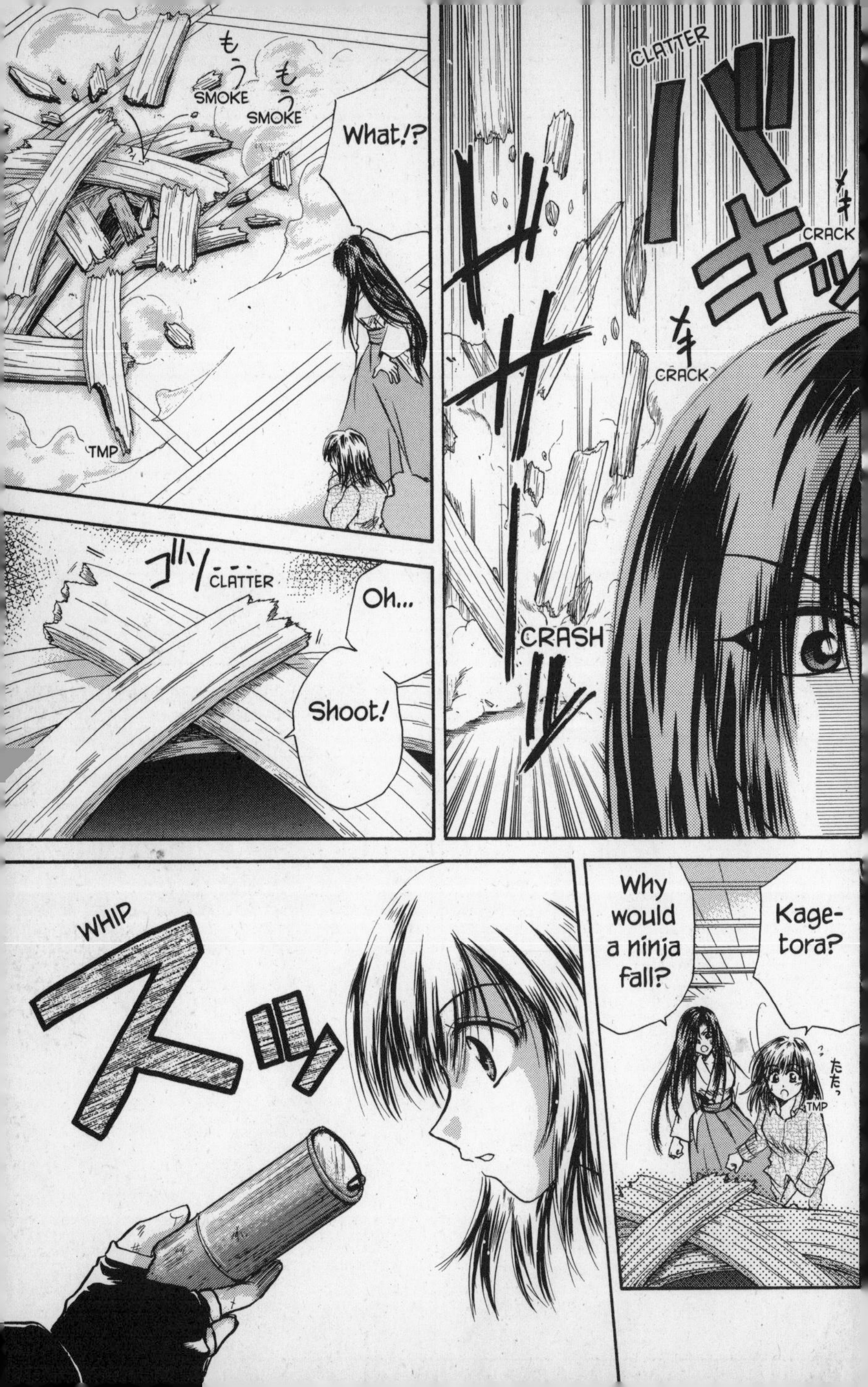

CLATTER
バキッ
メキ
CRACK
メキ
CRACK
CRASH
もう
SMOKE
もう
SMOKE
What!?
TMP
CLATTER
Oh...
Shoot!
Kage-tora?
Why would a ninja fall?
たたっ
TMP
WHIP
スッ

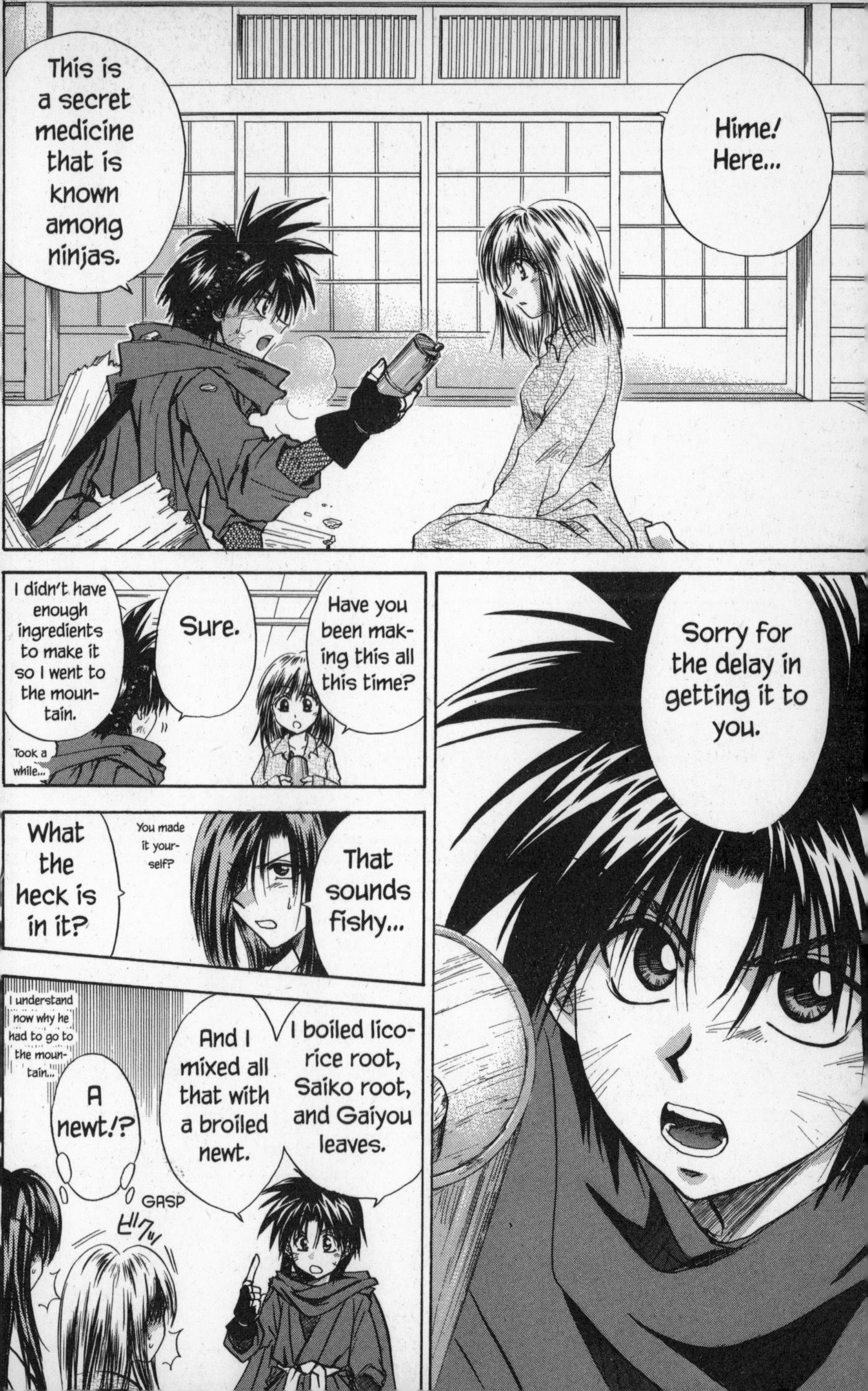
Hime! Here...
This is a secret medicine that is known among ninjas.
Sorry for the delay in getting it to you.
Have you been mak-ing this all this time?
Sure.
I didn't have enough ingredients to make it so I went to the moun-tain.
Took a while...
That sounds fishy...
You made it your-self?
What the heck is in it?
I boiled lico-rice root, Saiko root, and Gaiyou leaves.
And I mixed all that with a broiled newt.
A newt!?
GASP
ビクッ
I understand now why he had to go to the moun-tain...

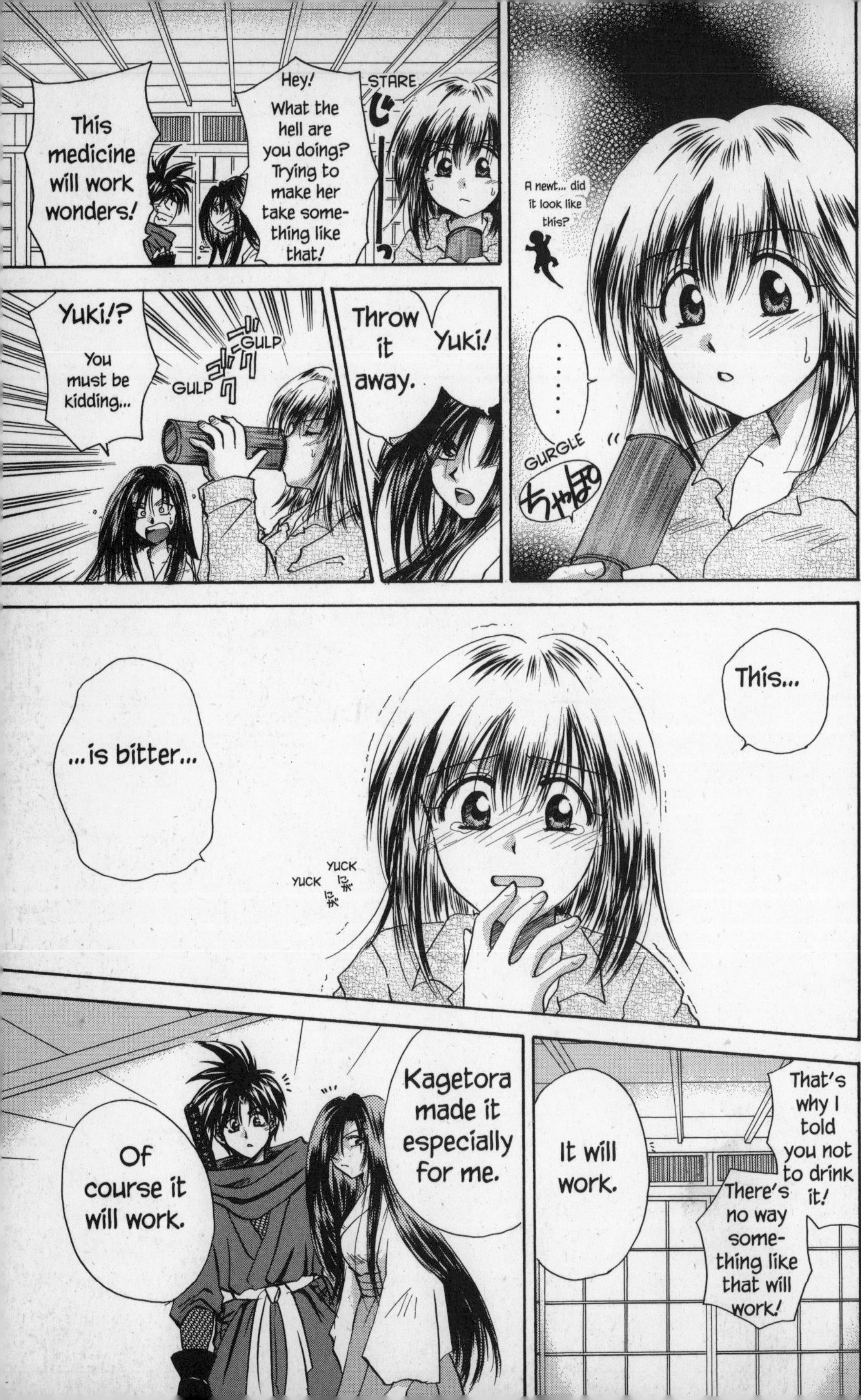
A newt... did it look like this?
......
GURGLE
ちゃぽ
STARE
Hey! What the hell are you doing? Trying to make her take something like that!
This medicine will work wonders!
Yuki!
Throw it away.
GULP
GULP
Yuki!? You must be kidding...
This...
...is bitter...
YUCK
YUCK
にがにが
That's why I told you not to drink it!
There's no way something like that will work!
It will work.
Kagetora made it especially for me.
Of course it will work.

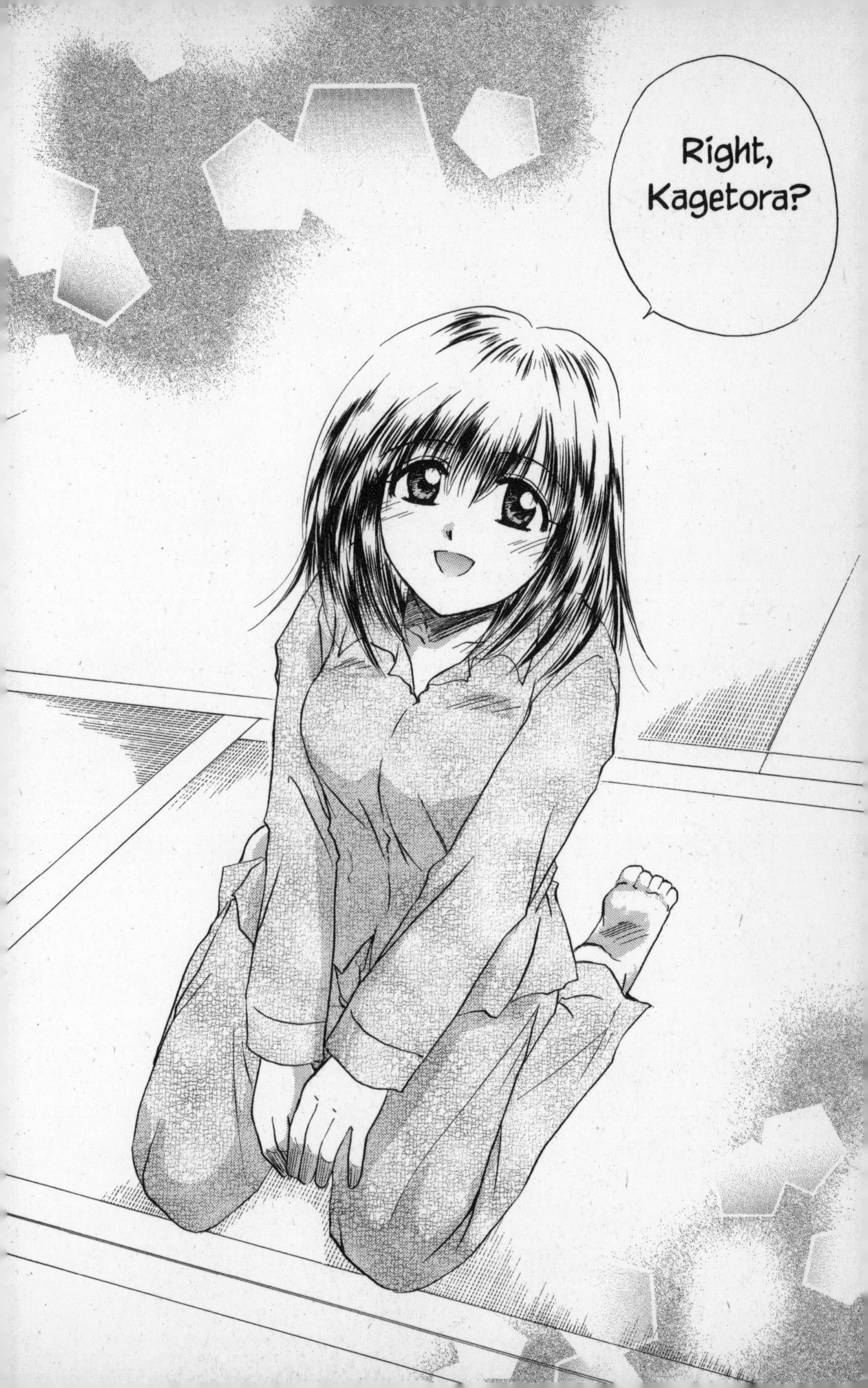
Right, Kagetora?

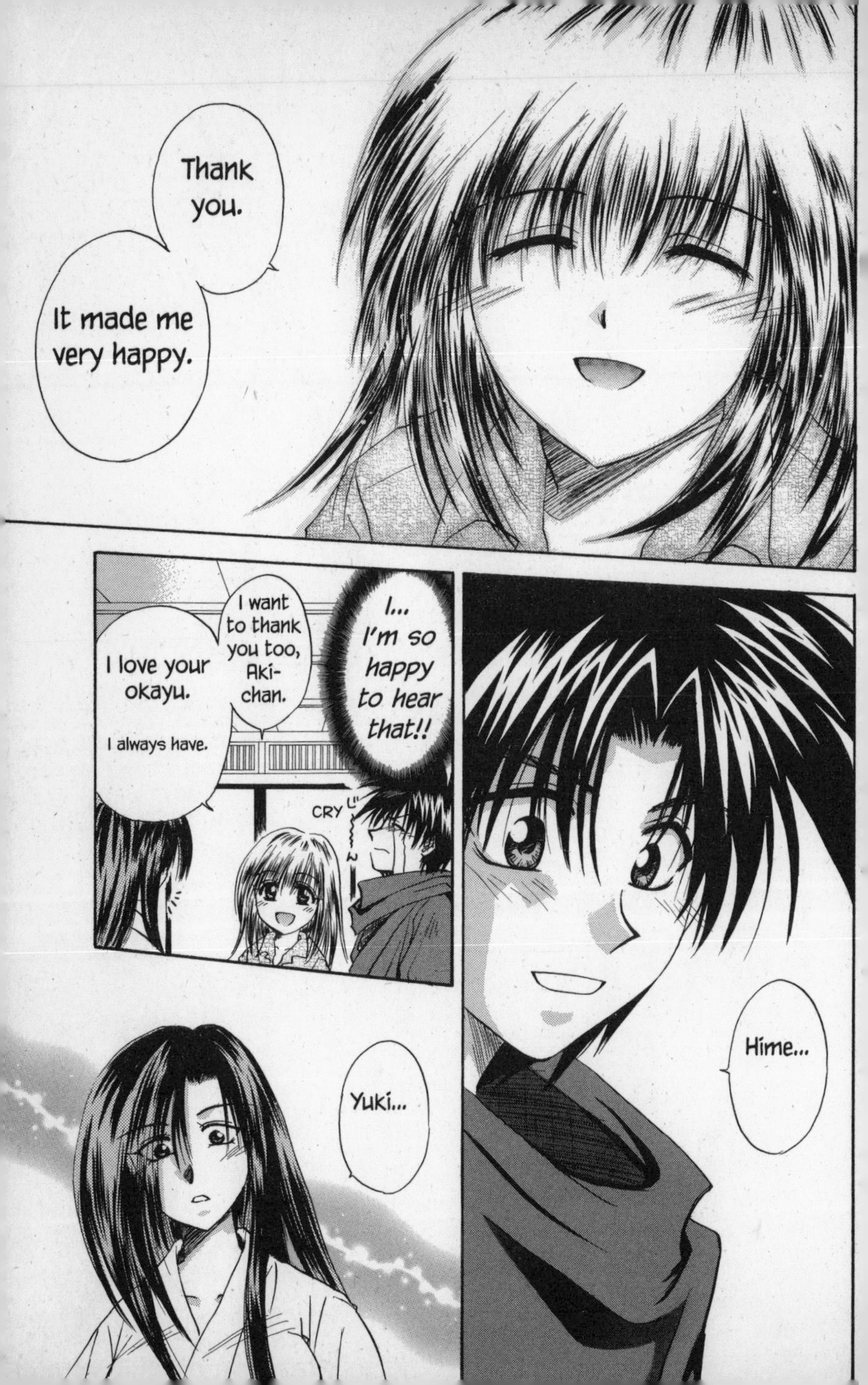
Thank you.
It made me very happy.
Hime...
I... I'm so happy to hear that!!
CRY
I want to thank you too, Aki-chan.
I love your okayu.
I always have.
Yuki...

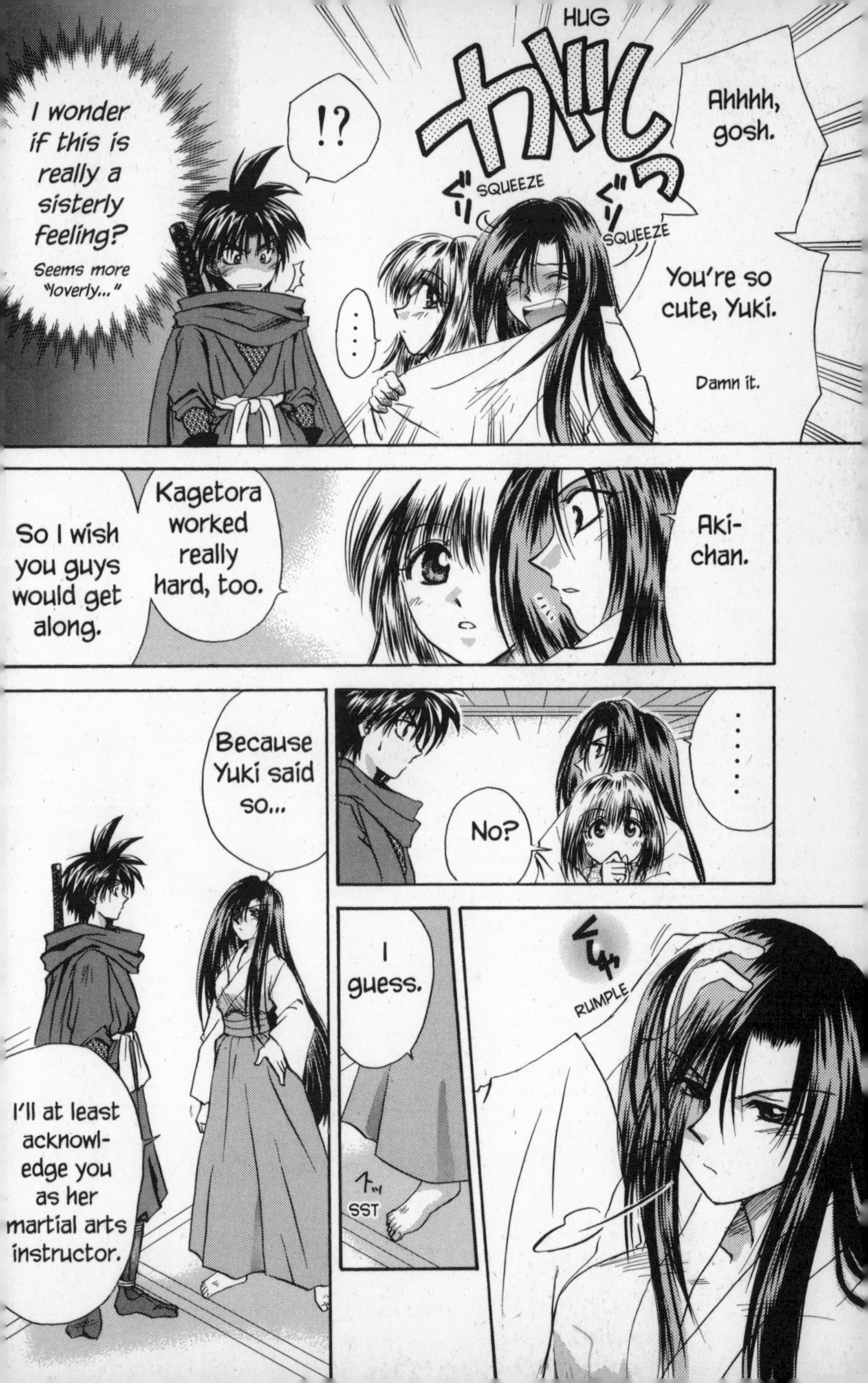
HUG
Ahhhh, gosh.
SQUEEZE
SQUEEZE
You're so cute, Yuki.
Damn it.
!?
. . . .
I wonder if this is really a sisterly feeling?
Seems more "loverly..."
Aki-chan.
Kagetora worked really hard, too.
So I wish you guys would get along.
. . . . . .
No?
RUMPLE
I guess.
SST
Because Yuki said so...
I'll at least acknowledge you as her martial arts instructor.

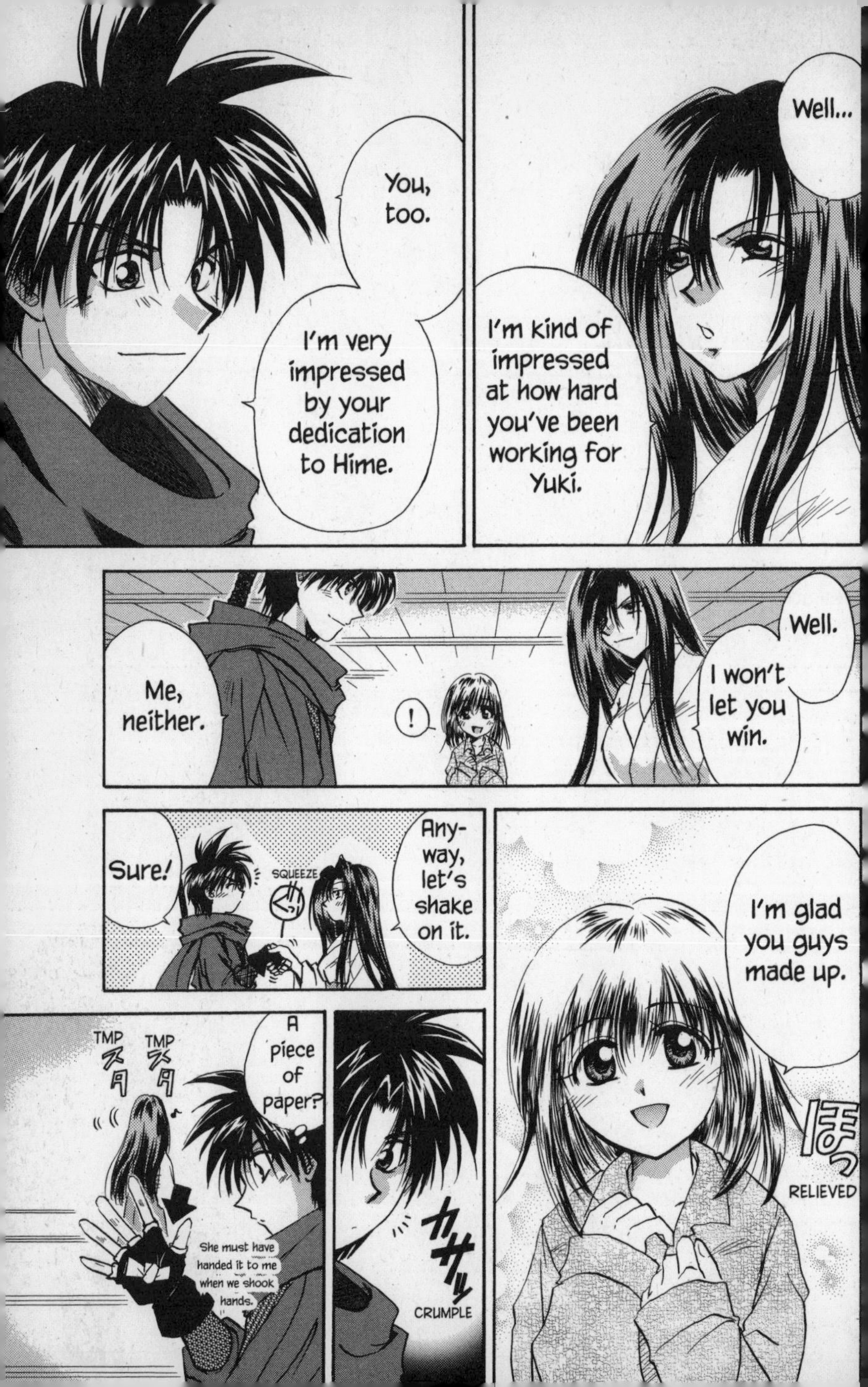
Well...
I'm kind of impressed at how hard you've been working for Yuki.
You, too.
I'm very impressed by your dedication to Hime.
Well.
I won't let you win.
!
Me, neither.
I'm glad you guys made up.
ほっ
RELIEVED
Any-way, let's shake on it.
SQUEEZE
Sure!
A piece of paper?
カサッ
CRUMPLE
TMP
スタ
TMP
スタ
She must have handed it to me when we shook hands.

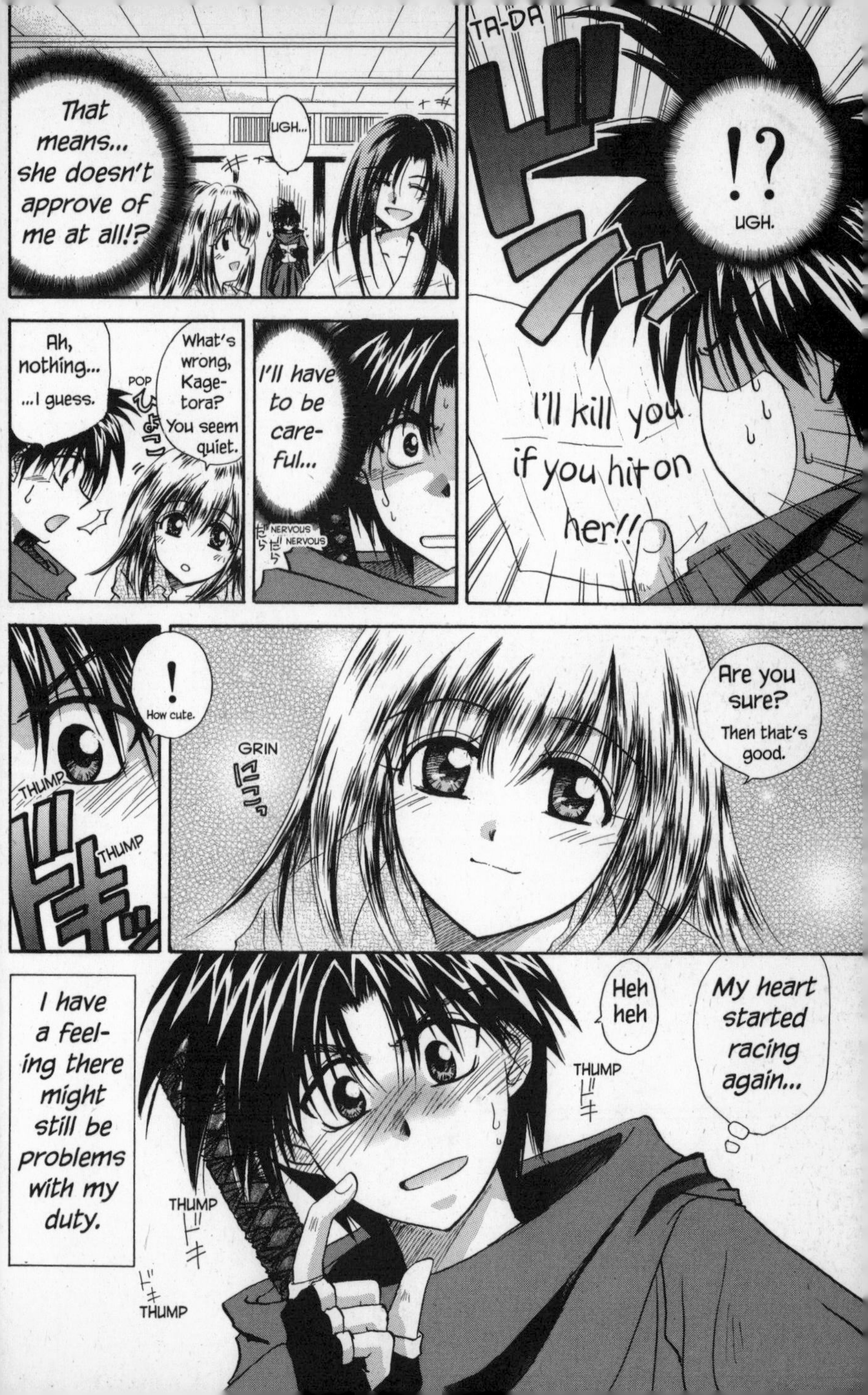
TA-DA
!?
UGH.
I'll kill you if you hit on her!!
That means... she doesn't approve of me at all!?
UGH...
I'll have to be care-ful...
NERVOUS NERVOUS
What's wrong, Kage-tora? You seem quiet.
POP
Ah, nothing... ...I guess.
Are you sure? Then that's good.
GRIN
! How cute.
THUMP
THUMP
My heart started racing again...
Heh heh
THUMP
I have a feel-ing there might still be problems with my duty.
THUMP
THUMP

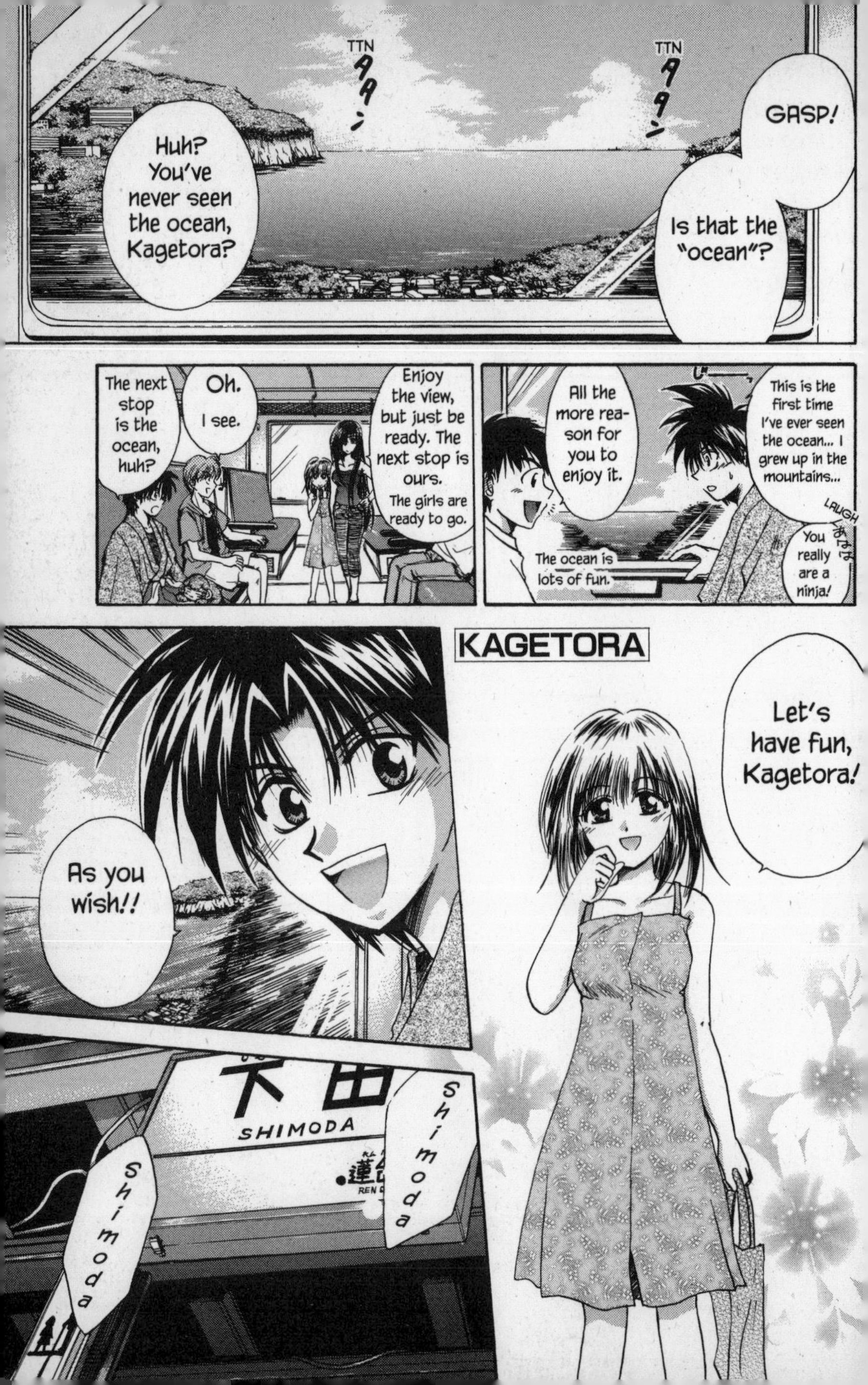
TTN
TTN
GASP!
Is that the "ocean"?
Huh? You've never seen the ocean, Kagetora?
This is the first time I've ever seen the ocean... I grew up in the mountains...
LAUGH
You really are a ninja!
All the more reason for you to enjoy it.
The ocean is lots of fun.
Enjoy the view, but just be ready. The next stop is ours.
The girls are ready to go.
Oh.
I see.
The next stop is the ocean, huh?
KAGETORA
Let's have fun, Kagetora!
As you wish!!
SHIMODA
Shimoda
Shimoda

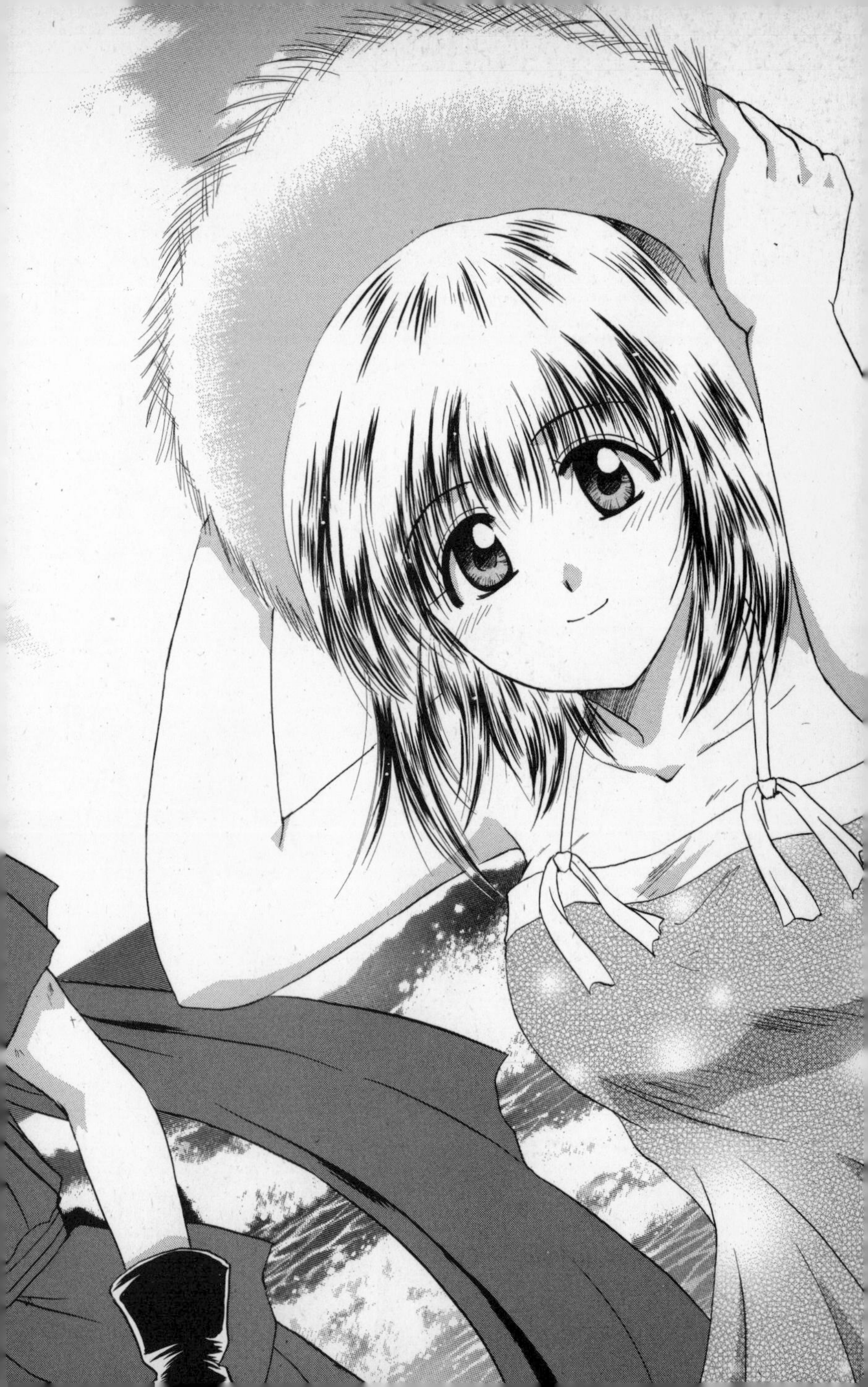

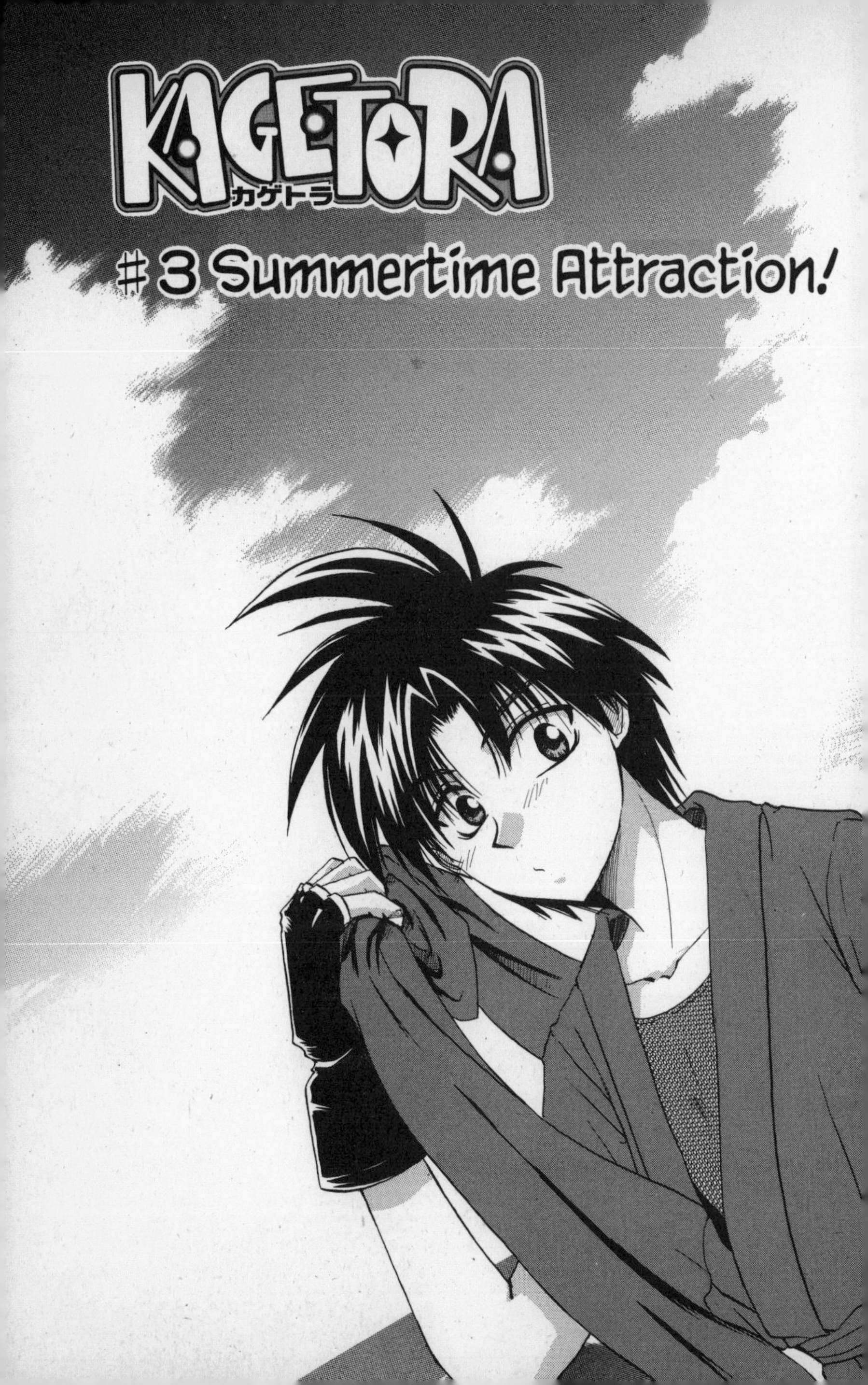
KAGETORA
カゲトラ
3 Summertime Attraction!

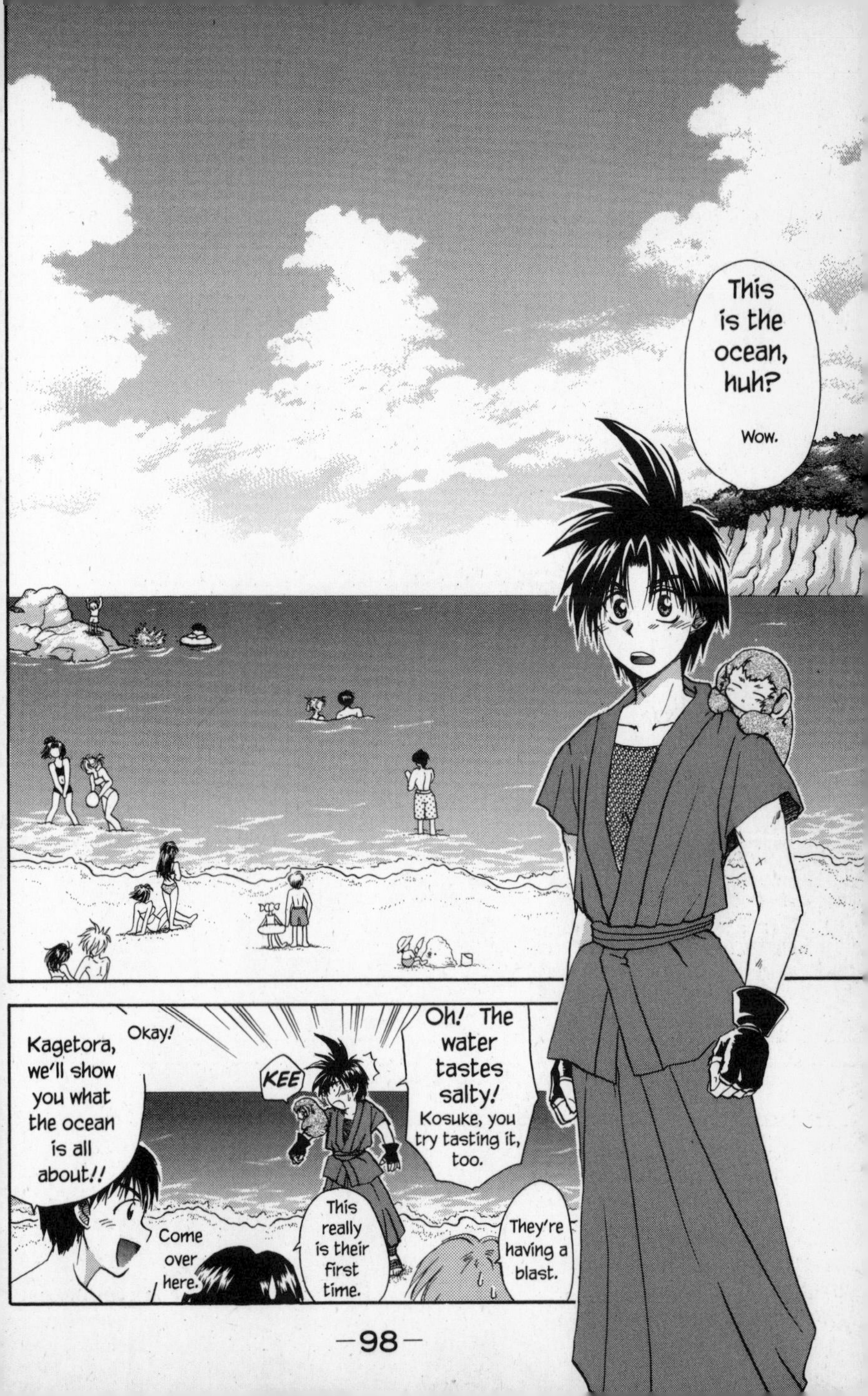
This is the ocean, huh?
Wow.
Oh! The water tastes salty!
Kosuke, you try tasting it, too.
KEE
Okay!
Kagetora, we'll show you what the ocean is all about!!
They're having a blast.
This really is their first time.
Come over here.

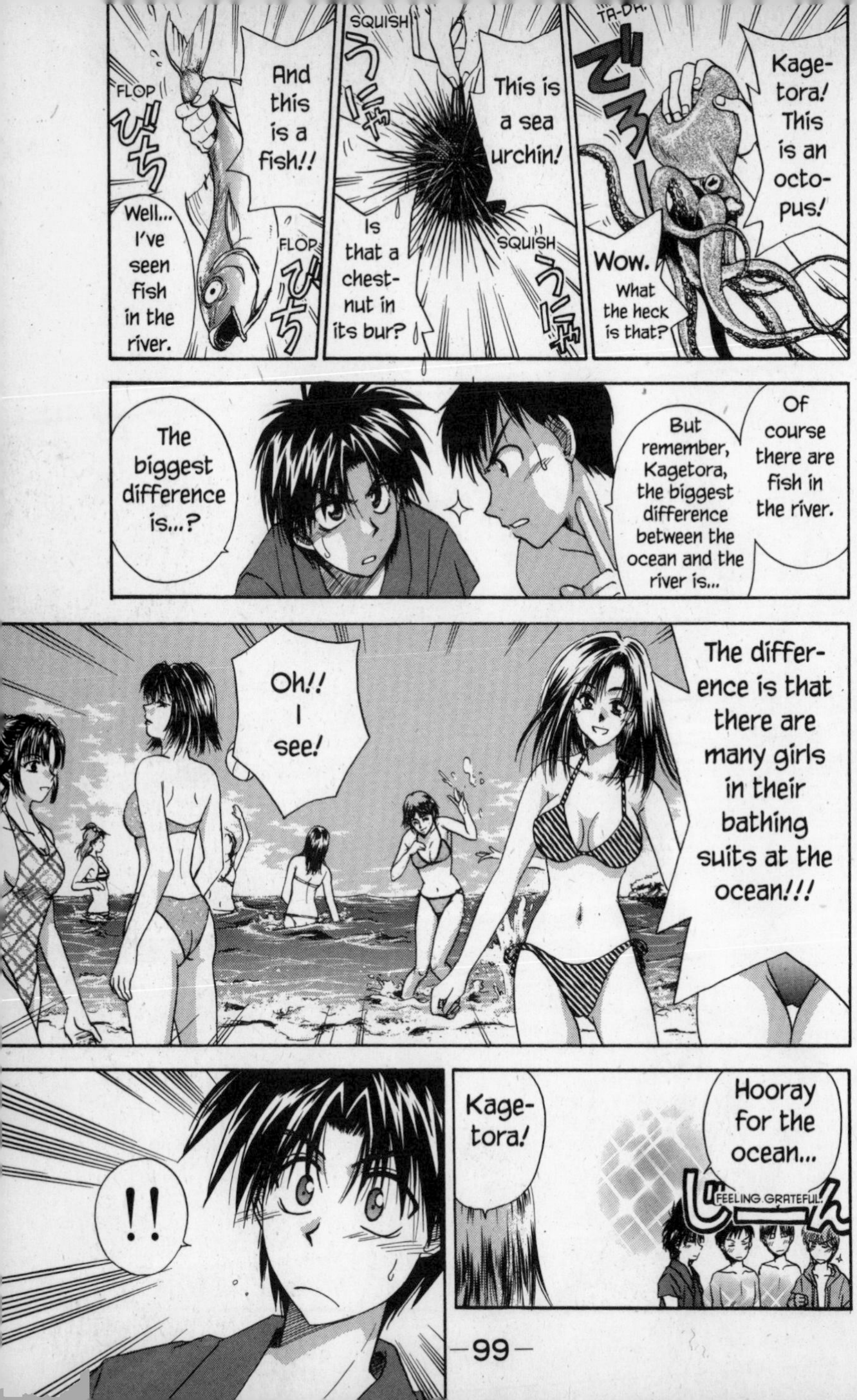
Kagetora! This is an octopus!
TA-DA.
Wow. What the heck is that?
This is a sea urchin!
SQUISH
Is that a chestnut in its bur?
SQUISH
And this is a fish!!
FLOP
Well... I've seen fish in the river.
FLOP
Of course there are fish in the river.
But remember, Kagetora, the biggest difference between the ocean and the river is...
The biggest difference is...?
The difference is that there are many girls in their bathing suits at the ocean!!!
Oh!! I see!
Hooray for the ocean...
FEELING GRATEFUL
Kagetora!
!!

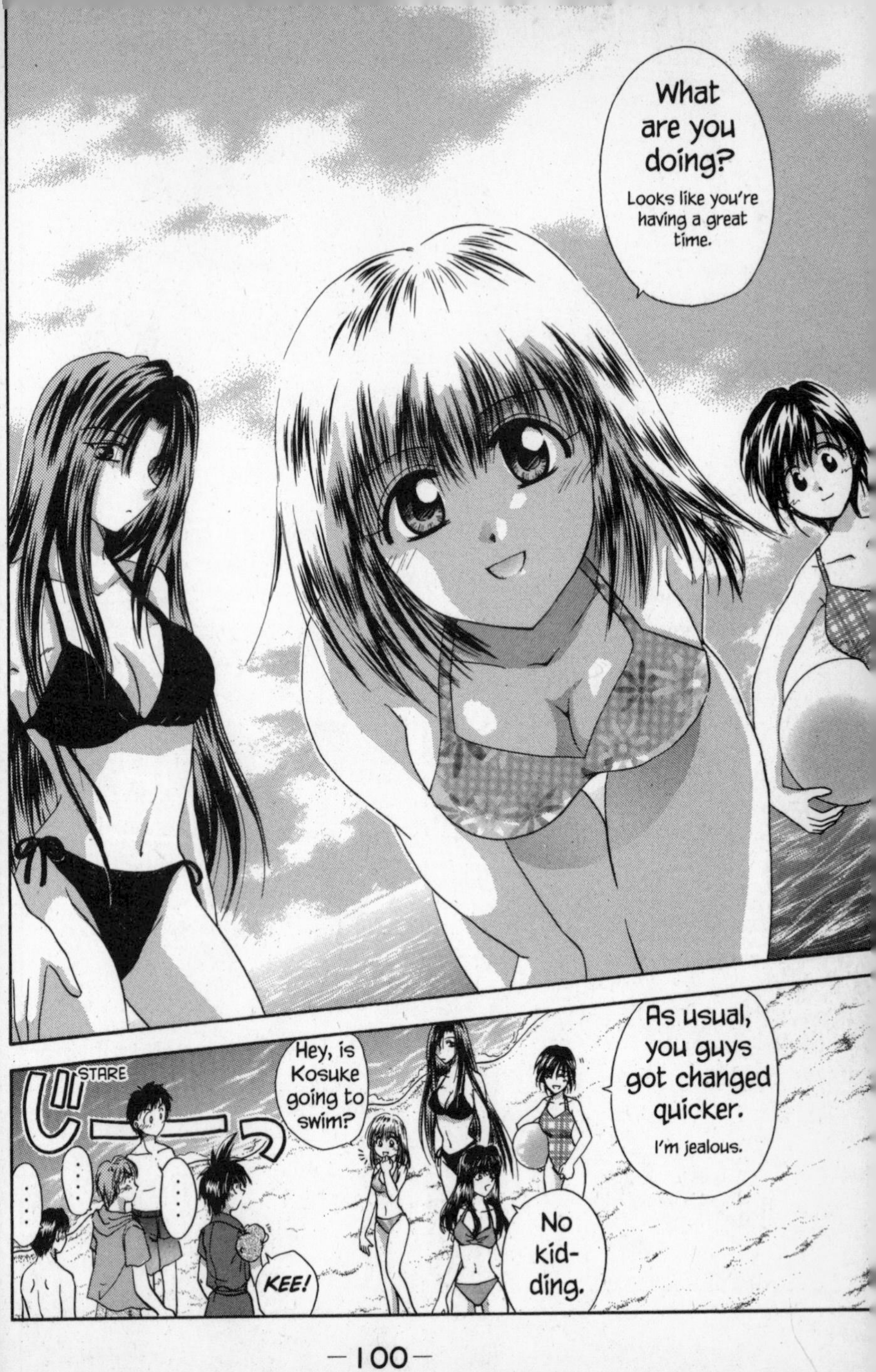
What are you doing?
Looks like you're having a great time.
As usual, you guys got changed quicker.
I'm jealous.
No kid-ding.
Hey, is Kosuke going to swim?
KEE!
STARE
...
...
...

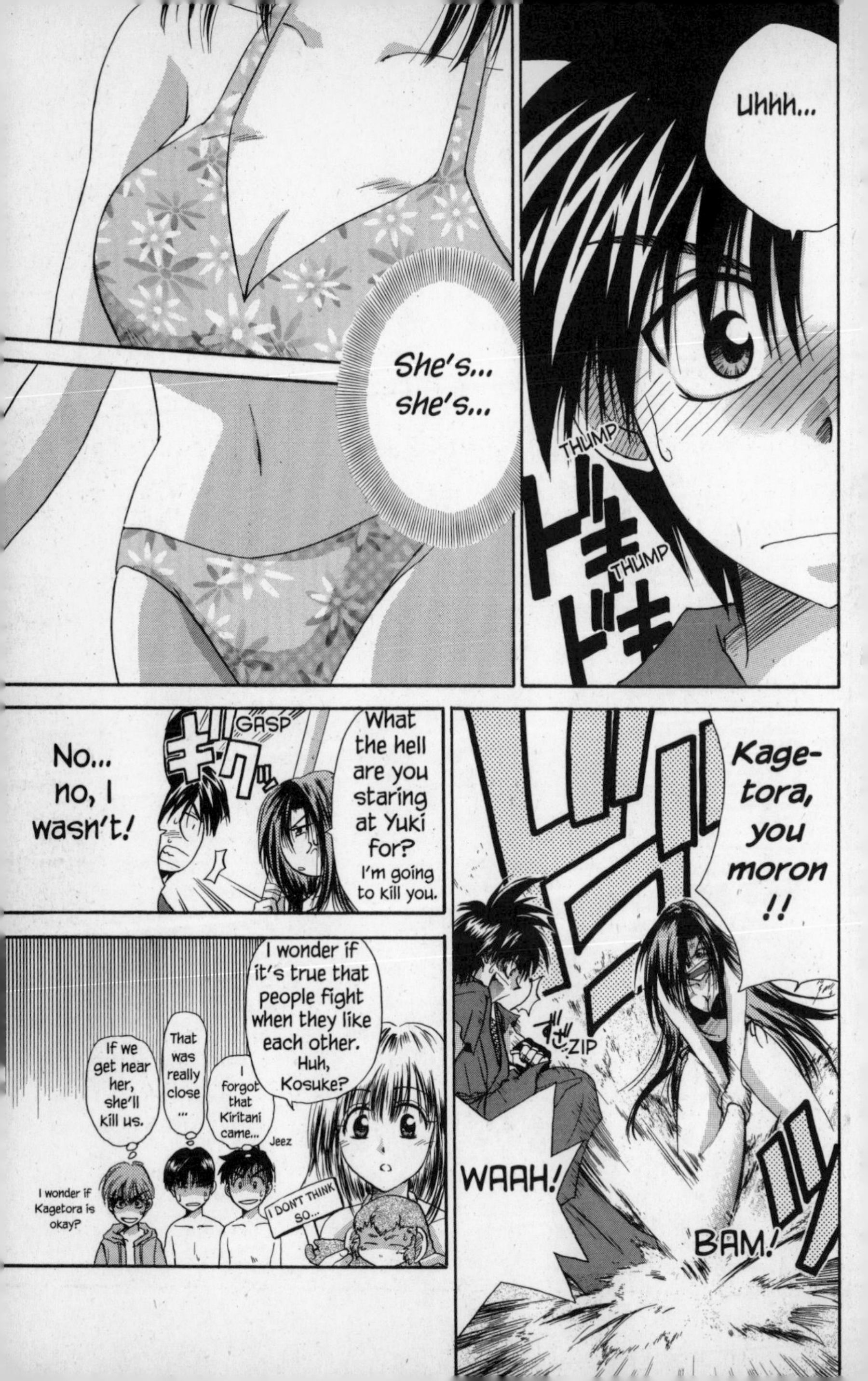
Uhhh...
THUMP
THUMP
She's... she's...
What the hell are you staring at Yuki for?
I'm going to kill you.
GASP
No... no, I wasn't!
Kage-tora, you moron!!
ZIP
WAAH!
BAM!
I wonder if it's true that people fight when they like each other. Huh, Kosuke?
I DON'T THINK SO...
I forgot that Kiritani came...
Jeez
That was really close...
If we get near her, she'll kill us.
I wonder if Kagetora is okay?

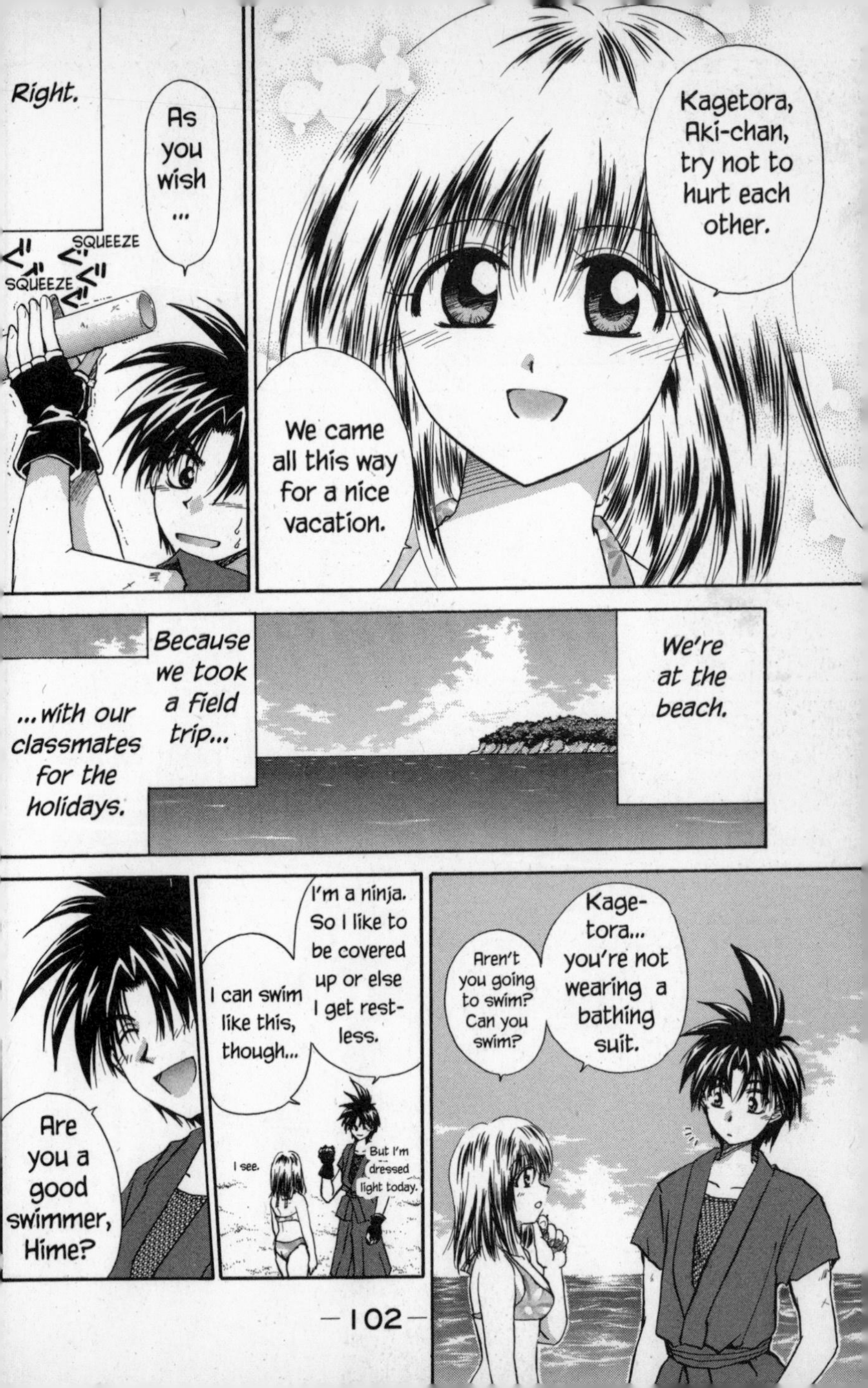
Kagetora, Aki-chan, try not to hurt each other.
We came all this way for a nice vacation.
As you wish...
Right.
SQUEEZE
SQUEEZE
We're at the beach.
Because we took a field trip...
...with our classmates for the holidays.
Kage-tora... you're not wearing a bathing suit.
Aren't you going to swim? Can you swim?
I'm a ninja. So I like to be covered up or else I get rest-less.
I can swim like this, though...
But I'm dressed light today.
I see.
Are you a good swimmer, Hime?

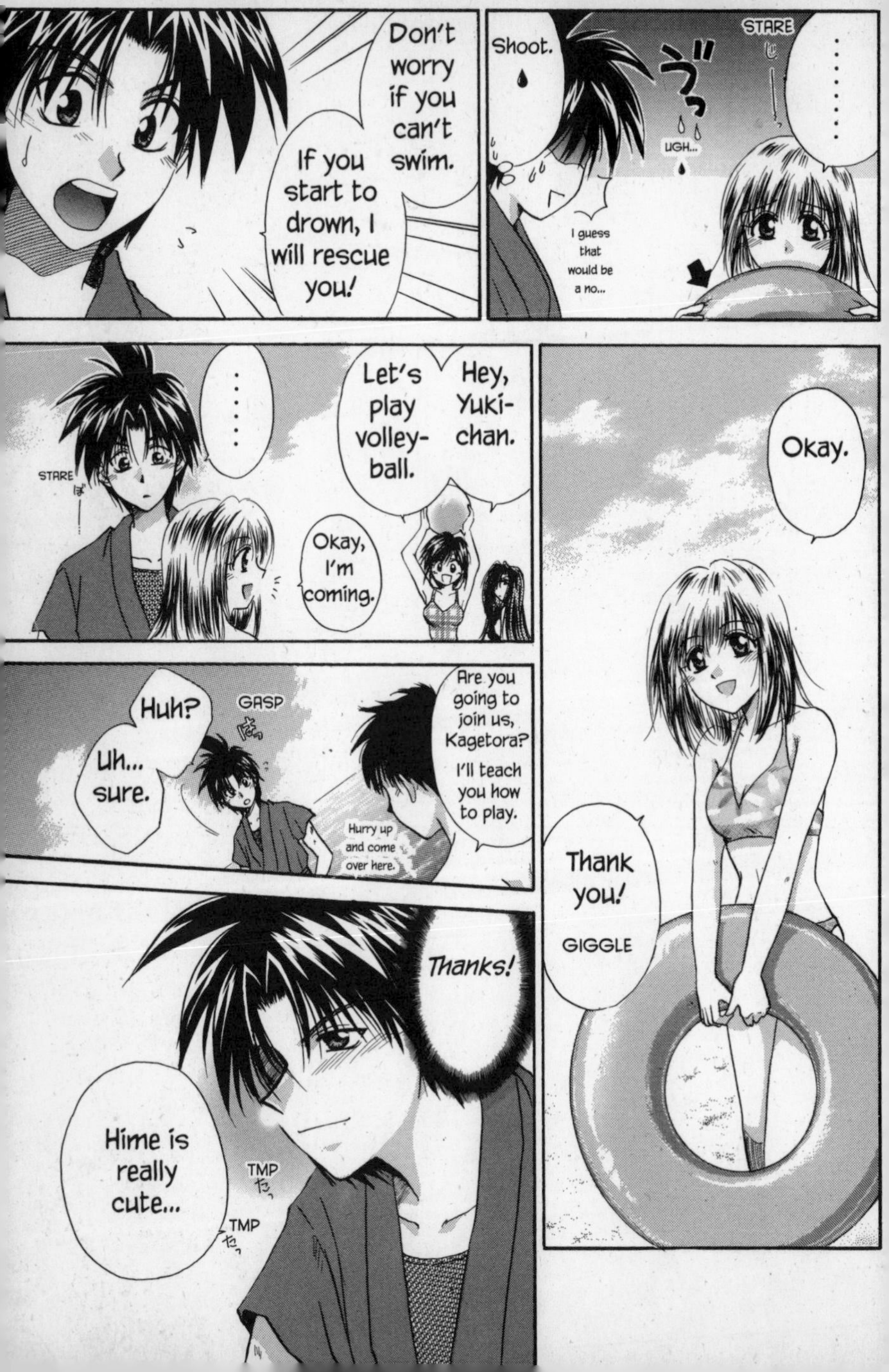
......
STARE
UGH...
Shoot.
I guess that would be a no...
Don't worry if you can't swim.
If you start to drown, I will rescue you!
Okay.
Thank you!
GIGGLE
Hey, Yuki-chan.
Let's play volley-ball.
Okay, I'm coming.
......
STARE
Are you going to join us, Kagetora?
I'll teach you how to play.
Hurry up and come over here.
GASP
Huh?
Uh... sure.
Thanks!
TMP
TMP
Hime is really cute...

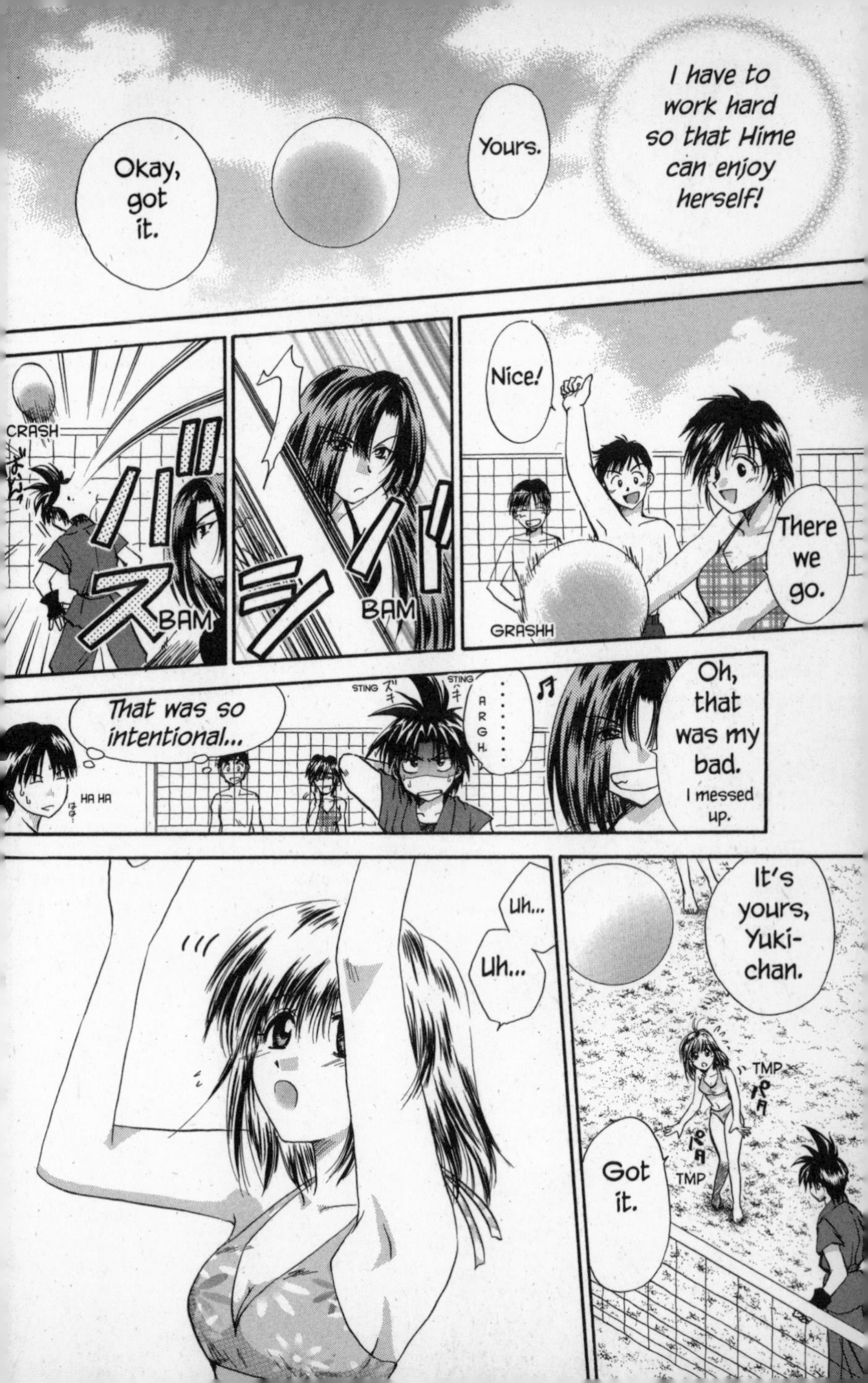
I have to work hard so that Hime can enjoy herself!
Yours.
Okay, got it.
Nice!
There we go.
GRASHH
BAM
CRASH
BAM
Oh, that was my bad.
I messed up.
♪
ARGH......
STING
STING
That was so intentional...
HA HA
It's yours, Yuki-chan.
TMP
TMP
Got it.
Uh...
Uh...

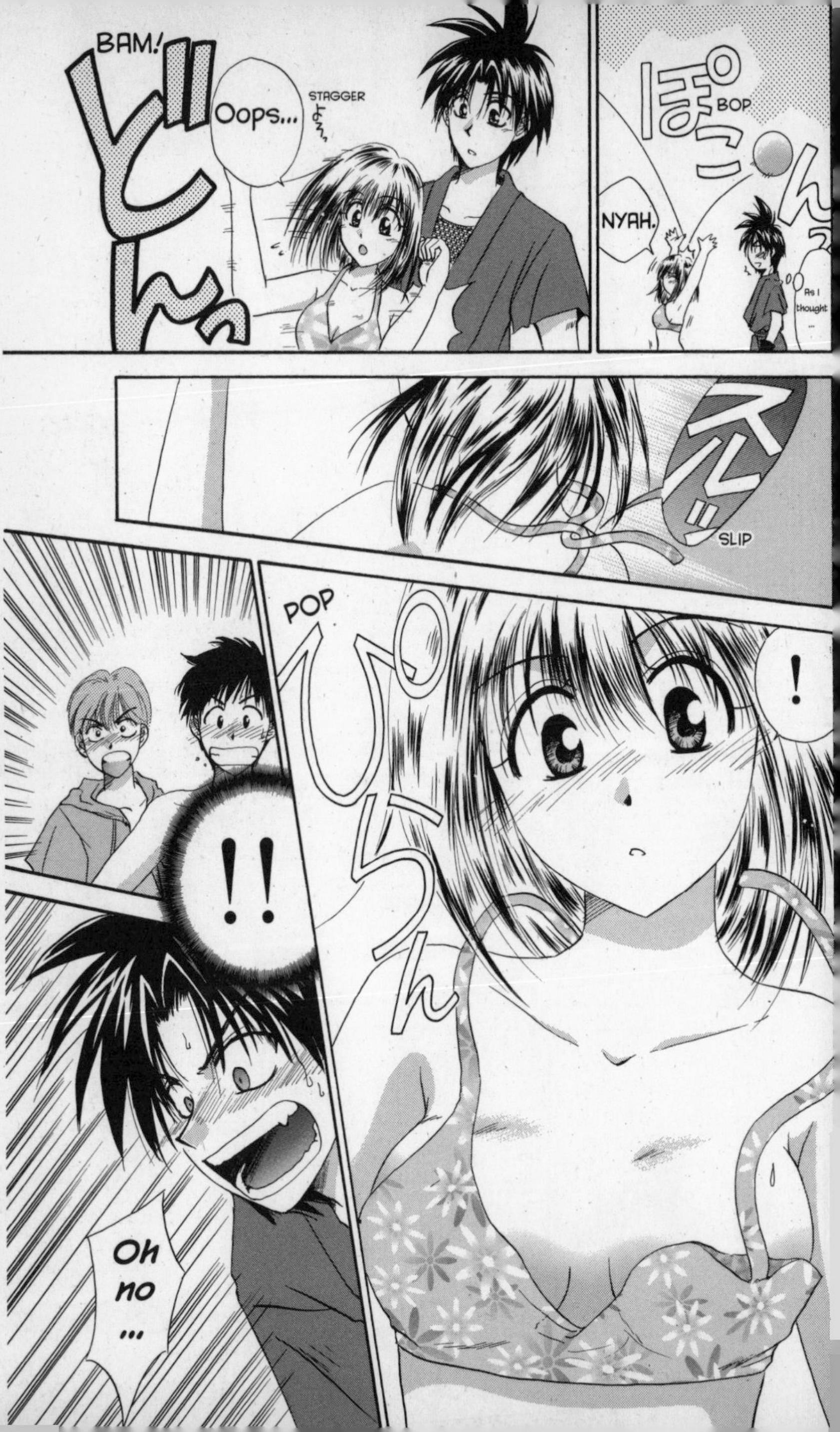
BOP
NYAH.
As I thought ...
BAM!
Oops...
STAGGER
SLIP
POP
!
!!
Oh no ...

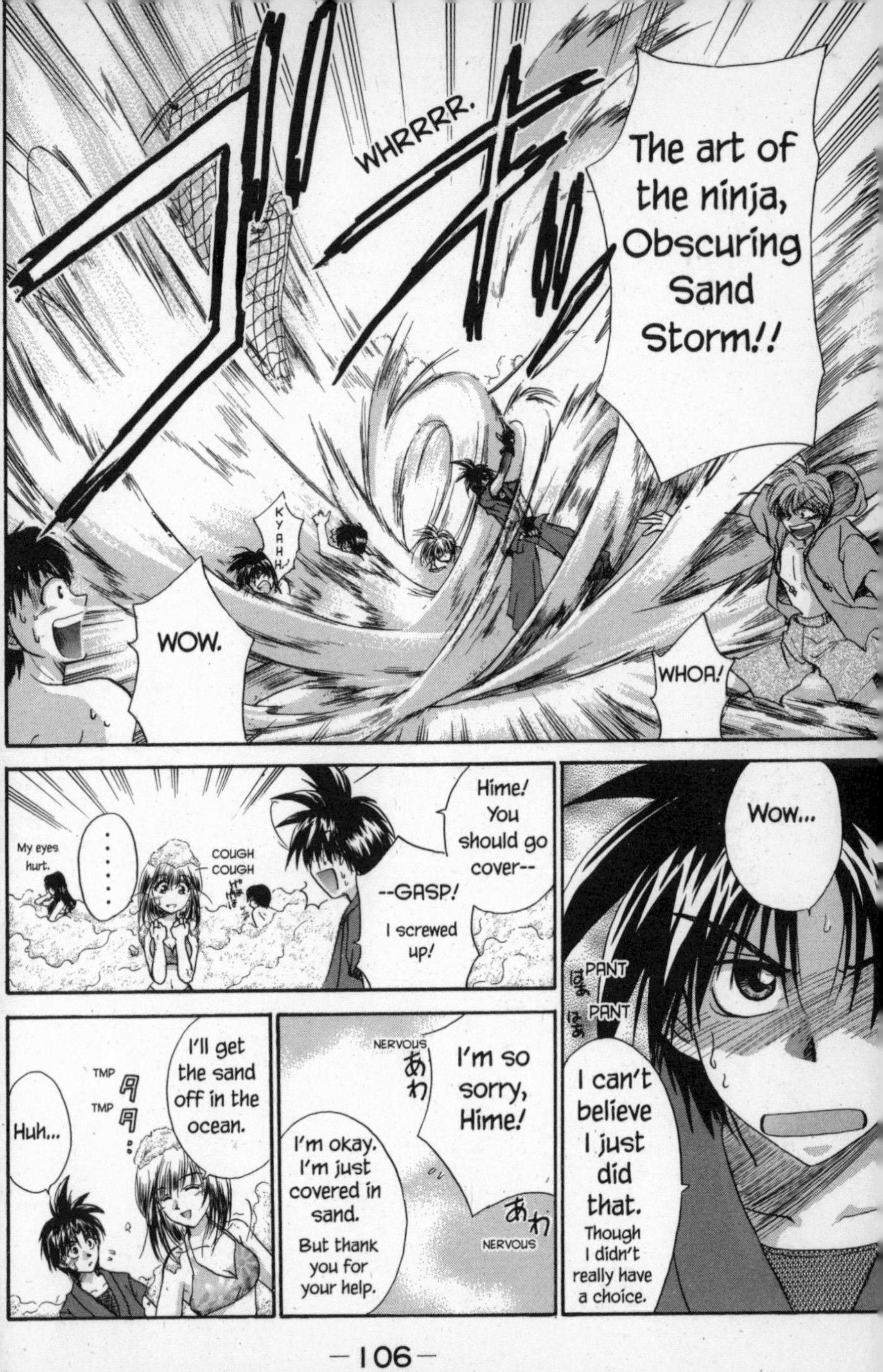

The art of the ninja, Obscuring Sand Storm!!
WHRRRR.
WHOA!
KYAHH!
WOW.
Wow...
PANT
PANT
I can't believe I just did that.
Though I didn't really have a choice.
Hime! You should go cover--
--GASP!
I screwed up!
COUGH
COUGH
......
My eyes hurt.
I'm so sorry, Hime!
あわ
NERVOUS
I'm okay. I'm just covered in sand.
But thank you for your help.
あわ
NERVOUS
I'll get the sand off in the ocean.
タタ
TMP
TMP
Huh...

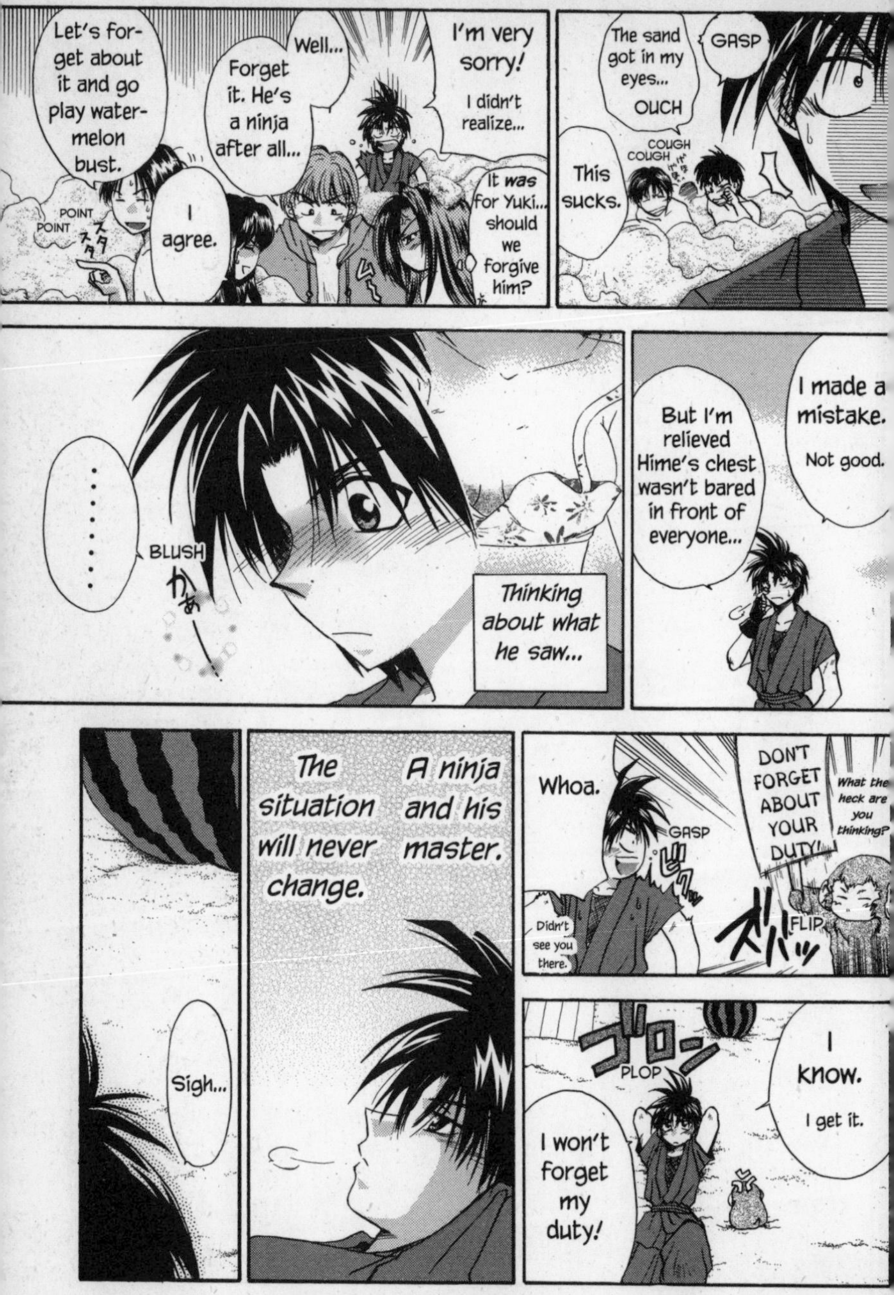
GASP
The sand got in my eyes... OUCH
COUGH COUGH
This sucks.
I'm very sorry! I didn't realize...
It was for Yuki... should we forgive him?
Well...
Forget it. He's a ninja after all...
Let's forget about it and go play watermelon bust.
I agree.
POINT POINT
I made a mistake. Not good.
But I'm relieved Hime's chest wasn't bared in front of everyone...
Thinking about what he saw...
......
BLUSH
DON'T FORGET ABOUT YOUR DUTY!
What the heck are you thinking?
FLIP
Whoa.
GASP
Didn't see you there.
I know. I get it.
PLOP
I won't forget my duty!
A ninja and his master.
The situation will never change.
Sigh...

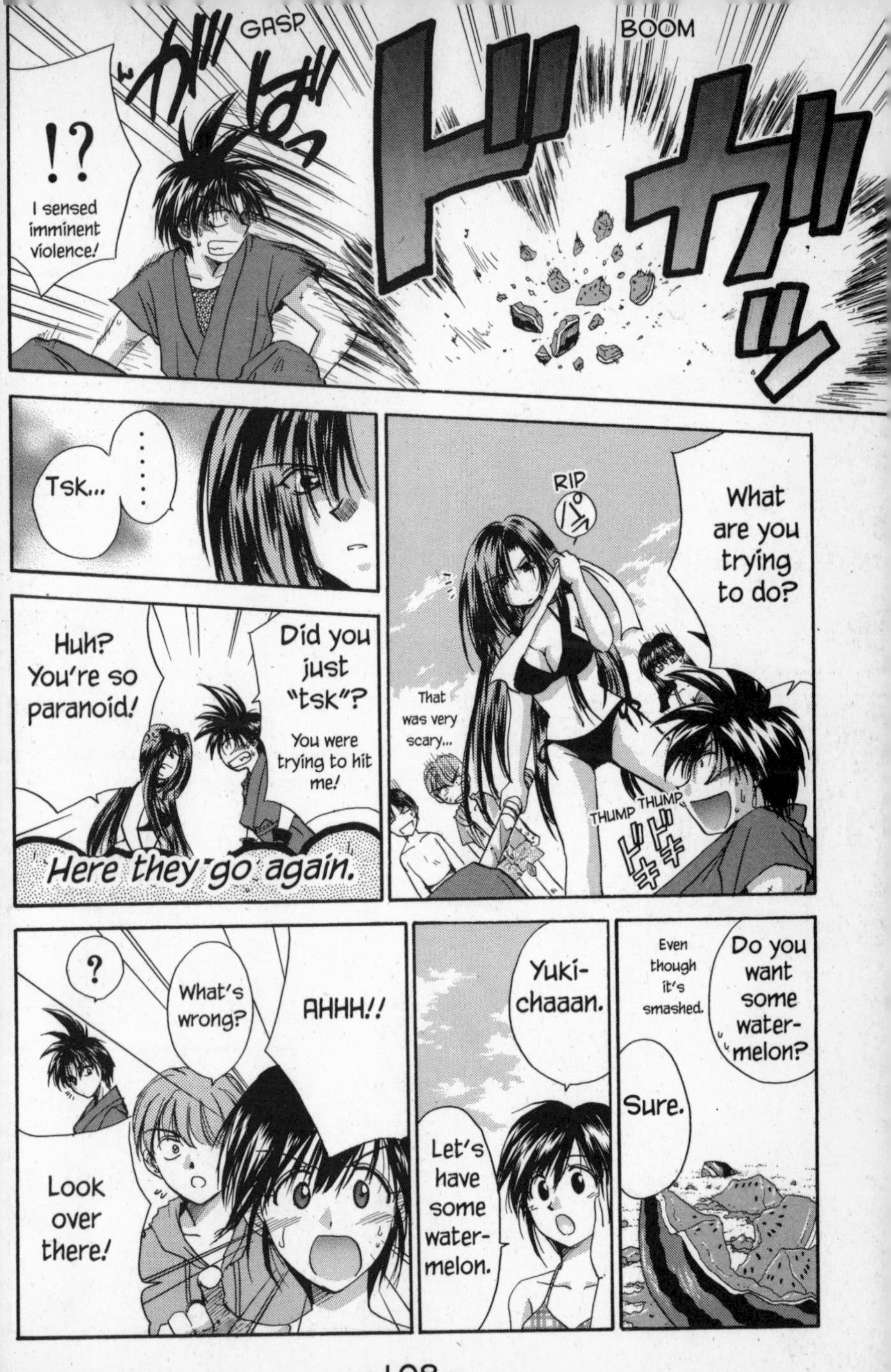
BOOM
ドガッ
GASP
がばっ
!?
I sensed imminent violence!
What are you trying to do?
RIP
That was very scary...
THUMP THUMP
ドキドキ
......
Tsk...
Did you just "tsk"?
You were trying to hit me!
Huh? You're so paranoid!
Here they go again.
Do you want some water-melon?
Even though it's smashed.
Sure.
Yuki-chaaan.
Let's have some water-melon.
AHHH!!
What's wrong?
?
Look over there!

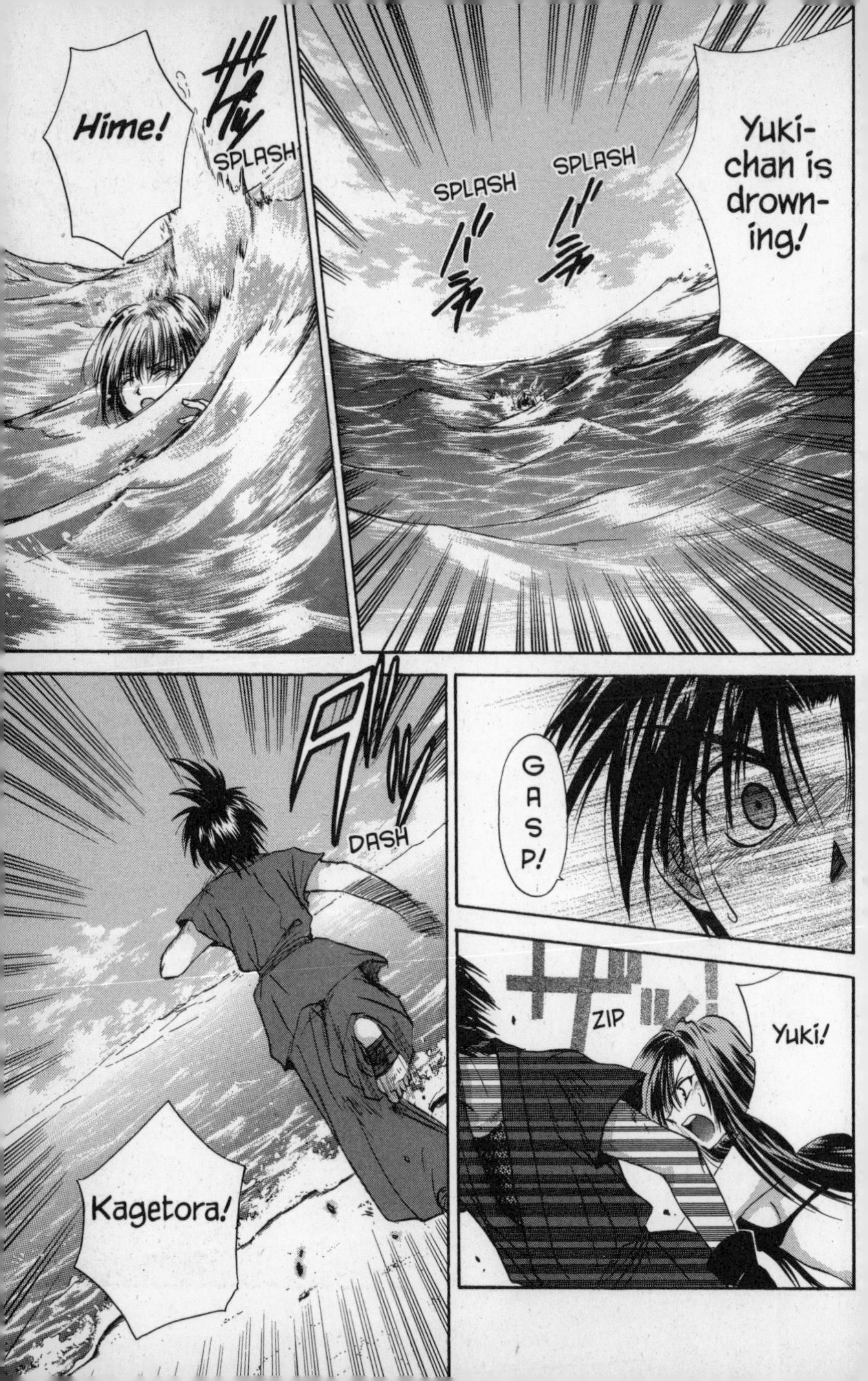
Yuki-chan is drowning!
SPLASH
SPLASH
Hime!
SPLASH
GASP!
Yuki!
ZIP
DASH
Kagetora!

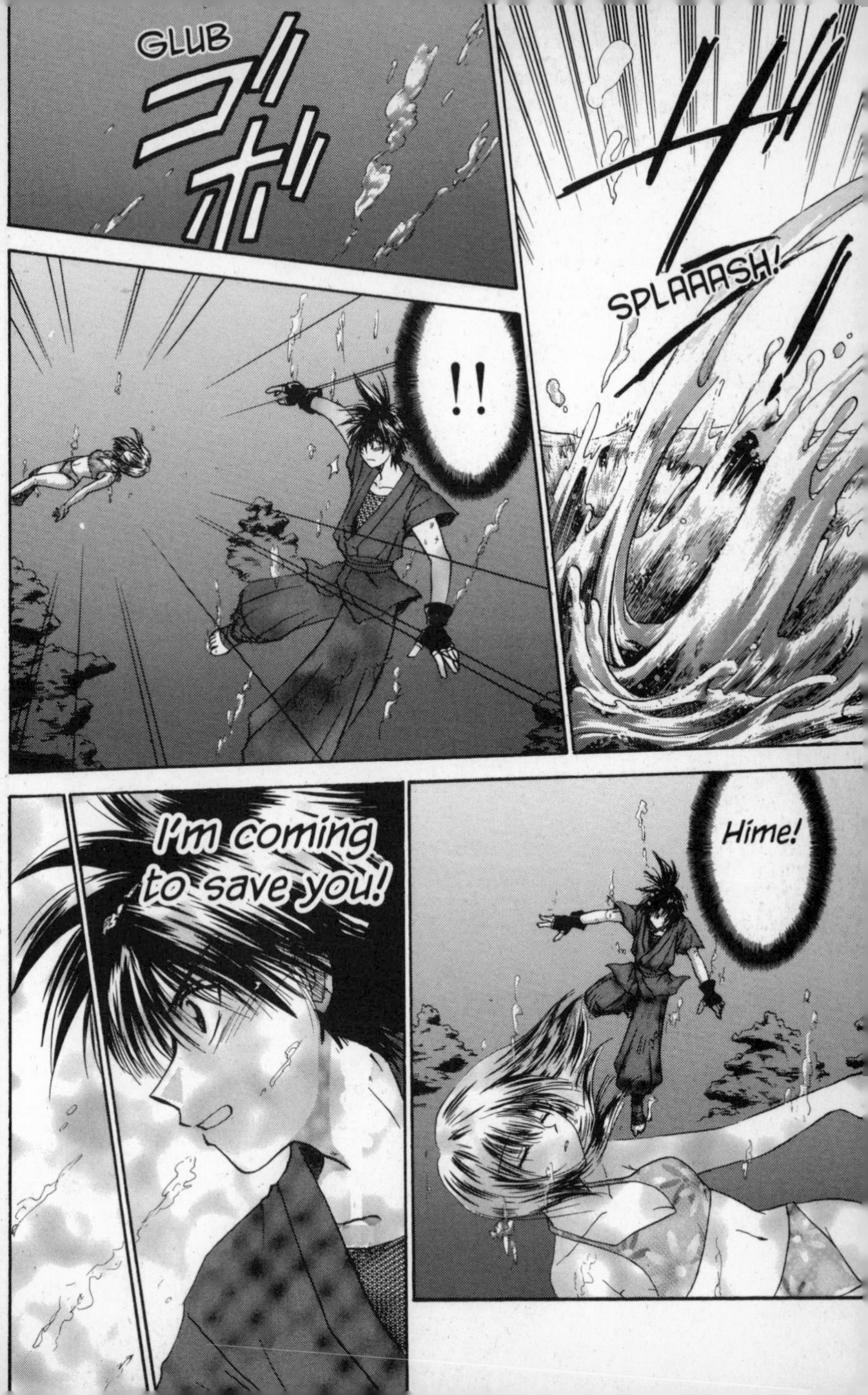
SPLAAASH!
GLUB
!!
Hime!
I'm coming to save you!

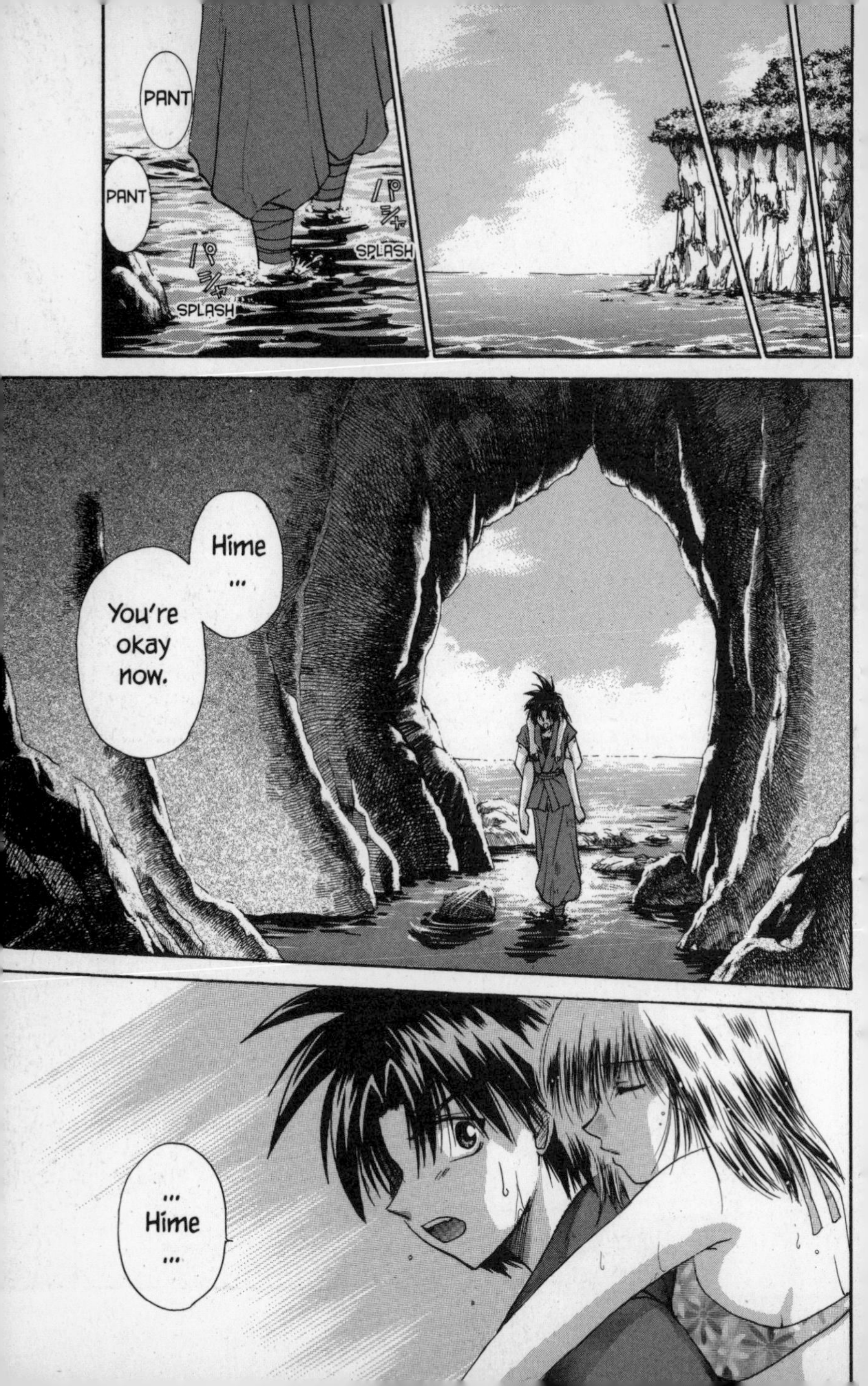
PANT
PANT
パシャ
SPLASH
パシャ
SPLASH
Hime ...
You're okay now.
... Hime ...

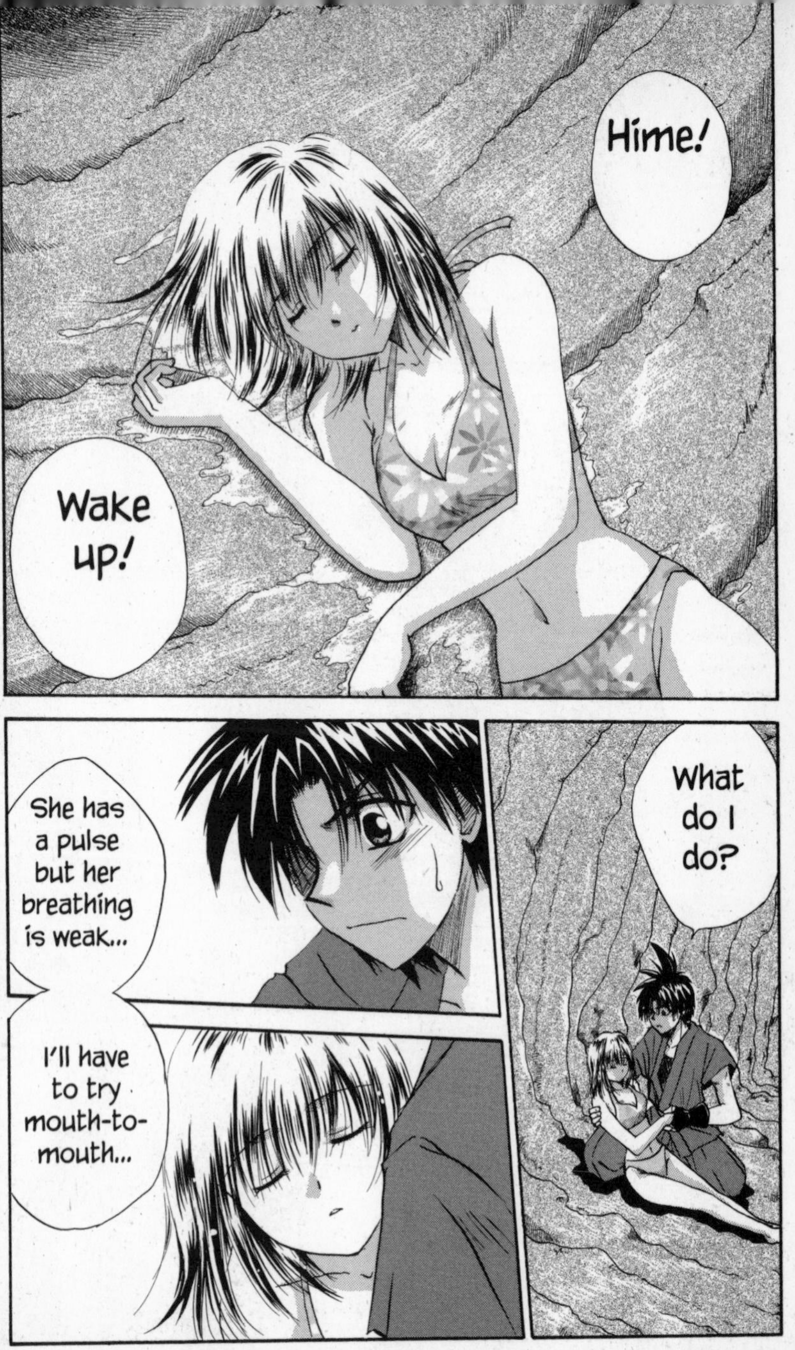
Hime!
Wake up!
What do I do?
She has a pulse but her breathing is weak...
I'll have to try mouth-to-mouth...

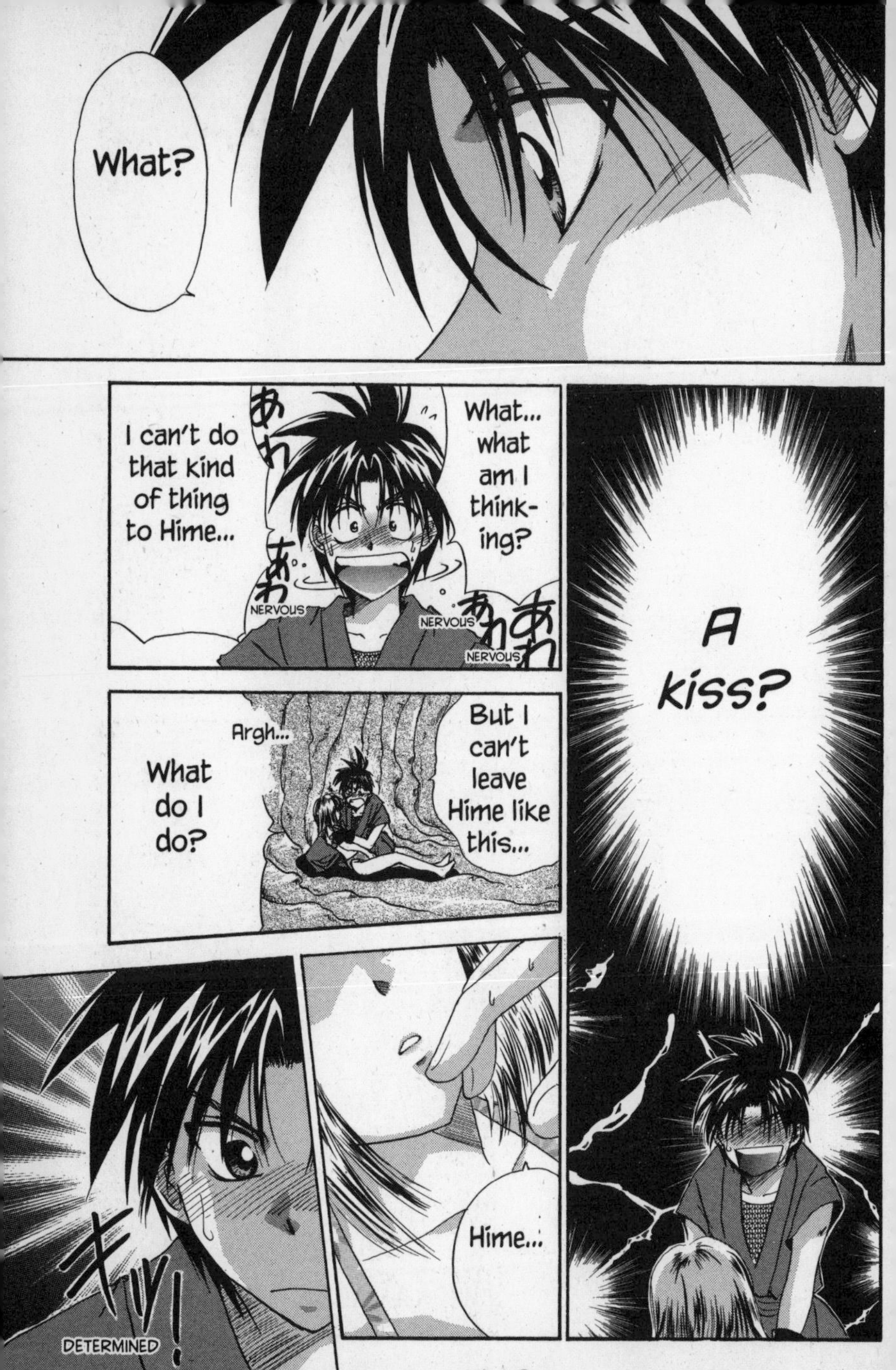
What?
A kiss?
What... what am I thinking?
あわ
NERVOUS
あわ
NERVOUS
I can't do that kind of thing to Hime...
あわ
NERVOUS
あわ
But I can't leave Hime like this...
Argh...
What do I do?
Hime...
キッ!
DETERMINED

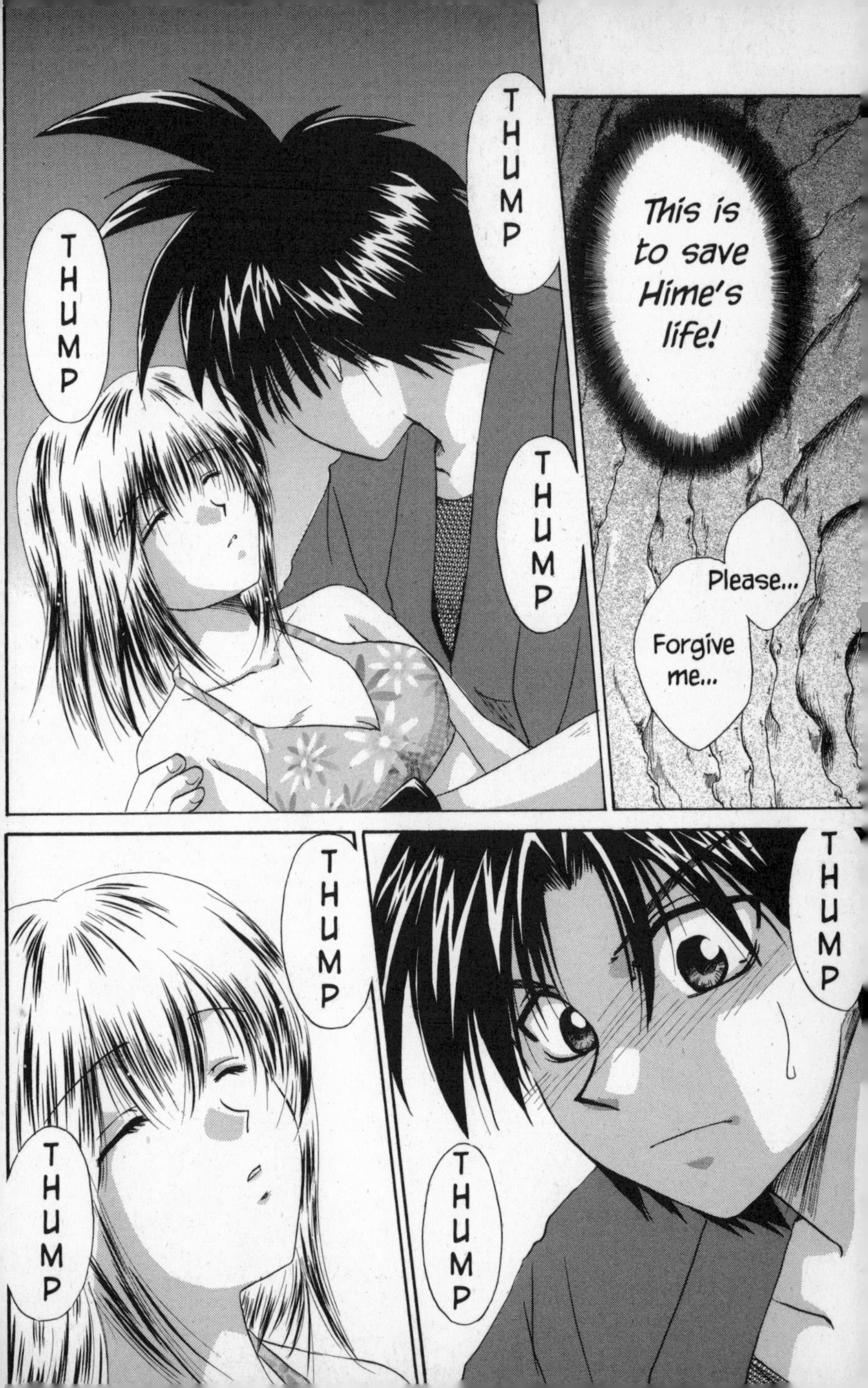
This is to save Hime's life!
Please...
Forgive me...
THUMP
THUMP
THUMP
THUMP
THUMP
THUMP
THUMP

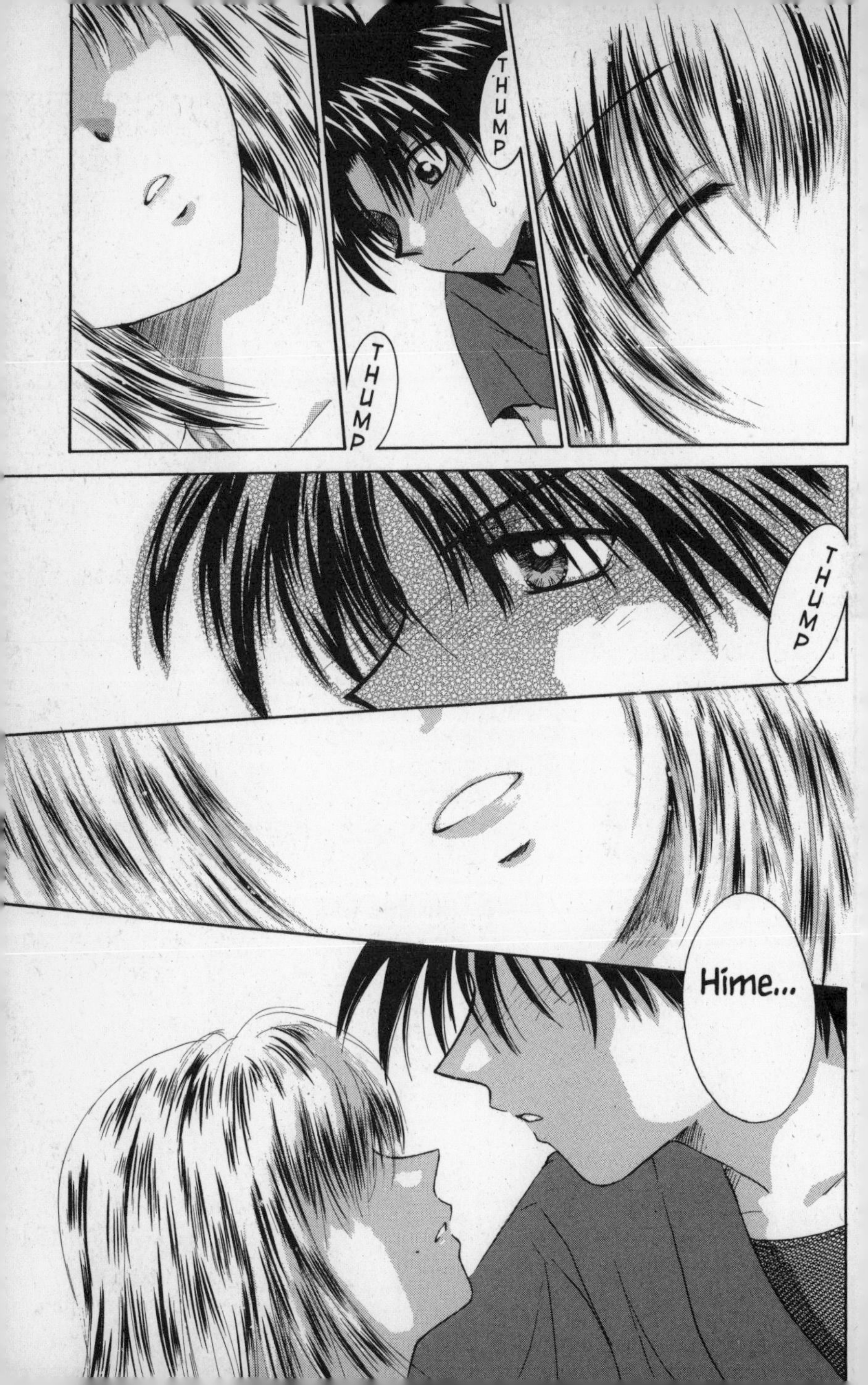
THUMP
THUMP
THUMP
Hime...

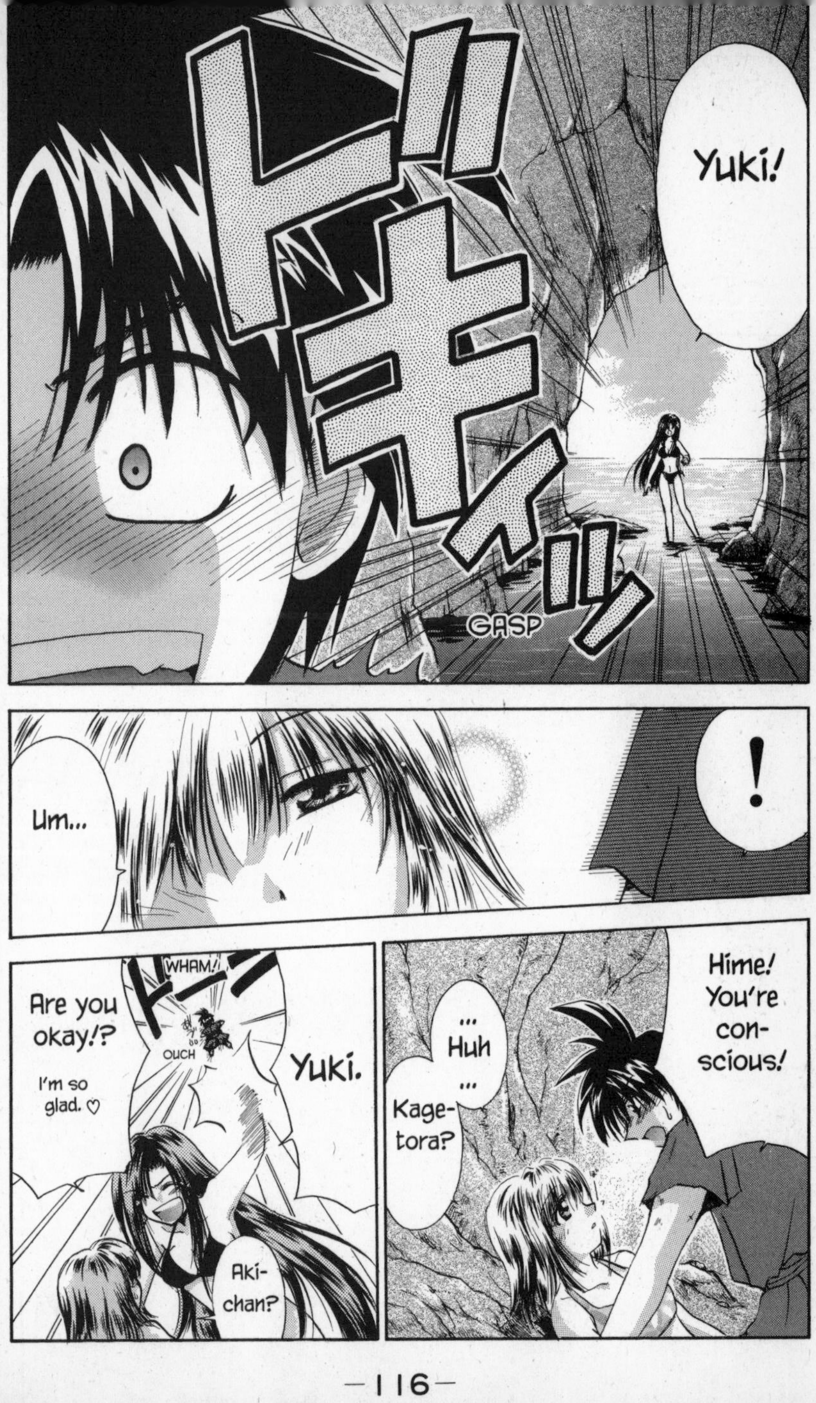
Yuki!
ドキィッ
GASP
!
Um...
Hime! You're con-scious!
... Huh ... Kage-tora?
WHAM!
Yuki.
Are you okay!?
OUCH
I'm so glad. ♡
Aki-chan?

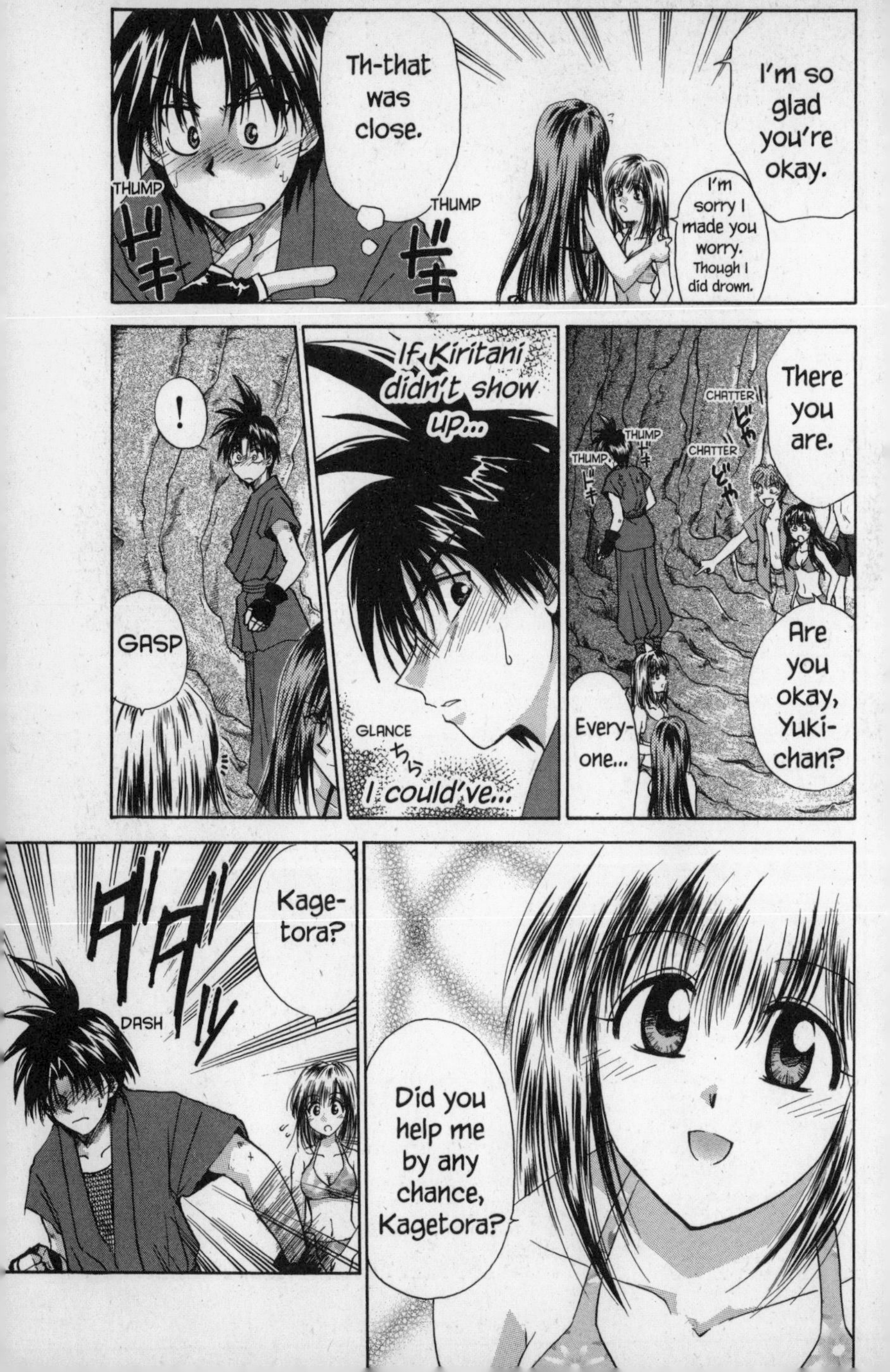
I'm so glad you're okay.
I'm sorry I made you worry. Though I did drown.
Th-that was close.
THUMP
THUMP
There you are.
CHATTER
CHATTER
THUMP
THUMP
Are you okay, Yuki-chan?
Every-one...
If Kiritani didn't show up...
GLANCE
I could've...
!
GASP
Did you help me by any chance, Kagetora?
Kage-tora?
DASH

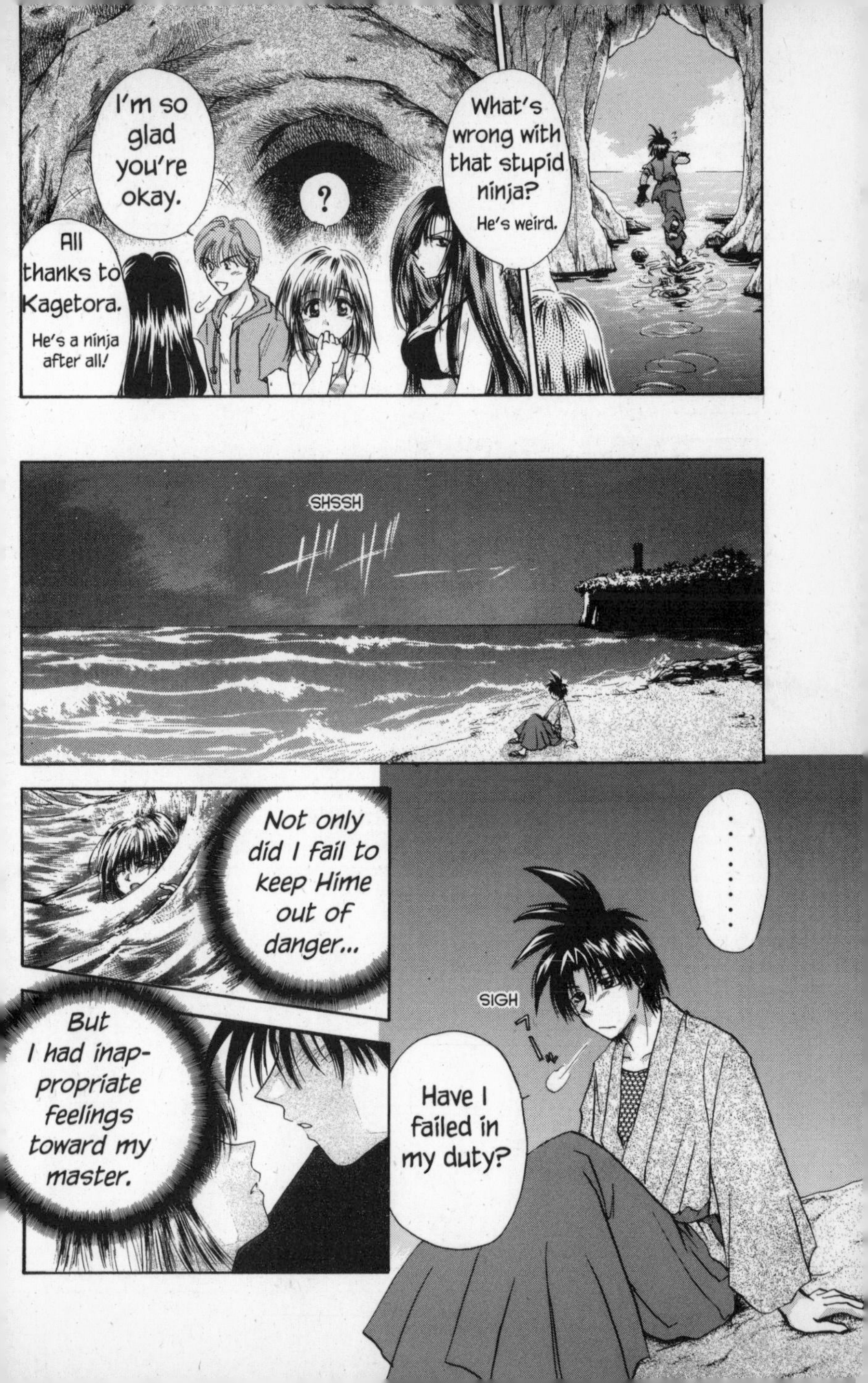

What's wrong with that stupid ninja?
He's weird.
?
I'm so glad you're okay.
All thanks to Kagetora.
He's a ninja after all!
SHSSH
......
SIGH
Have I failed in my duty?
Not only did I fail to keep Hime out of danger...
But I had inap-propriate feelings toward my master.

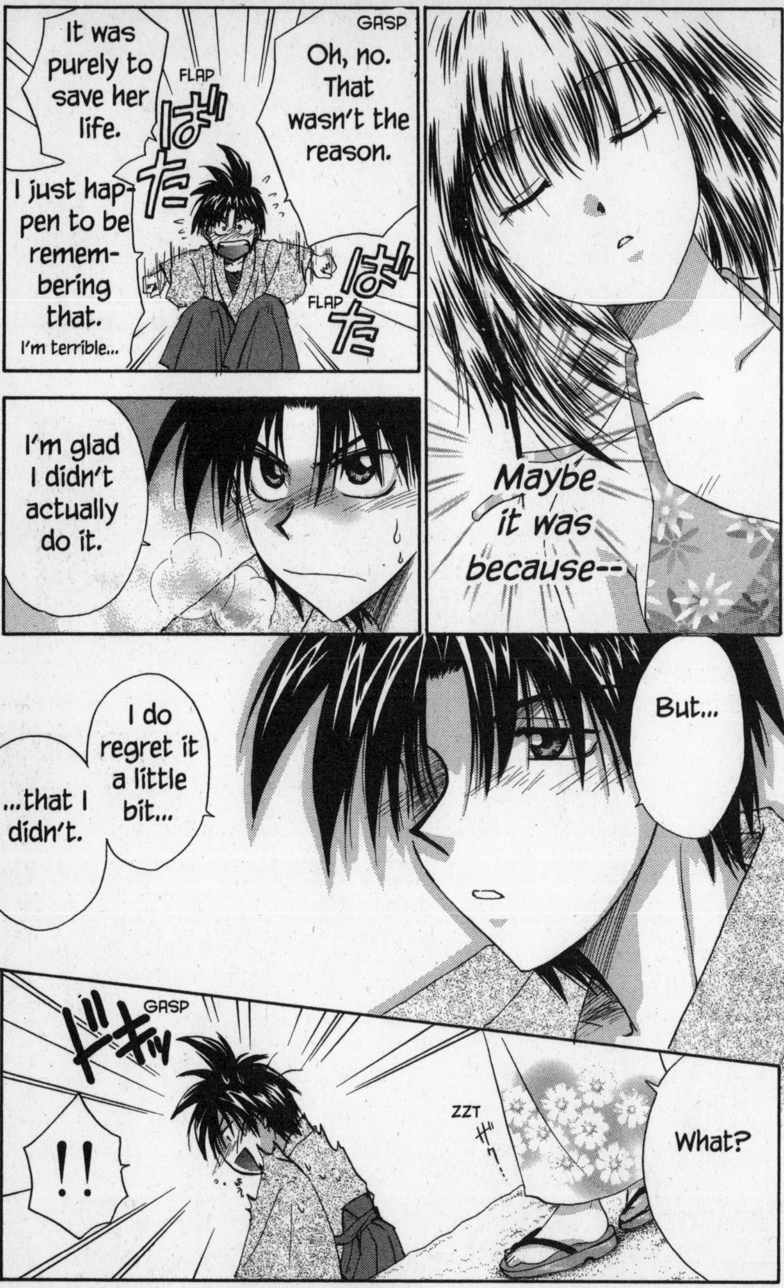
Maybe it was because--
GASP
Oh, no. That wasn't the reason.
FLAP
ばた
It was purely to save her life.
I just happen to be remembering that.
I'm terrible...
ばた
FLAP
I'm glad I didn't actually do it.
But...
I do regret it a little bit...
...that I didn't.
What?
ZZT
ザク
GASP
ドキッ
!!

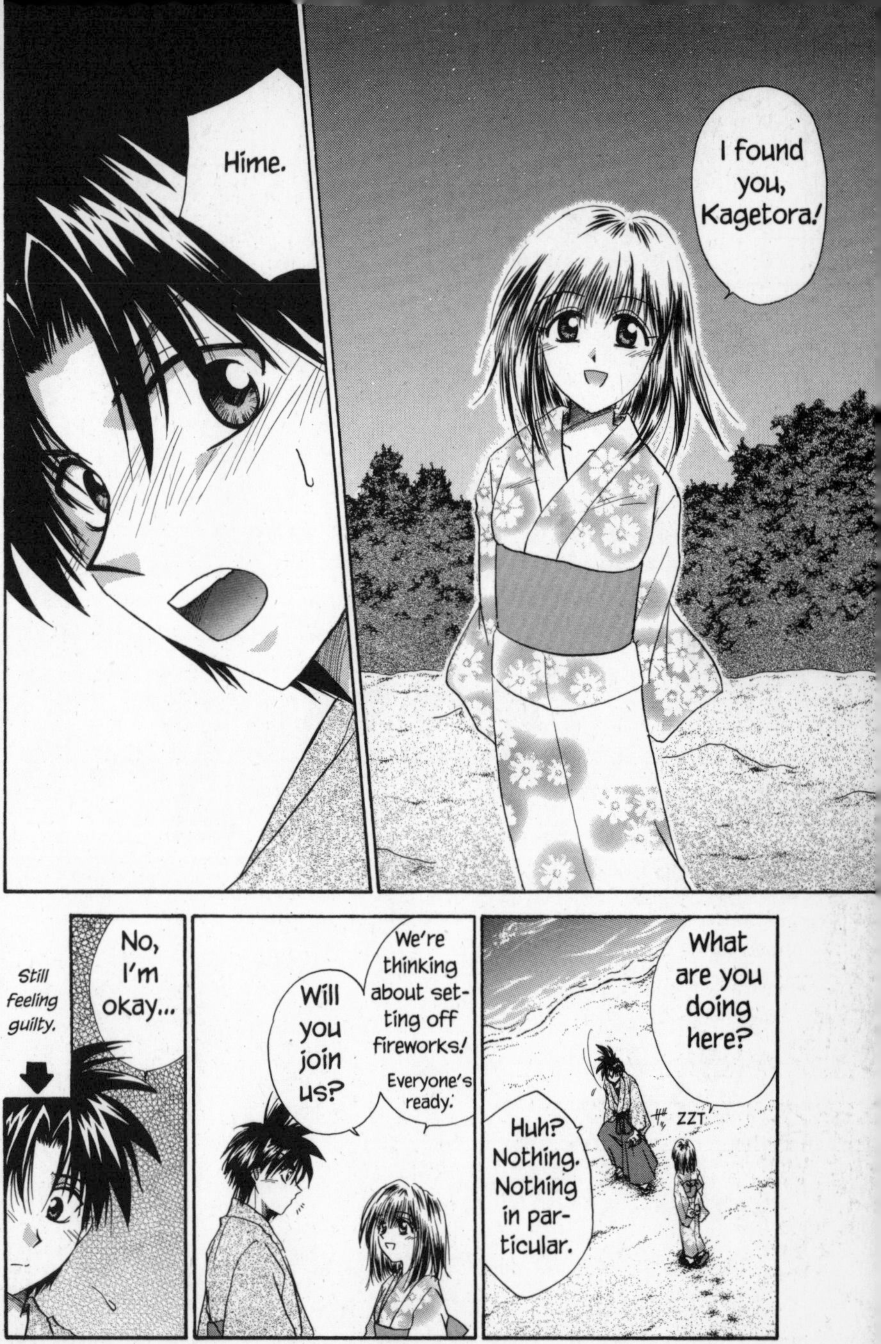
I found you, Kagetora!
Hime.
What are you doing here?
ZZT
Huh? Nothing. Nothing in par-ticular.
We're thinking about set-ting off fireworks!
Everyone's ready.
Will you join us?
No, I'm okay...
Still feeling guilty.

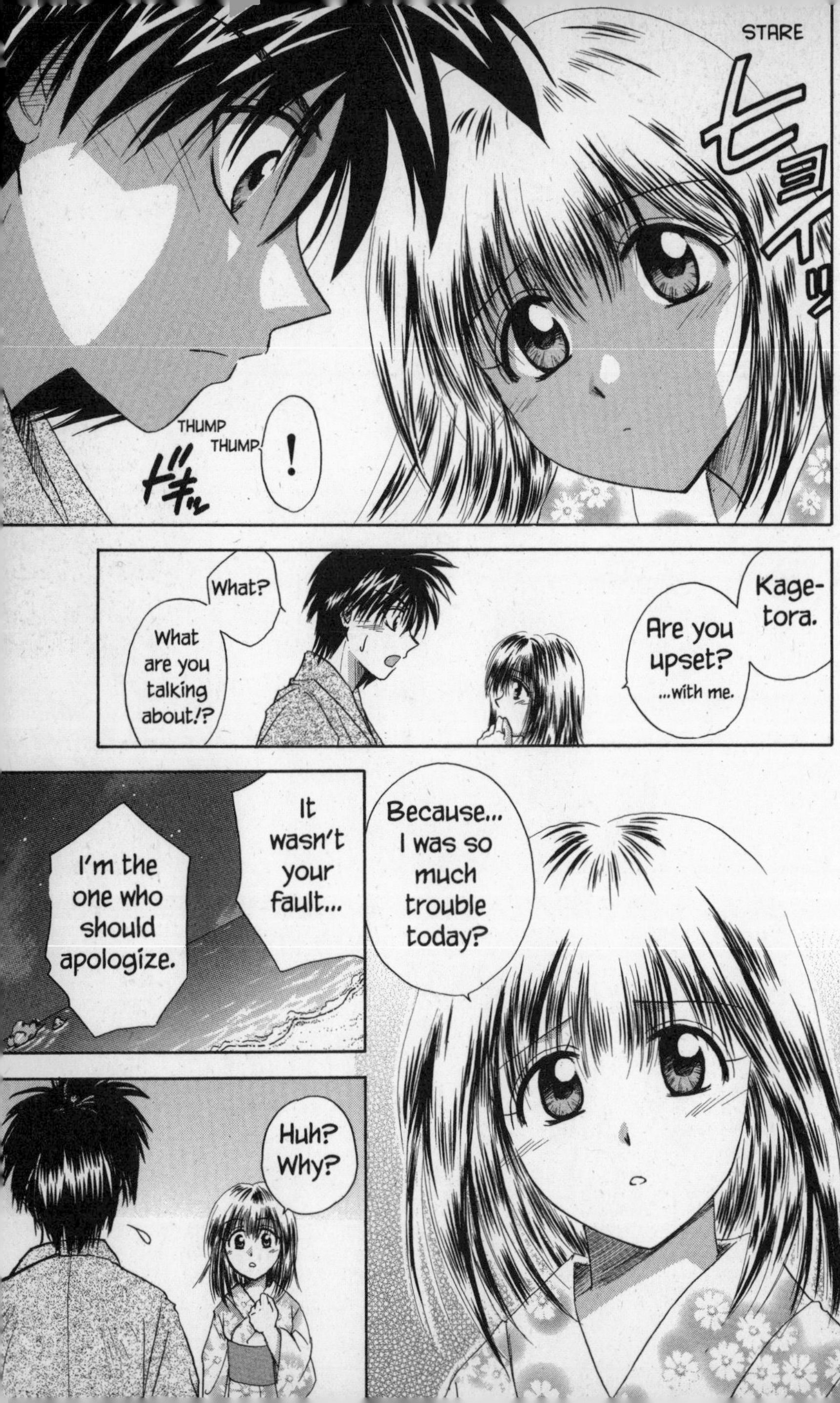
STARE
THUMP THUMP
!
Kage-tora.
Are you upset? ...with me.
What?
What are you talking about!?
Because... I was so much trouble today?
It wasn't your fault...
I'm the one who should apologize.
Huh? Why?

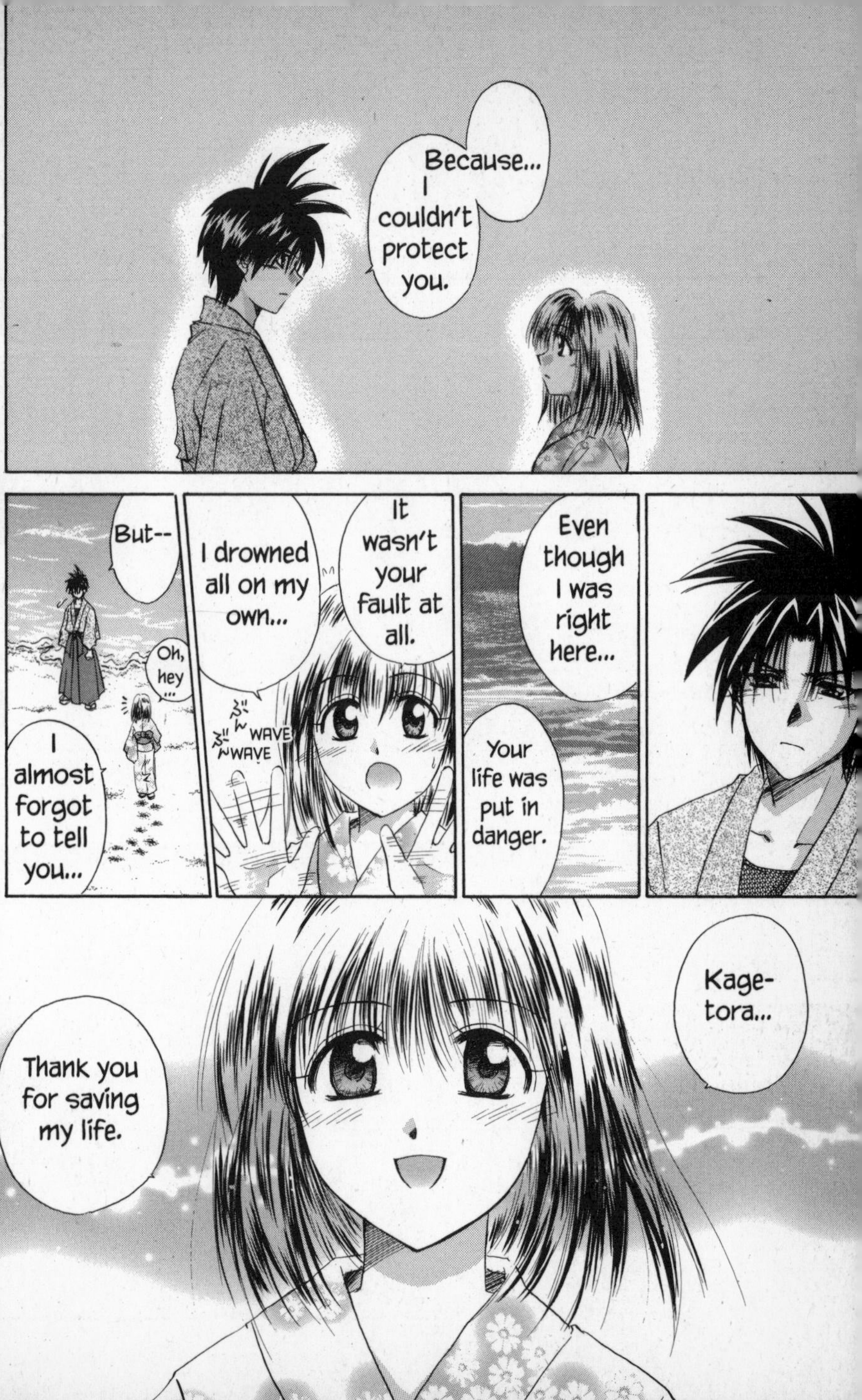
Because... I couldn't protect you.
Even though I was right here...
Your life was put in danger.
It wasn't your fault at all.
I drowned all on my own...
WAVE WAVE
But--
Oh, hey...
I almost forgot to tell you...
Kage-tora...
Thank you for saving my life.

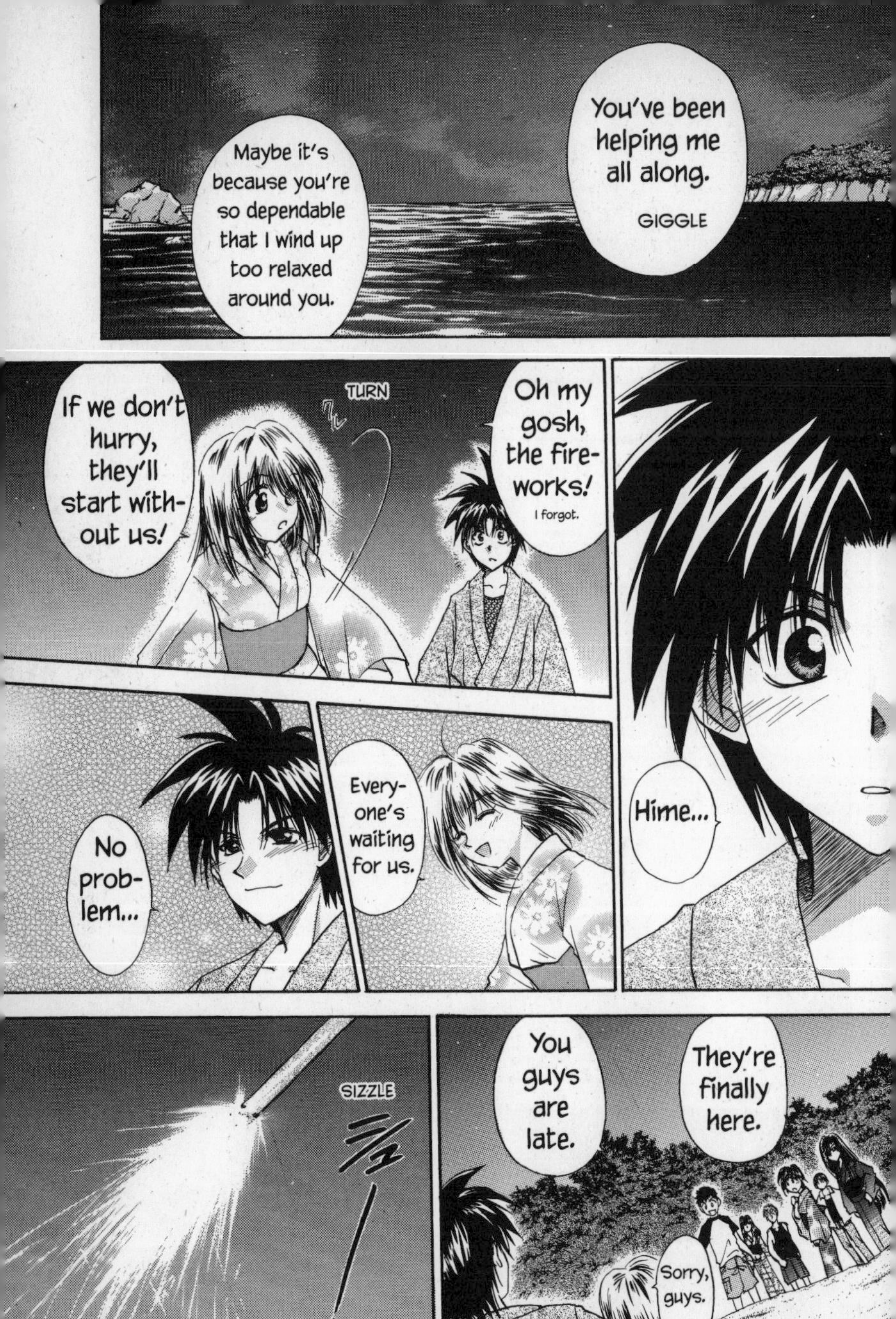
You've been helping me all along.
GIGGLE
Maybe it's because you're so dependable that I wind up too relaxed around you.
Hime...
Oh my gosh, the fire-works!
I forgot.
TURN
If we don't hurry, they'll start with-out us!
Every-one's waiting for us.
No prob-lem...
They're finally here.
You guys are late.
Sorry, guys.
SIZZLE

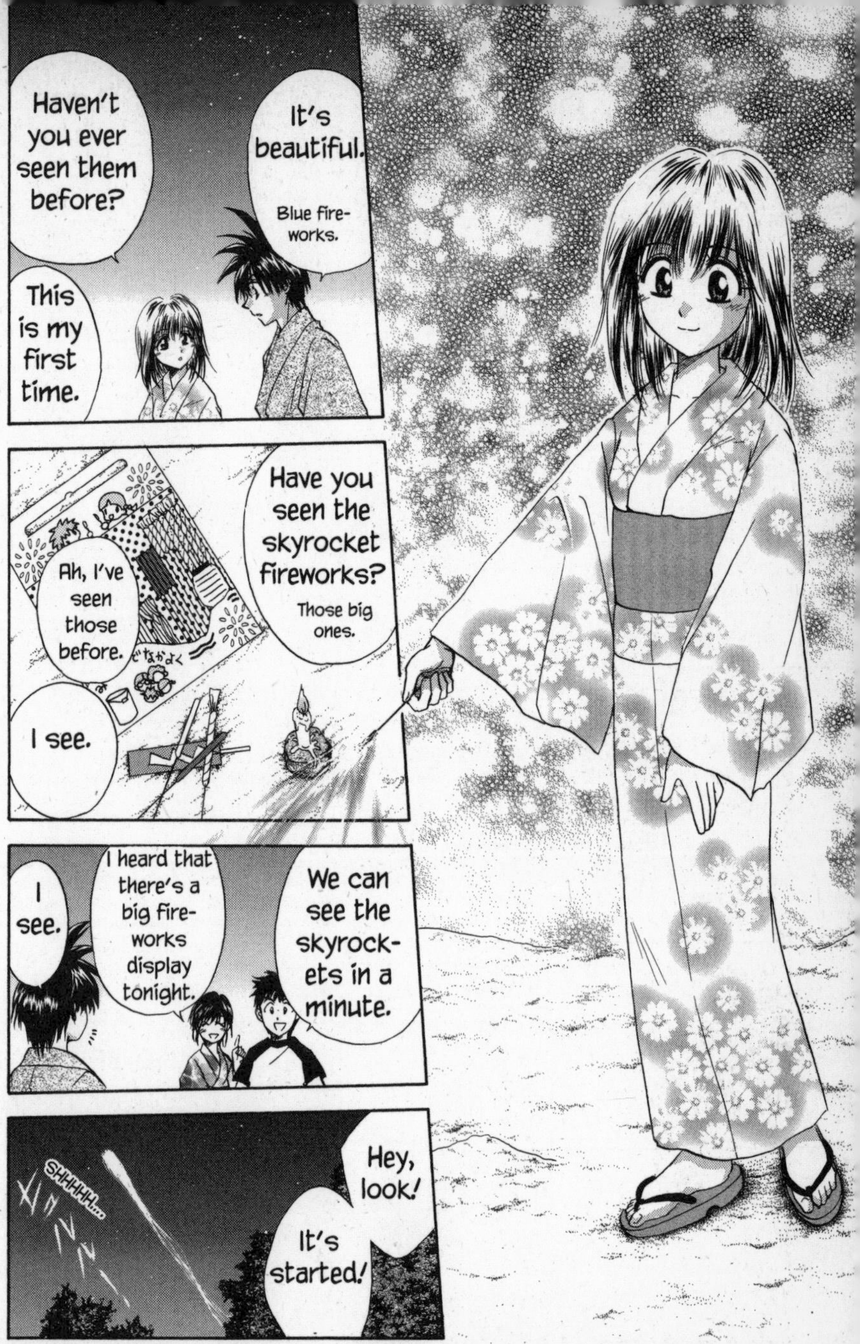
It's beautiful.
Blue fire-works.
Haven't you ever seen them before?
This is my first time.
Have you seen the skyrocket fireworks?
Those big ones.
Ah, I've seen those before.
I see.
We can see the skyrock-ets in a minute.
I heard that there's a big fire-works display tonight.
I see.
Hey, look!
It's started!
SHHHHH...

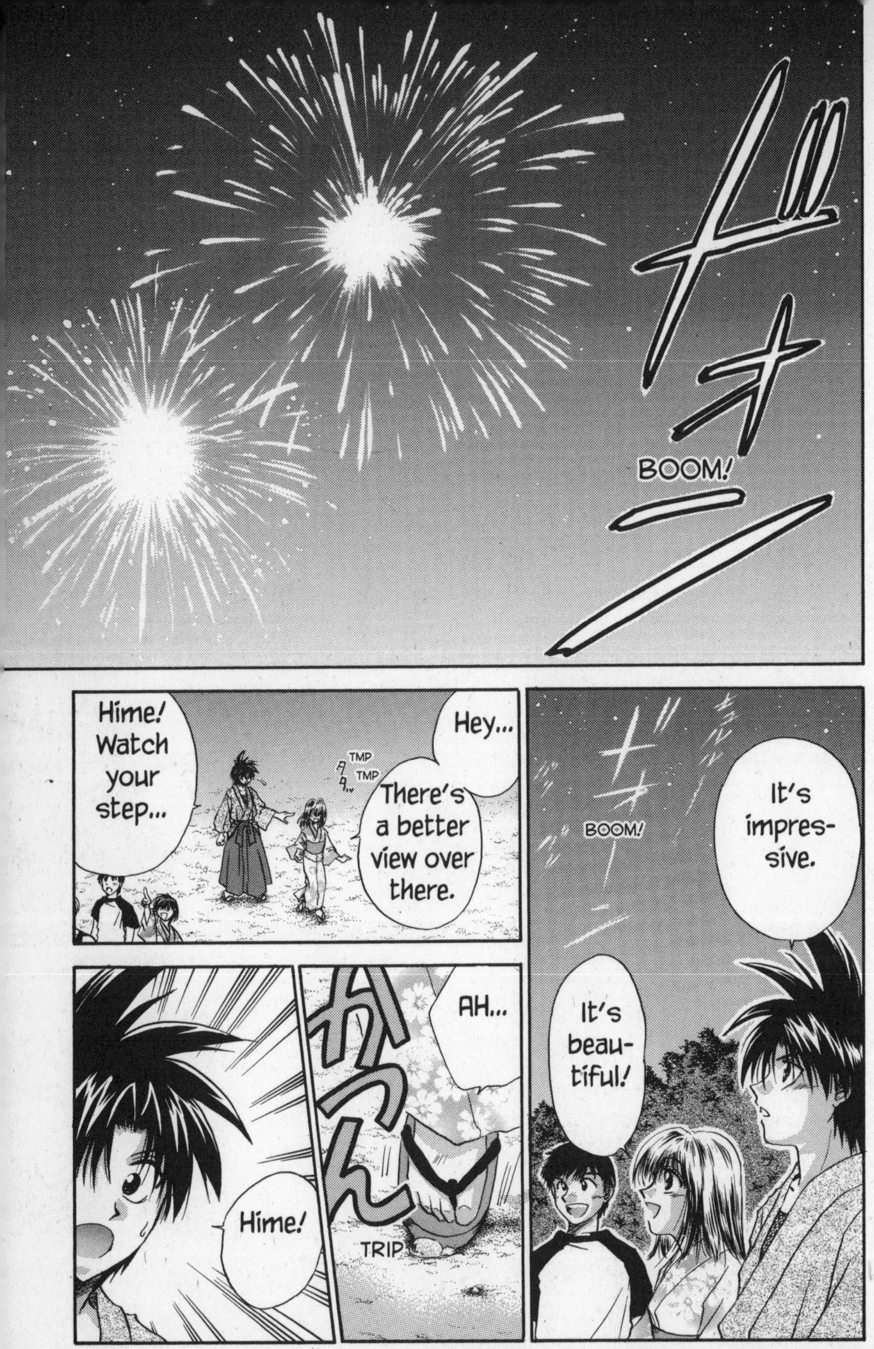
BOOM!
BOOM!
It's impressive.
It's beautiful!
Hey...
There's a better view over there.
TMP TMP
Hime! Watch your step...
AH...
TRIP
Hime!

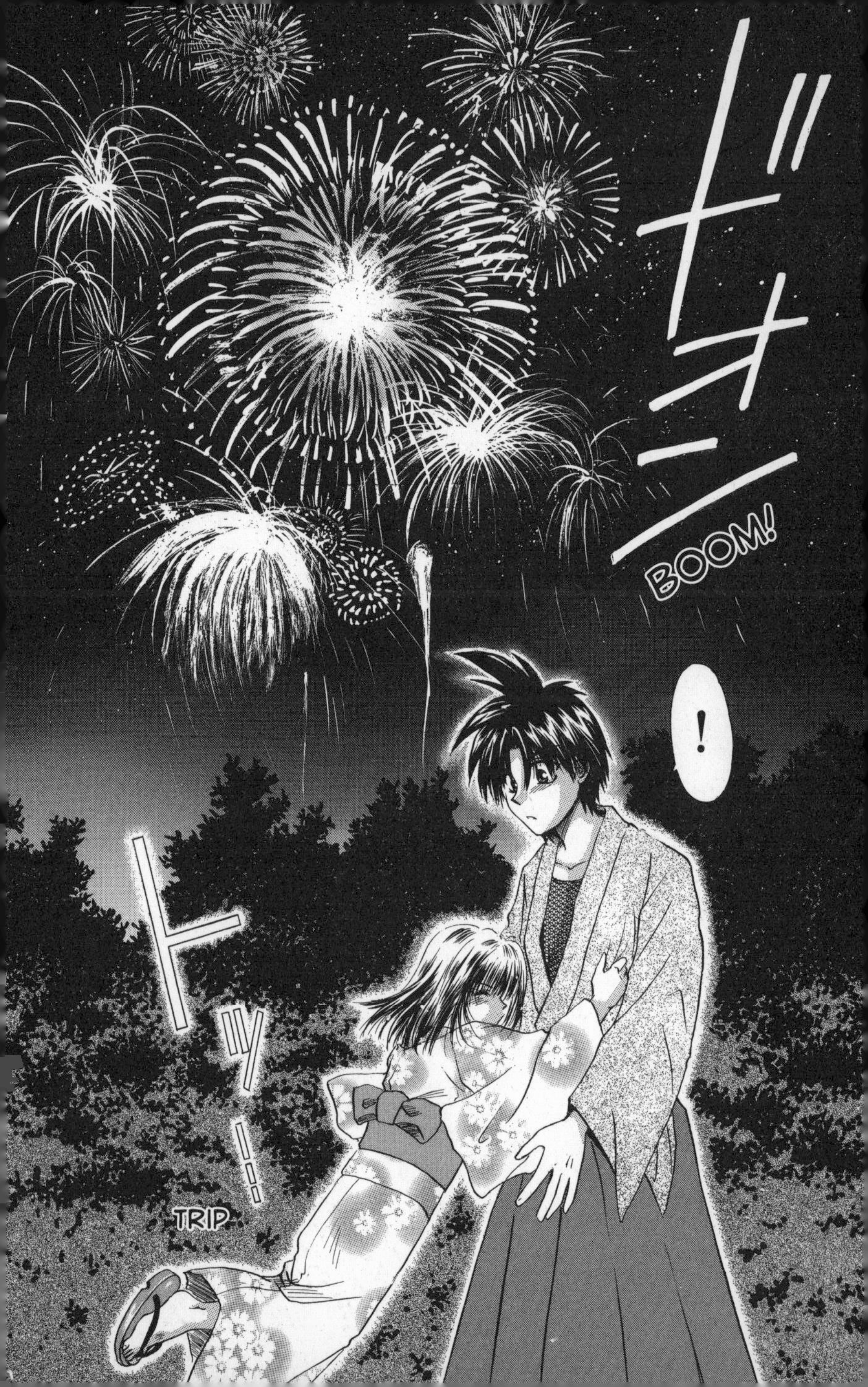
BOOM!
!
TRIP

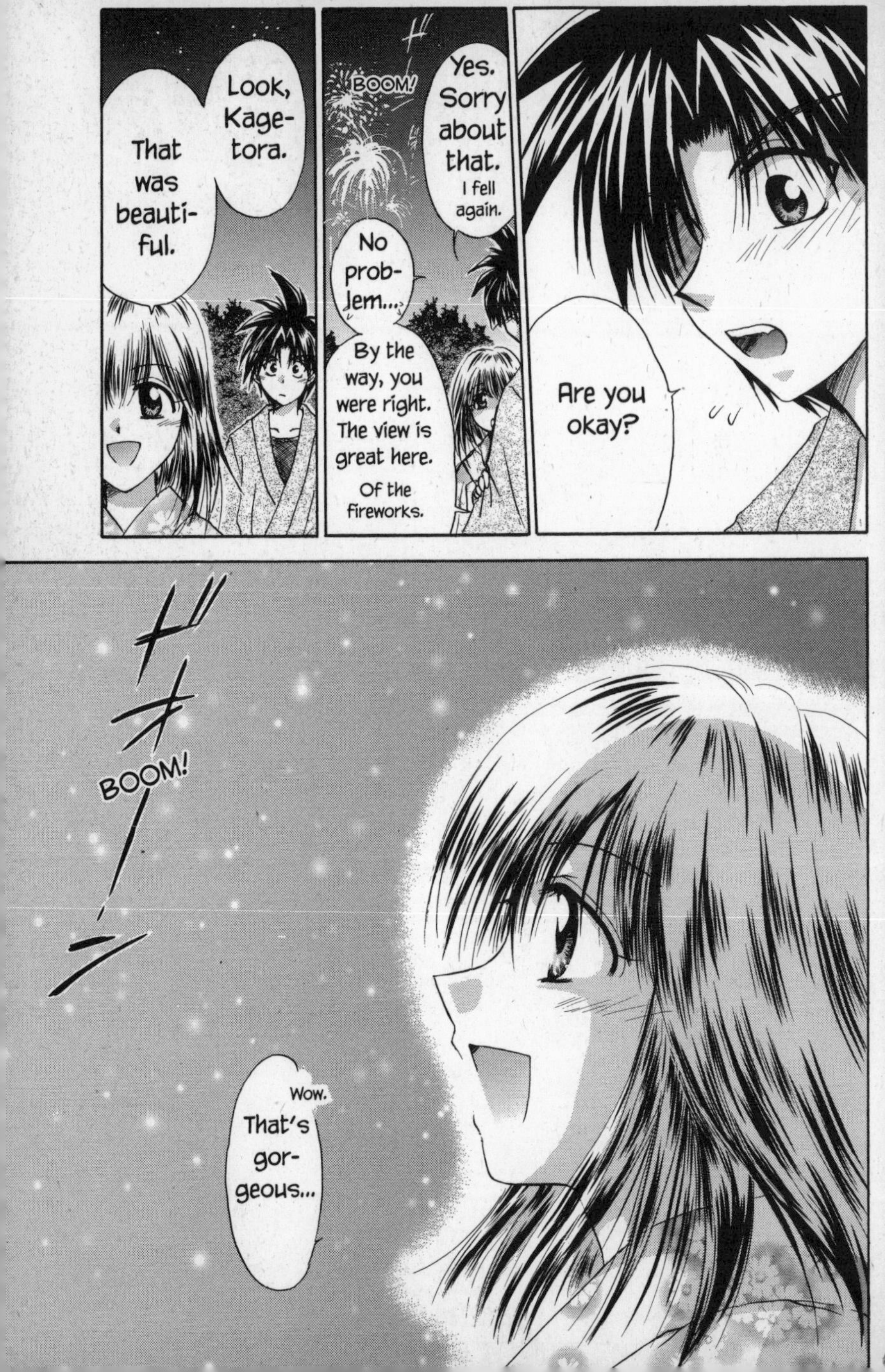
Are you okay?
Yes. Sorry about that.
I fell again.
BOOM!
No problem...
By the way, you were right. The view is great here.
Of the fireworks.
Look, Kagetora.
That was beautiful.
BOOM!
Wow.
That's gorgeous...

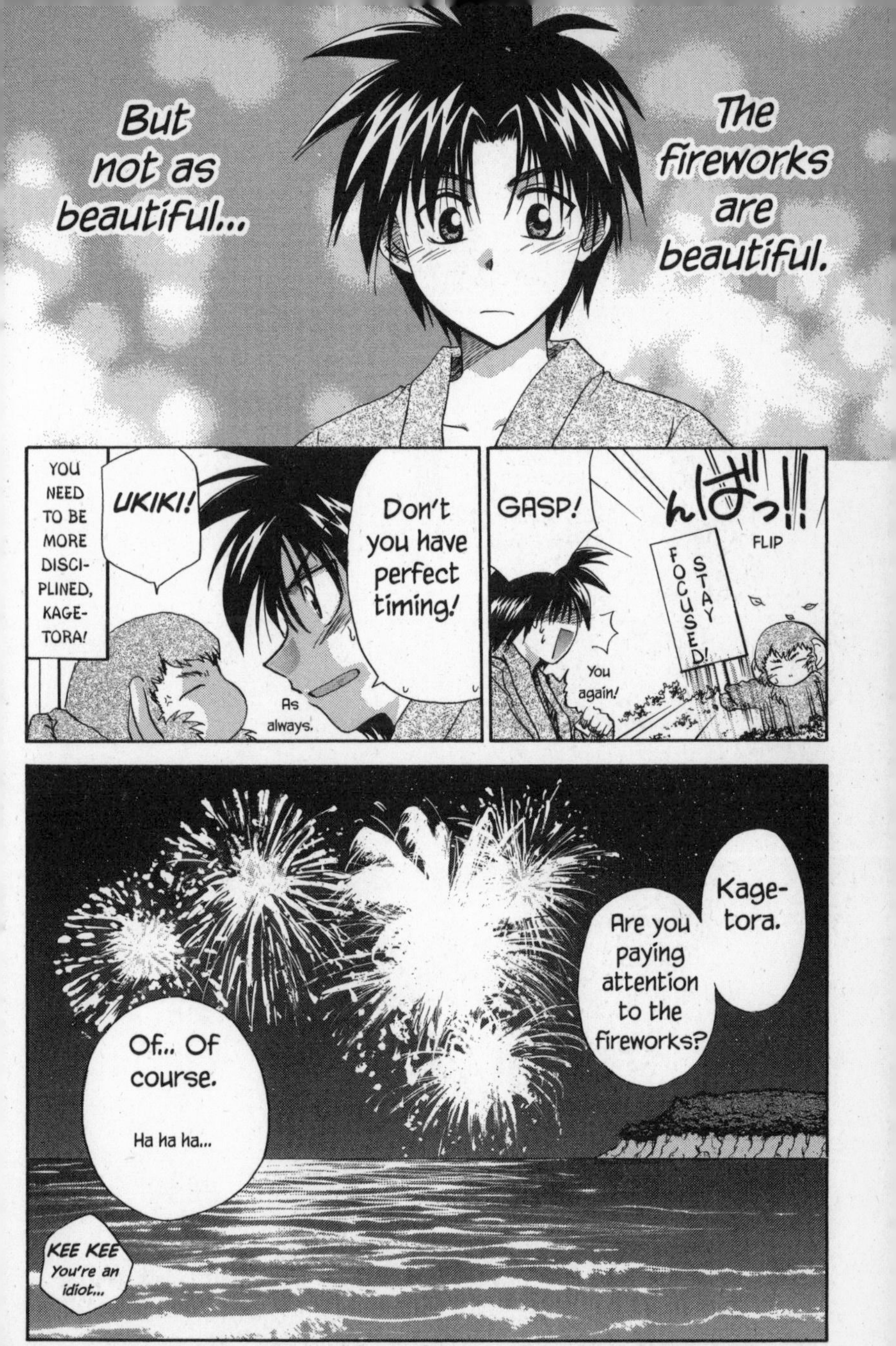
The fireworks are beautiful.
But not as beautiful...
GASP!
んばっ!!
FLIP
STAY FOCUSED!
You again!
Don't you have perfect timing!
UKIKI!
YOU NEED TO BE MORE DISCIPLINED, KAGETORA!
As always.
Kage-tora.
Are you paying attention to the fireworks?
Of... Of course.
Ha ha ha...
KEE KEE You're an idiot...

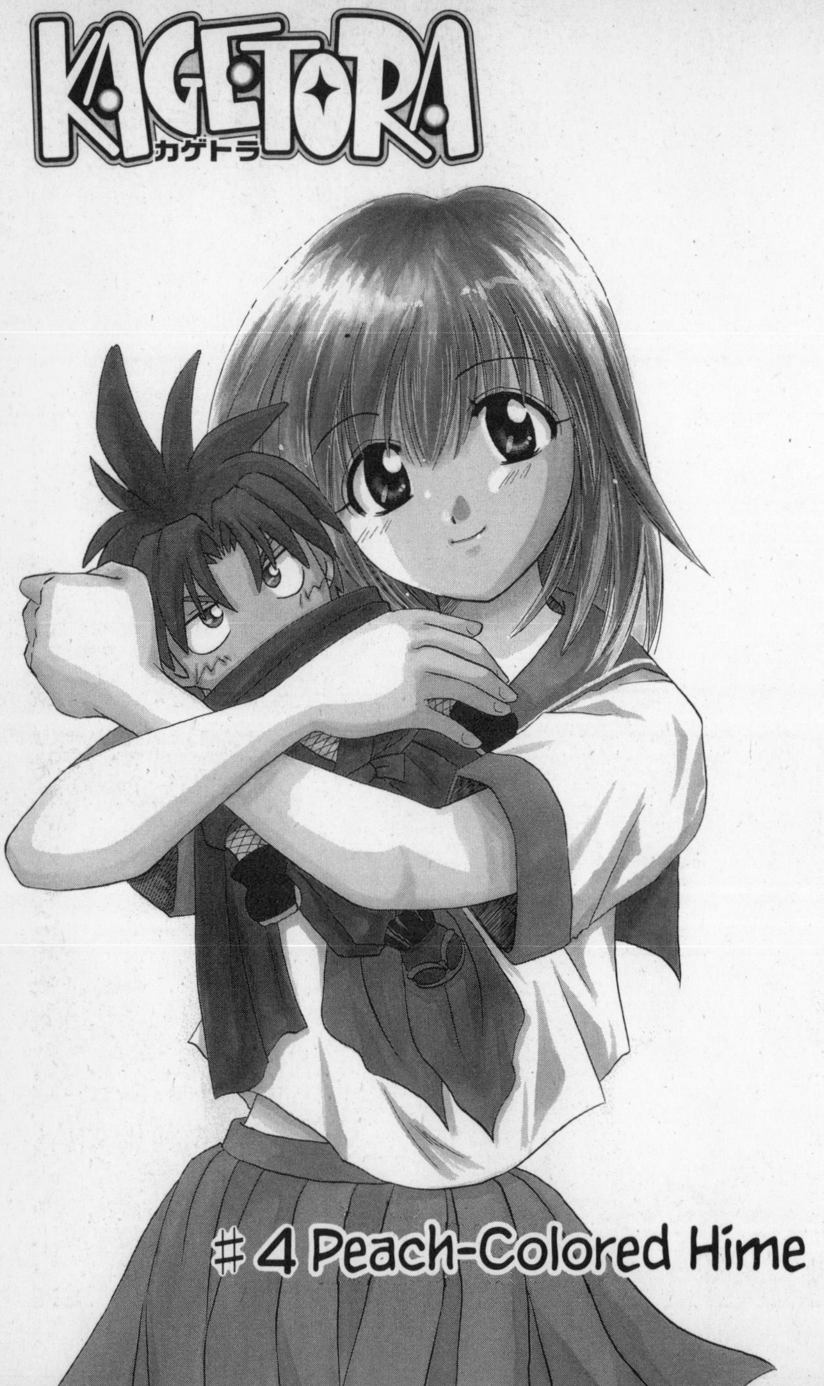
KAGETORA
カゲトラ
4 Peach-Colored Hime

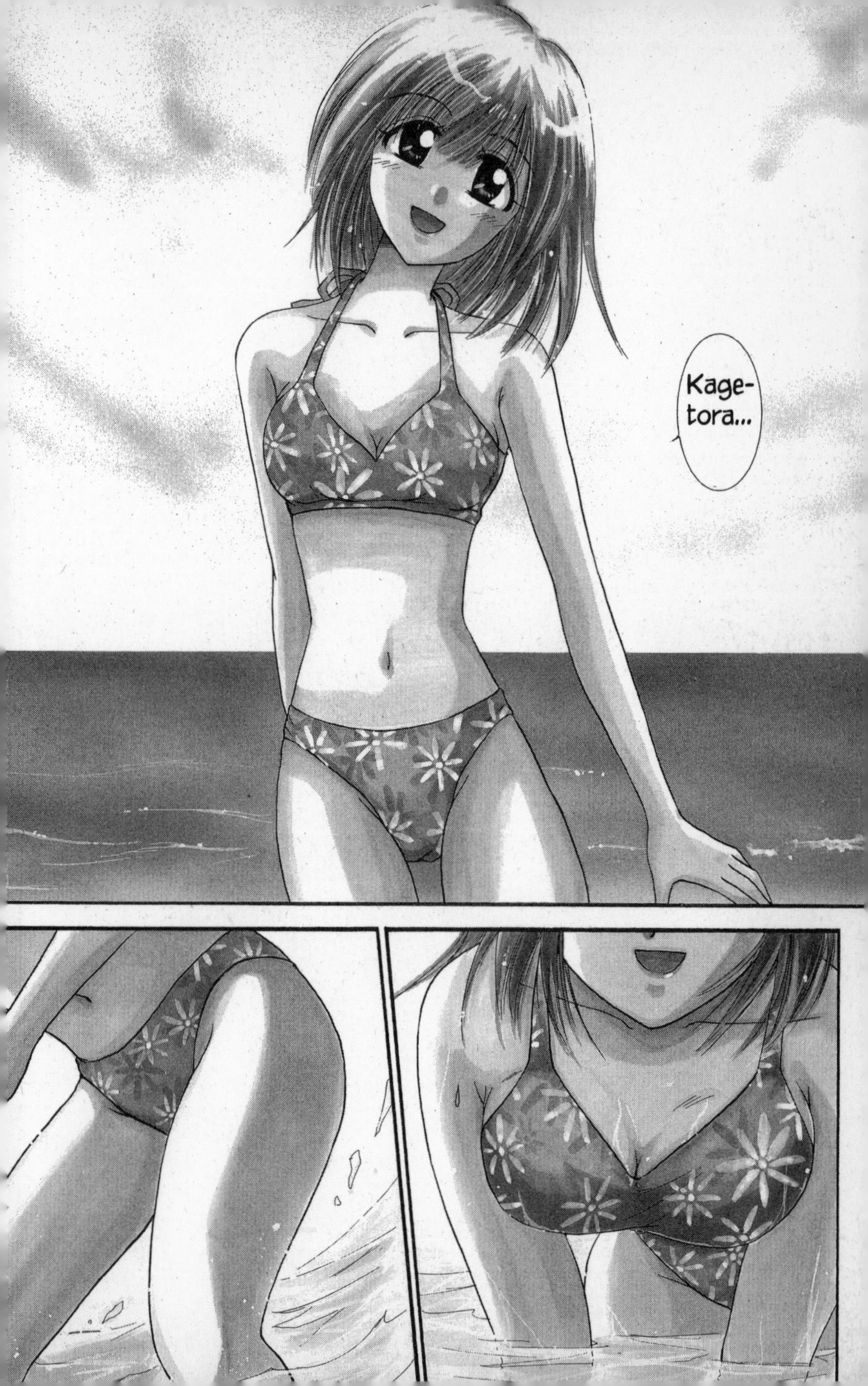
Kage-
tora...

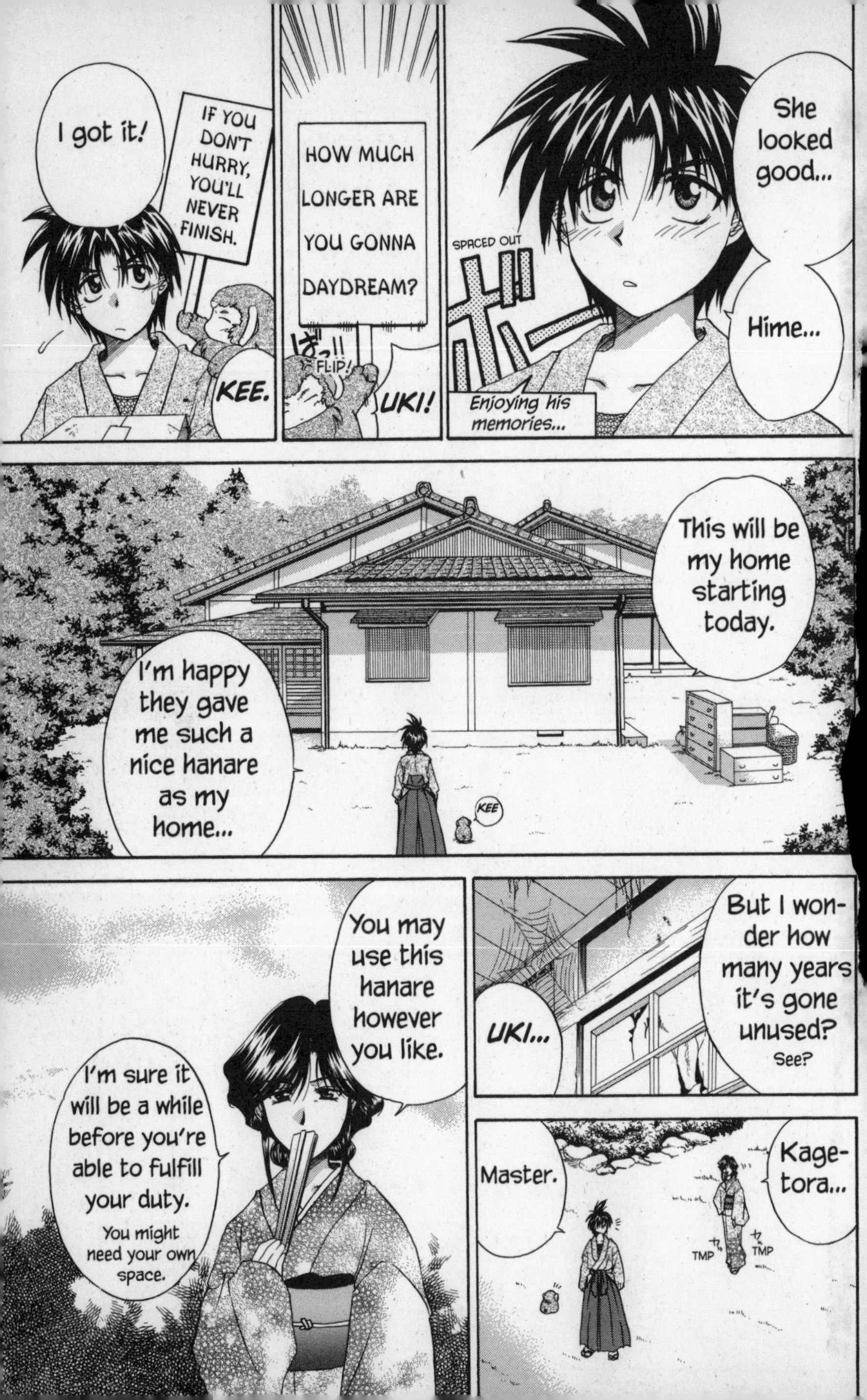
SPACED OUT
She looked good...
Hime...
Enjoying his memories...
HOW MUCH LONGER ARE YOU GONNA DAYDREAM?
FLIP!
UKI!
IF YOU DON'T HURRY, YOU'LL NEVER FINISH.
KEE.
I got it!
This will be my home starting today.
I'm happy they gave me such a nice hanare as my home...
KEE
But I wonder how many years it's gone unused?
See?
UKI...
Kagetora...
Master.
TMP
TMP
You may use this hanare however you like.
I'm sure it will be a while before you're able to fulfill your duty.
You might need your own space.

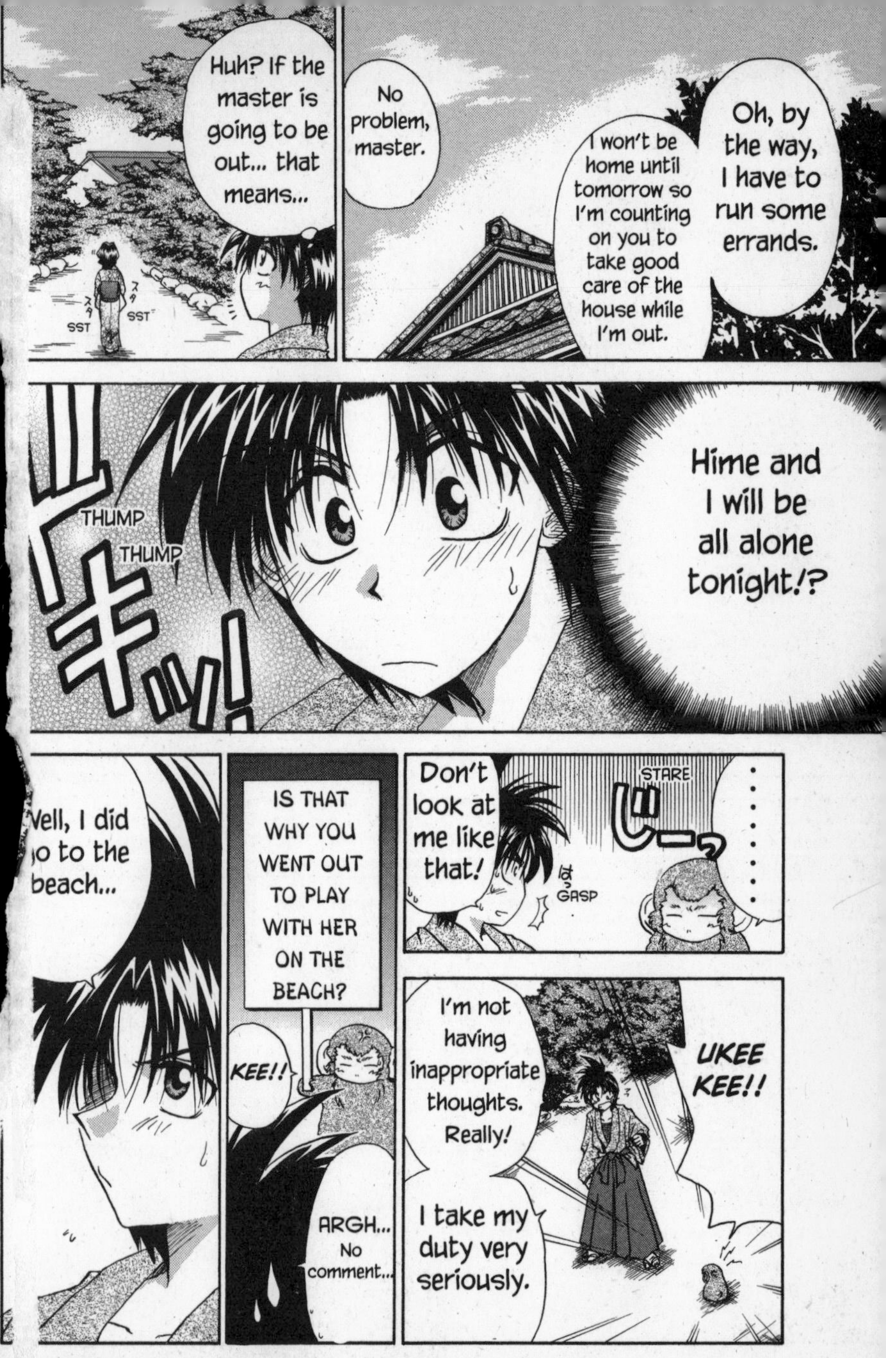
Oh, by the way, I have to run some errands.
I won't be home until tomorrow so I'm counting on you to take good care of the house while I'm out.
No problem, master.
Huh? If the master is going to be out... that means...
SST
SST
Hime and I will be all alone tonight!?
THUMP
THUMP
......
STARE
GASP
Don't look at me like that!
UKEE KEE!!
I'm not having inappropriate thoughts. Really!
I take my duty very seriously.
IS THAT WHY YOU WENT OUT TO PLAY WITH HER ON THE BEACH?
KEE!!
ARGH... No comment...
Vell, I did jo to the beach...

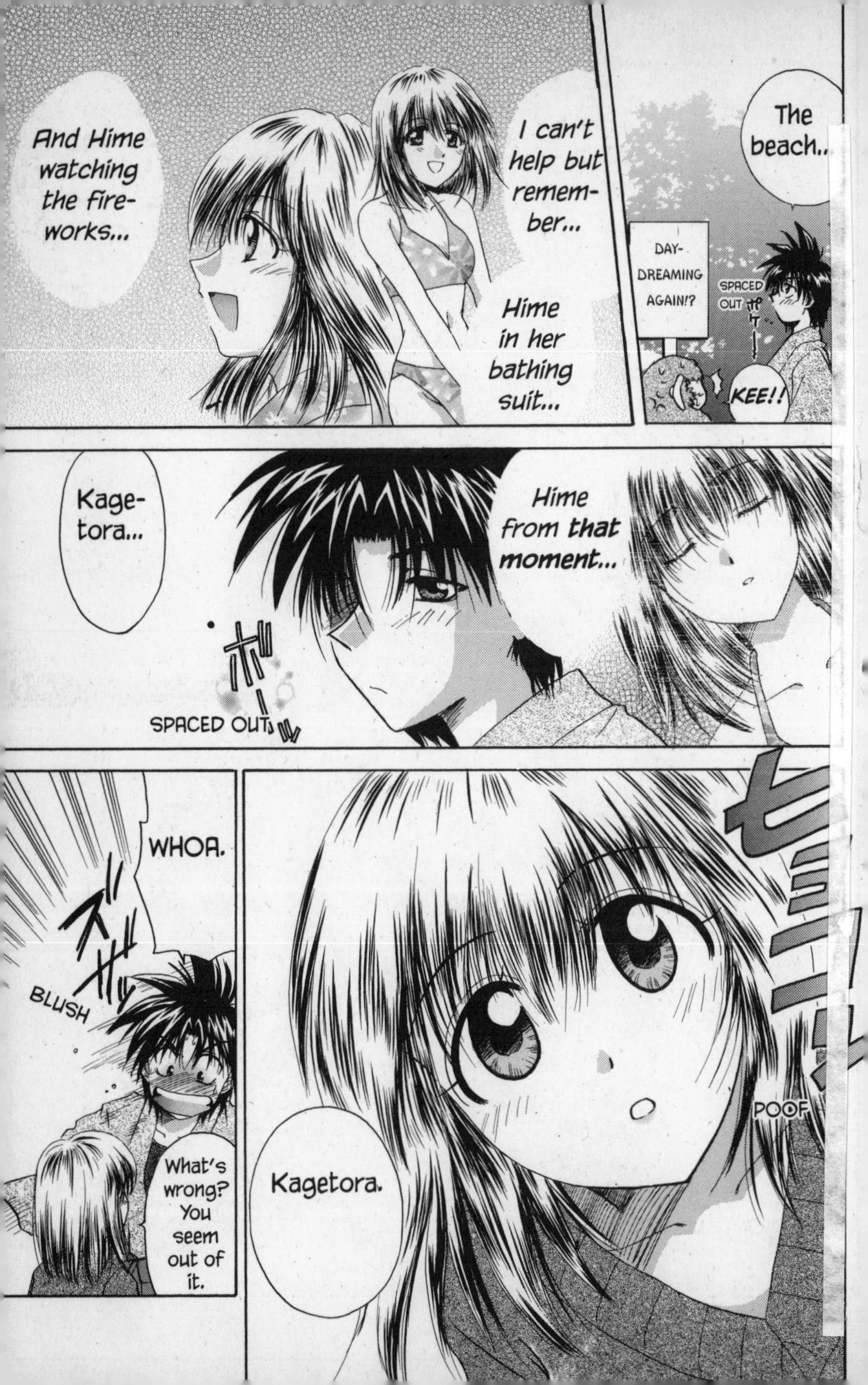
The beach..
DAY-DREAMING AGAIN!?
SPACED OUT
KEE!!
I can't help but remem-ber...
Hime in her bathing suit...
And Hime watching the fire-works...
Hime from **that moment**...
Kage-tora...
SPACED OUT
POOF
Kagetora.
WHOA.
BLUSH
What's wrong? You seem out of it.

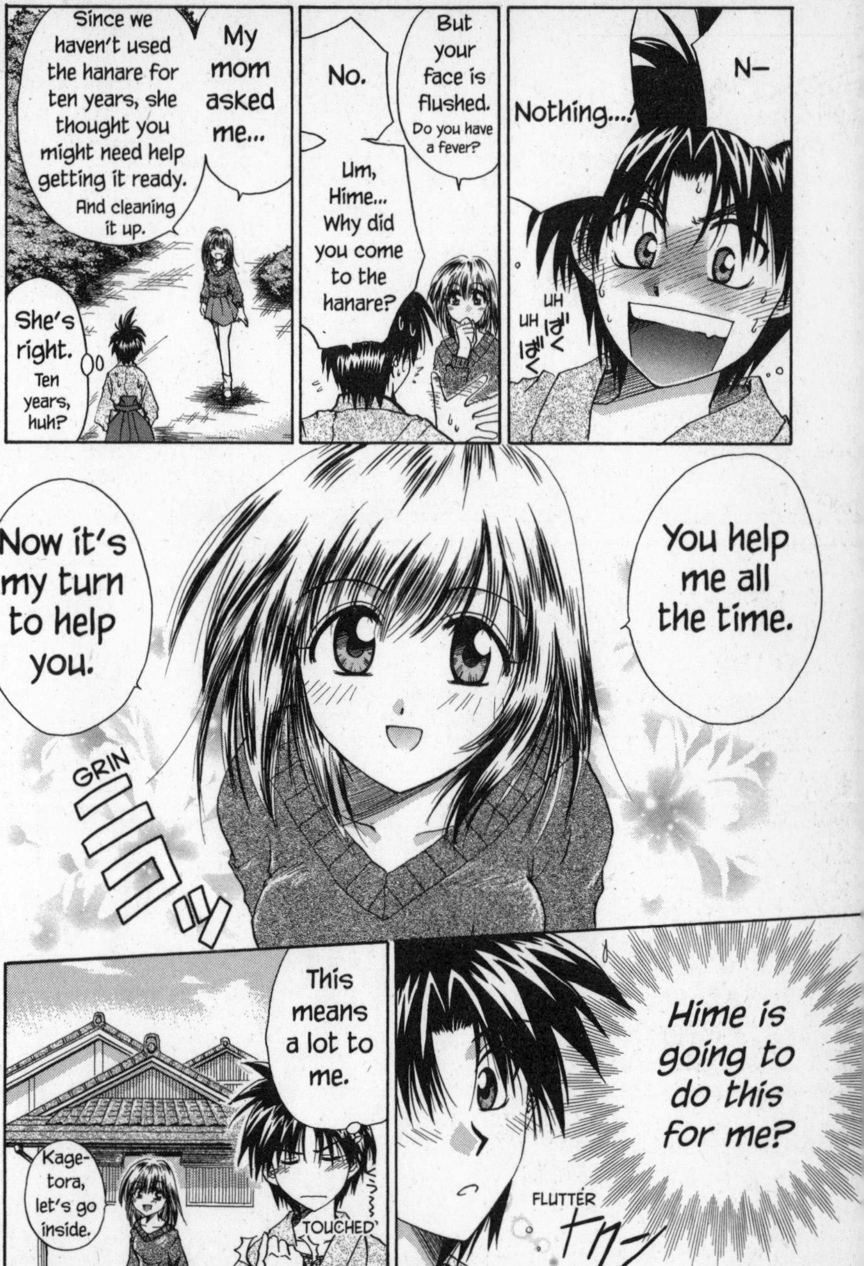
N–
Nothing...!
UH UH
But your face is flushed. Do you have a fever?
No.
Um, Hime... Why did you come to the hanare?
My mom asked me...
Since we haven't used the hanare for ten years, she thought you might need help getting it ready. And cleaning it up.
She's right. Ten years, huh?
You help me all the time.
Now it's my turn to help you.
GRIN
Hime is going to do this for me?
FLUTTER
This means a lot to me.
TOUCHED
Kagetora, let's go inside.

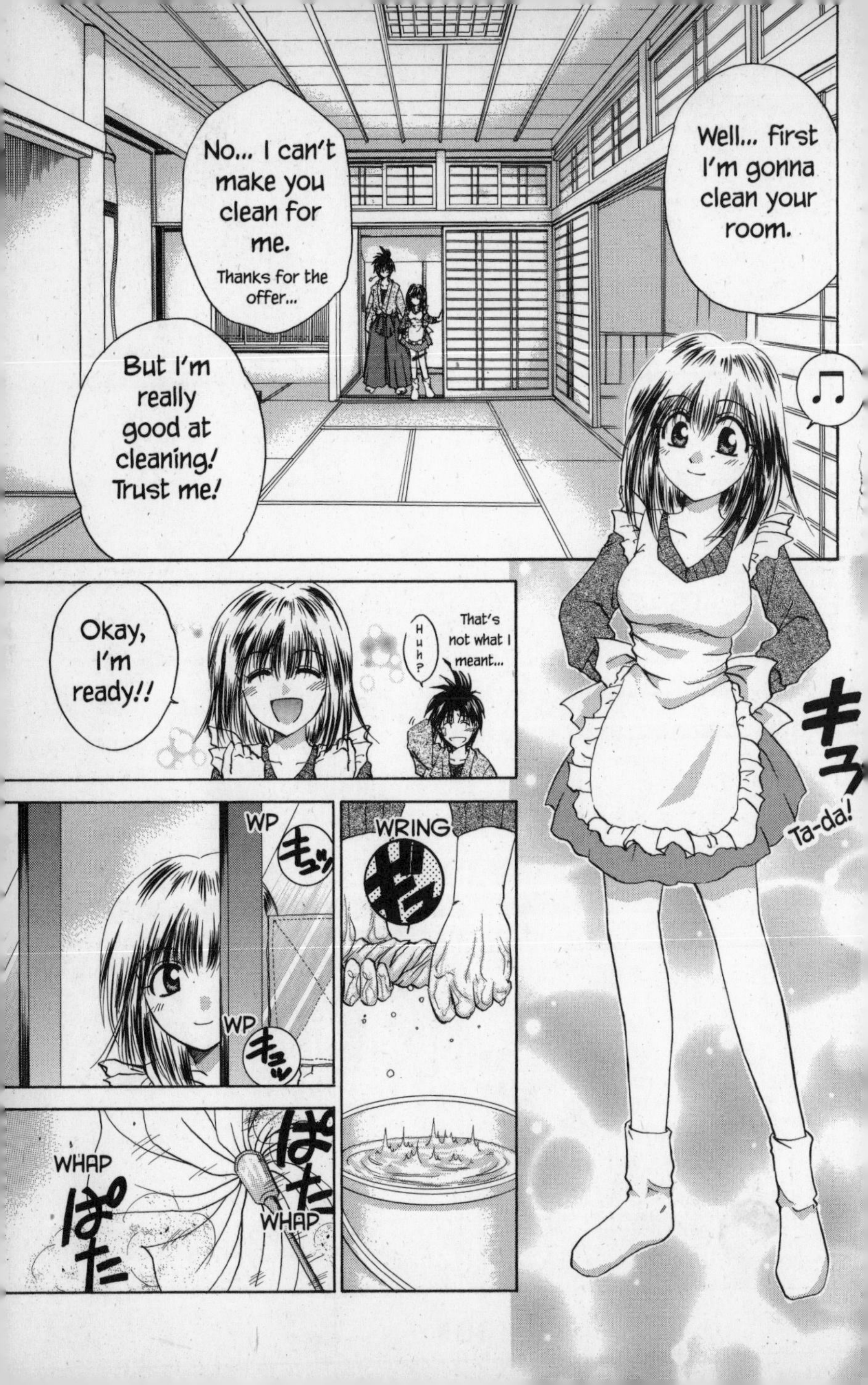
Well... first I'm gonna clean your room.
No... I can't make you clean for me.
Thanks for the offer...
But I'm really good at cleaning! Trust me!
♫
Ta-da!
That's not what I meant...
Huh?
Okay, I'm ready!!
WRING
WP
WP
WHAP
ぱた
WHAP
ぱた

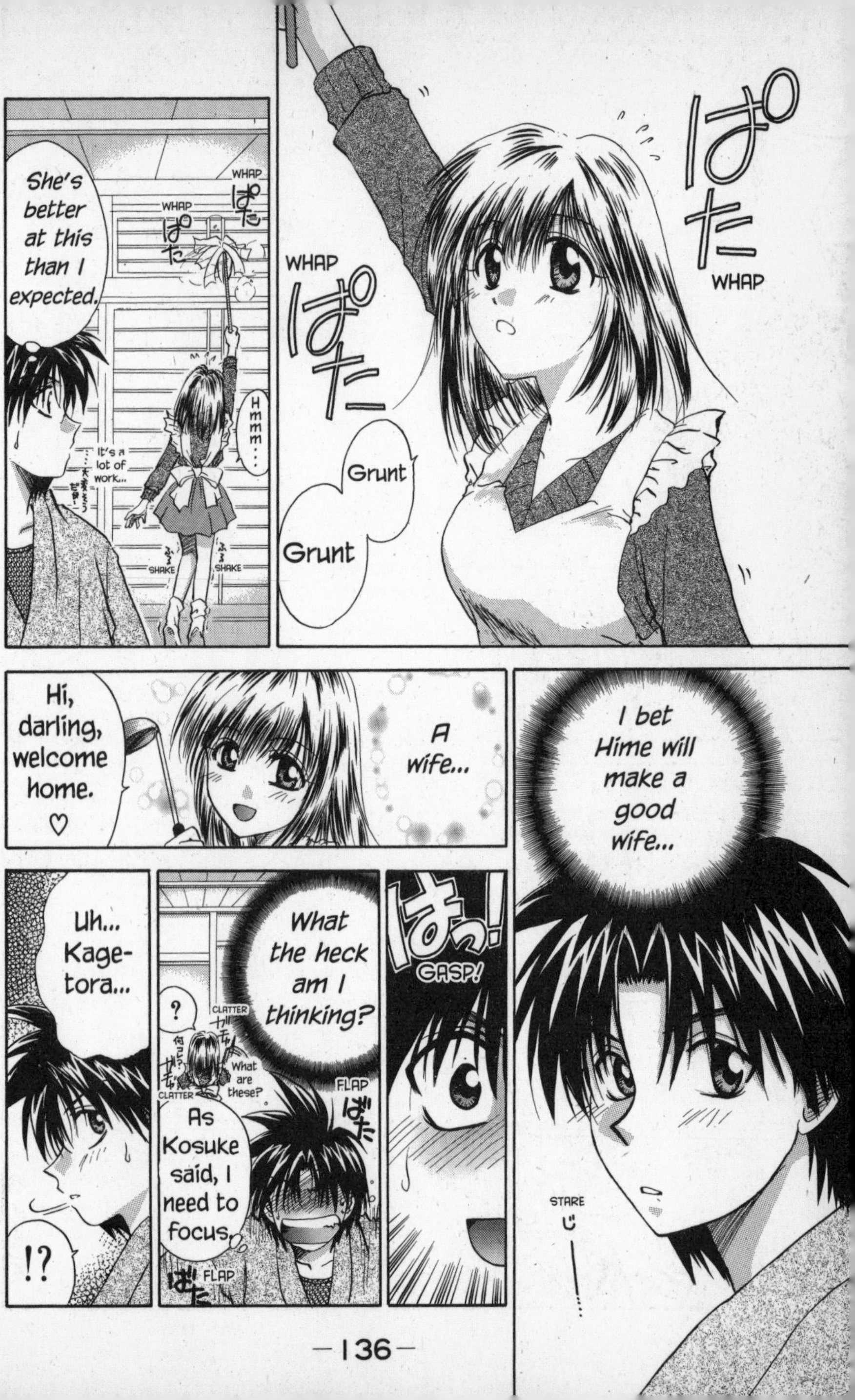
ぱた
WHAP
WHAP
ぱたー
Grunt
Grunt
WHAP
ぱた
WHAP
ぱた
She's better at this than I expected.
Hmmm...
It's a lot of work...
SHAKE
SHAKE
I bet Hime will make a good wife...
STARE
じー
A wife...
Hi, darling, welcome home. ♡
はっ!
GASP!
What the heck am I thinking?
FLAP
ばた
?
CLATTER
What are these?
CLATTER
As Kosuke said, I need to focus.
ばた
FLAP
Uh... Kagetora...
!?

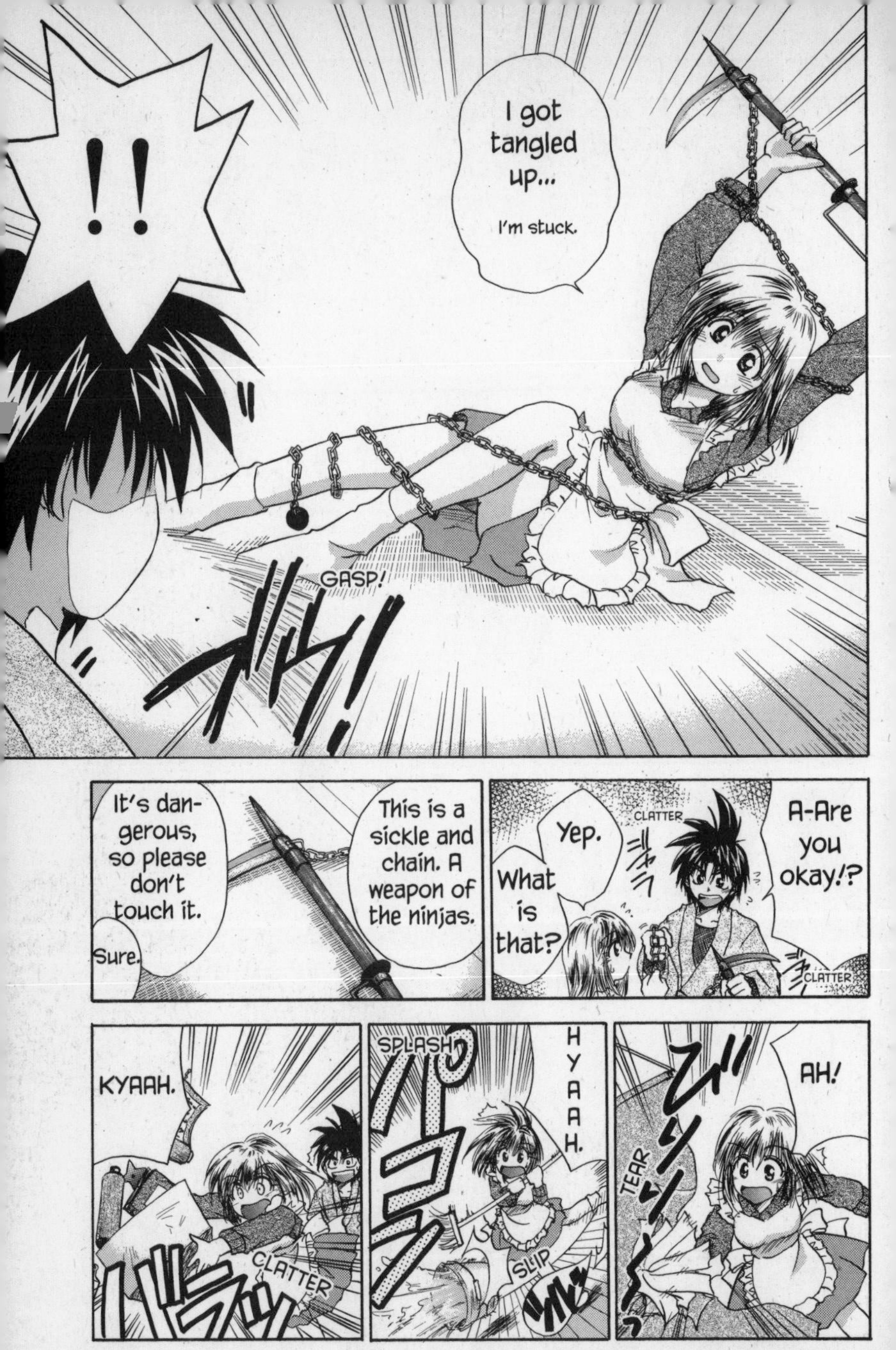
I got tangled up...
I'm stuck.
!!
GASP!
A-Are you okay!?
CLATTER
Yep.
What is that?
CLATTER
This is a sickle and chain. A weapon of the ninjas.
It's dangerous, so please don't touch it.
Sure.
AH!
TEAR
HYAAAH.
SPLASH
SLIP
KYAAH.
CLATTER

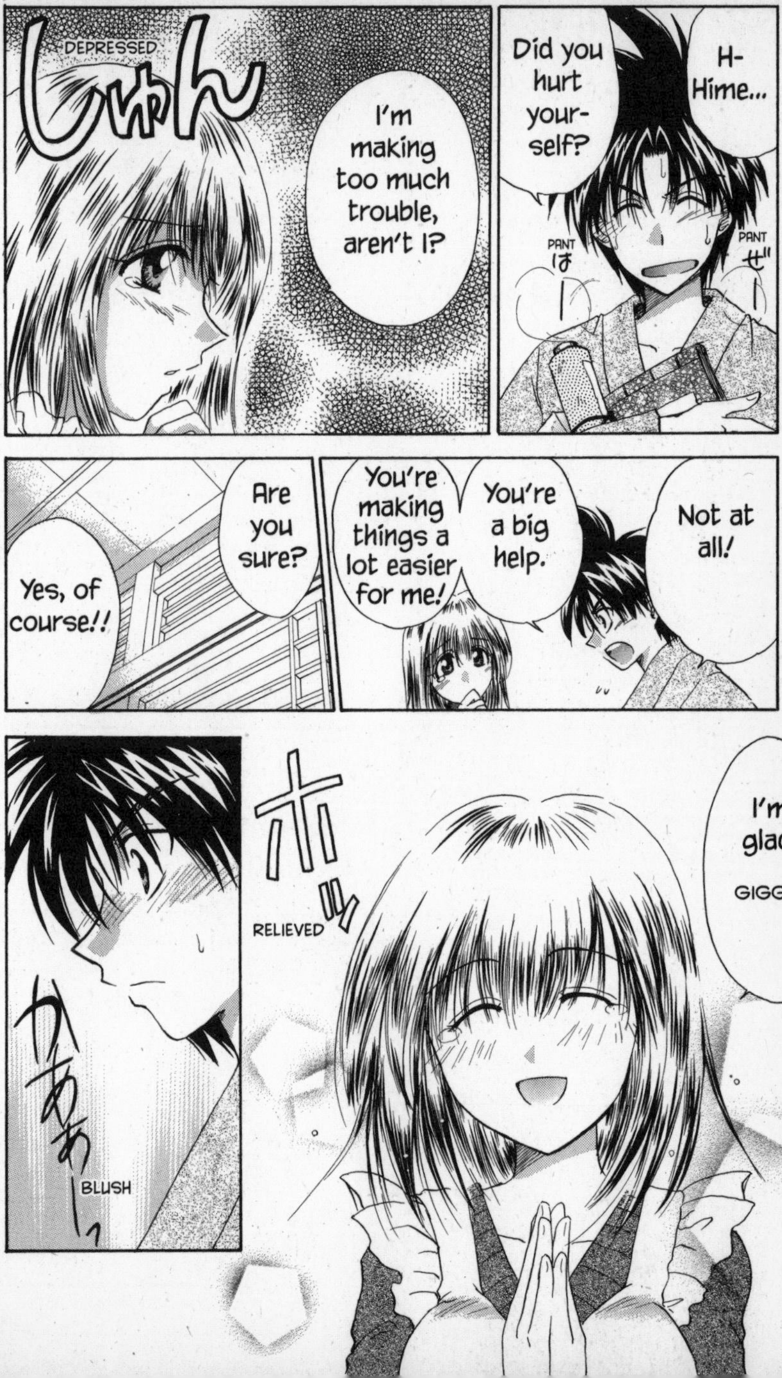
H-Hime...
Did you hurt your-self?
PANT
ぜー
PANT
はー
DEPRESSED
しゅん
I'm making too much trouble, aren't I?
Not at all!
You're a big help.
You're making things a lot easier for me!
Are you sure?
Yes, of course!!
I'm glad.
GIGGLE
ホッ
RELIEVED
かあああ
BLUSH

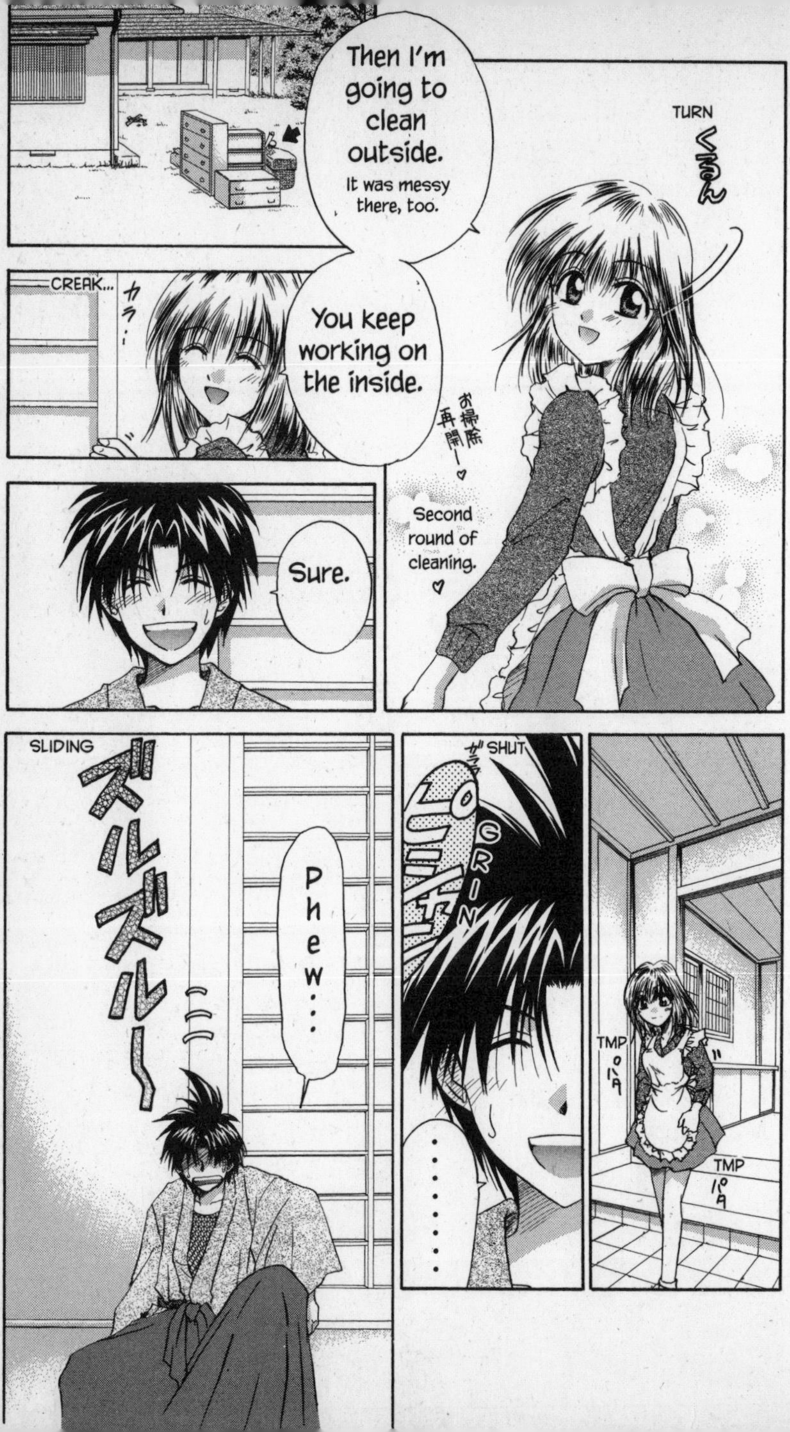

TURN
くるん
お掃除再開ー♡
Second round of cleaning. ♡
Then I'm going to clean outside. It was messy there, too.
CREAK...
カラ…
You keep working on the inside.
Sure.
TMP
パ
TMP
パ
SHUT
ガラ
ニコ
GRIN
......
SLIDING
ズルズルー
Phew...

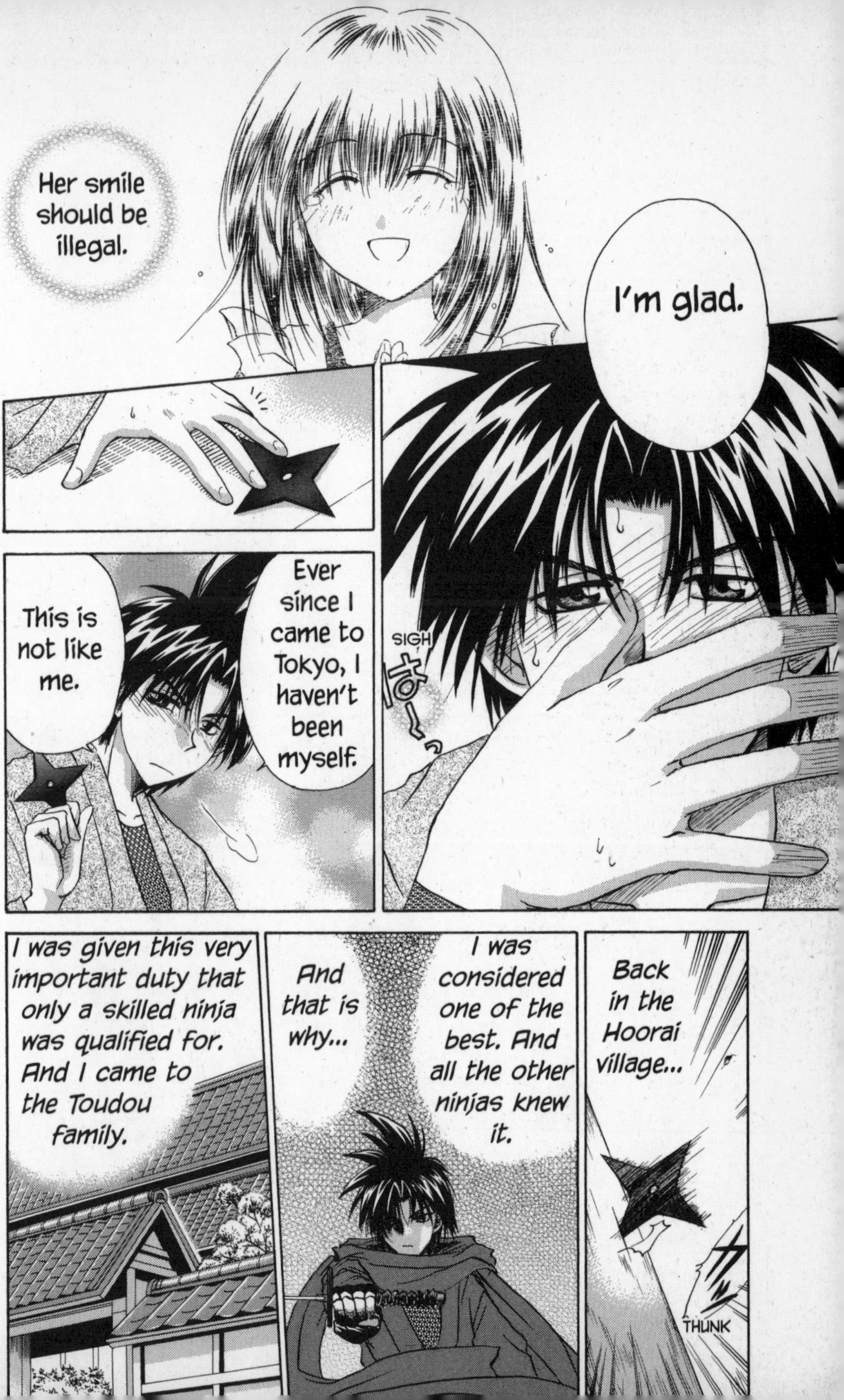
I'm glad.
Her smile should be illegal.
SIGH
Ever since I came to Tokyo, I haven't been myself.
This is not like me.
Back in the Hoorai village...
THUNK
I was considered one of the best. And all the other ninjas knew it.
And that is why...
I was given this very important duty that only a skilled ninja was qualified for. And I came to the Toudou family.

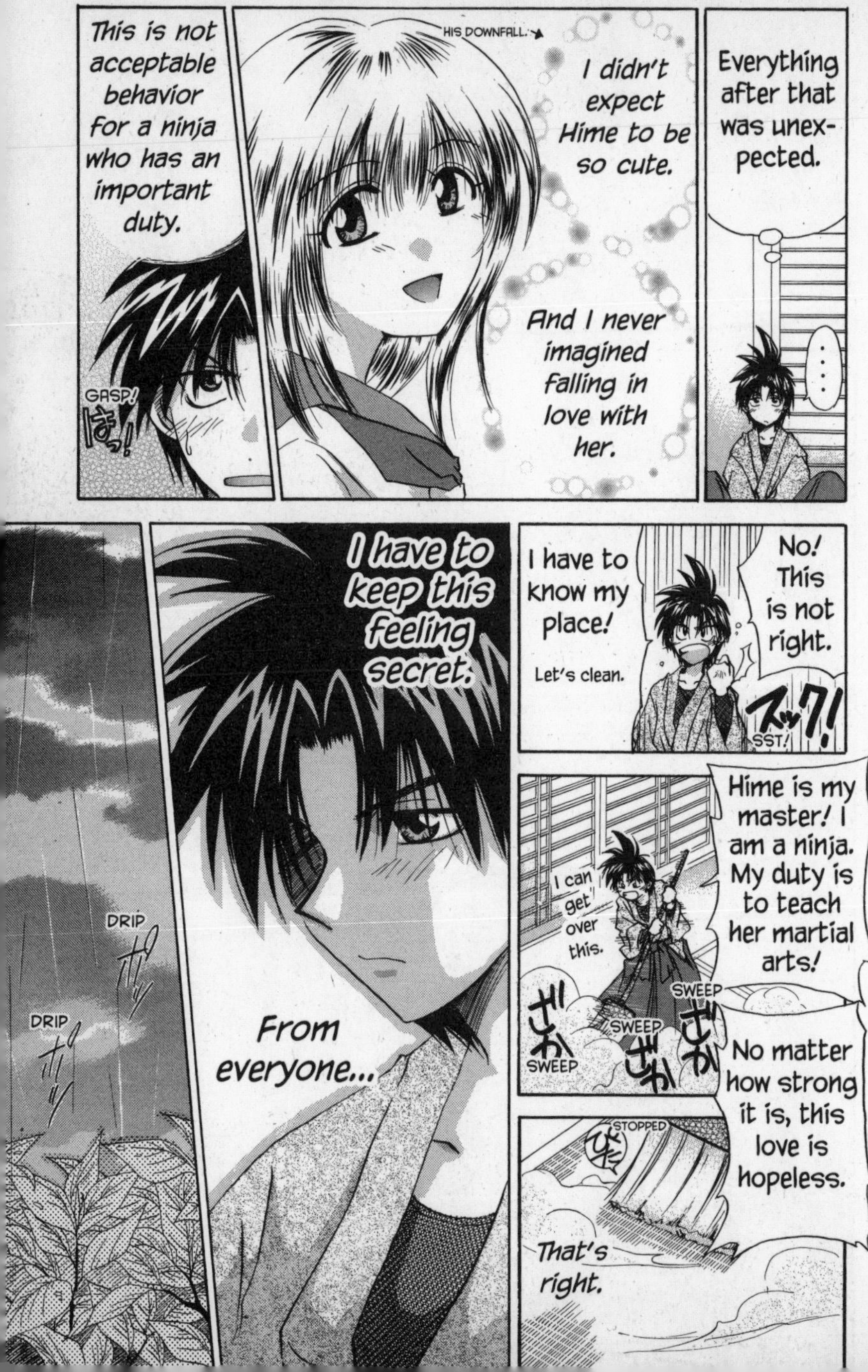
Everything after that was unexpected.
....
HIS DOWNFALL.
I didn't expect Hime to be so cute.
And I never imagined falling in love with her.
This is not acceptable behavior for a ninja who has an important duty.
GASP!
はっ!
No! This is not right.
I have to know my place!
Let's clean.
SST!
Hime is my master! I am a ninja. My duty is to teach her martial arts!
I can get over this.
SWEEP
SWEEP
SWEEP
No matter how strong it is, this love is hopeless.
STOPPED
That's right.
I have to keep this feeling secret.
From everyone...
DRIP
DRIP

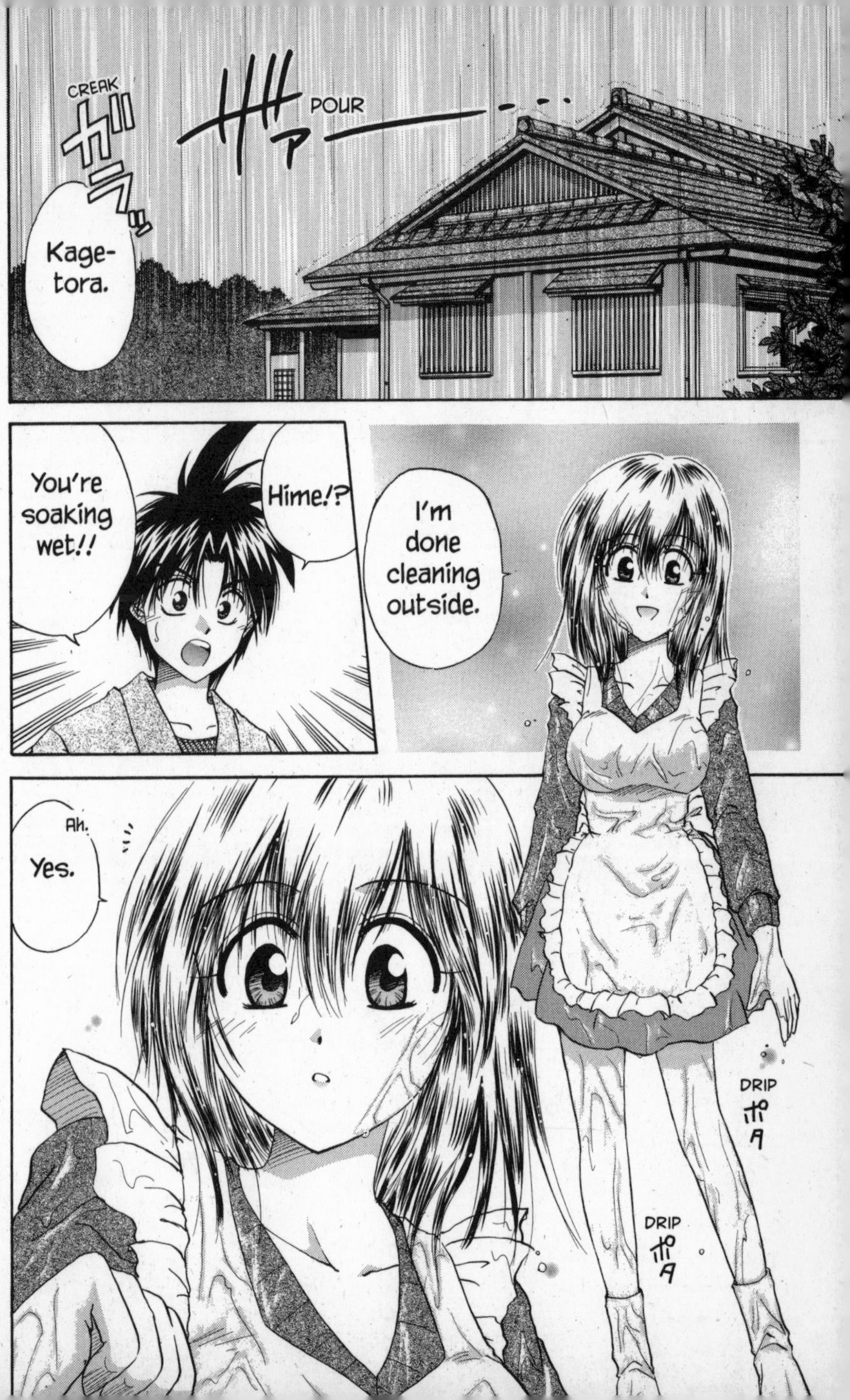
POUR
CREAK
Kage-tora.
I'm done cleaning outside.
Hime!?
You're soaking wet!!
DRIP
DRIP
Ah.
Yes.

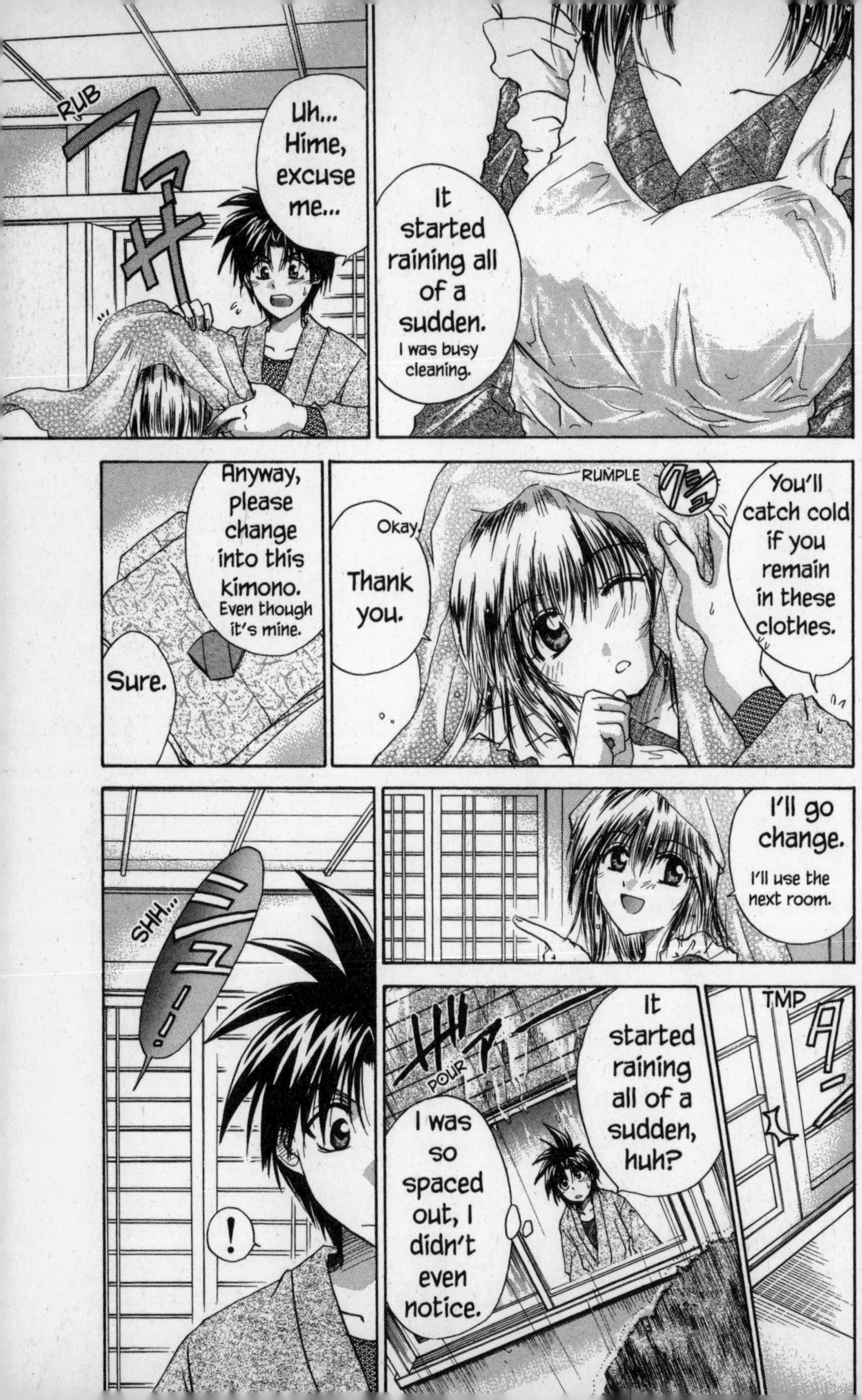
It started raining all of a sudden.
I was busy cleaning.
RUB
Uh... Hime, excuse me...
RUMPLE
You'll catch cold if you remain in these clothes.
Okay.
Thank you.
Anyway, please change into this kimono.
Even though it's mine.
Sure.
I'll go change.
I'll use the next room.
TMP
It started raining all of a sudden, huh?
POUR
I was so spaced out, I didn't even notice.
SHH...
!

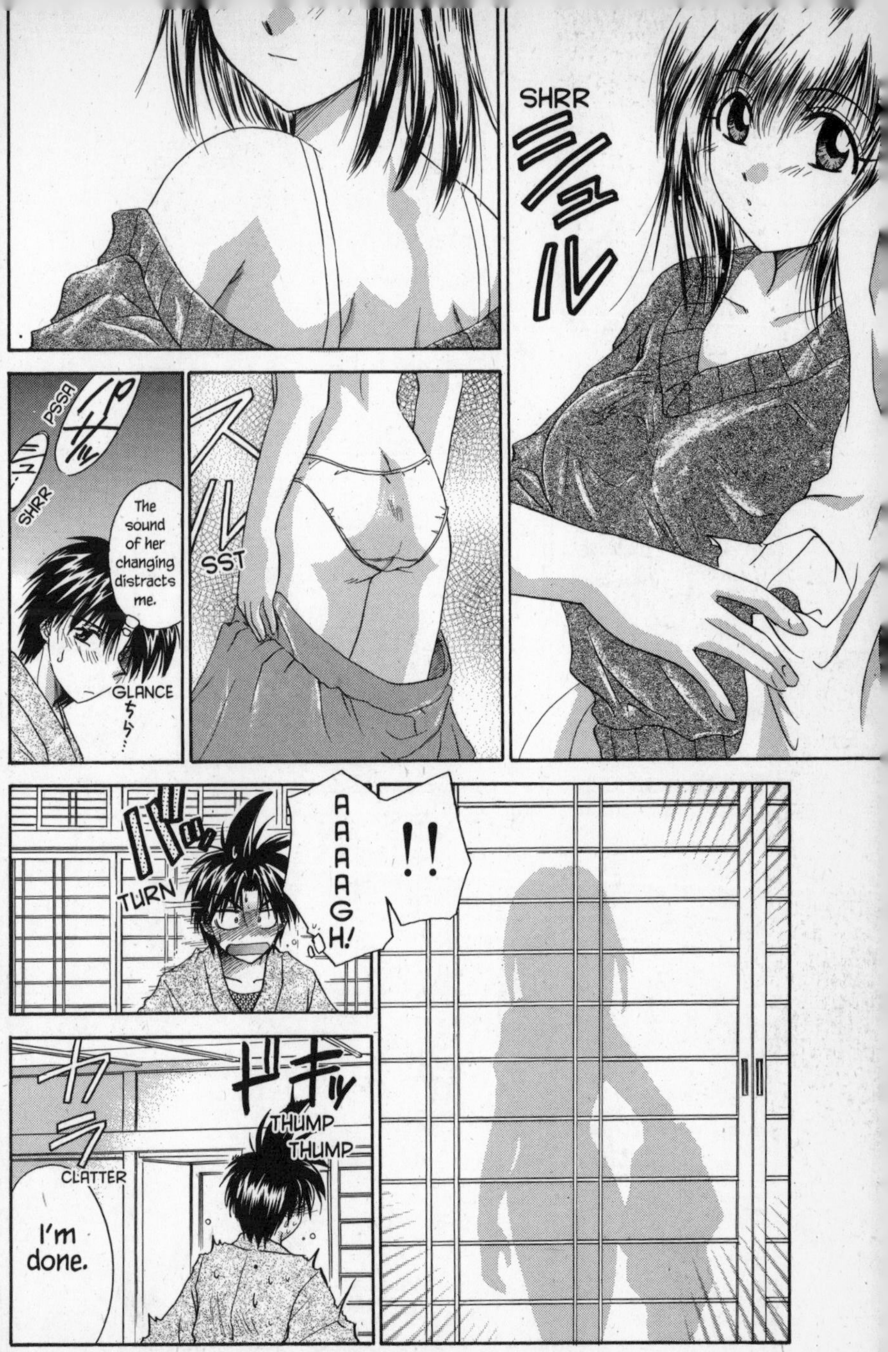

SHRR
シュル
スル
SST
PSSA
SHRR
The sound of her changing distracts me.
GLANCE
ちら…
!!
AAAAAGH!
バッ
TURN
ドキッ
THUMP THUMP
カラ
CLATTER
I'm done.

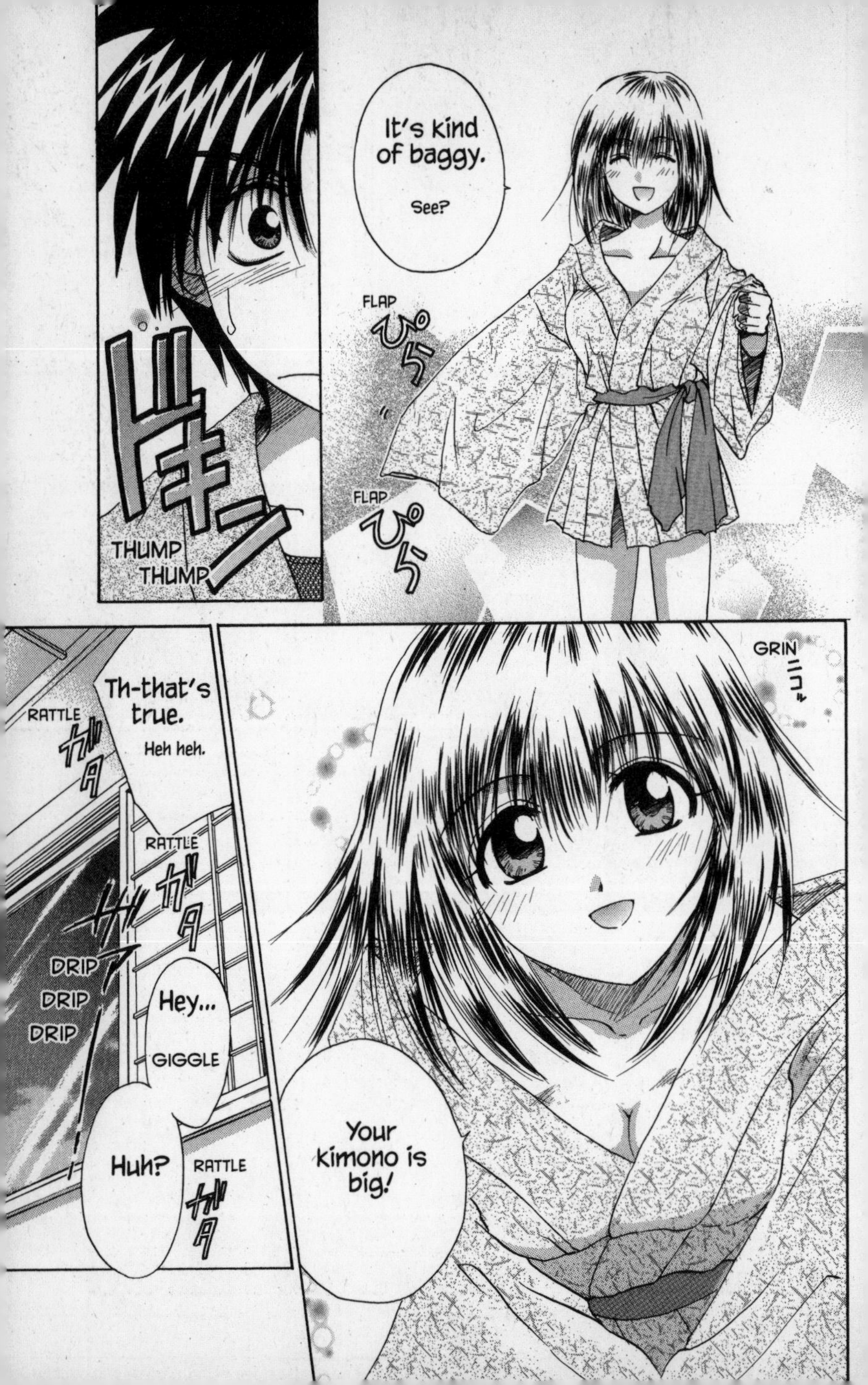
It's kind of baggy.
See?
FLAP
ぴら
FLAP
ぴら
ドキーン
THUMP THUMP
GRIN
ニコッ
Your kimono is big!
Th-that's true.
Heh heh.
RATTLE
ガタ
RATTLE
ガタ
ザァ
DRIP DRIP DRIP
Hey...
GIGGLE
Huh?
RATTLE
ガタ

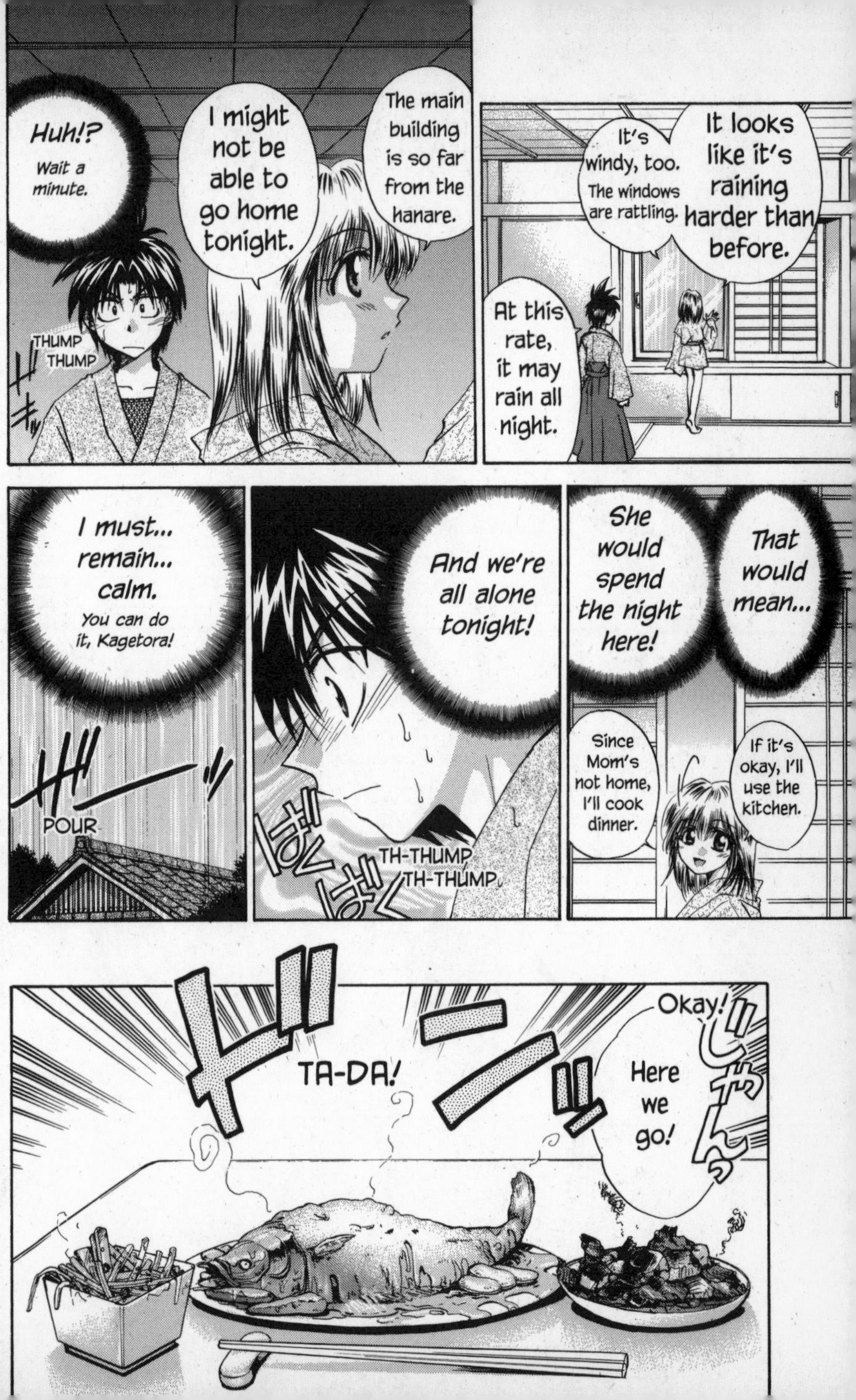
It looks like it's raining harder than before.
It's windy, too. The windows are rattling.
At this rate, it may rain all night.
The main building is so far from the hanare.
I might not be able to go home tonight.
Huh!? Wait a minute.
THUMP THUMP
That would mean...
She would spend the night here!
If it's okay, I'll use the kitchen.
Since Mom's not home, I'll cook dinner.
And we're all alone tonight!
TH-THUMP TH-THUMP
I must... remain... calm. You can do it, Kagetora!
POUR
Okay! Here we go!
TA-DA!

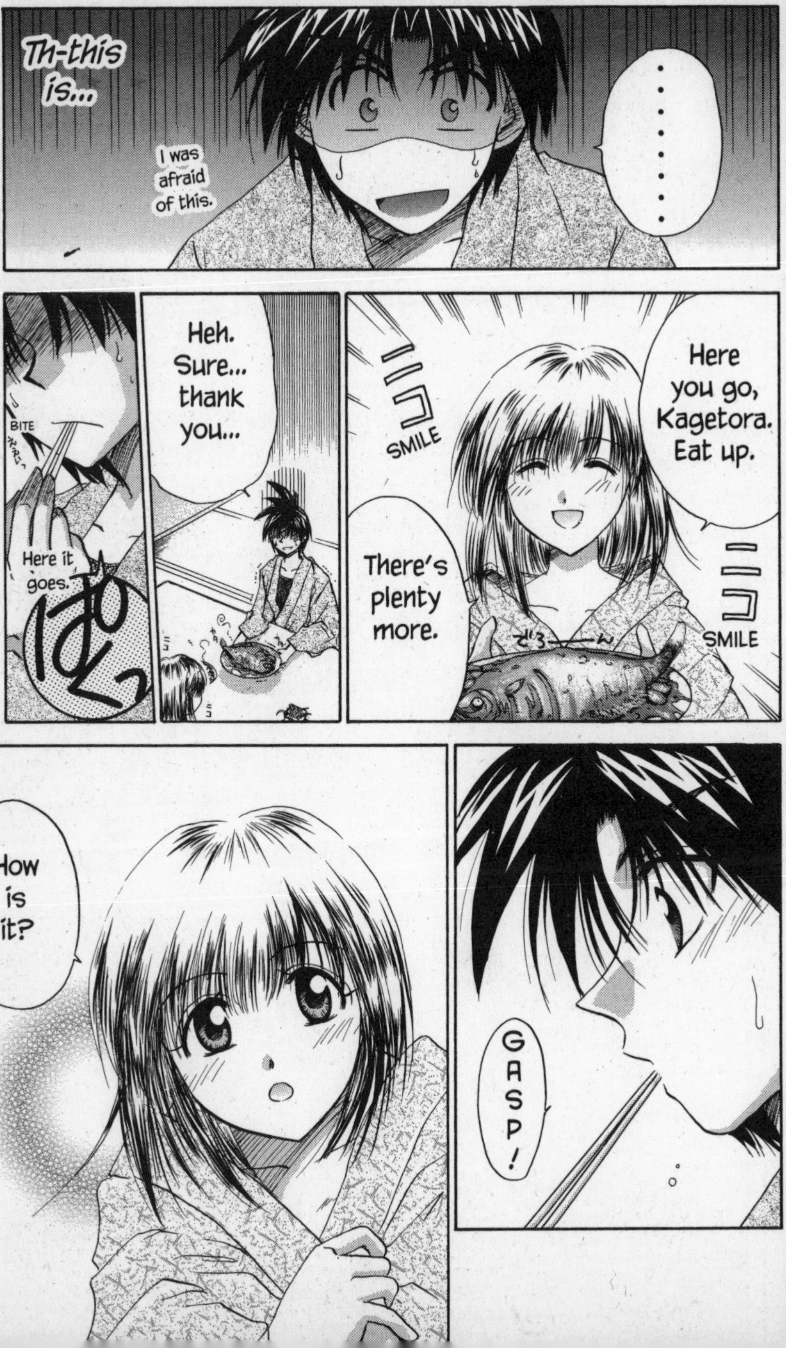
....
Th-this is...
I was afraid of this.
ニコ
SMILE
Here you go, Kagetora. Eat up.
ニコ
SMILE
There's plenty more.
Heh. Sure... thank you...
BITE
Here it goes.
GASP!
How is it?

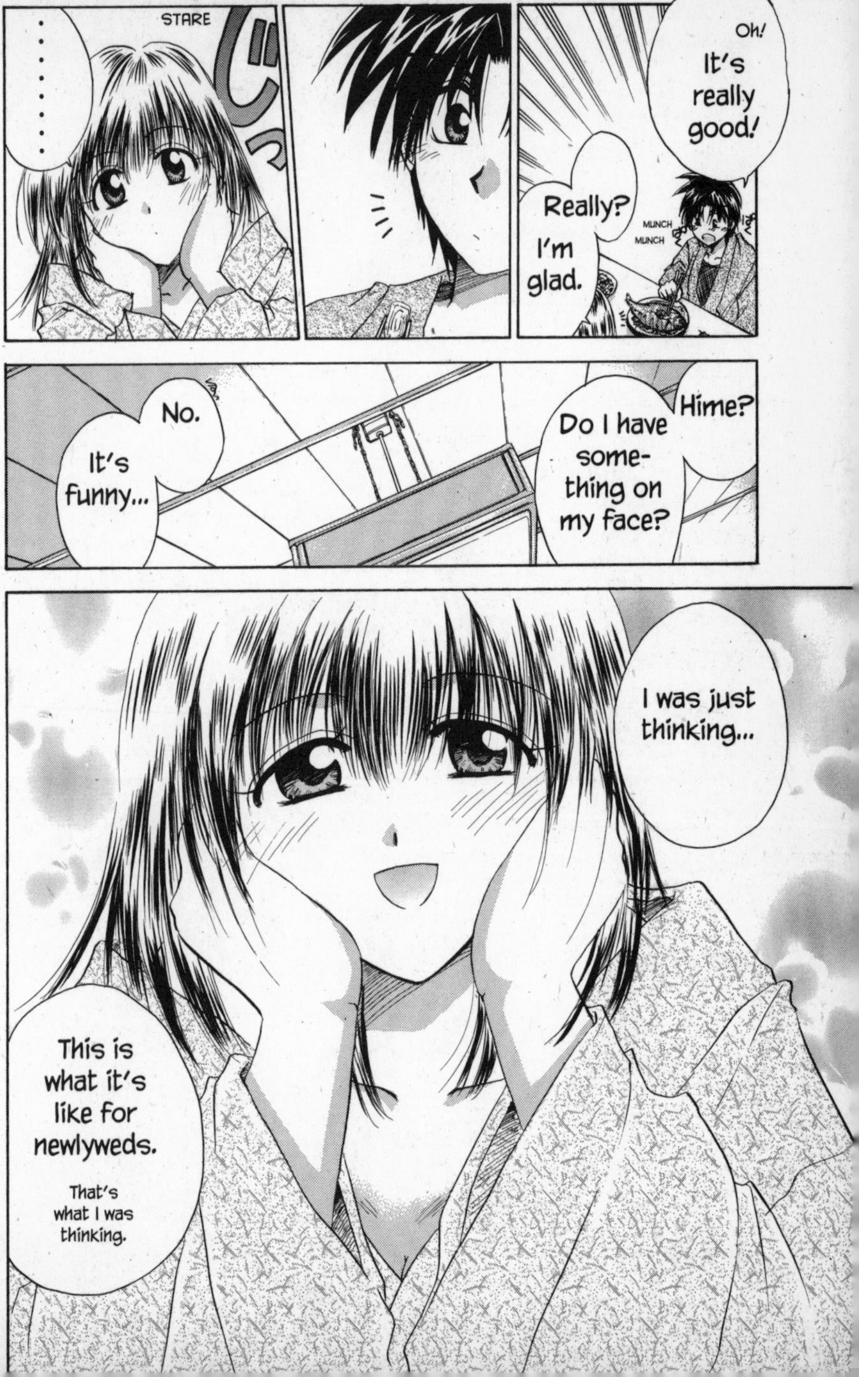
Oh! It's really good!
Really? I'm glad.
MUNCH MUNCH
STARE
....
Hime?
Do I have some-thing on my face?
No.
It's funny...
I was just thinking...
This is what it's like for newlyweds.
That's what I was thinking.

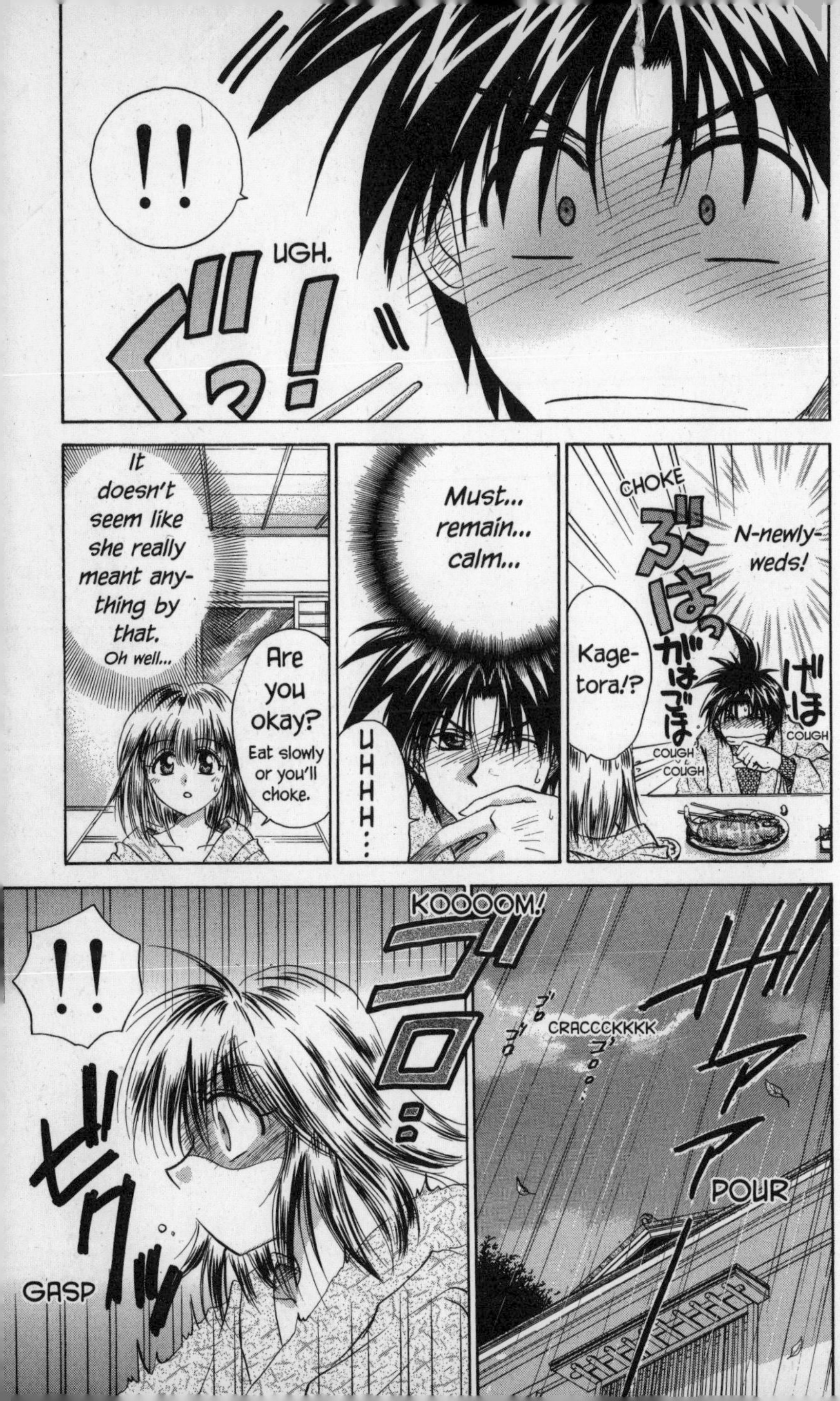

!!
UGH.
ぐっ!
CHOKE
ぶはっ
N-newlyweds!
Kage-tora!?
がはごほ
ぜほ
COUGH
COUGH
COUGH
Must... remain... calm...
UHHHH...
It doesn't seem like she really meant anything by that.
Oh well...
Are you okay?
Eat slowly or you'll choke.
ザアア
POUR
KOOOOM!
ゴロ…
CRACCCKKKK
!!
ビクッ
GASP

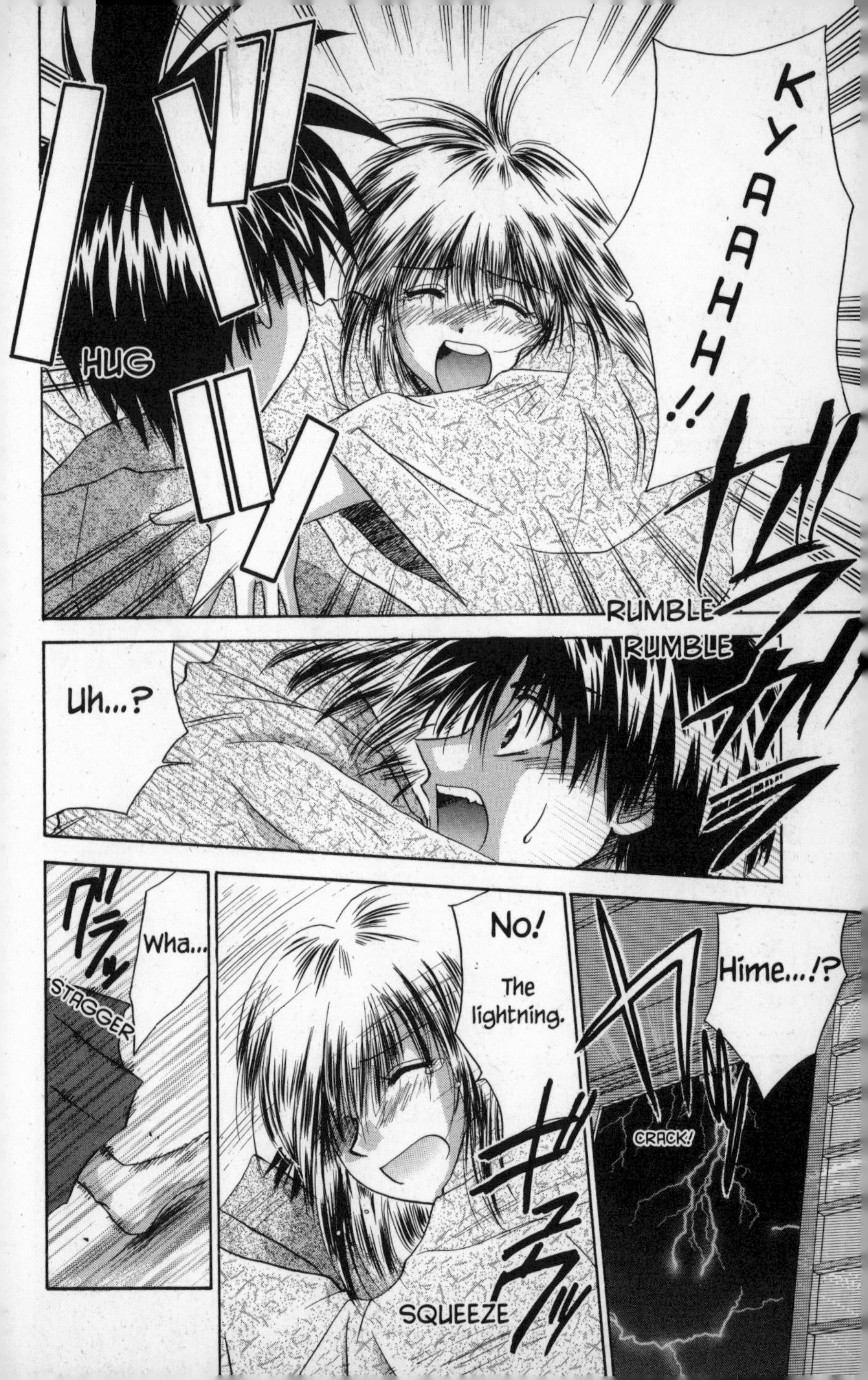
KYAAHH!!
HUG
RUMBLE
RUMBLE
Uh...?
Hime...!?
CRACK!
No!
The lightning.
SQUEEZE
Wha...
STAGGER

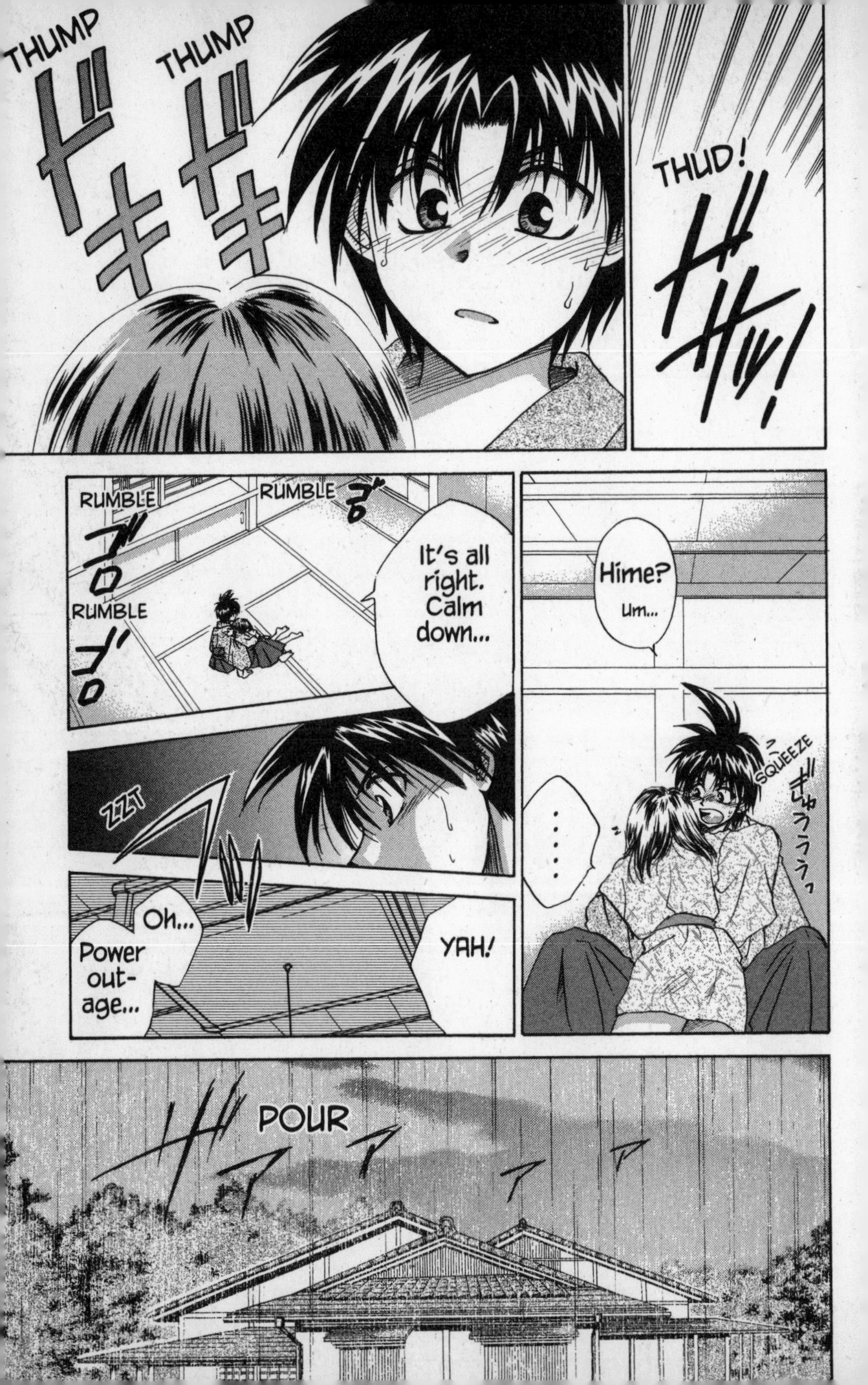
THUD!
THUMP
THUMP
Hime?
um...
. . . . .
SQUEEZE
RUMBLE
RUMBLE
RUMBLE
It's all right. Calm down...
ZZT
YAH!
Oh...
Power out-age...
POUR

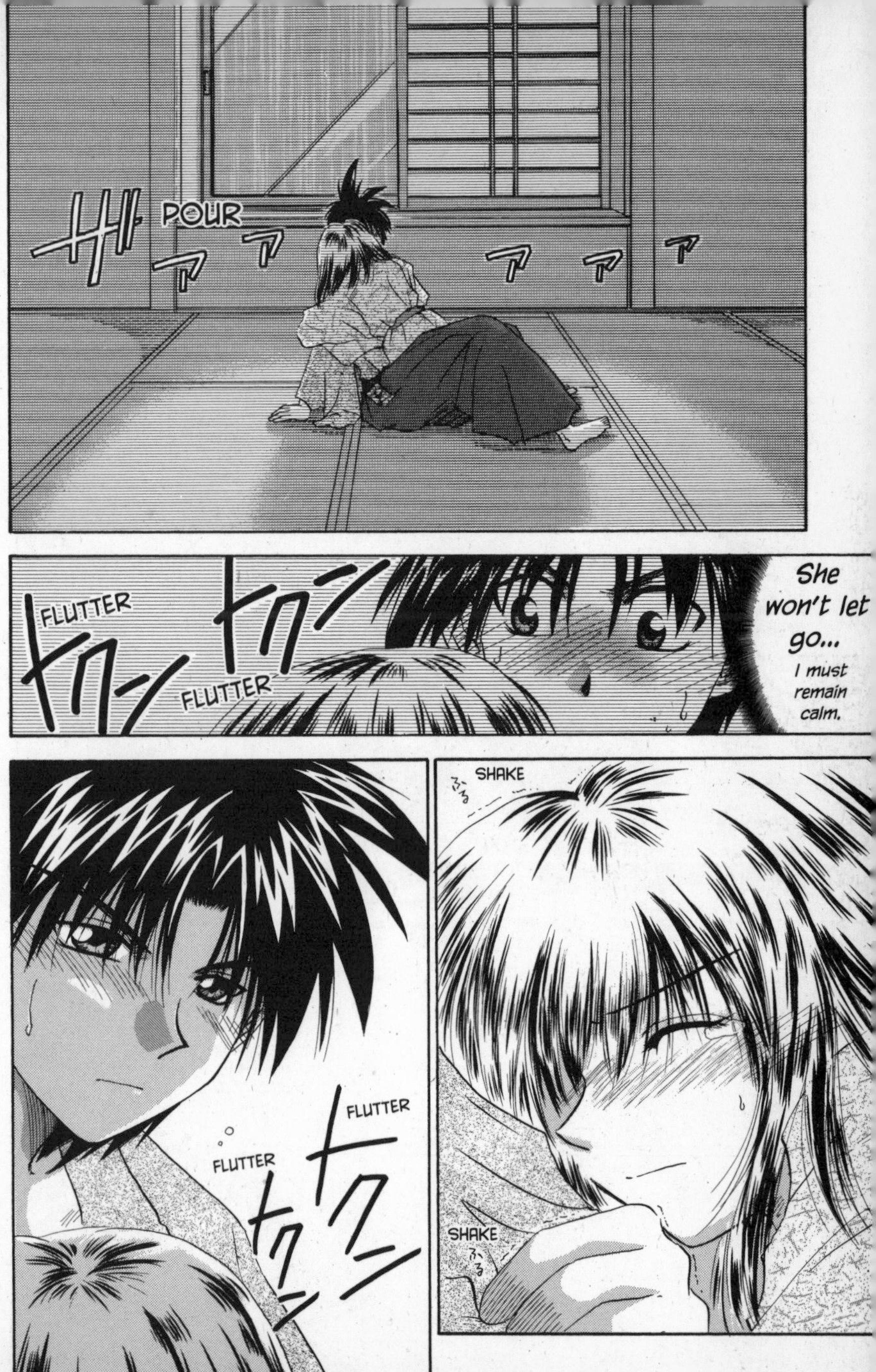
POUR
FLUTTER
FLUTTER
She won't let go...
I must remain calm.
SHAKE
ふる
SHAKE
ふる
FLUTTER
FLUTTER

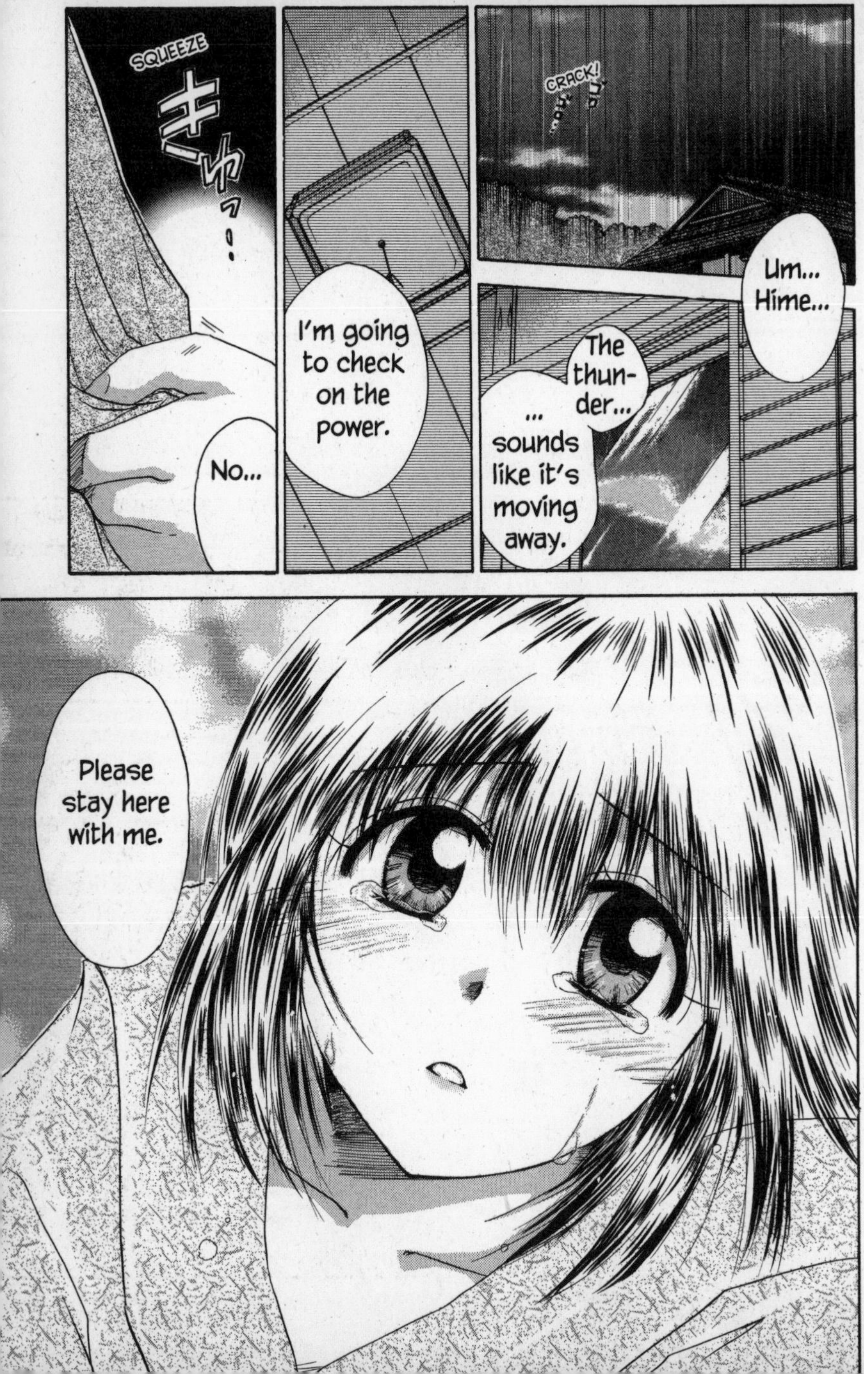
CRACK!
Um... Hime...
The thunder...
... sounds like it's moving away.
I'm going to check on the power.
SQUEEZE
No...
Please stay here with me.

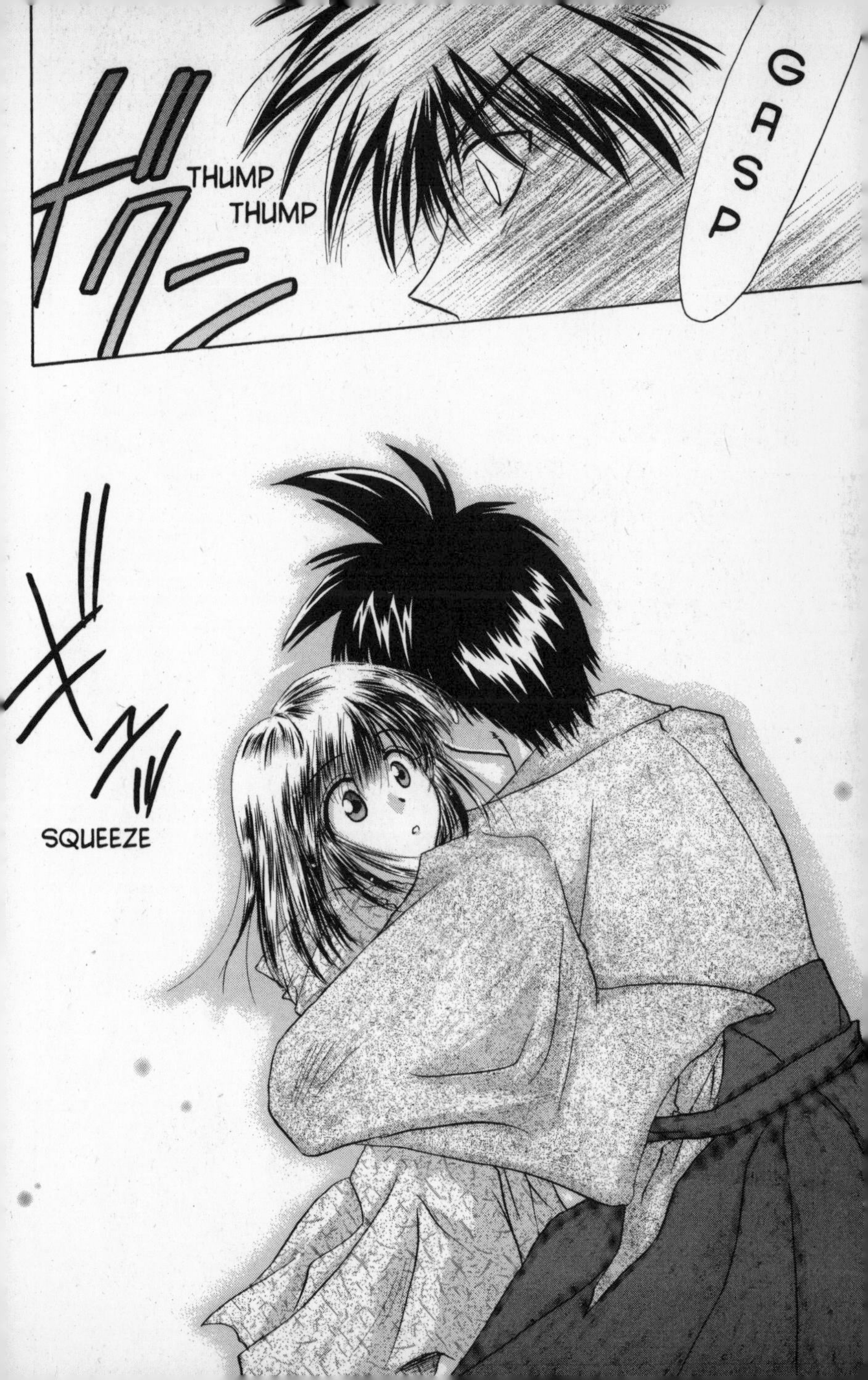
GASP
THUMP THUMP
SQUEEZE

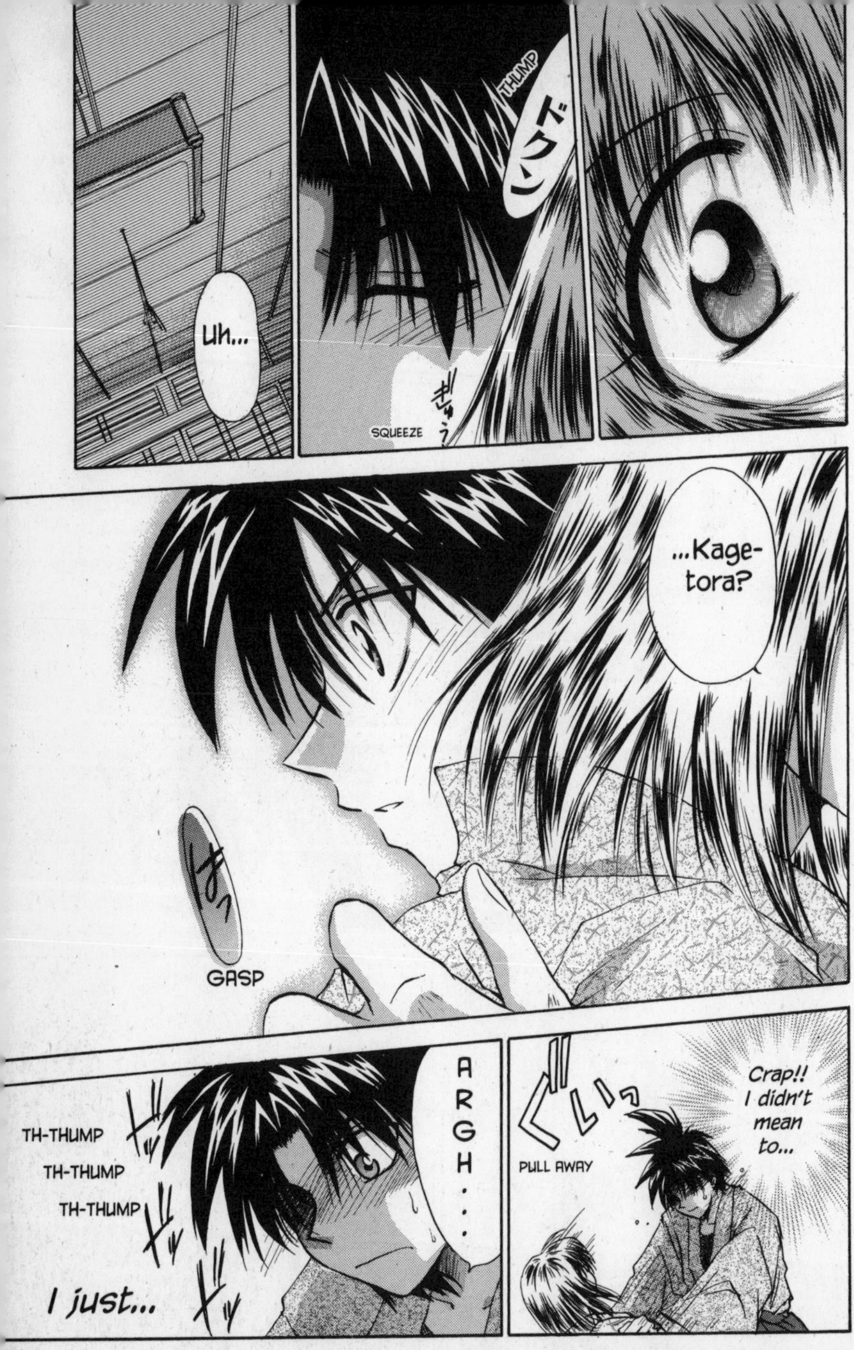
THUMP
ドクン
SQUEEZE
Uh...
...Kage-tora?
GASP
Crap!! I didn't mean to...
PULL AWAY
ARGH...
TH-THUMP
TH-THUMP
TH-THUMP
I just...

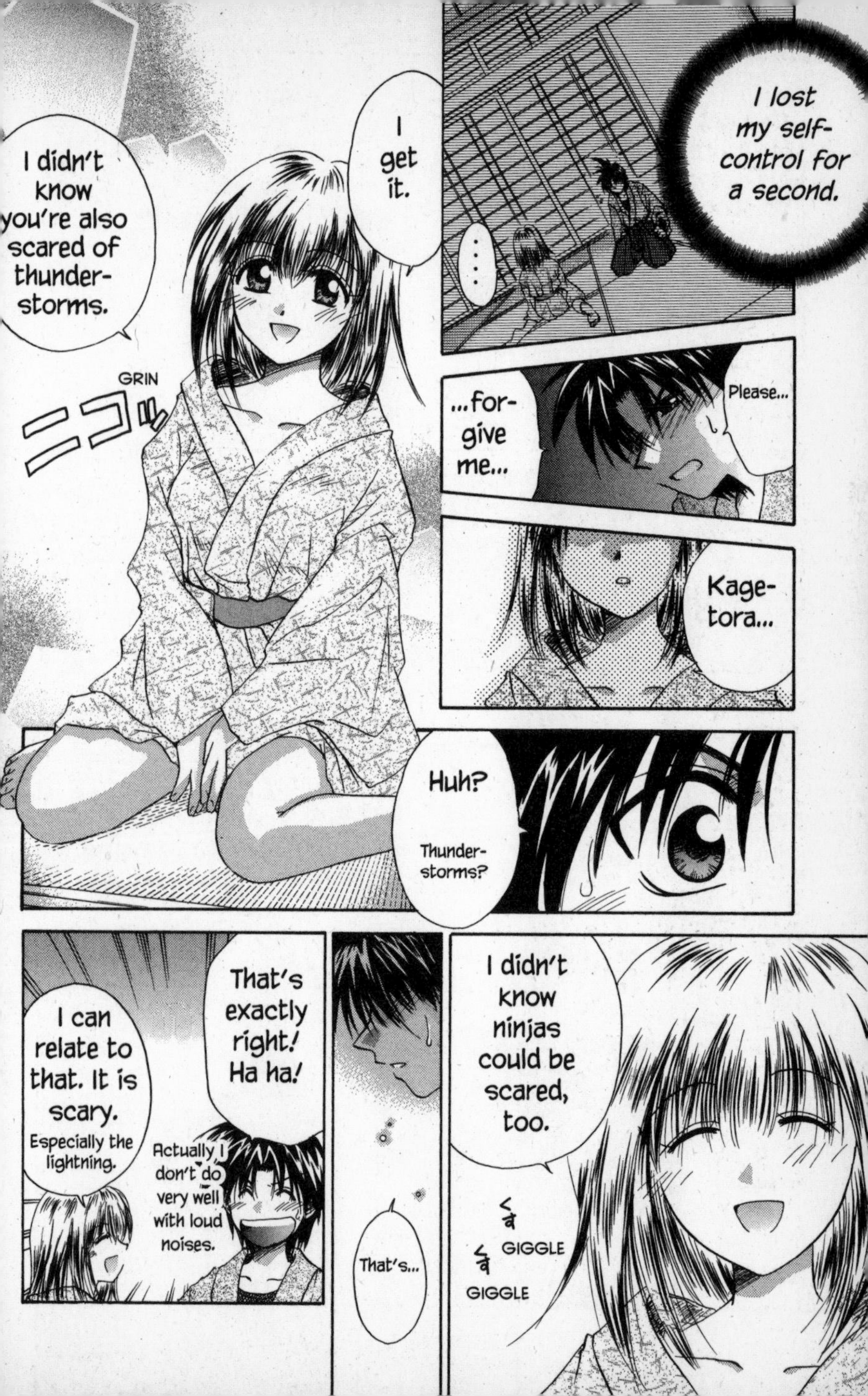
I lost my self-control for a second.
...
Please...
...forgive me...
Kagetora...
Huh?
Thunderstorms?
I get it.
I didn't know you're also scared of thunderstorms.
ニコッ
GRIN
I didn't know ninjas could be scared, too.
くす GIGGLE
くす GIGGLE
That's...
That's exactly right! Ha ha!
I can relate to that. It is scary.
Especially the lightning.
Actually I don't do very well with loud noises.

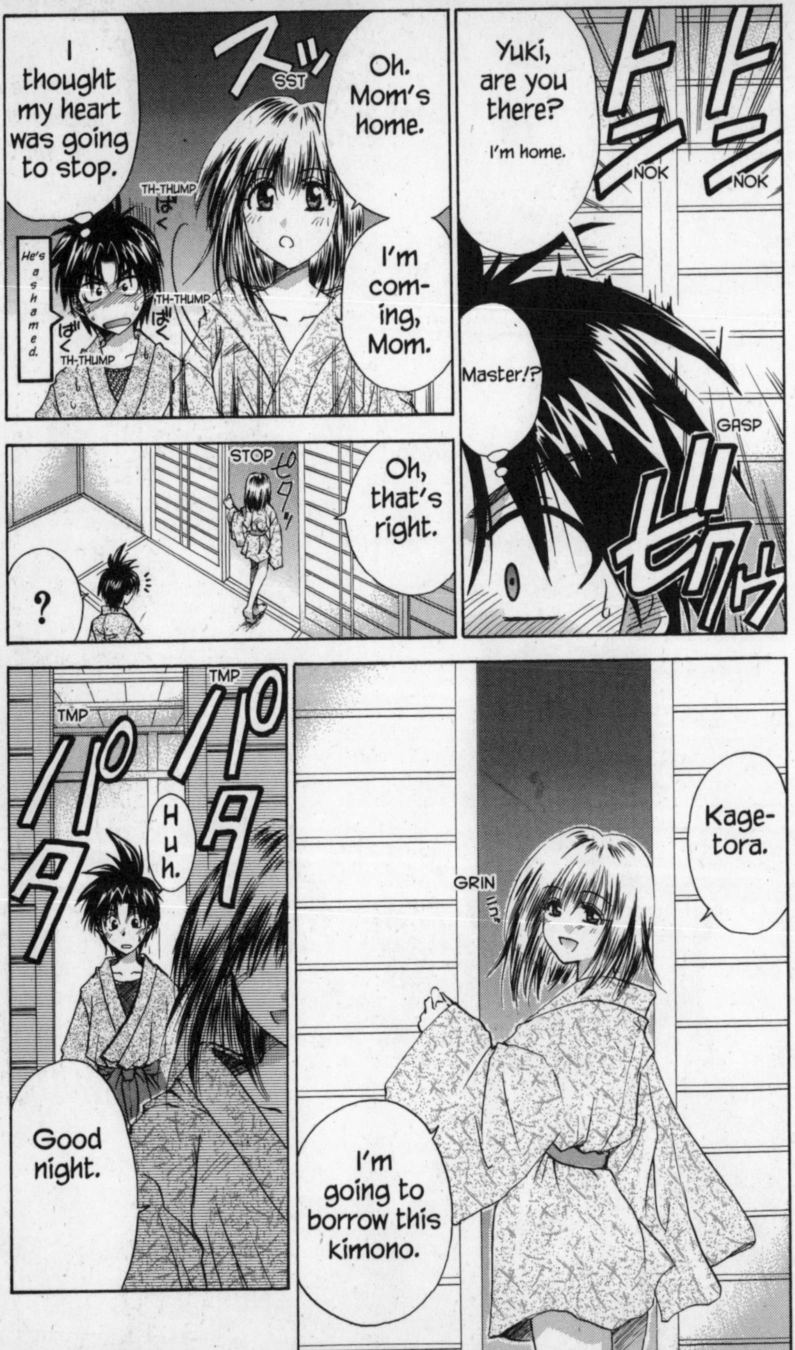
NOK
NOK
Yuki, are you there?
I'm home.
Master!?
GASP
SST
Oh. Mom's home.
I'm coming, Mom.
I thought my heart was going to stop.
TH-THUMP
TH-THUMP
TH-THUMP
He's ashamed.
STOP
Oh, that's right.
?
Kagetora.
GRIN
I'm going to borrow this kimono.
TMP
TMP
Huh.
Good night.

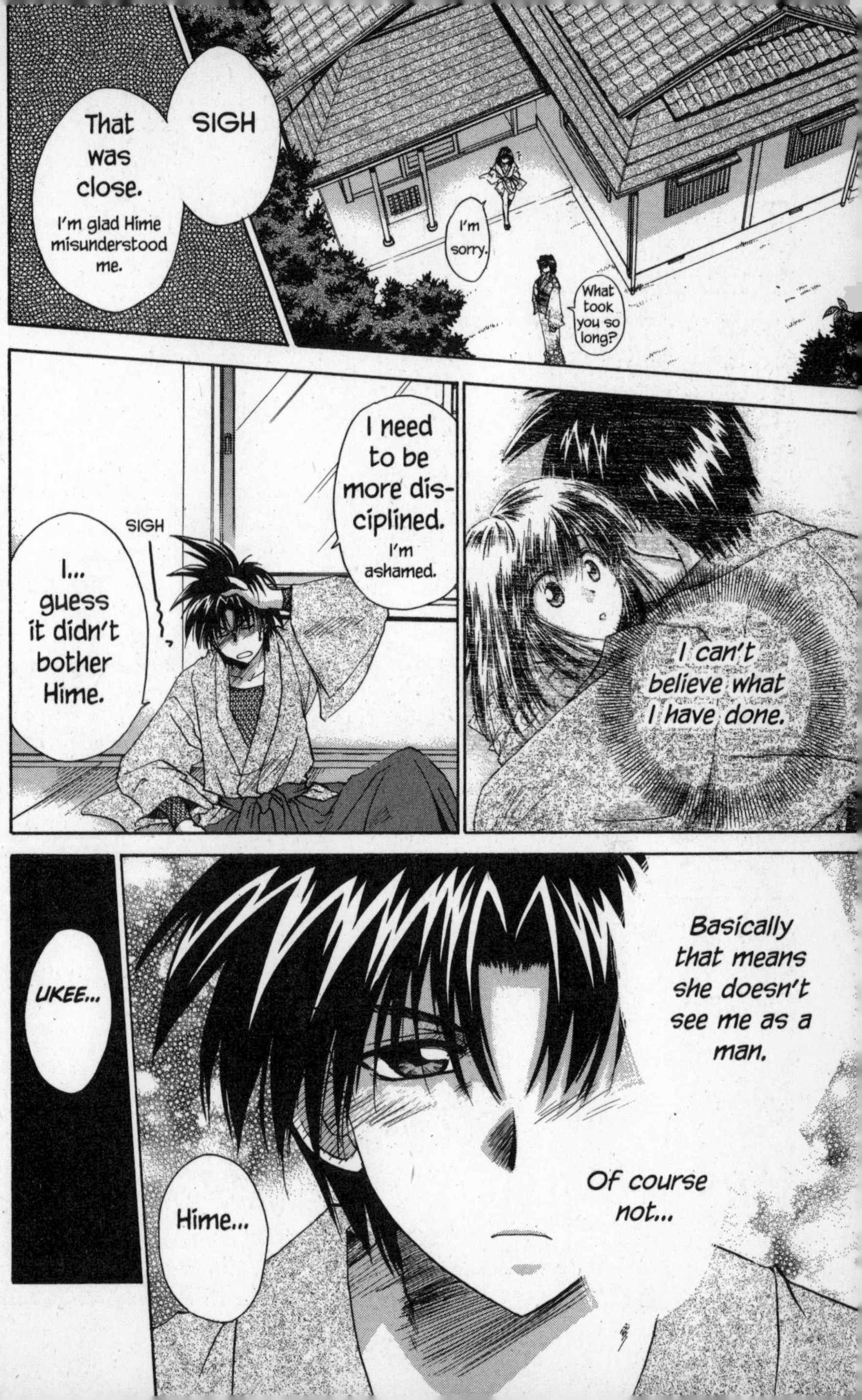
What took you so long?
I'm sorry.
SIGH
That was close.
I'm glad Hime misunderstood me.
I can't believe what I have done.
I need to be more disciplined.
I'm ashamed.
SIGH
I... guess it didn't bother Hime.
Basically that means she doesn't see me as a man.
Of course not...
UKEE...
Hime...

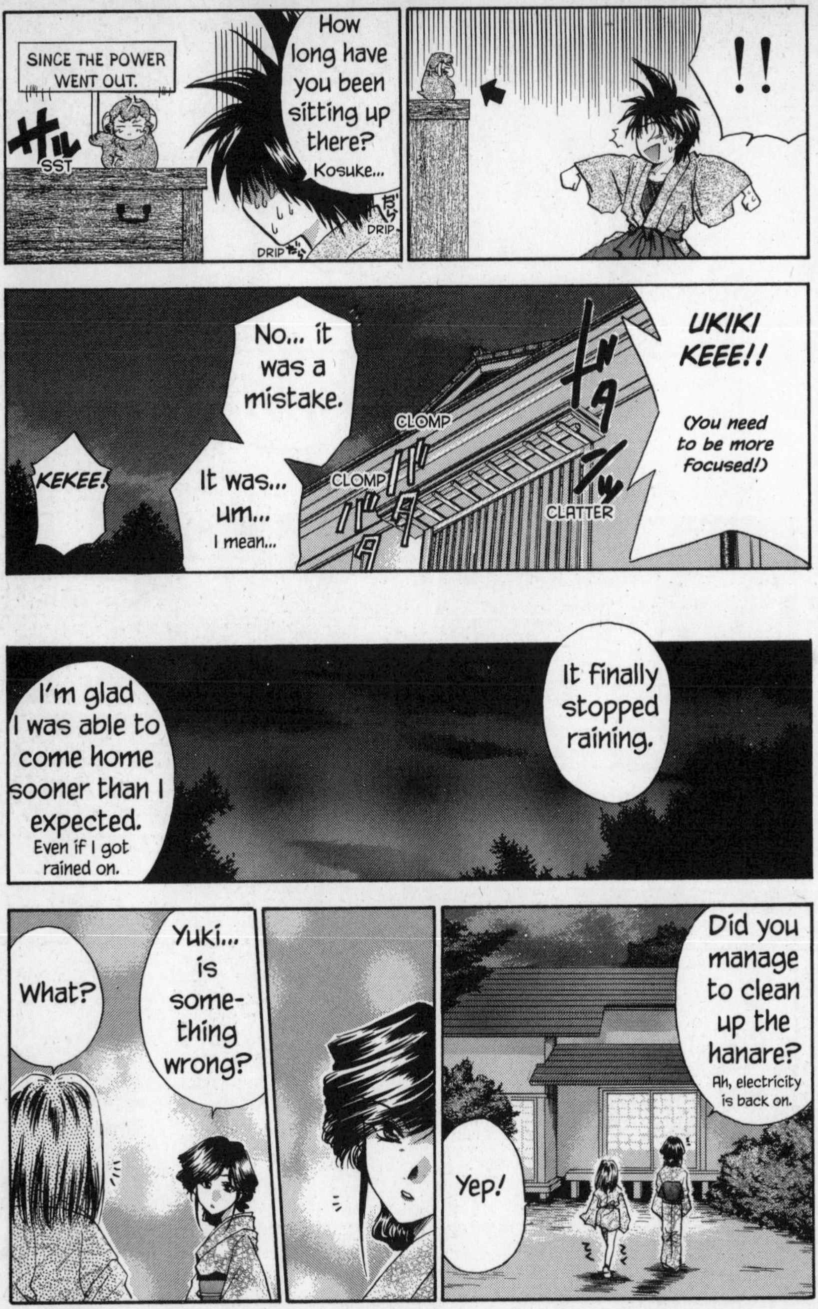
!!
How long have you been sitting up there?
Kosuke...
SINCE THE POWER WENT OUT.
SST
DRIP
DRIP
UKIKI KEEE!!
(You need to be more focused!)
CLATTER
CLOMP
CLOMP
No... it was a mistake.
It was... um...
I mean...
KEKEE!
It finally stopped raining.
I'm glad I was able to come home sooner than I expected.
Even if I got rained on.
Did you manage to clean up the hanare?
Ah, electricity is back on.
Yep!
Yuki... is something wrong?
What?

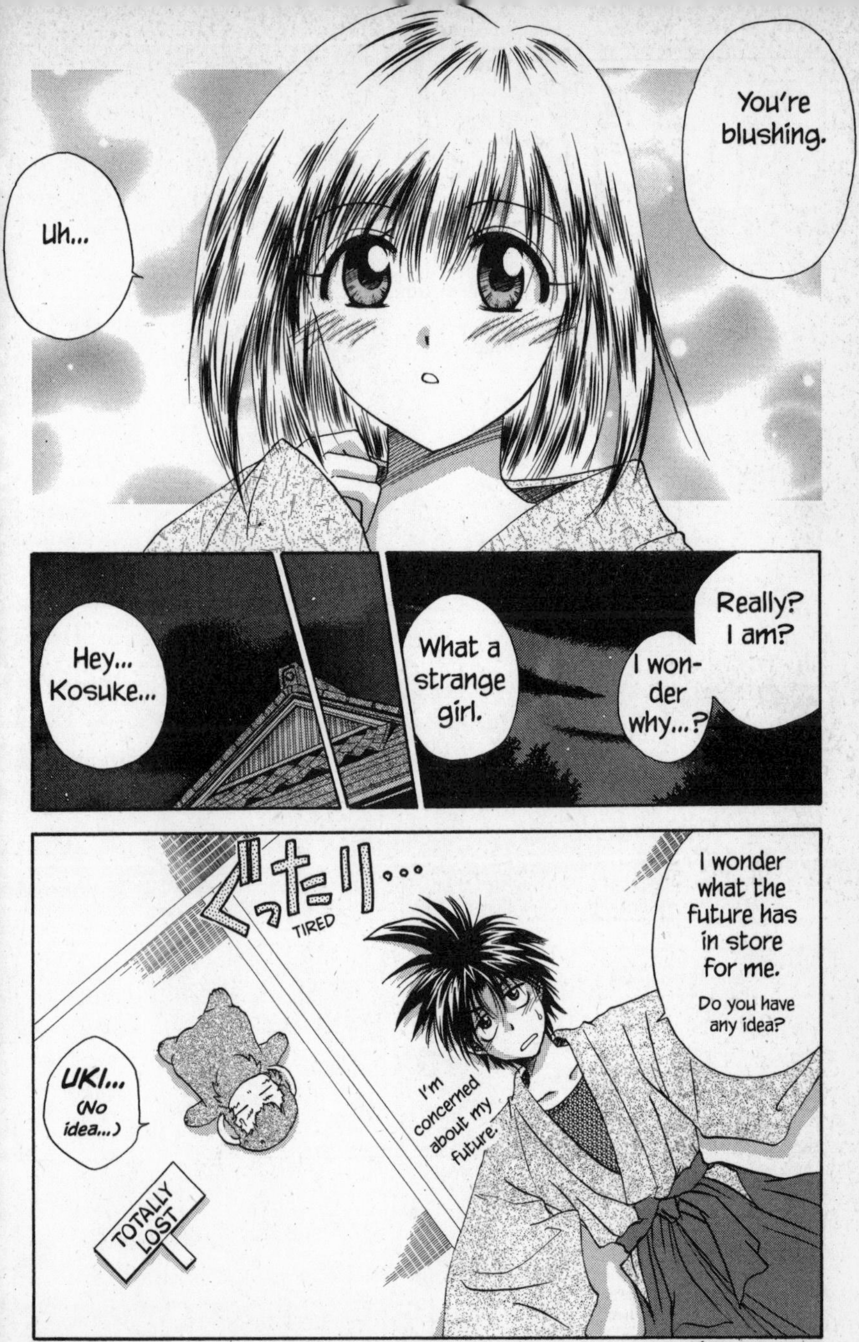
You're blushing.
Uh...
Really? I am?
I wonder why...?
What a strange girl.
Hey... Kosuke...
I wonder what the future has in store for me.
Do you have any idea?
ぐったり...
TIRED
I'm concerned about my future.
UKI... (No idea...)
TOTALLY LOST

↖This chapter was pretty exciting for Kagetora...

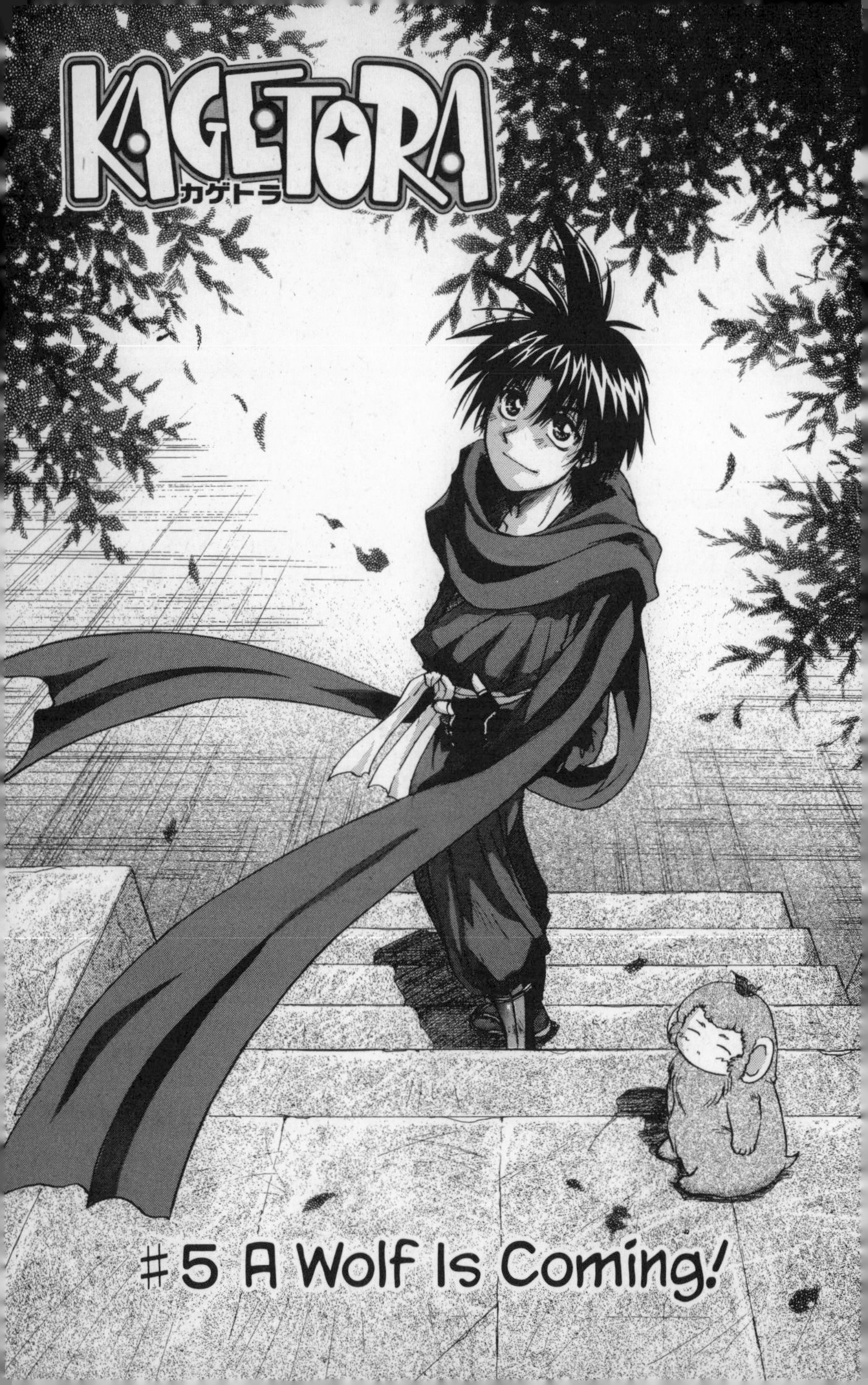
KAGETORA
カゲトラ
#5 A Wolf Is Coming!

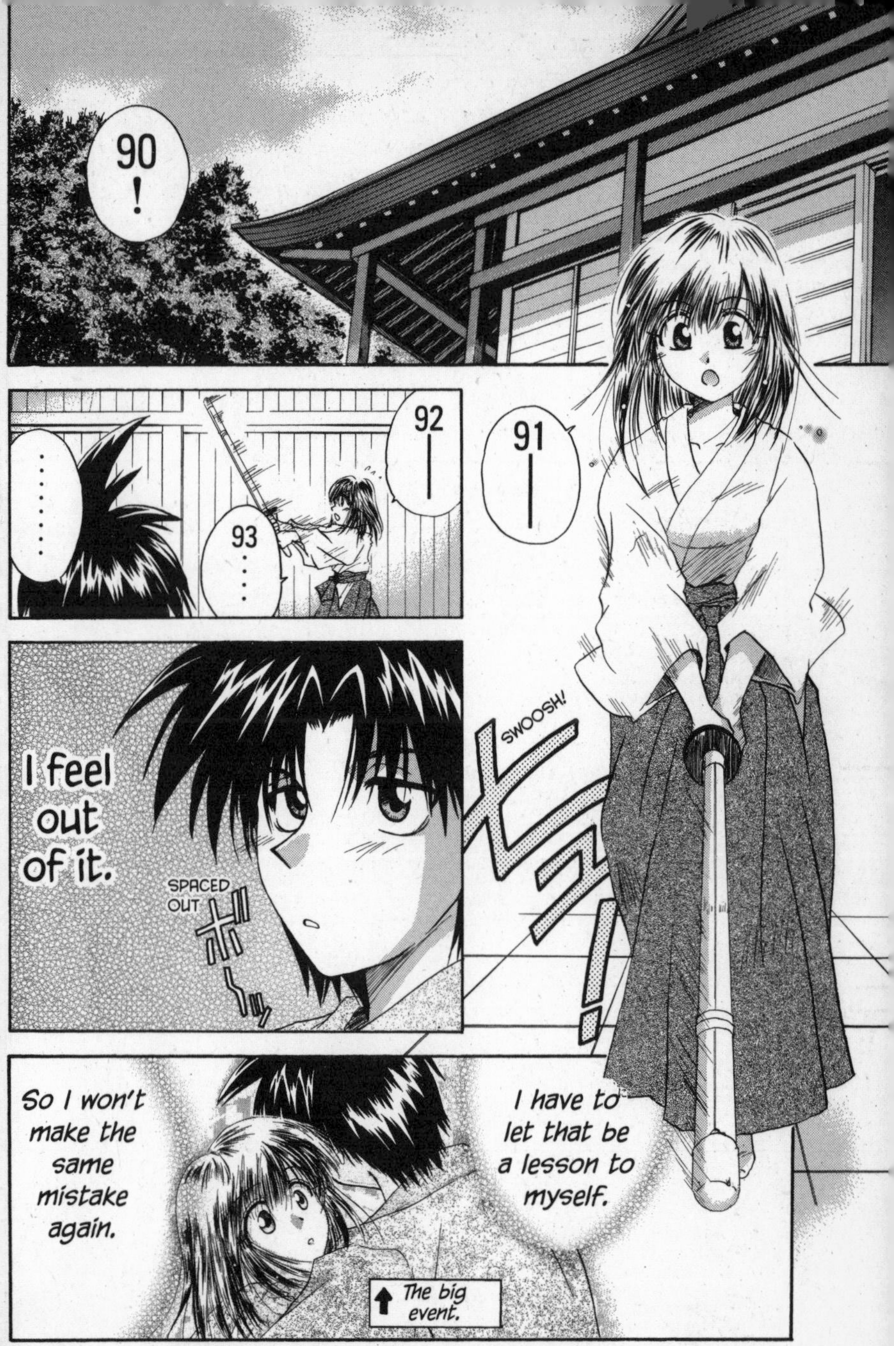
90 !
91 —
SWOOSH!
92 —
93 . . .
. . . . . .
I feel out of it.
SPACED OUT
I have to let that be a lesson to myself.
So I won't make the same mistake again.
The big event.

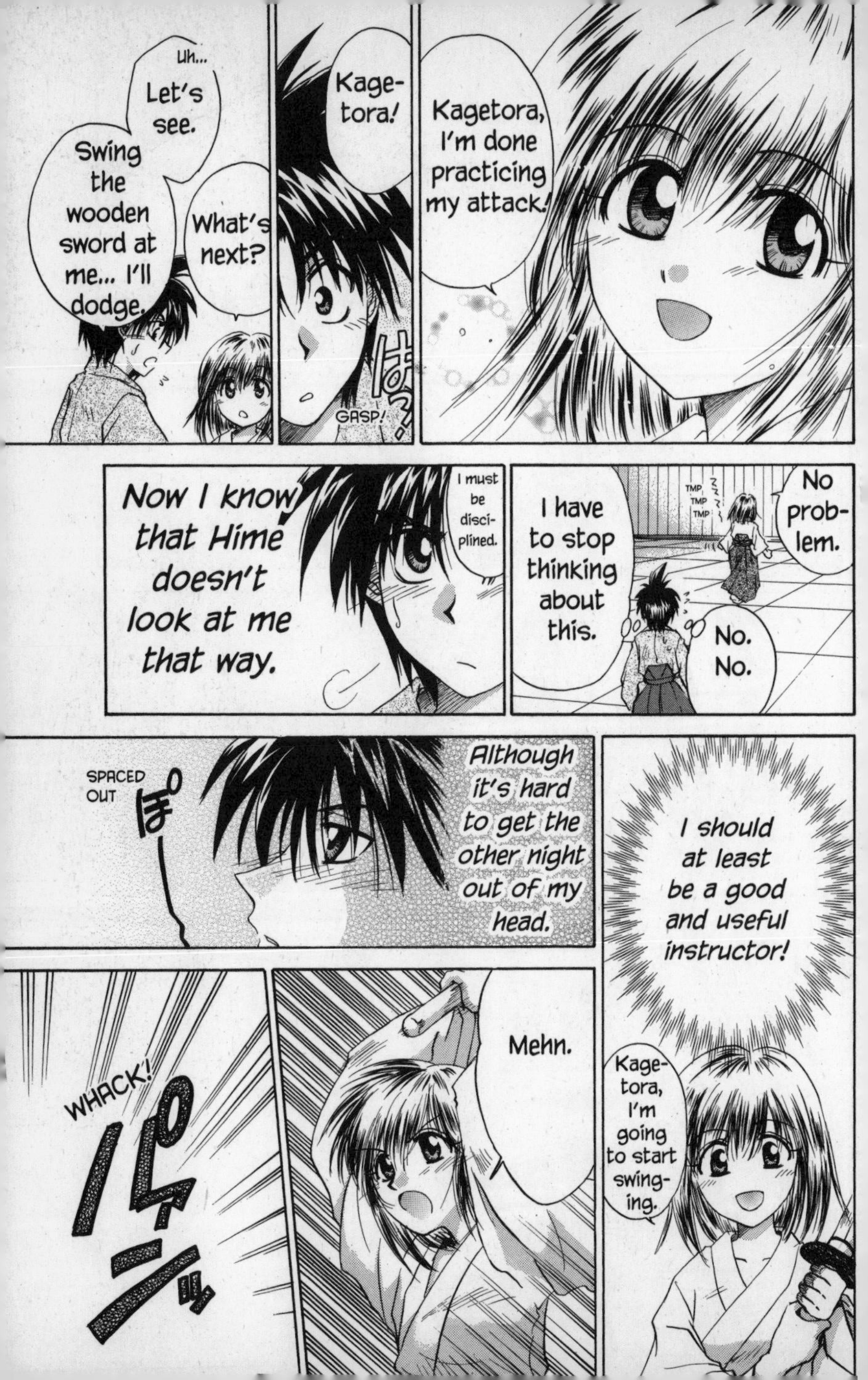
Kagetora, I'm done practicing my attack!
Kage-tora!
GASP!
What's next?
Uh... Let's see. Swing the wooden sword at me... I'll dodge.
No problem.
TMP TMP TMP
I have to stop thinking about this.
No. No.
I must be disciplined.
Now I know that Hime doesn't look at me that way.
I should at least be a good and useful instructor!
Kagetora, I'm going to start swinging.
Although it's hard to get the other night out of my head.
SPACED OUT
Mehn.
WHACK!

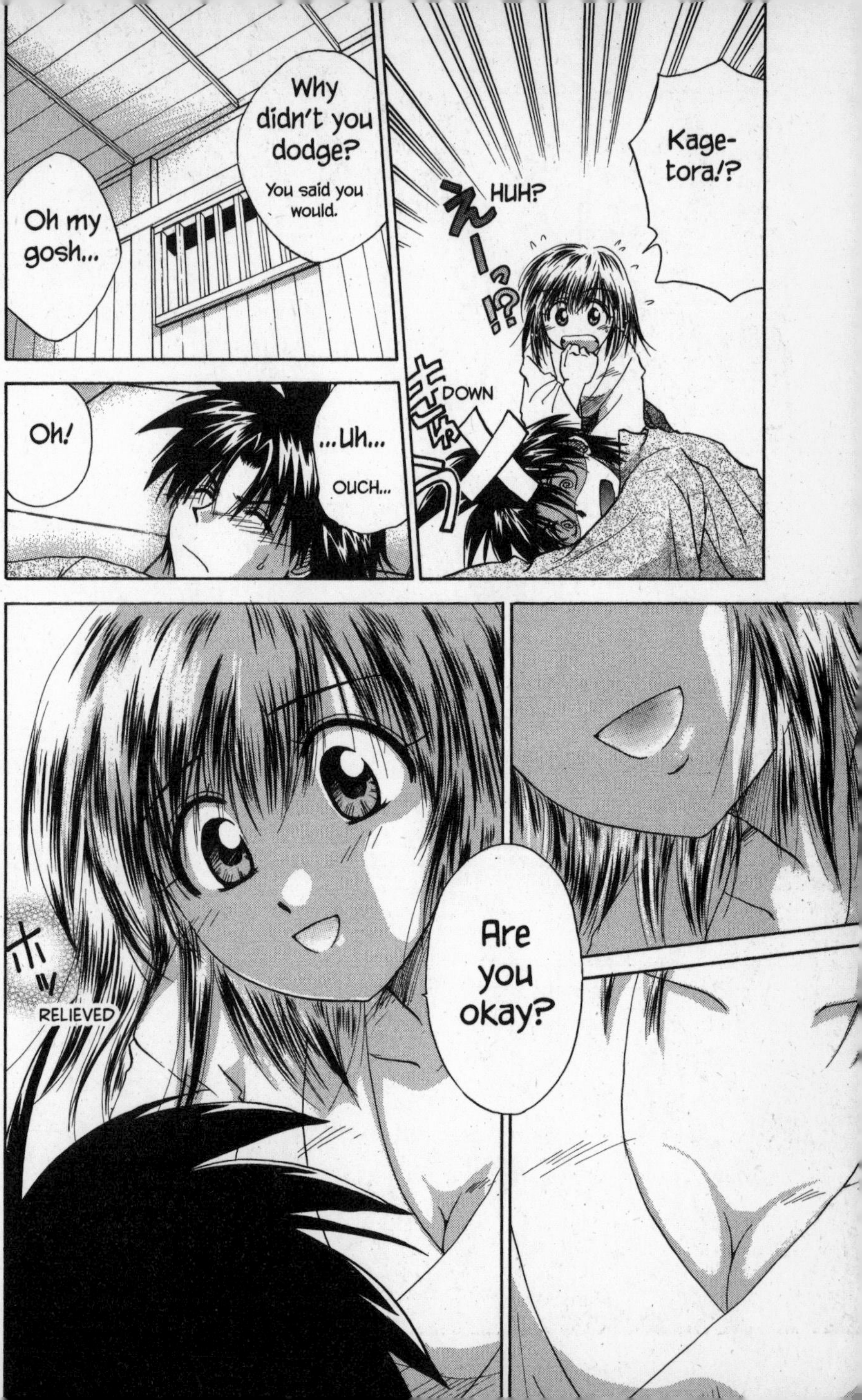
Kage-
tora!?
えーっ!?
HUH?
DOWN
Why didn't you dodge?
You said you would.
Oh my gosh...
...uh...
OUCH...
Oh!
Are you okay?
ホッ
RELIEVED

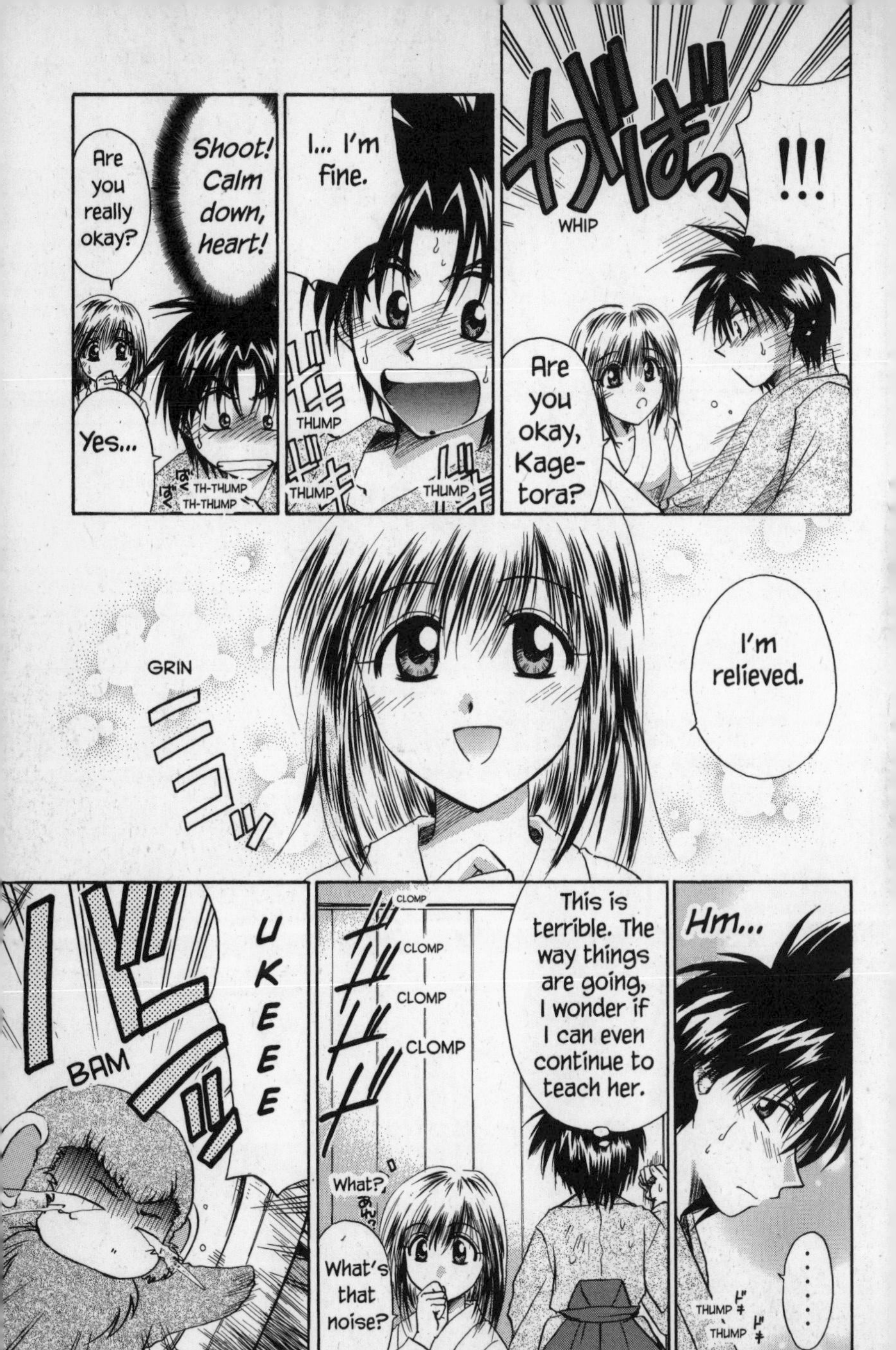

WHIP
!!!
Are you okay, Kage-tora?
I... I'm fine.
THUMP
THUMP
THUMP
Shoot! Calm down, heart!
Are you really okay?
Yes...
TH-THUMP
TH-THUMP
I'm relieved.
GRIN
Hm...
......
THUMP
THUMP
This is terrible. The way things are going, I wonder if I can even continue to teach her.
CLOMP
CLOMP
CLOMP
CLOMP
What?
What's that noise?
UKEEE
BAM

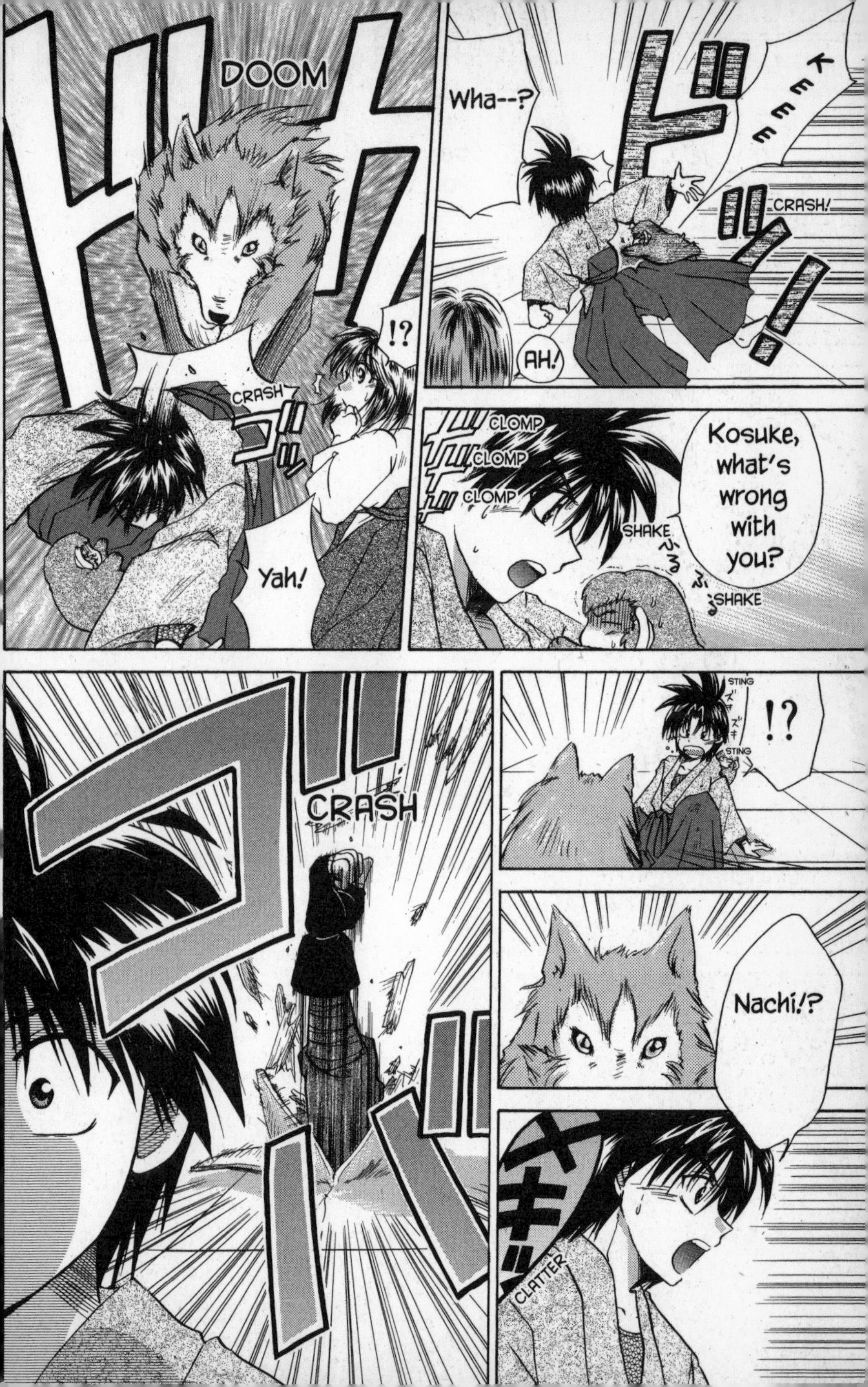

KEEEE
CRASH!
Wha--?
AH!
Kosuke, what's wrong with you?
CLOMP
CLOMP
CLOMP
SHAKE
SHAKE
DOOM
!?
CRASH
Yah!
!?
STING
STING
Nachi!?
CLATTER
CRASH

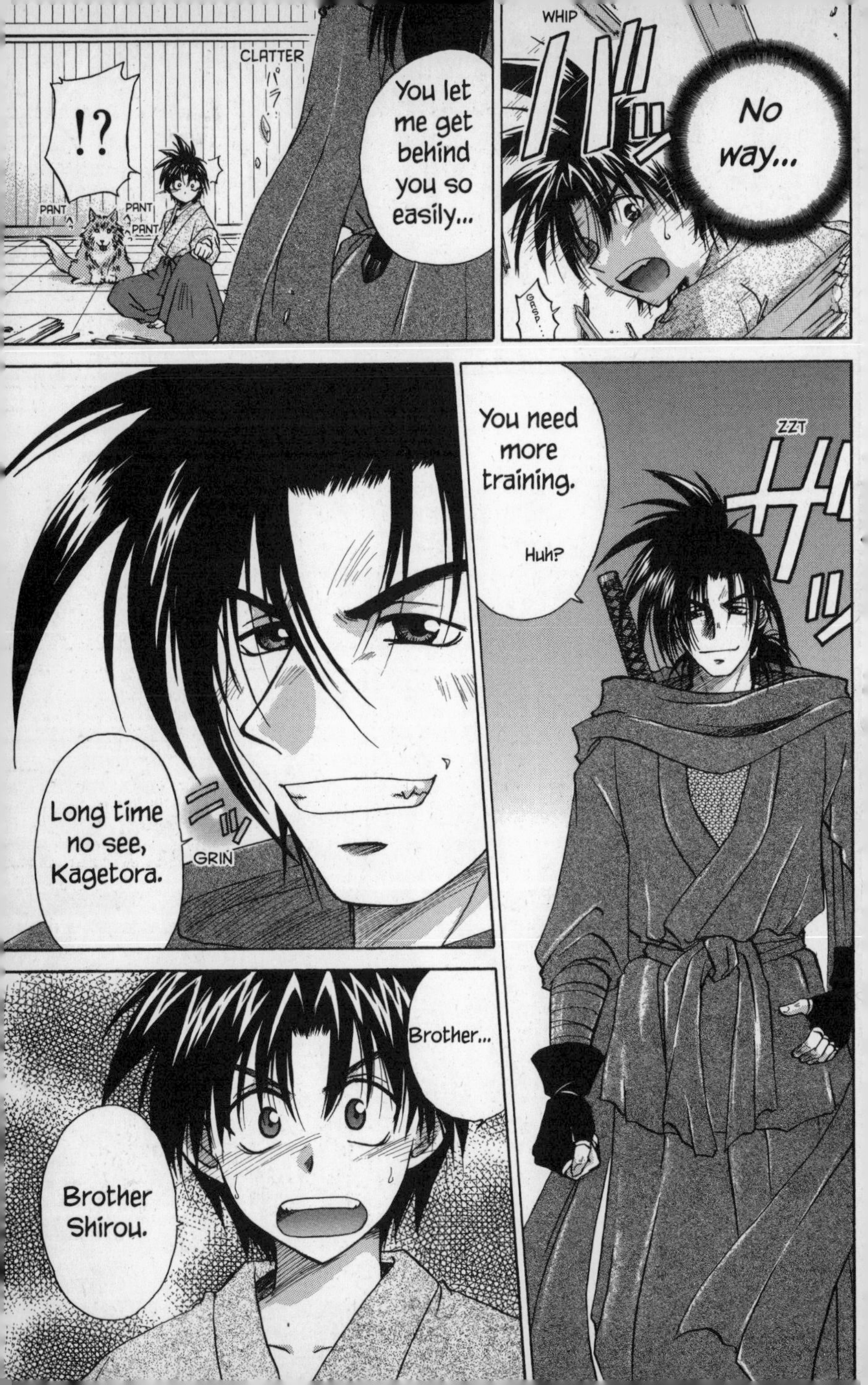
WHIP
No way...
GASP...
CLATTER
You let me get behind you so easily...
!?
PANT
PANT
PANT
ZZT
You need more training.
Huh?
Long time no see, Kagetora.
GRIN
Brother...
Brother Shirou.

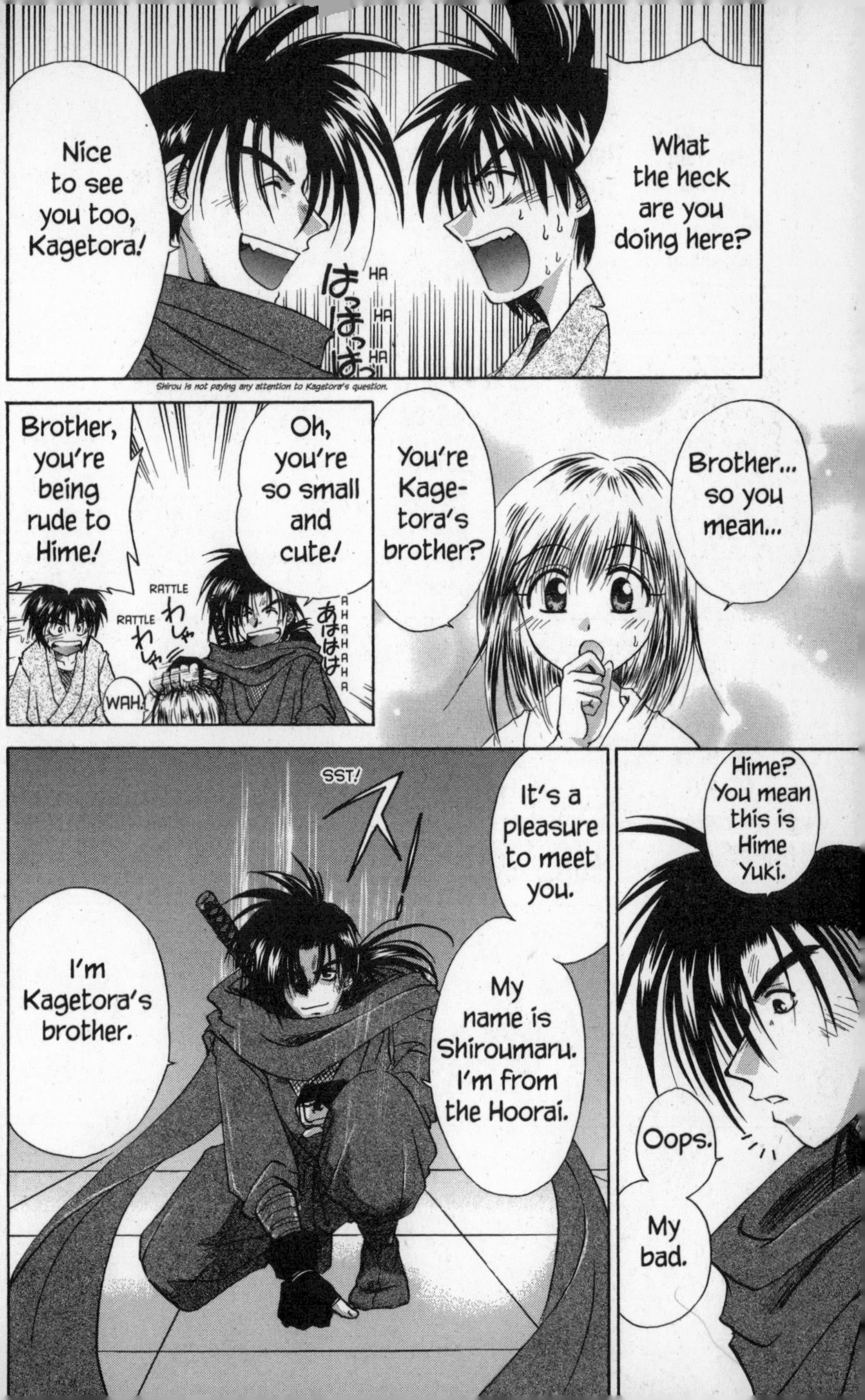
What the heck are you doing here?
Nice to see you too, Kagetora!
HA HA HA
Shirou is not paying any attention to Kagetora's question.
Brother... so you mean...
You're Kage-tora's brother?
Oh, you're so small and cute!
AHAHAHAHA
RATTLE RATTLE
WAH!
Brother, you're being rude to Hime!
Hime? You mean this is Hime Yuki.
Oops.
My bad.
SST!
It's a pleasure to meet you.
My name is Shiroumaru. I'm from the Hoorai.
I'm Kagetora's brother.

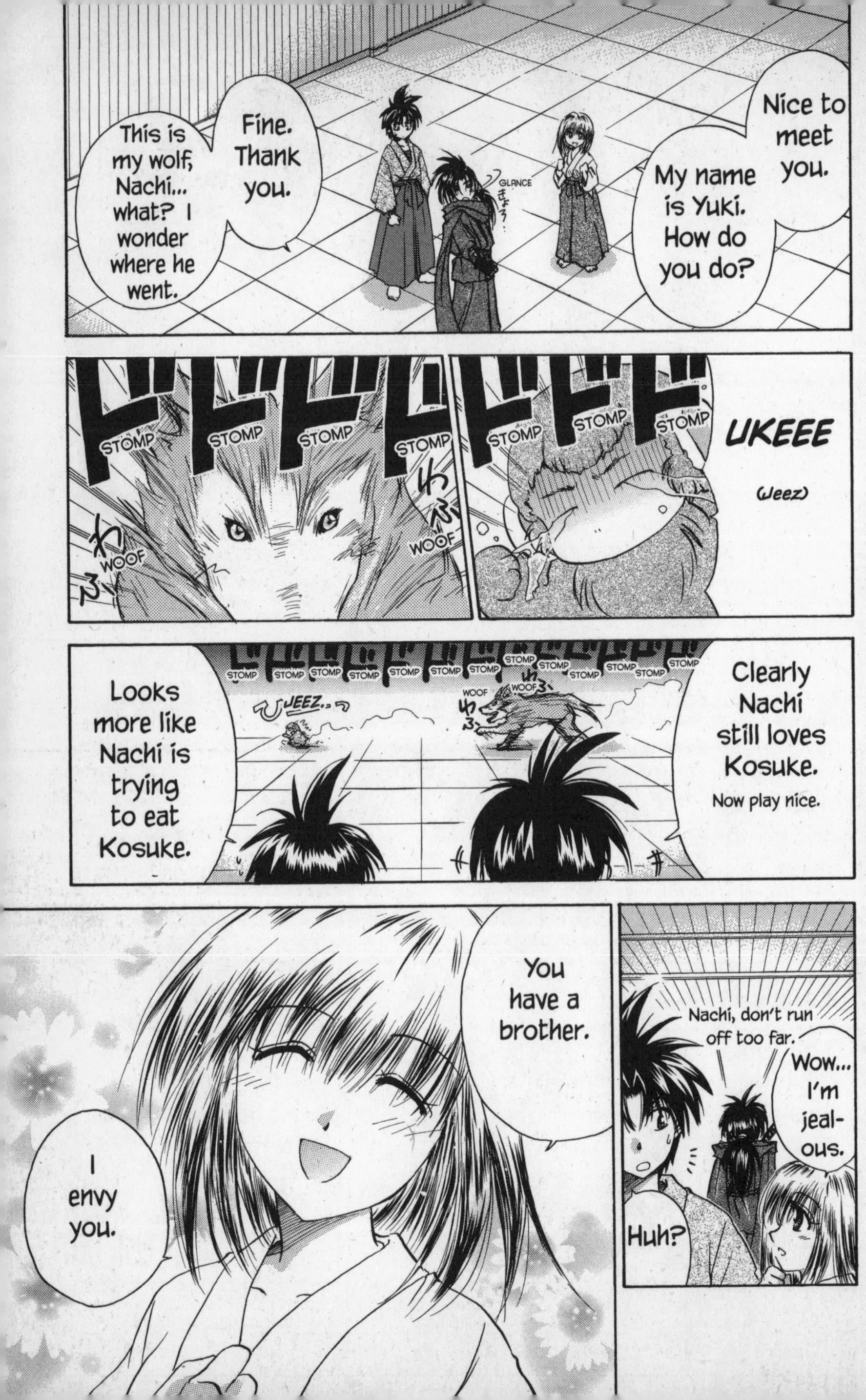
Nice to meet you.
My name is Yuki. How do you do?
GLANCE
Fine. Thank you.
This is my wolf, Nachi... what? I wonder where he went.
UKEEE
(Jeez)
STOMP STOMP STOMP
STOMP STOMP STOMP STOMP
WOOF
WOOF
Clearly Nachi still loves Kosuke.
Now play nice.
STOMP STOMP STOMP STOMP STOMP STOMP STOMP STOMP STOMP STOMP STOMP STOMP STOMP STOMP
WOOF
WOOF
JEEZ..
Looks more like Nachi is trying to eat Kosuke.
Nachi, don't run off too far.
Wow... I'm jeal-ous.
Huh?
You have a brother.
I envy you.

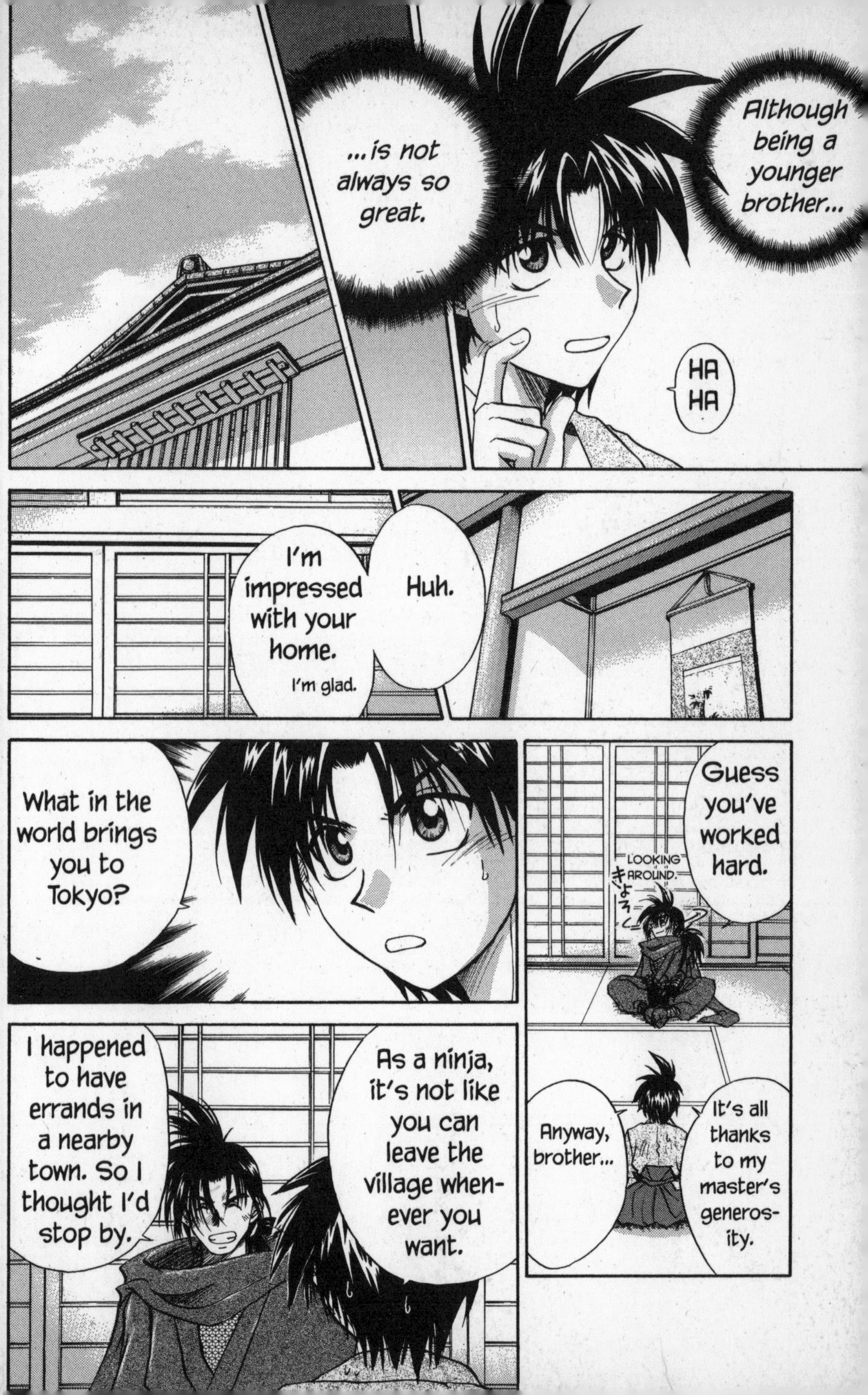

Although being a younger brother...
...is not always so great.
HA HA
Huh.
I'm impressed with your home.
I'm glad.
Guess you've worked hard.
LOOKING AROUND
It's all thanks to my master's generosity.
Anyway, brother...
What in the world brings you to Tokyo?
As a ninja, it's not like you can leave the village whenever you want.
I happened to have errands in a nearby town. So I thought I'd stop by.

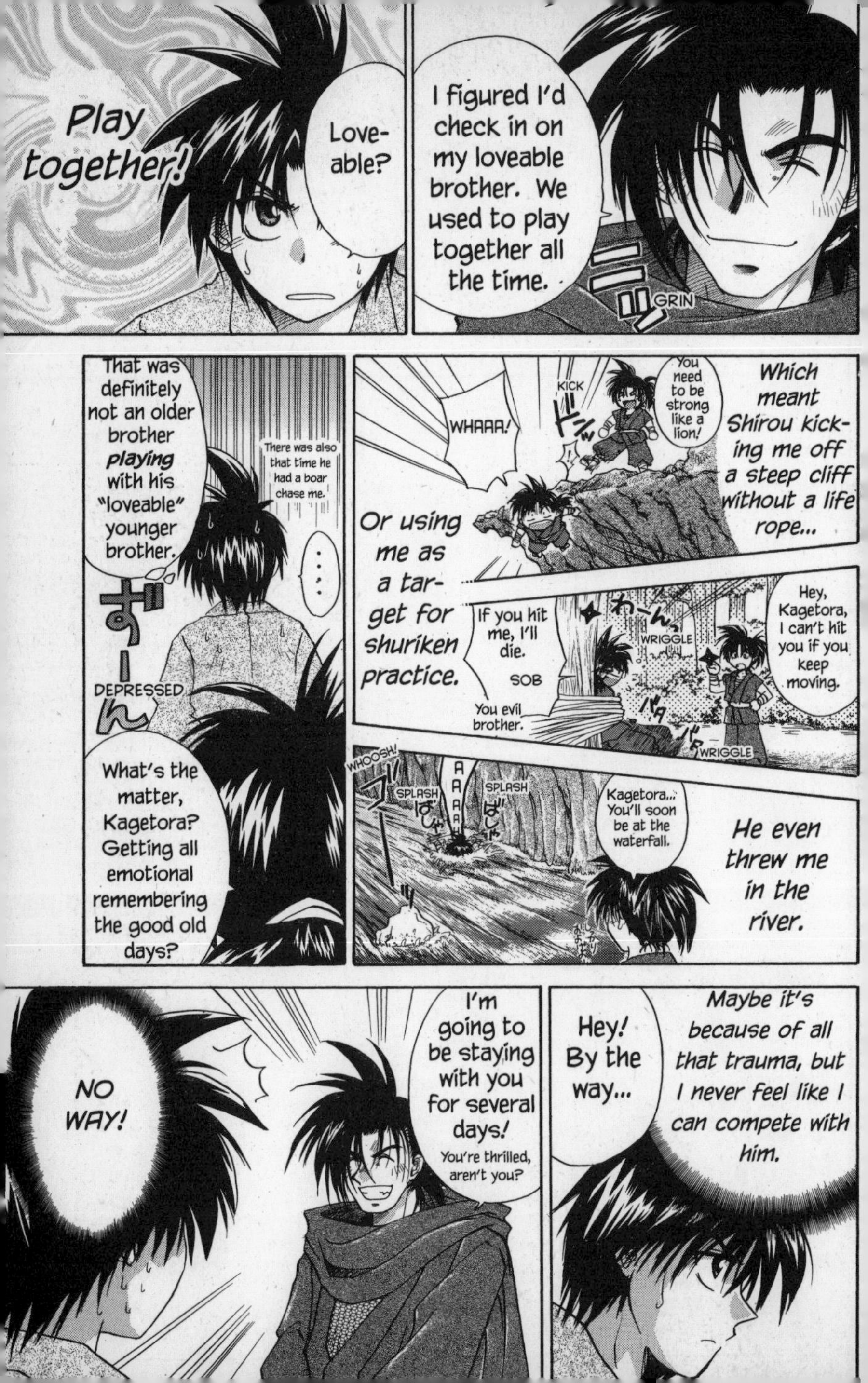
I figured I'd check in on my loveable brother. We used to play together all the time.
GRIN
Love-able?
Play together!
Which meant Shirou kick-ing me off a steep cliff without a life rope...
You need to be strong like a lion!
KICK
WHAAA!
Hey, Kagetora, I can't hit you if you keep moving.
WRIGGLE
WRIGGLE
If you hit me, I'll die.
SOB
You evil brother.
Or using me as a tar-get for shuriken practice.
He even threw me in the river.
Kagetora... You'll soon be at the waterfall.
SPLASH
SPLASH
AAAAA
WHOOSH!
That was definitely not an older brother *playing* with his "loveable" younger brother.
There was also that time he had a boar chase me.
...
DEPRESSED
What's the matter, Kagetora? Getting all emotional remembering the good old days?
Maybe it's because of all that trauma, but I never feel like I can compete with him.
Hey! By the way...
I'm going to be staying with you for several days!
You're thrilled, aren't you?
NO WAY!

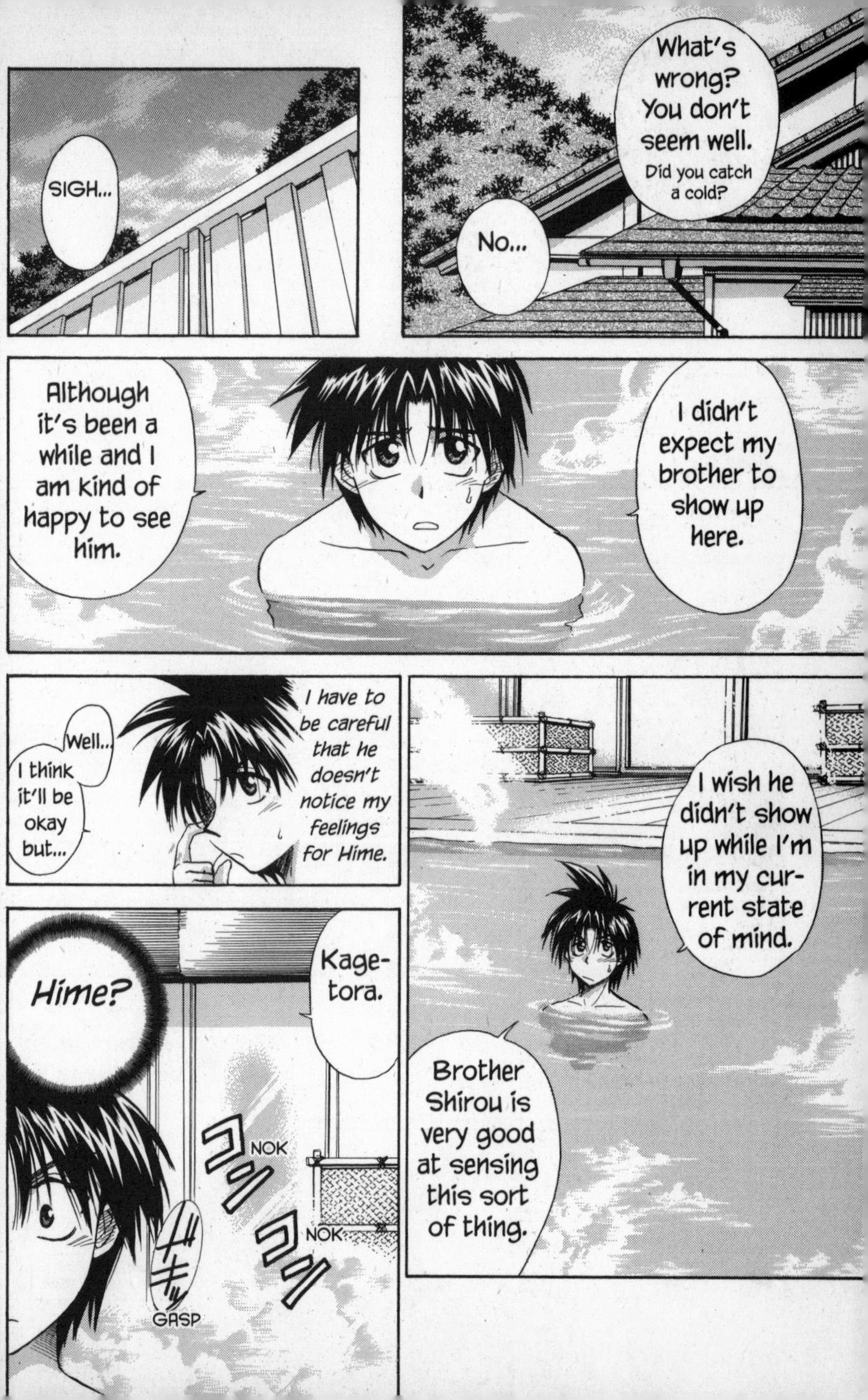

What's wrong? You don't seem well.
Did you catch a cold?
No...
SIGH...
I didn't expect my brother to show up here.
Although it's been a while and I am kind of happy to see him.
I wish he didn't show up while I'm in my current state of mind.
Brother Shirou is very good at sensing this sort of thing.
I have to be careful that he doesn't notice my feelings for Hime.
Well...
I think it'll be okay but...
Kage-tora.
Hime?
NOK
NOK
GASP

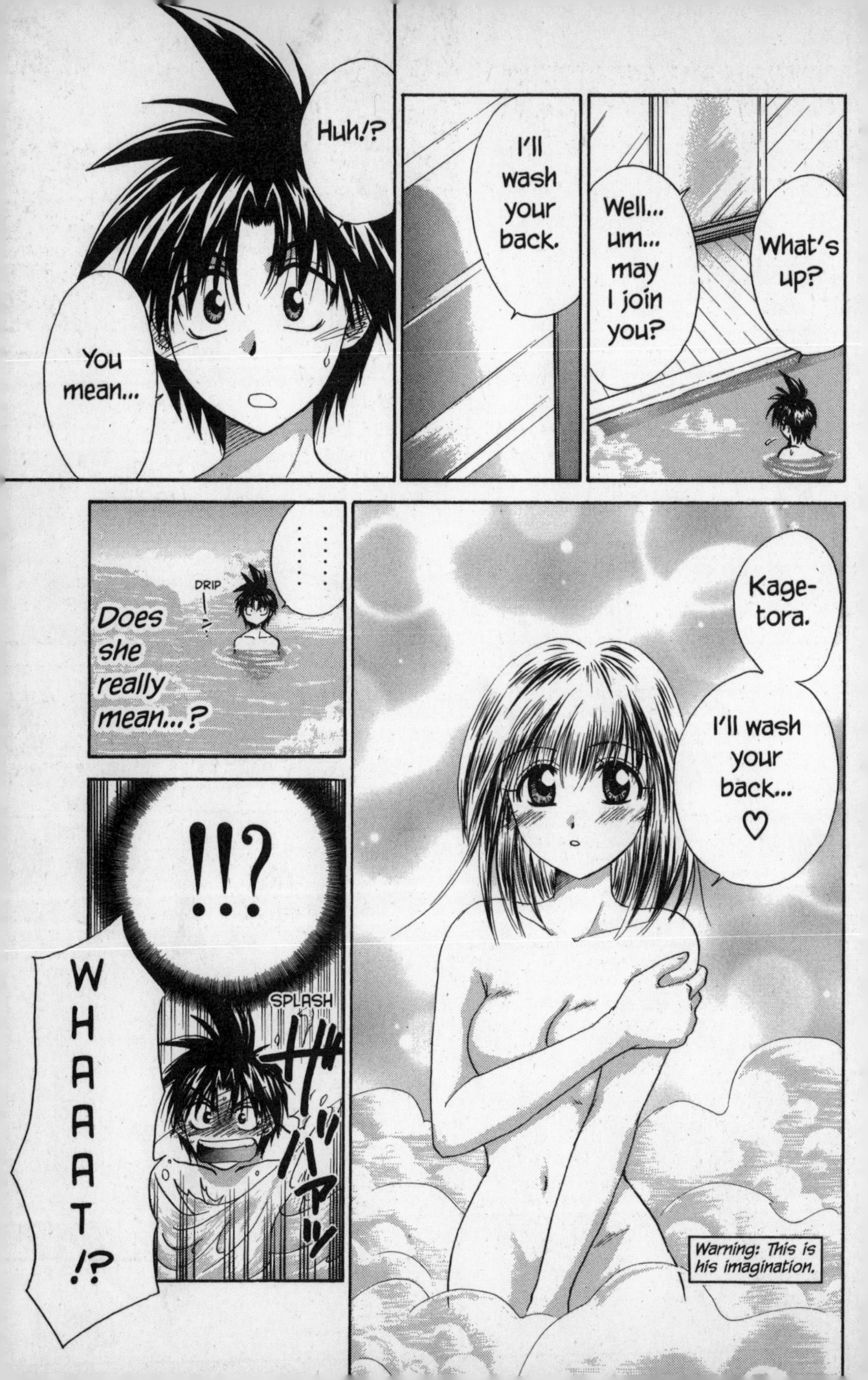
What's up?
Well... um... may I join you?
I'll wash your back.
Huh!?
You mean...
Kage-tora.
I'll wash your back... ♡
Warning: This is his imagination.
......
DRIP
Does she really mean...?
!!?
SPLASH
WHAAAAT!?

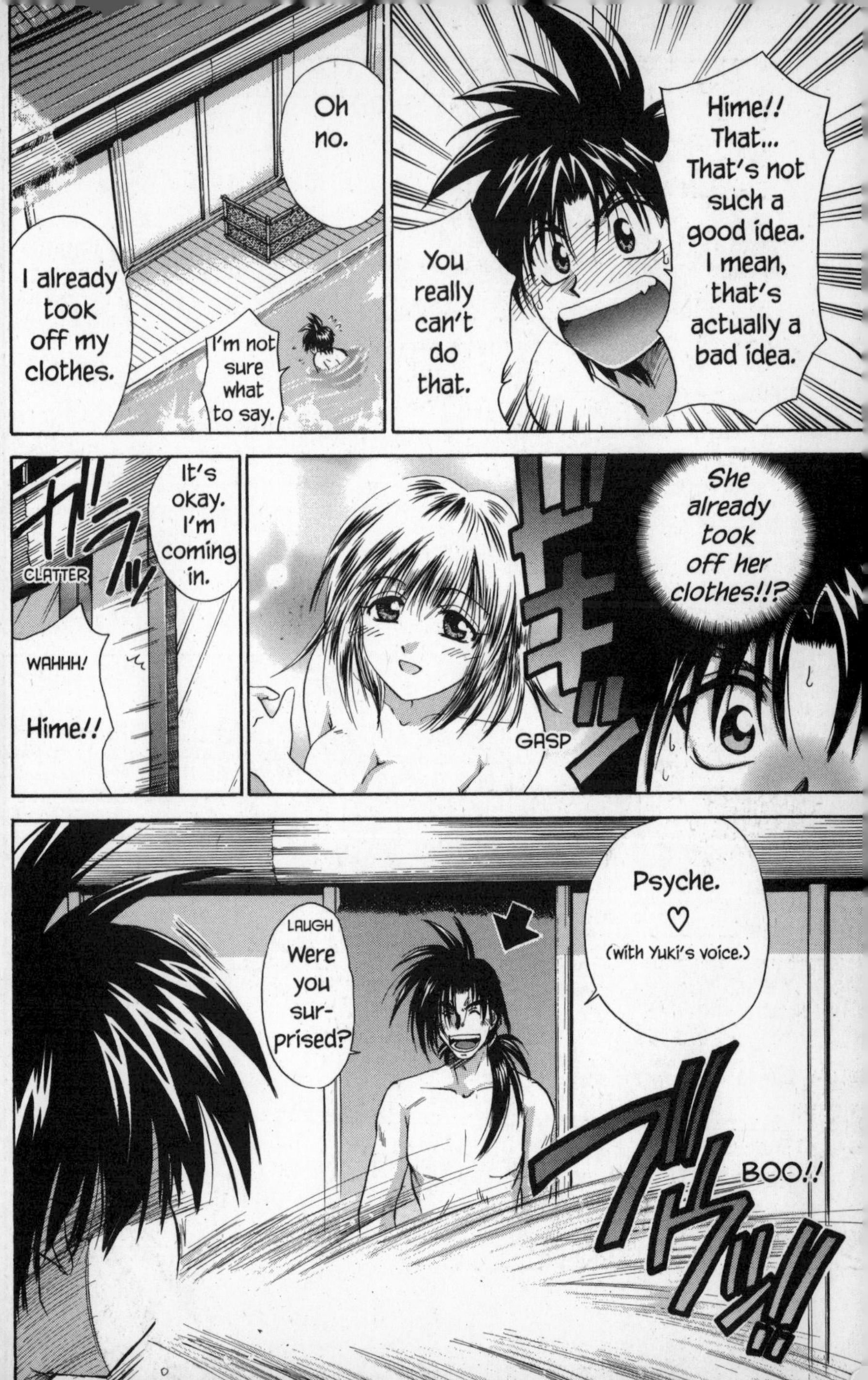
Hime!! That... That's not such a good idea. I mean, that's actually a bad idea.
You really can't do that.
Oh no.
I already took off my clothes.
I'm not sure what to say.
She already took off her clothes!!?
GASP
It's okay. I'm coming in.
CLATTER
WAHHH!
Hime!!
Psyche. ♡
(with Yuki's voice.)
LAUGH
Were you surprised?
BOO!!

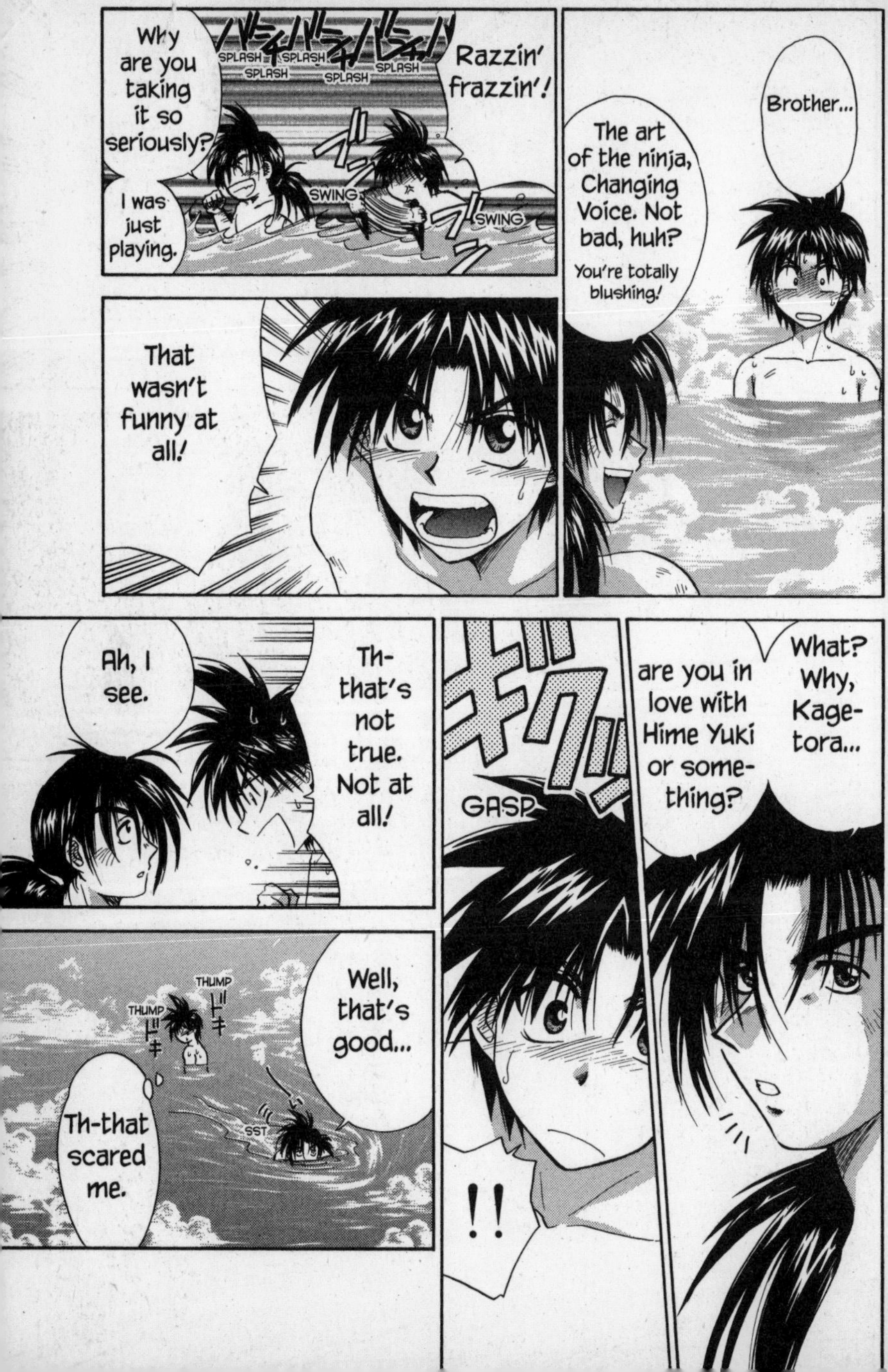
Brother...
The art of the ninja, Changing Voice. Not bad, huh?
You're totally blushing!
Razzin' frazzin'!
SPLASH SPLASH SPLASH SPLASH SPLASH
Why are you taking it so seriously?
SWING
SWING
I was just playing.
That wasn't funny at all!
What? Why, Kagetora...
are you in love with Hime Yuki or some-thing?
GASP
!!
Th- that's not true. Not at all!
Ah, I see.
Well, that's good...
THUMP
THUMP
SST
Th-that scared me.

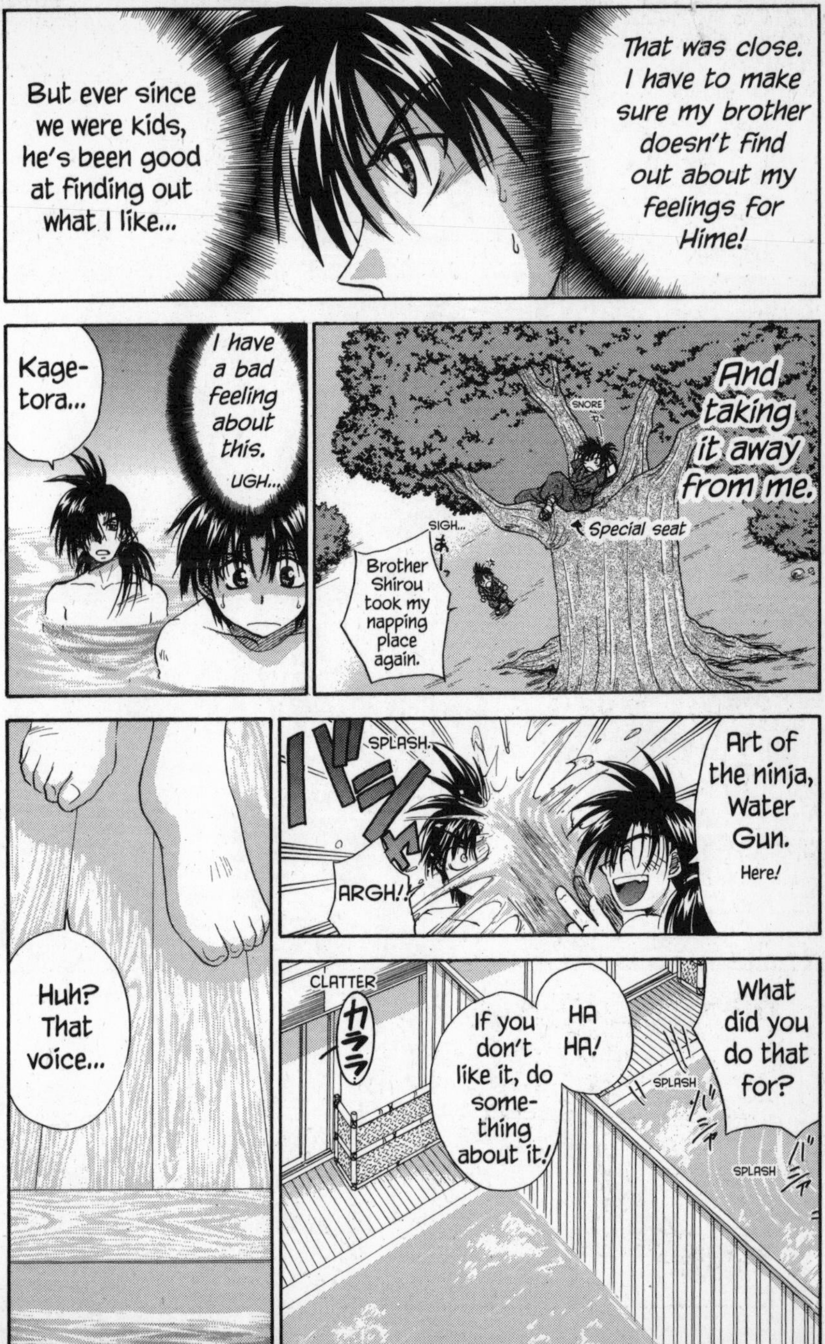

That was close. I have to make sure my brother doesn't find out about my feelings for Hime!
But ever since we were kids, he's been good at finding out what I like...
And taking it away from me.
SNORE
Special seat
SIGH...
Brother Shirou took my napping place again.
I have a bad feeling about this.
UGH...
Kage-tora...
Art of the ninja, Water Gun.
Here!
SPLASH
ARGH!!
What did you do that for?
SPLASH
SPLASH
HA HA!
If you don't like it, do some-thing about it!
CLATTER
カララ
Huh? That voice...

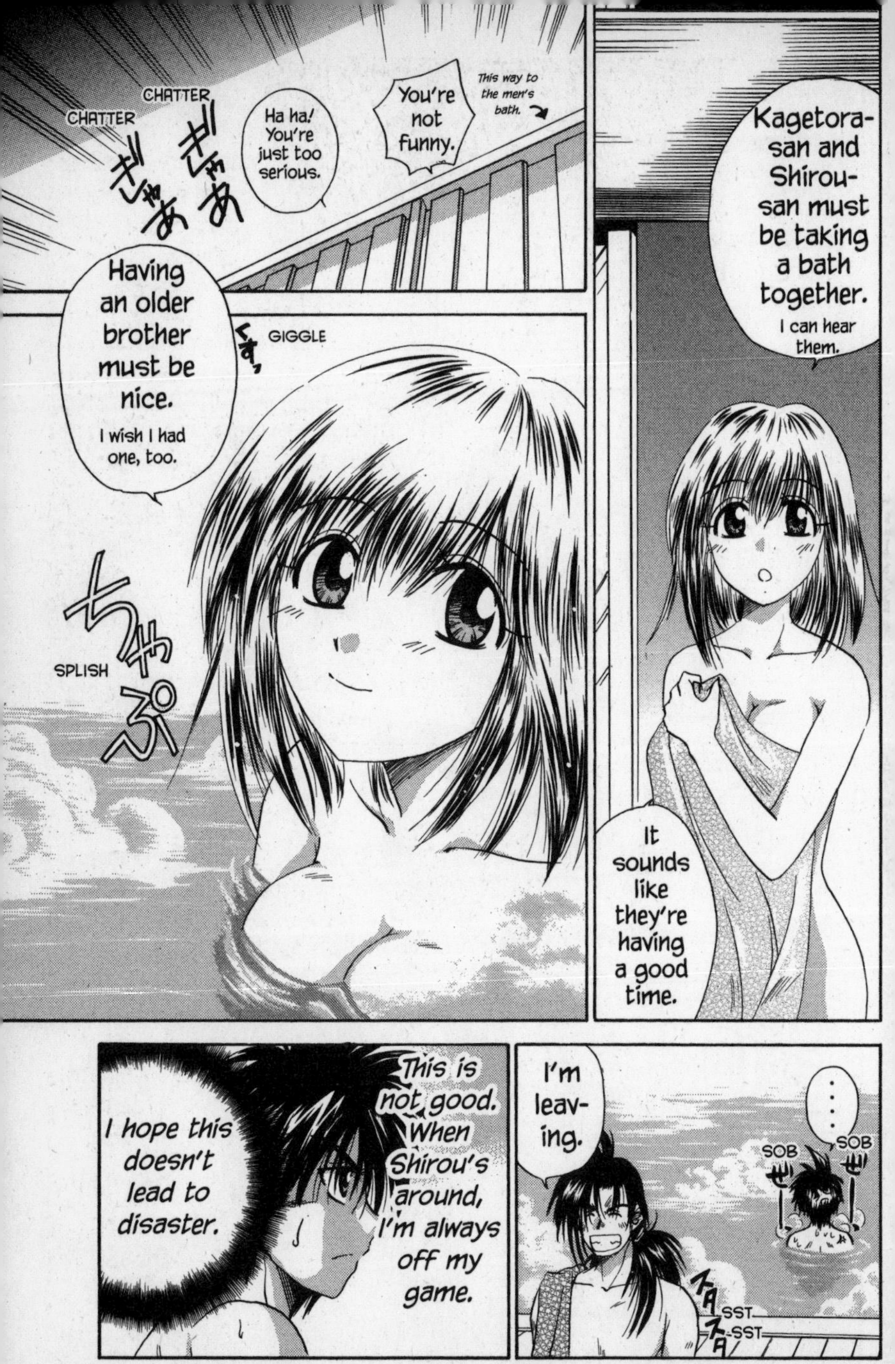
Kagetora-san and Shirou-san must be taking a bath together.
I can hear them.
It sounds like they're having a good time.
This way to the men's bath.
You're not funny.
Ha ha! You're just too serious.
CHATTER
CHATTER
ぎゃあぎゃあ
Having an older brother must be nice.
I wish I had one, too.
GIGGLE
くすっ
SPLISH
ちゃぷ
...
SOB
SOB
I'm leav-ing.
SST
SST
This is not good. When Shirou's around, I'm always off my game.
I hope this doesn't lead to disaster.

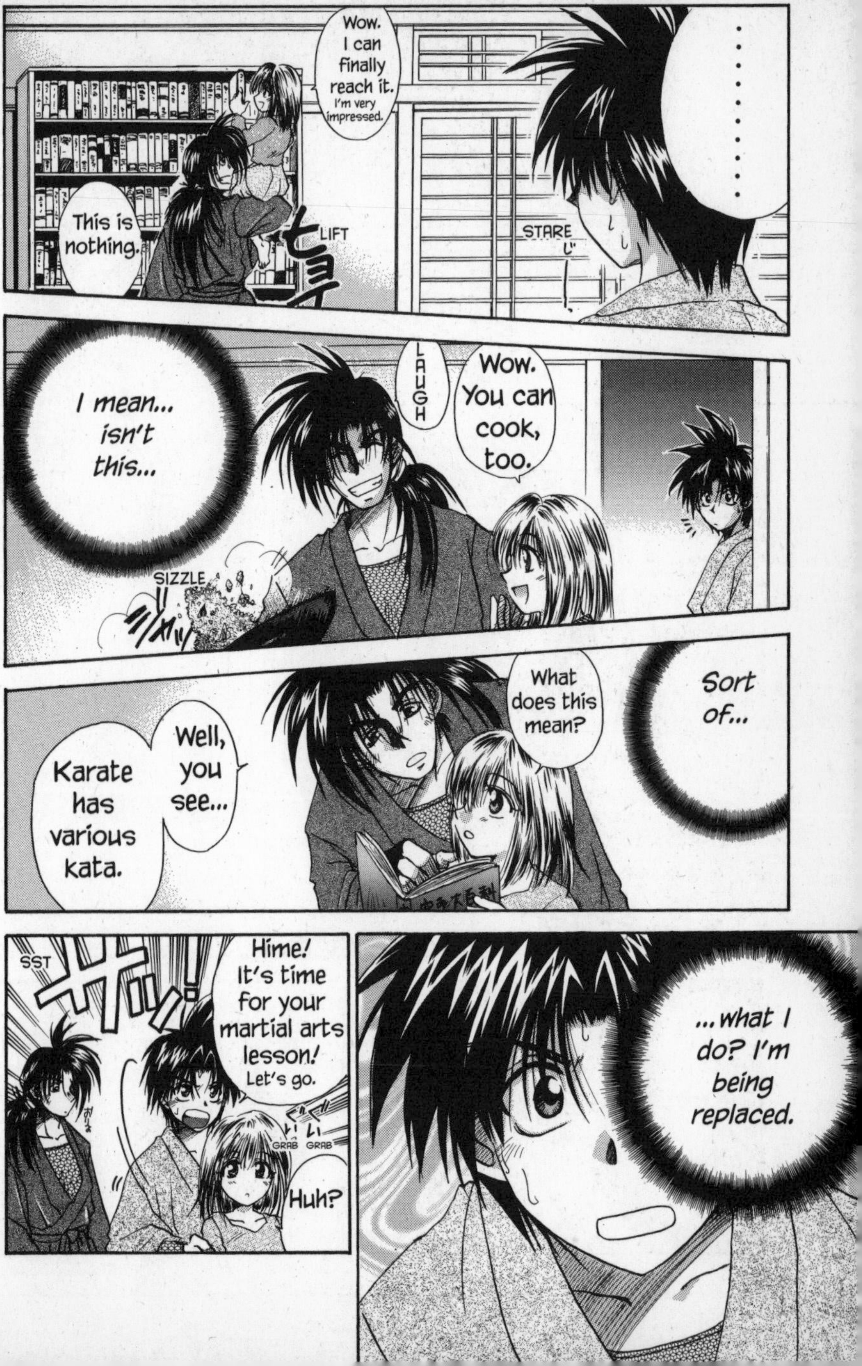
......
STARE
Wow. I can finally reach it. I'm very impressed.
LIFT
This is nothing.
Wow. You can cook, too.
LAUGH
I mean... isn't this...
SIZZLE
Sort of...
What does this mean?
Well, you see...
Karate has various kata.
...what I do? I'm being replaced.
Hime! It's time for your martial arts lesson! Let's go.
SST
GRAB GRAB
Huh?

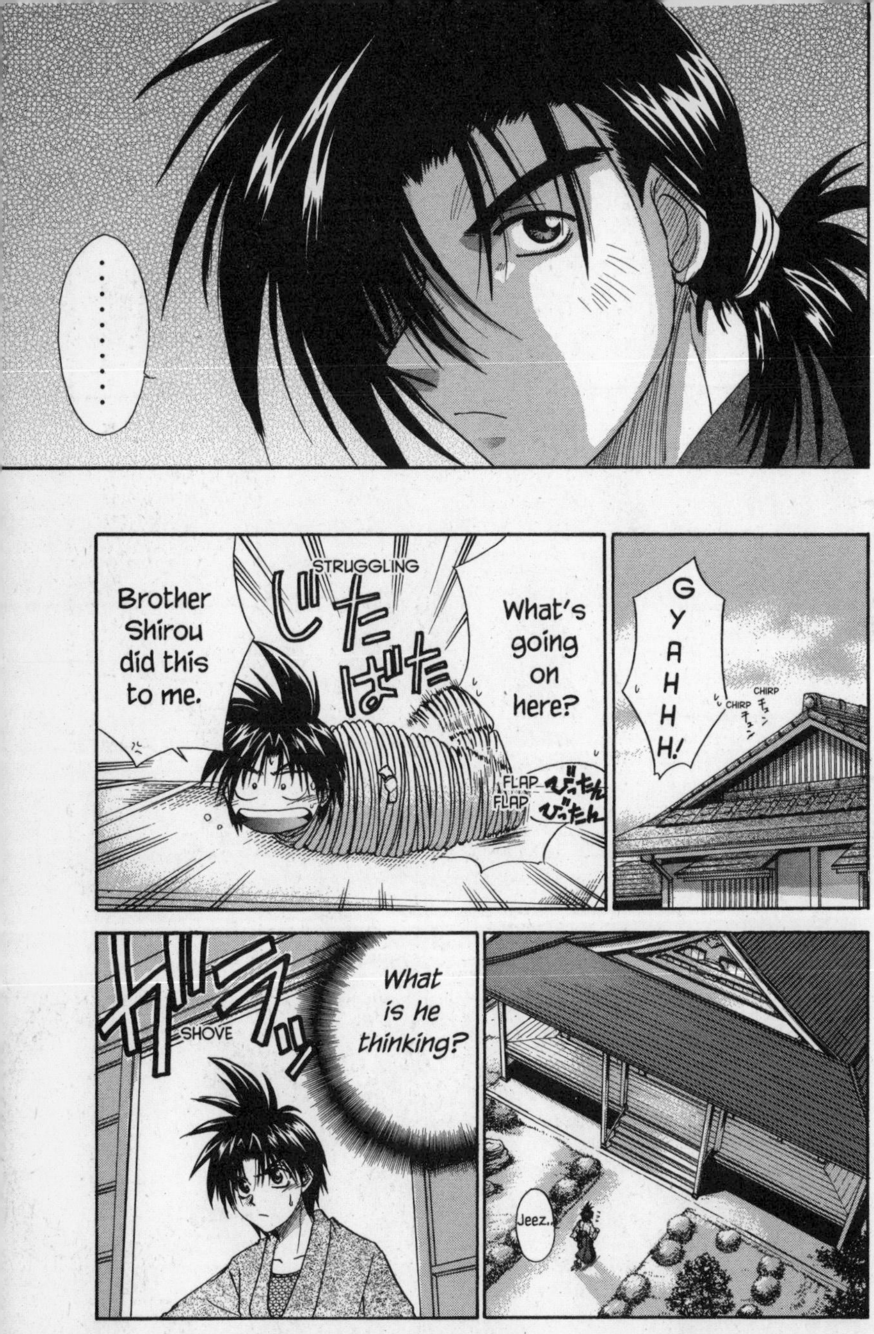
......
GYAHHH!
CHIRP CHIRP
チュン チュン
What's going on here?
STRUGGLING
じたばた
FLAP FLAP
びったん びったん
Brother Shirou did this to me.
Jeez...
What is he thinking?
SHOVE
ガラッ

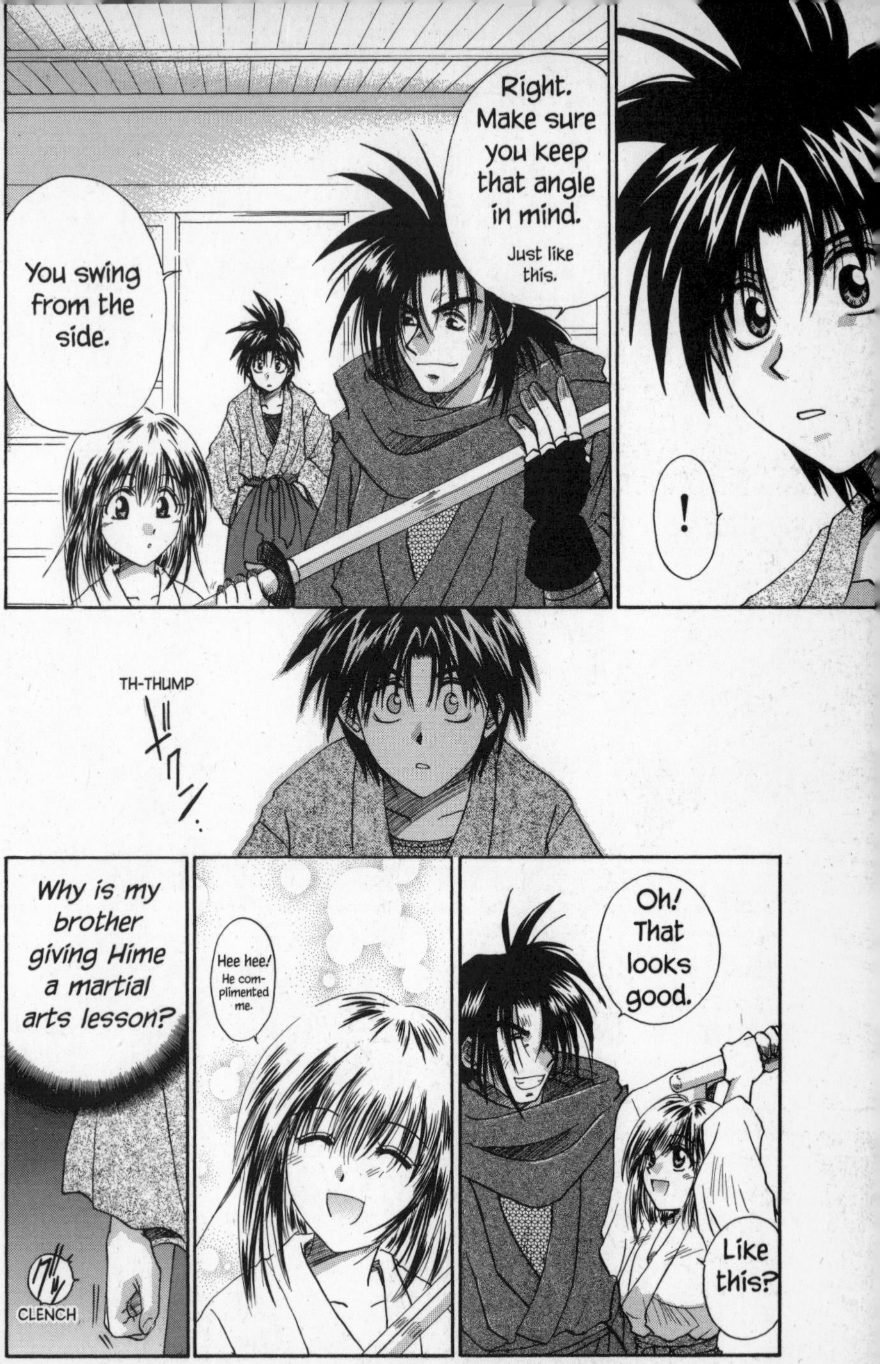
!
Right. Make sure you keep that angle in mind.
Just like this.
You swing from the side.
TH-THUMP
Oh! That looks good.
Like this?
Hee hee! He complimented me.
Why is my brother giving Hime a martial arts lesson?
CLENCH

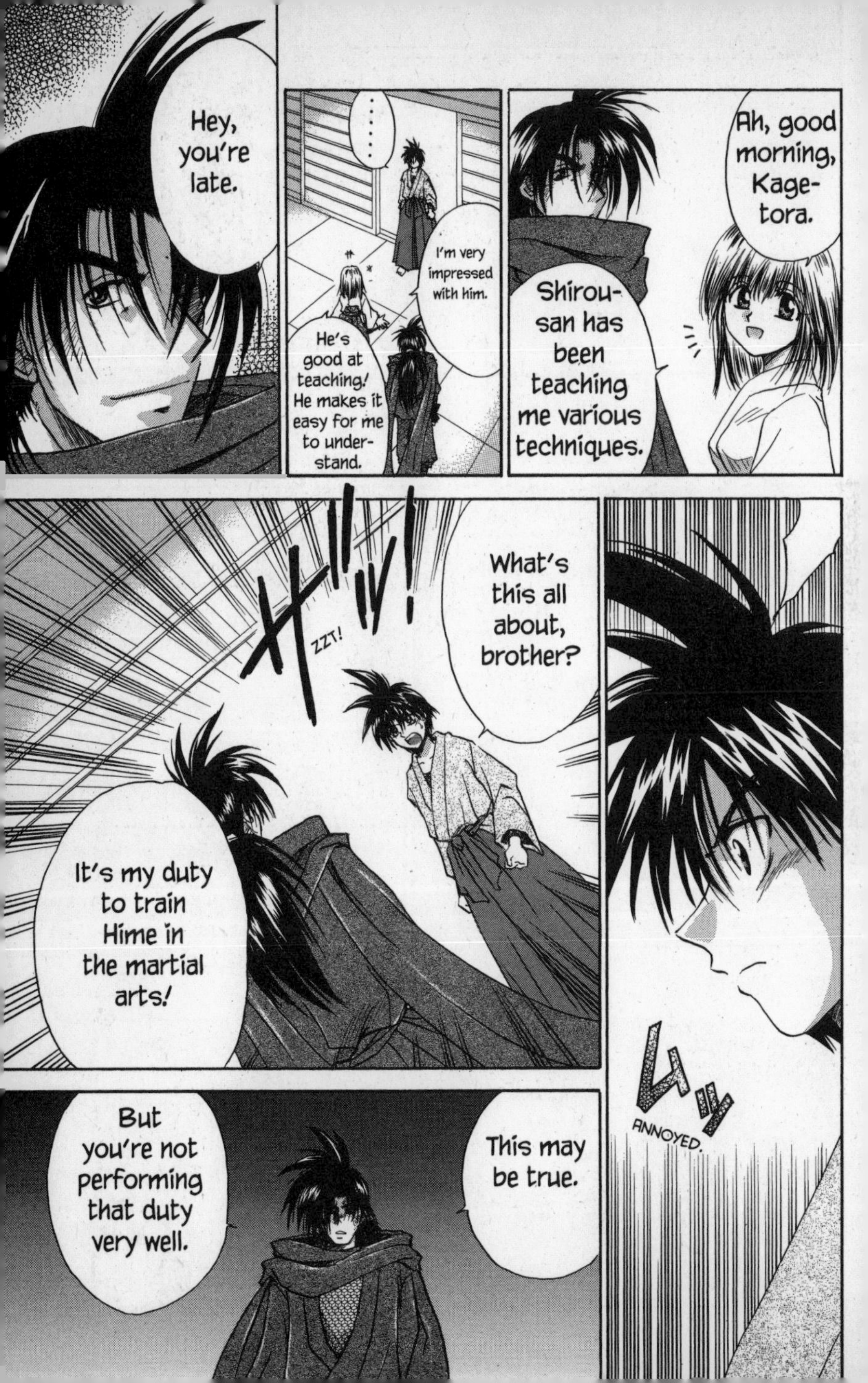

Ah, good morning, Kagetora.
Shirou-san has been teaching me various techniques.
......
I'm very impressed with him.
He's good at teaching! He makes it easy for me to understand.
Hey, you're late.
ANNOYED.
What's this all about, brother?
ZZT!
It's my duty to train Hime in the martial arts!
This may be true.
But you're not performing that duty very well.

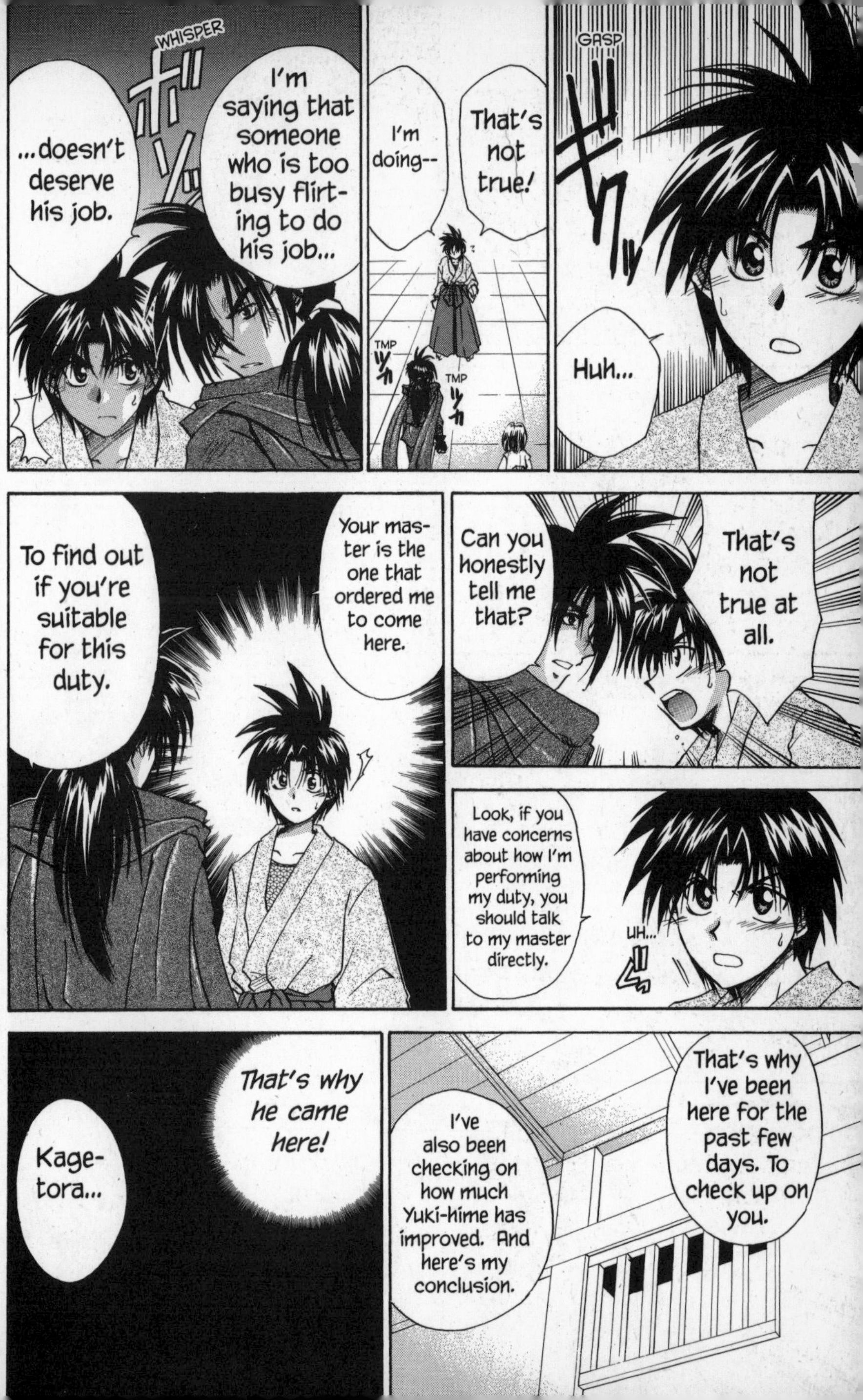
GASP
Huh...
That's not true!
I'm doing--
TMP
TMP
WHISPER
I'm saying that someone who is too busy flirting to do his job...
...doesn't deserve his job.
That's not true at all.
Can you honestly tell me that?
Look, if you have concerns about how I'm performing my duty, you should talk to my master directly.
UH...
Your master is the one that ordered me to come here.
To find out if you're suitable for this duty.
That's why I've been here for the past few days. To check up on you.
I've also been checking on how much Yuki-hime has improved. And here's my conclusion.
That's why he came here!
Kage-tora...

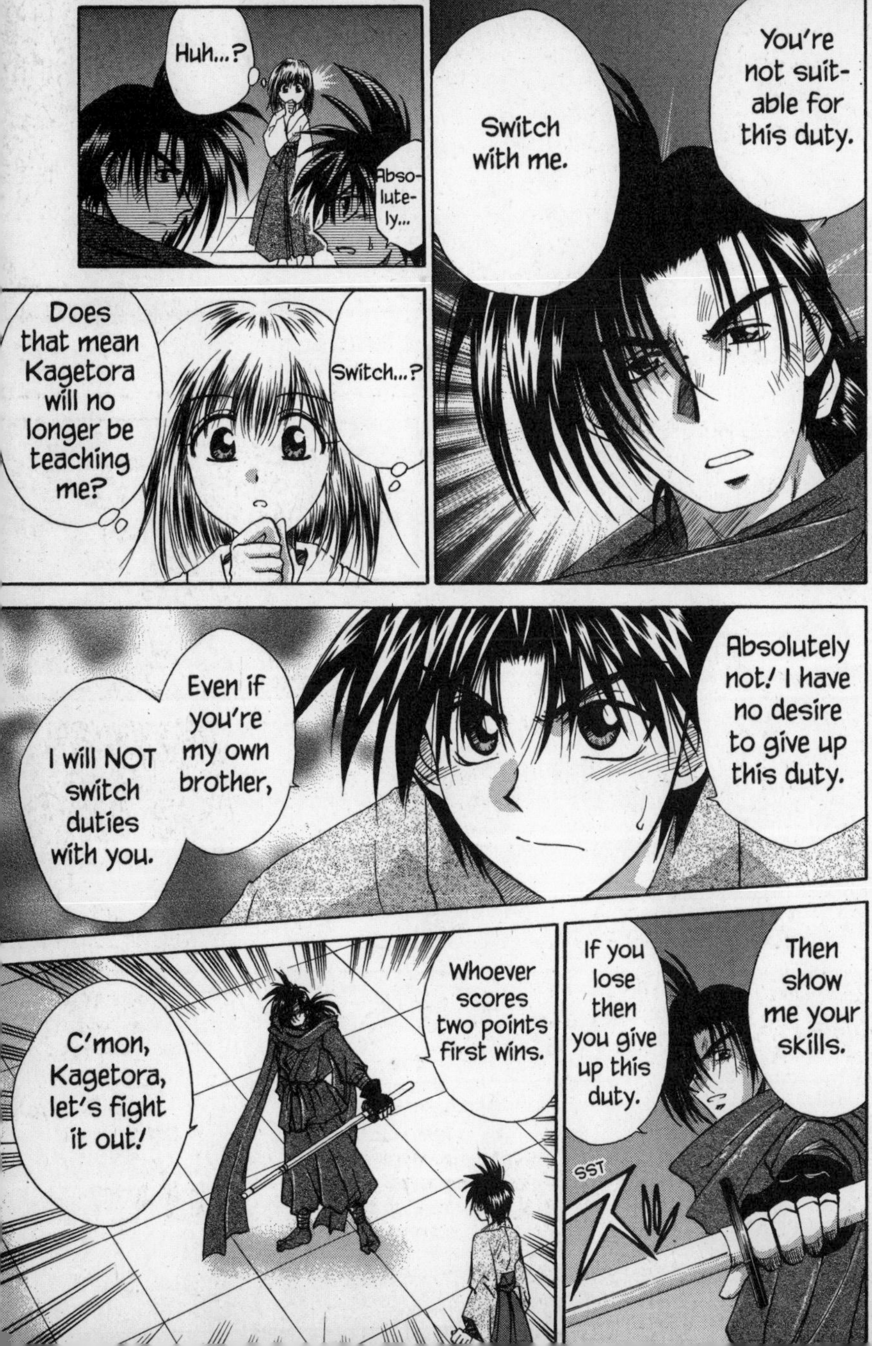
You're not suit-able for this duty.
Switch with me.
Huh...?
Abso-lute-ly...
Switch...?
Does that mean Kagetora will no longer be teaching me?
Absolutely not! I have no desire to give up this duty.
Even if you're my own brother,
I will NOT switch duties with you.
Then show me your skills.
If you lose then you give up this duty.
SST
Whoever scores two points first wins.
C'mon, Kagetora, let's fight it out!

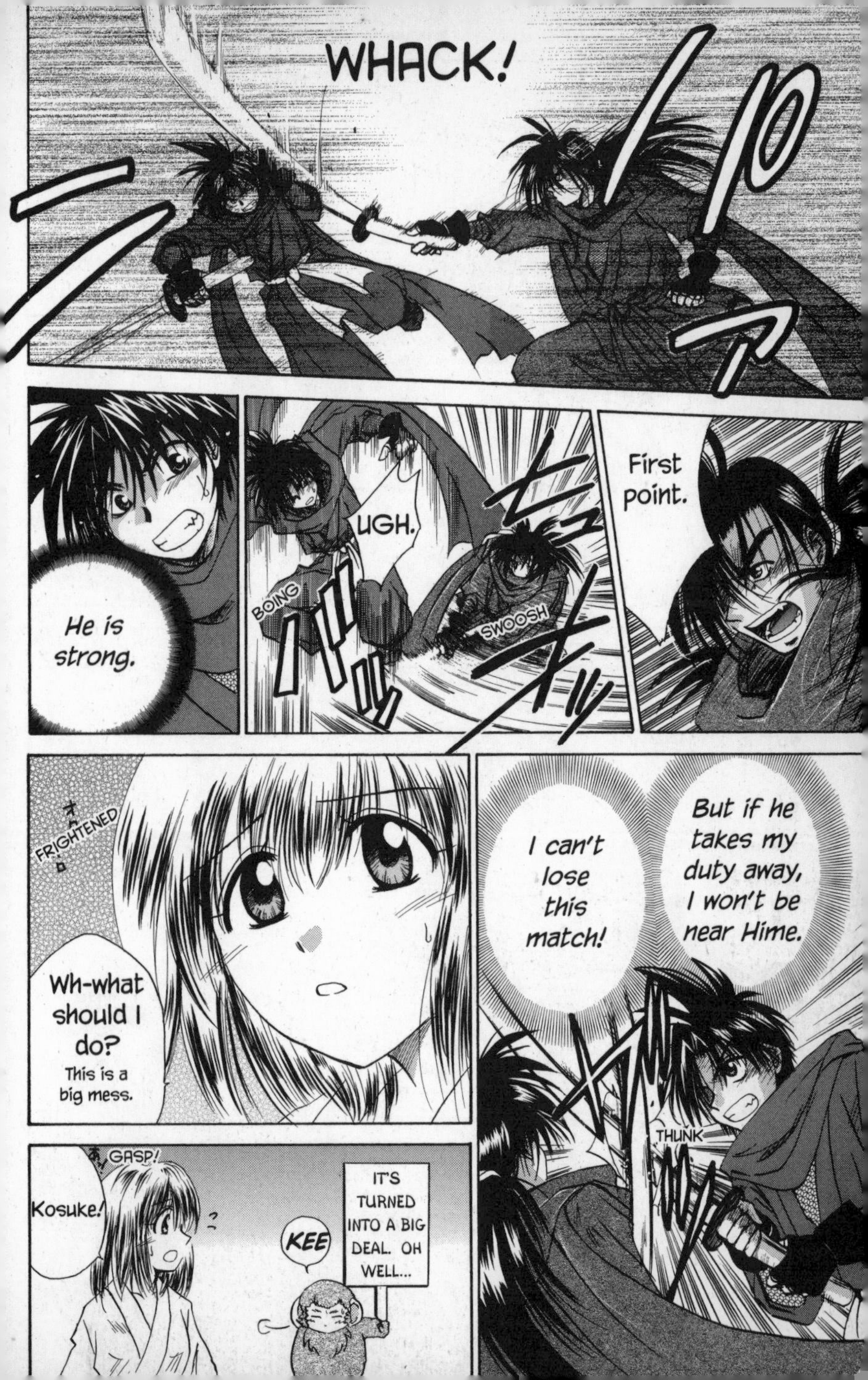
WHACK!
First point.
UGH.
SWOOSH
BOING
He is strong.
But if he takes my duty away, I won't be near Hime.
I can't lose this match!
THUNK
FRIGHTENED
Wh-what should I do?
This is a big mess.
IT'S TURNED INTO A BIG DEAL. OH WELL...
KEE
GASP!
Kosuke!

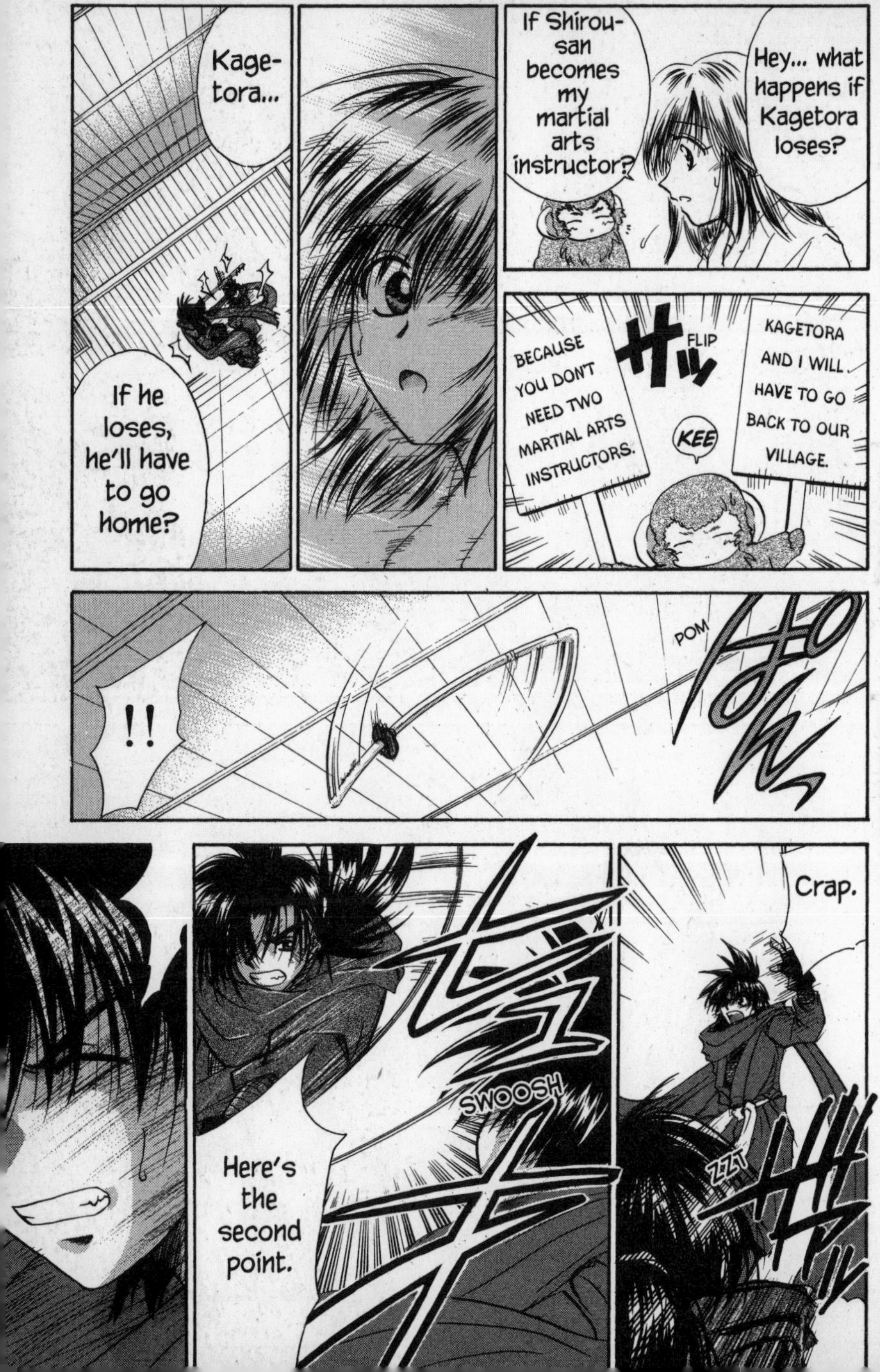
Hey... what happens if Kagetora loses?
If Shirou-san becomes my martial arts instructor?
KAGETORA AND I WILL HAVE TO GO BACK TO OUR VILLAGE.
FLIP
KEE
BECAUSE YOU DON'T NEED TWO MARTIAL ARTS INSTRUCTORS.
Kage-tora...
If he loses, he'll have to go home?
POM
!!
Crap.
ZZZT
SWOOSH
Here's the second point.

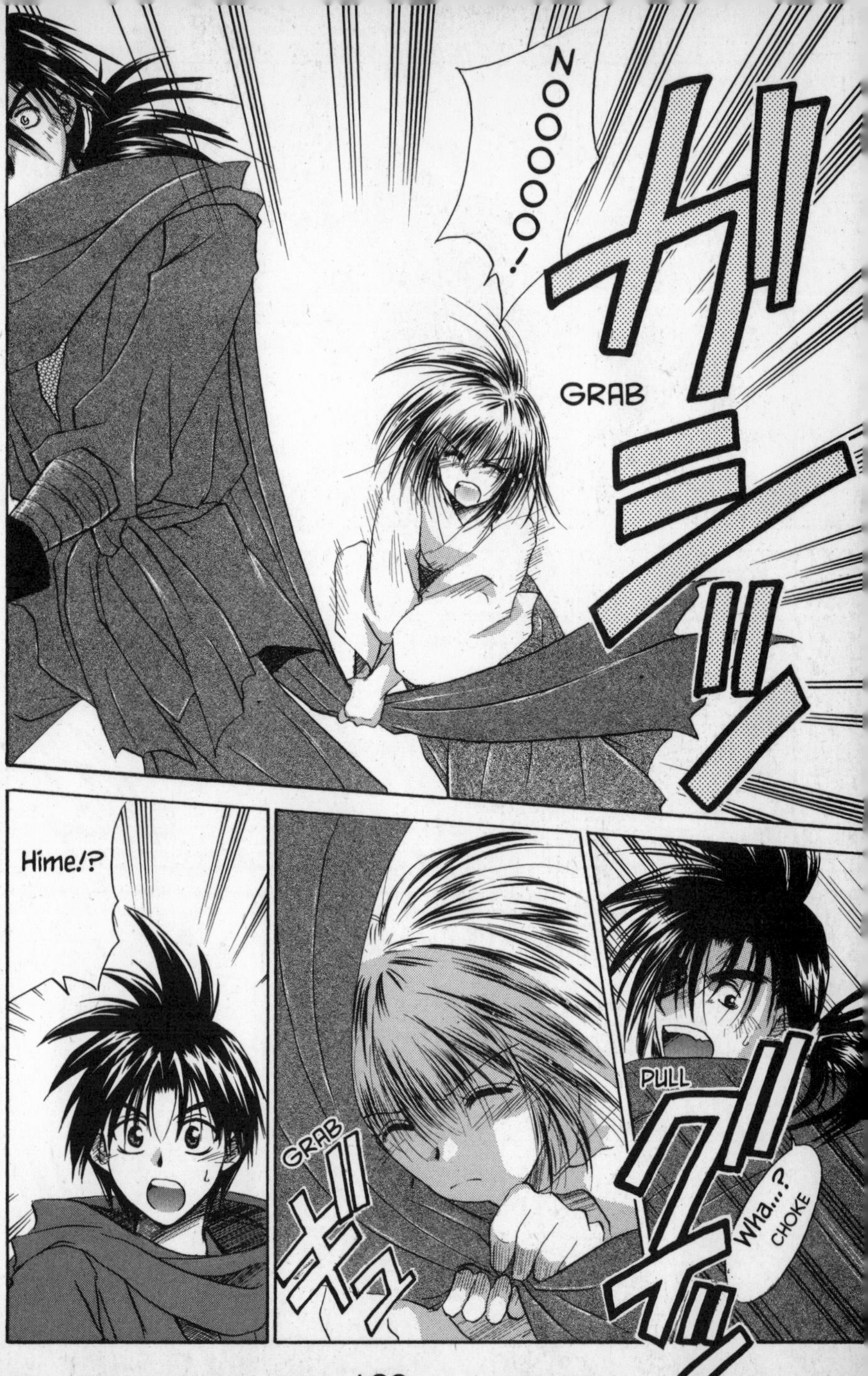
NOOOOOO!
GRAB
PULL
Wha...?
CHOKE
GRAB
Hime!?

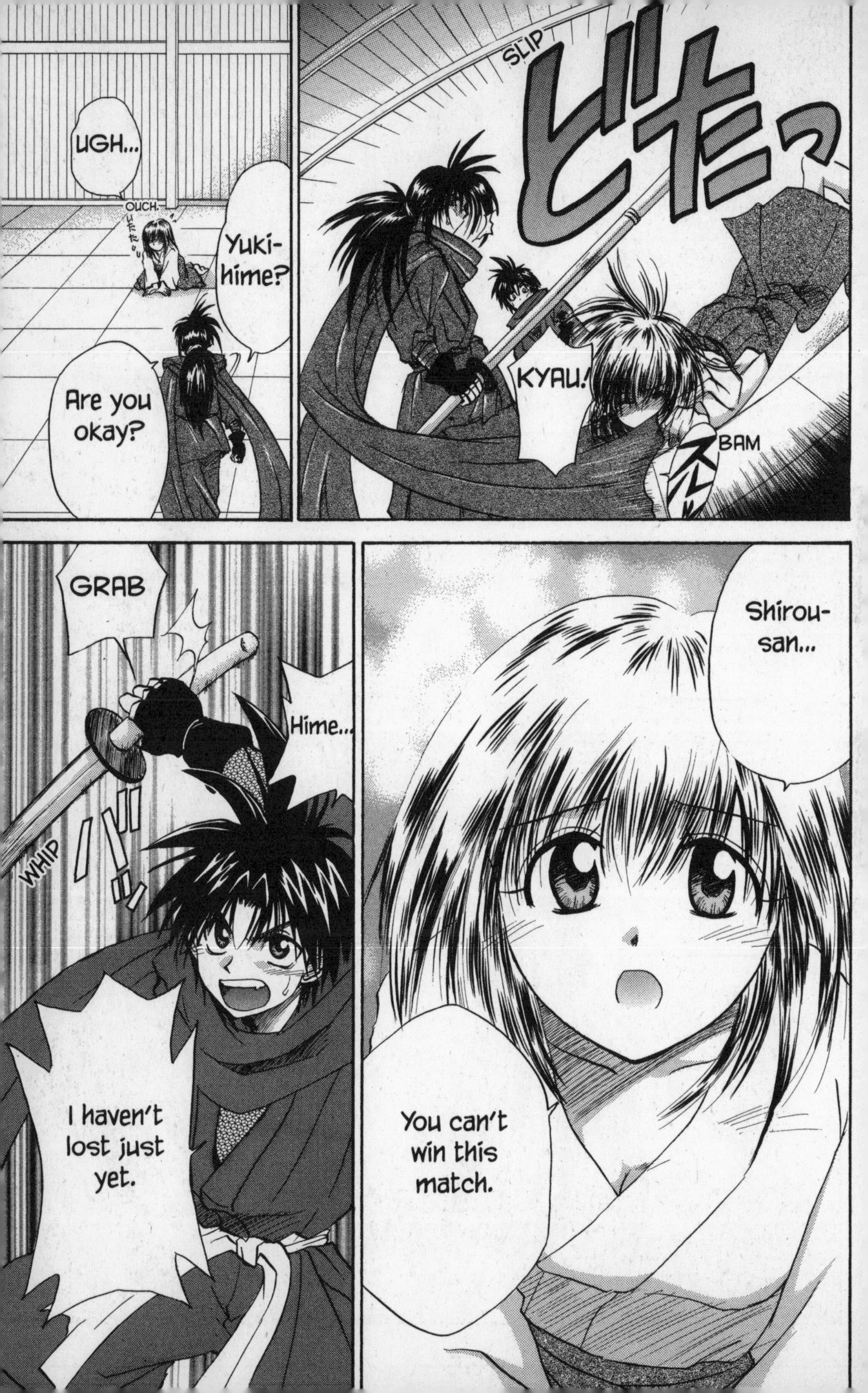
SLIP
どたっ
KYAU!
BAM
UGH...
OUCH
Yuki-hime?
Are you okay?
Shirou-san...
You can't win this match.
GRAB
Hime...
WHIP
I haven't lost just yet.

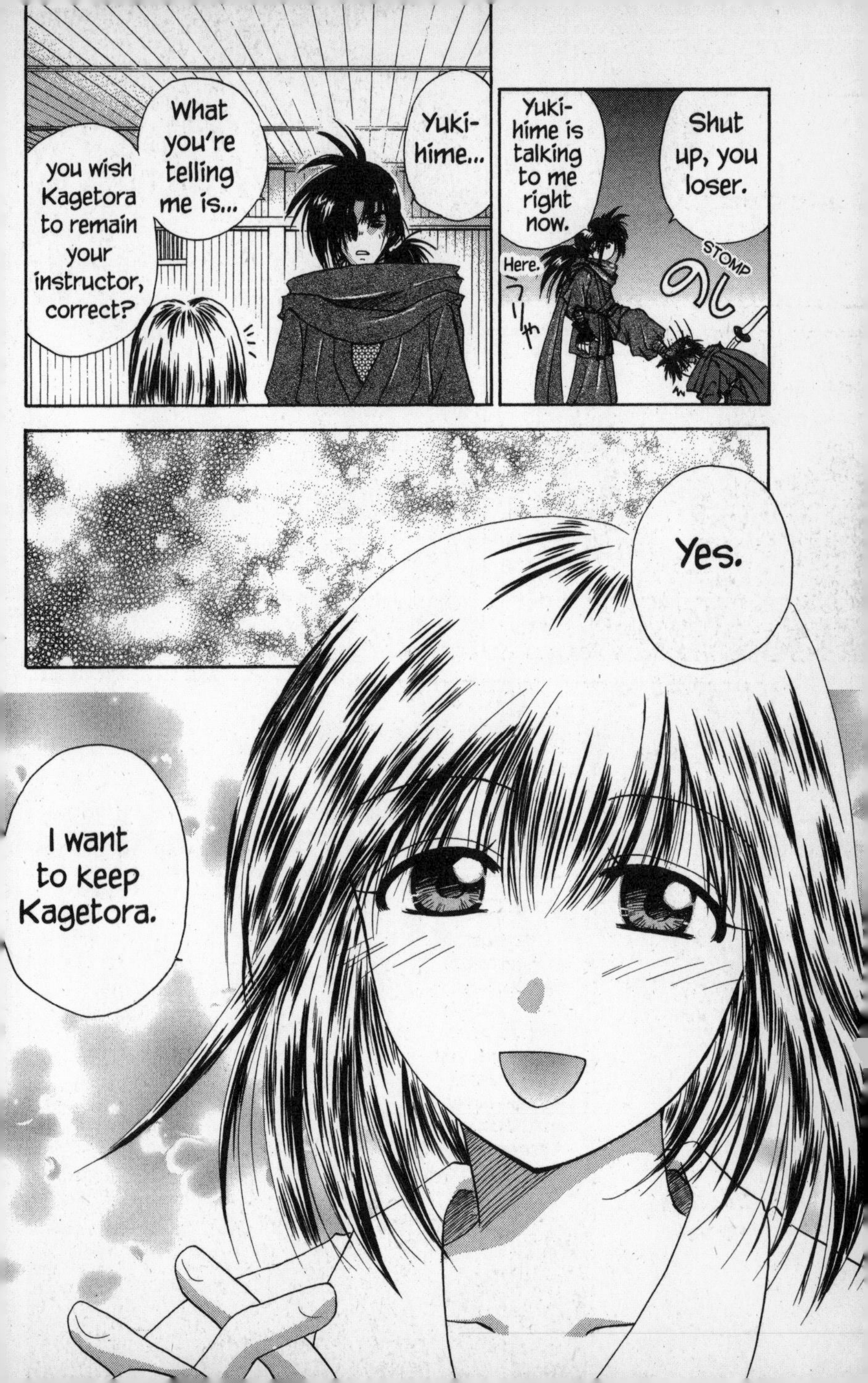
Shut up, you loser.
Yuki-hime is talking to me right now.
STOMP
Here.
Yuki-hime...
What you're telling me is...
you wish Kagetora to remain your instructor, correct?
Yes.
I want to keep Kagetora.

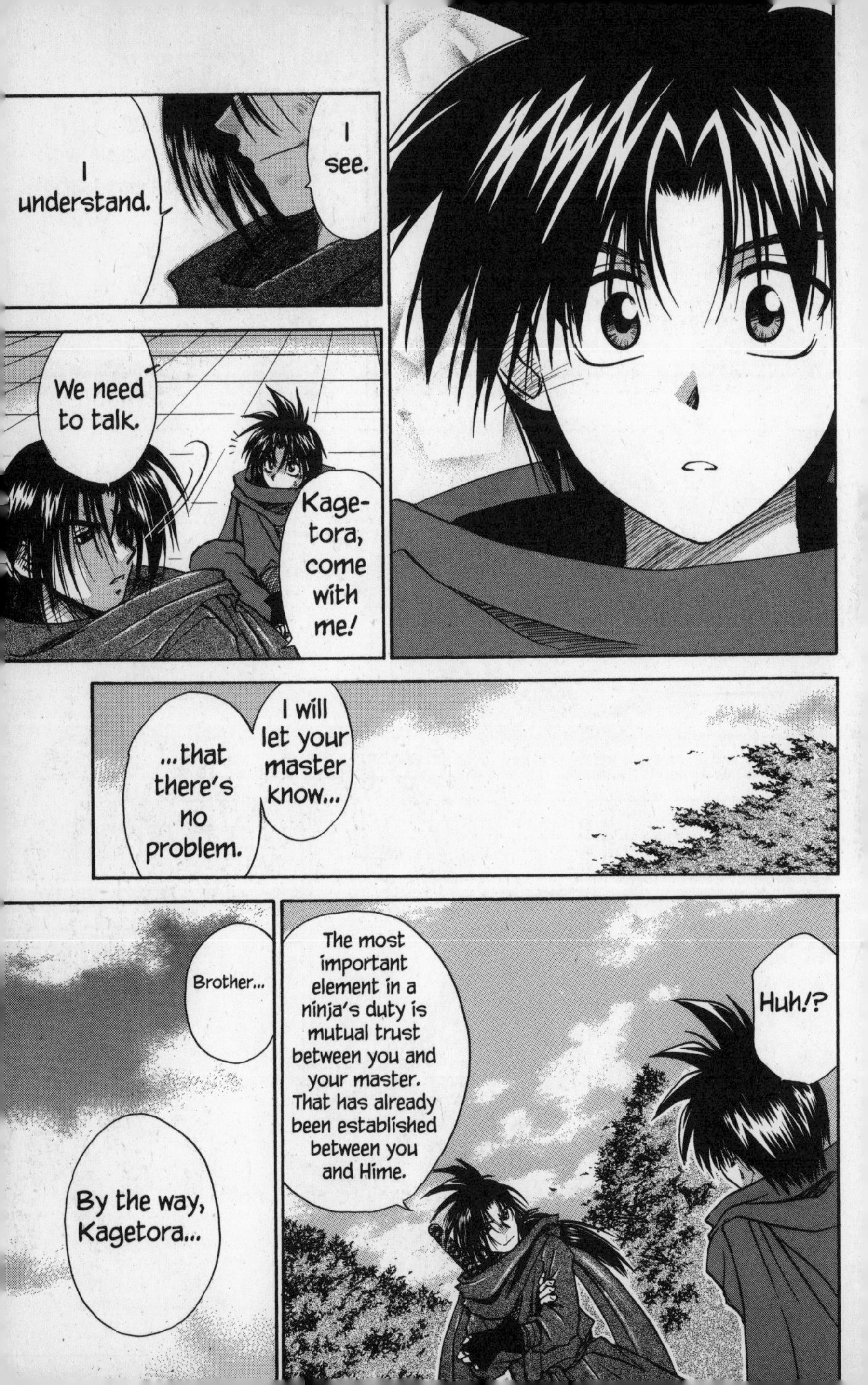
I see.
I understand.
Kagetora, come with me!
We need to talk.
I will let your master know...
...that there's no problem.
Huh!?
The most important element in a ninja's duty is mutual trust between you and your master. That has already been established between you and Hime.
Brother...
By the way, Kagetora...

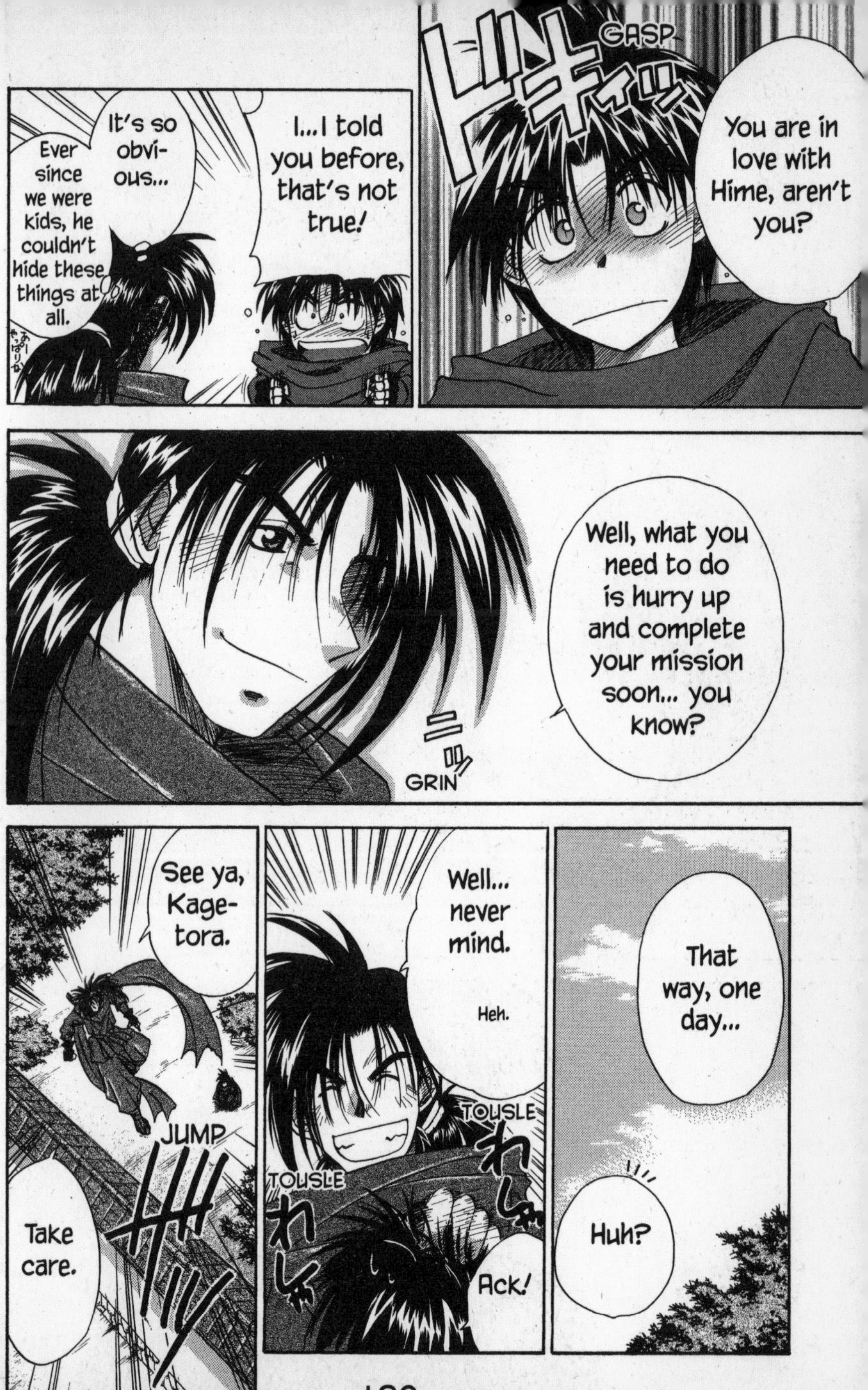
GASP
You are in love with Hime, aren't you?
I...I told you before, that's not true!
It's so obvious...
Ever since we were kids, he couldn't hide these things at all.
Well, what you need to do is hurry up and complete your mission soon... you know?
GRIN
That way, one day...
Huh?
Well... never mind.
Heh.
TOUSLE
TOUSLE
Ack!
See ya, Kage-tora.
JUMP
Take care.

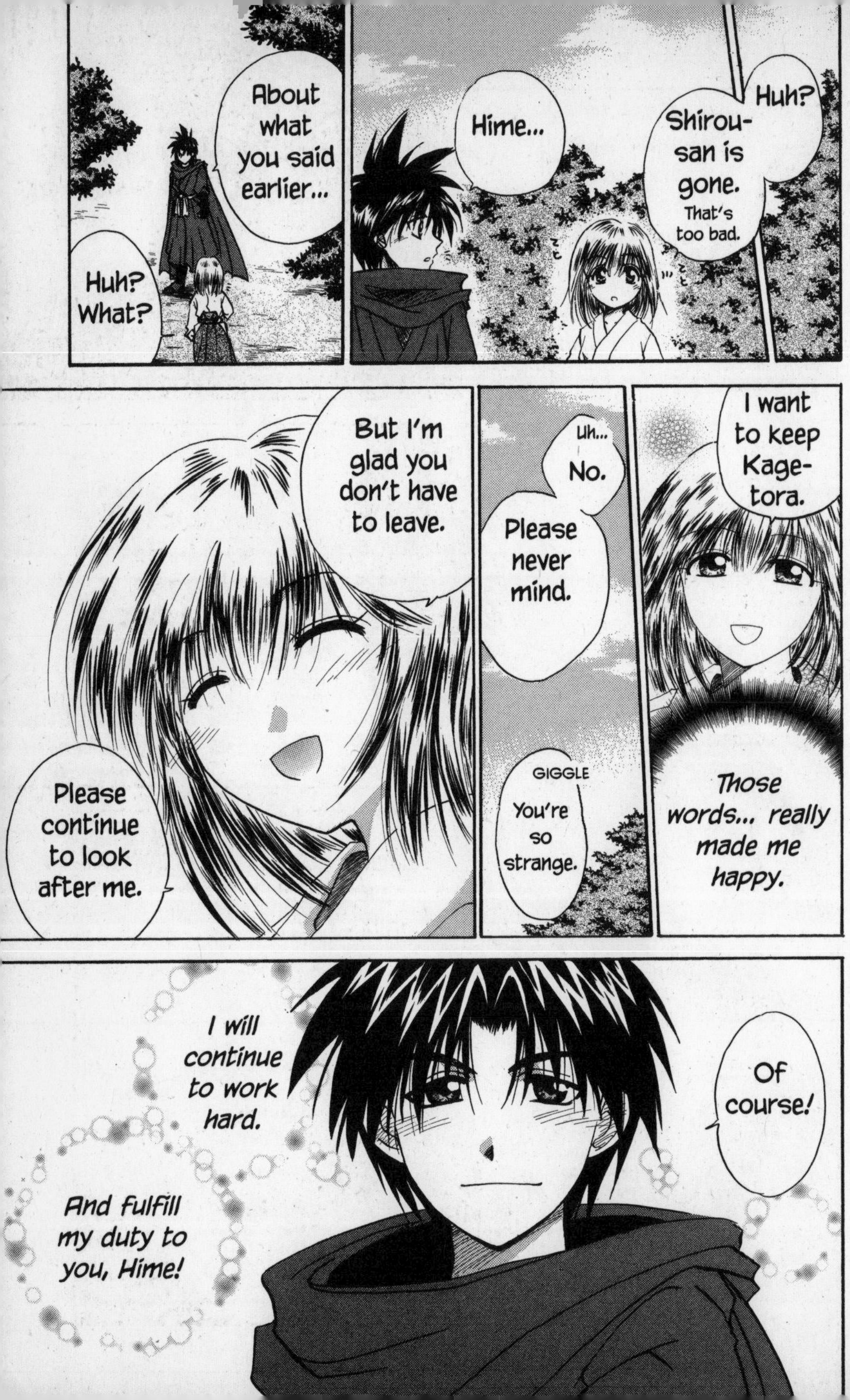
Huh?
Shirou-san is gone.
That's too bad.
Hime...
About what you said earlier...
Huh? What?
I want to keep Kagetora.
Those words... really made me happy.
Uh...
No.
Please never mind.
GIGGLE
You're so strange.
But I'm glad you don't have to leave.
Please continue to look after me.
Of course!
I will continue to work hard.
And fulfill my duty to you, Hime!

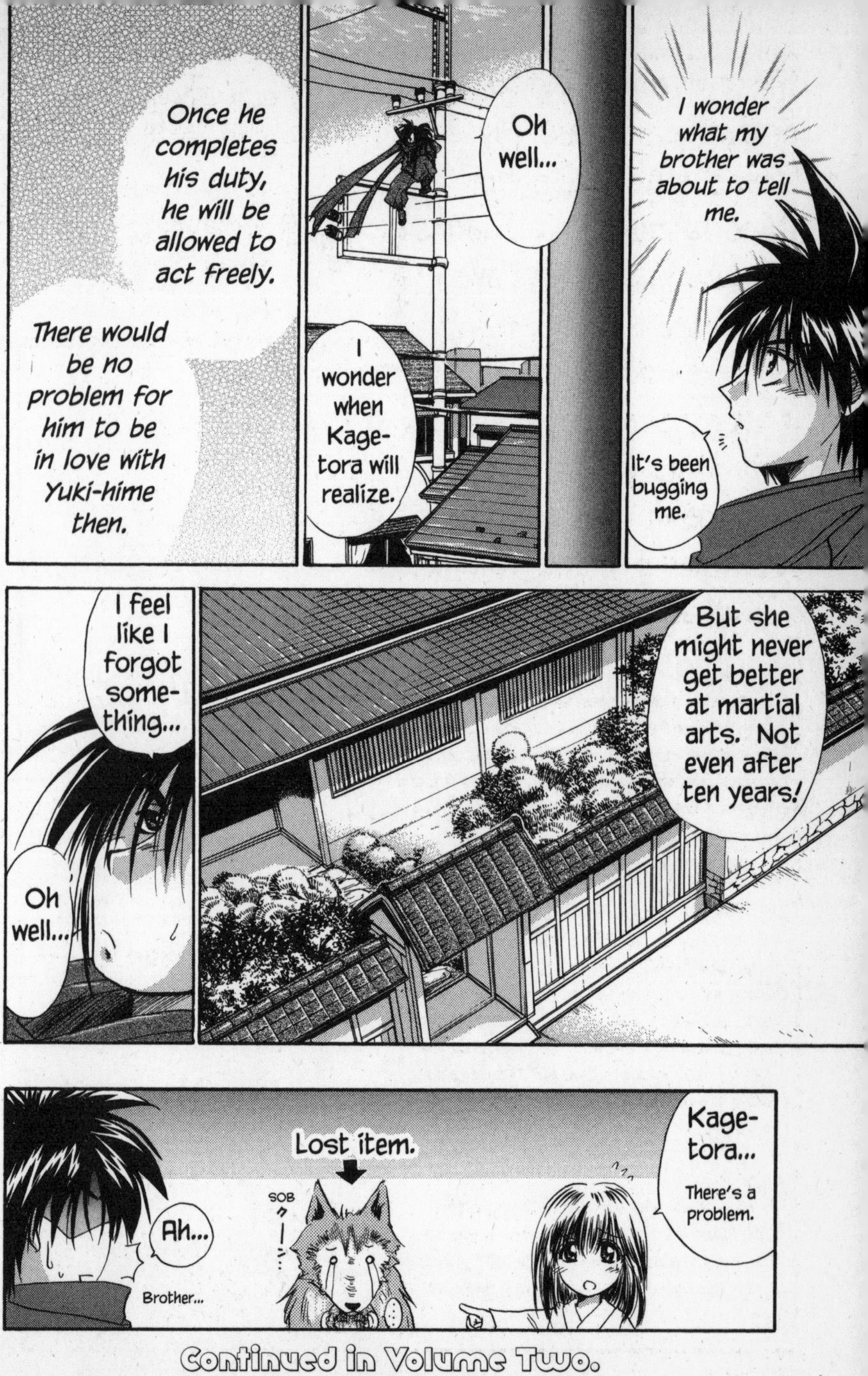
I wonder what my brother was about to tell me.
It's been bugging me.
Oh well...
I wonder when Kage-tora will realize.
Once he completes his duty, he will be allowed to act freely.
There would be no problem for him to be in love with Yuki-hime then.
But she might never get better at martial arts. Not even after ten years!
I feel like I forgot some-thing...
Oh well...
Kage-tora...
There's a problem.
Lost item.
SOB
Ah...
Brother...

Continued in Volume Two.

Extra Page

First of all, I'd like to introduce myself. My name is Akira Segami. Nice to meet you. Thanks to your support, I have managed to publish Volume 1 of Kagetora successfully. I can now say that my sleepless nights were worth it after all. (Although I did travel when I found the time...) Apparently there are some extra pages available at the end of this volume, so I'll write some stuff. Such as gag strips and silly stories... etc.

About Ninjas:
I discovered a strange snack when I went to a ninja village. It's a *Katayaki* (egg-flavored, hard-baked cake). Apparently this portable food was carried by ninjas, but it's super hard! It looks like *Karumeyaki* (Japanese sweet cake) but if you bite on it, worst case scenario, it can destroy your teeth. Seriously. I wonder how ninjas were able to eat them...

About Weapons:
I have many weapons in my office as research materials. Ninja swords, of course, shuriken, *Kunai* (an earth digger), *Makibishi* (caltrops), a samurai sword, and daggers (well, most of them are imitations). Ah, I think there's a common *kanzashi* (an ornamental hairpin), too (laugh). This way, I can fight even if a robber breaks into my office. But there's really nothing that would attract a robber in my office. I'm really broke.

Thank You
For those of you who have been sending letters to me, thank you! Your support is greatly appreciated. I'll work harder to make time to write you back. (S-san, thank you for all your letters. I always read them.)

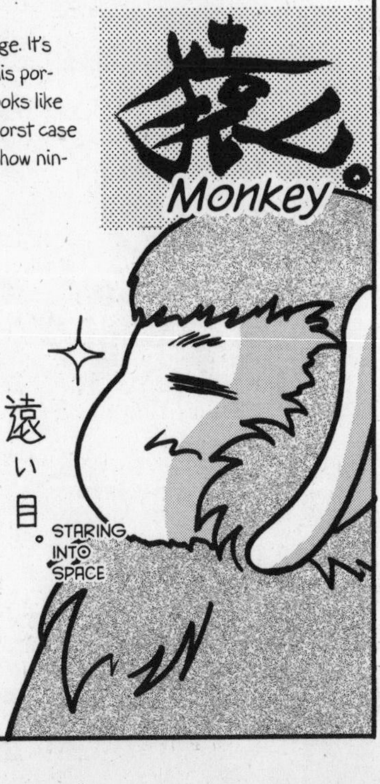
猿。
Monkey
遠い目。
STARING INTO SPACE

Interstitial 1:

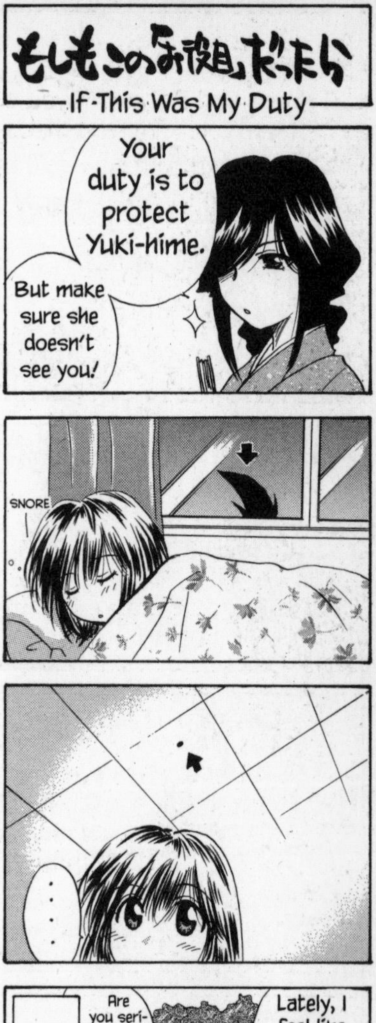
If This Was My Duty
Your duty is to protect Yuki-hime.
But make sure she doesn't see you!
SNORE
...
Lately, I feel like someone's always watching me.
It's creepy.
Are you serious!? I wonder if it's a stalker.
Wow.
There's no chance of romantic success here.

Interstitial 2:

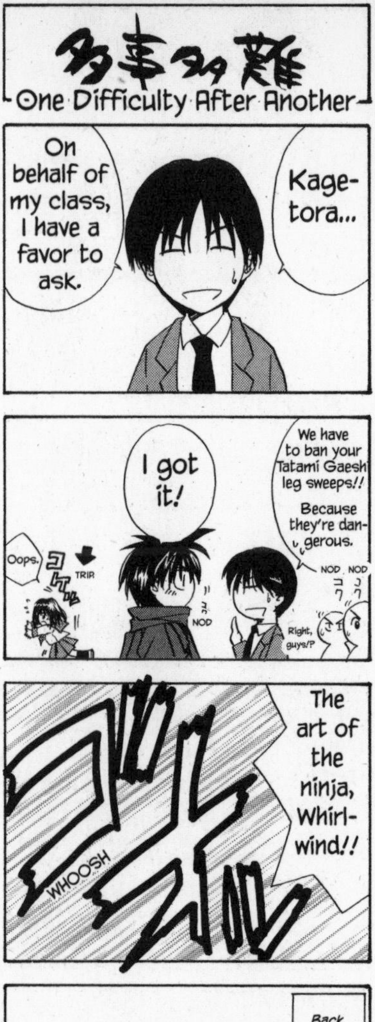
One Difficulty After Another
Kage-tora...
On behalf of my class, I have a favor to ask.
We have to ban your Tatami Gaesh leg sweeps!!
Because they're dangerous.
NOD NOD
Right, guys!?
I got it!
NOD
TRIP
Oops.
The art of the ninja, Whirlwind!!
WHOOSH
Back to the beginning...
Are you okay?
He doesn't get it.
Yes!
We're not okay!

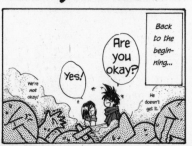

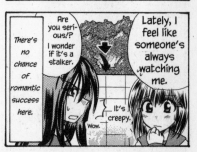

Interstitial 3:

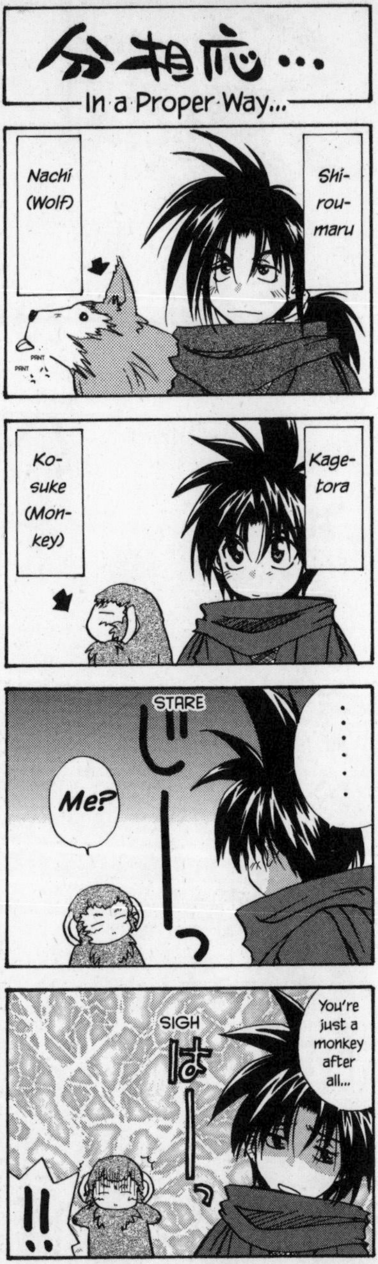
分相応…
In a Proper Way...
Shi-rou-maru
Nachi (Wolf)
PANT PANT
Kage-tora
Ko-suke (Mon-key)
......
STARE
Me?
You're just a monkey after all...
SIGH
!!

Interstitial 4:

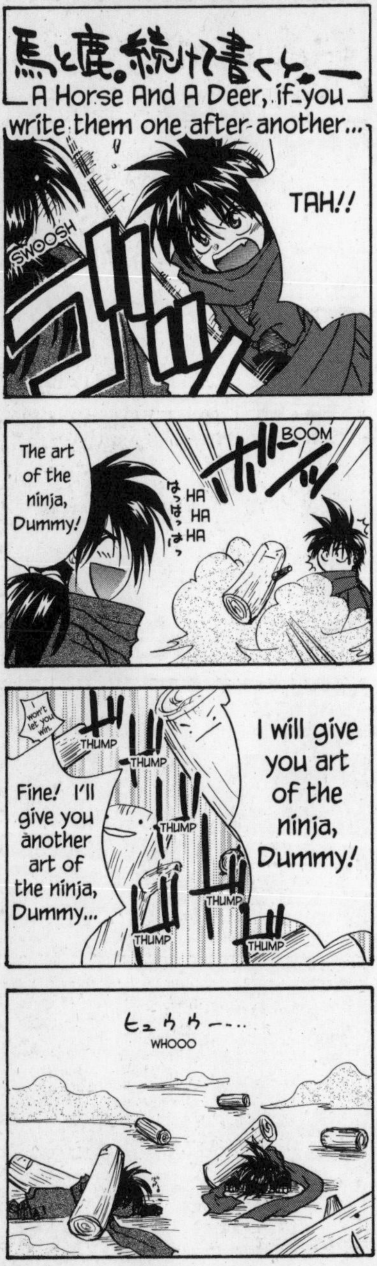
A Horse And A Deer, if you write them one after another...
TAH!!
SWOOSH
BOOM
The art of the ninja, Dummy!
HA HA HA
I will give you art of the ninja, Dummy!
Fine! I'll give you another art of the ninja, Dummy...
I won't let you win.
THUMP
THUMP
THUMP
THUMP
THUMP
WHOOO

Special Thanks

マシスタント・田中亮二 くん
Assistants: Ryouji Tanaka

大島 真弓 ちゃん
Mayumi Ooshima

担当
Editors:

森田氏
Mr. Morita

松木氏
Mr. Matsuki

コミックス担当
Comic editor:

法土さん
Hatto (Norito) -san

家族・猫・友人...etc.
Family, Cat, Friends... etc.

同居リスのトラ (笑)
A squirrel named Tora that lives with me (laugh)

読者の皆様
My fans

兎にも角にも 大感謝!!
Thanks to

the rabbit and Tsuno (horn)!!

風雷忍者。
Wind and Thunder Ninja.

Translation Notes

Japanese is a tricky language for most Westerners, and translation is often more art than science. For your edification and reading pleasure, here are notes on some of the places where we could have gone in a different direction in our translation of the work, or where a Japanese cultural reference is used.

Page 13, *Oyakume*

Oyakume translates as "a duty."

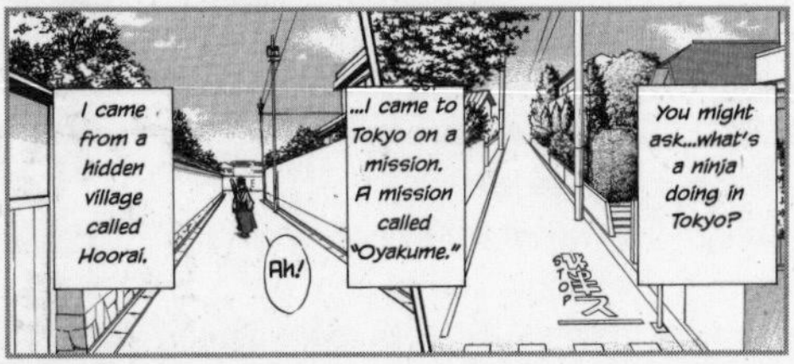
You might ask...what's a ninja doing in Tokyo?
...I came to Tokyo on a mission. A mission called "Oyakume."
Ah!
I came from a hidden village called Hoorai.

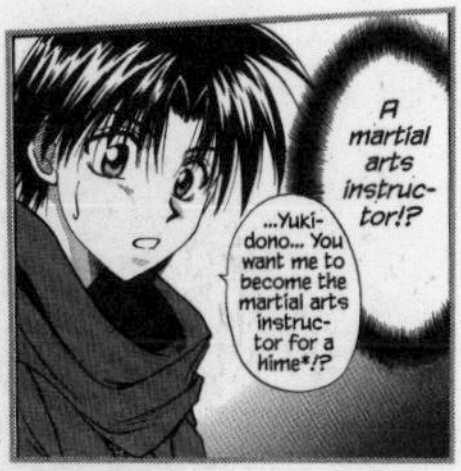
A martial arts instructor!?
...Yuki-dono... You want me to become the martial arts instructor for a hime*!?

Page 15, *Hime*

Literal translation of the word *"hime"* is a princess in Japanese. *Hime* can also be used as an honorific for a daughter of a high-class family. In this story, Kagetora refers to Yuki as a *hime,* as she's the daughter of a respected master of the martial arts, and from an honorable family.

Page 27, New Student Introduction at Japanese Schools

In the original manga, the teacher drew the character, *Kaze*— which means wind, as a part of Kagetora's last name, *Kazama.* In Japanese schools, when the new student is introduced to the class for the first time, it's common for the teacher to write down the student's name on the blackboard.

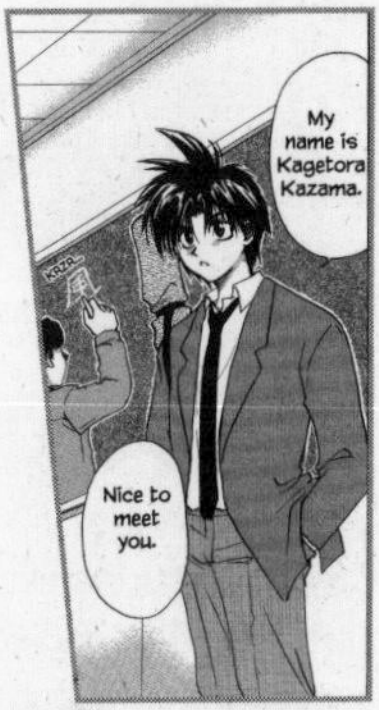
My name is Kagetora Kazama.
Nice to meet you.

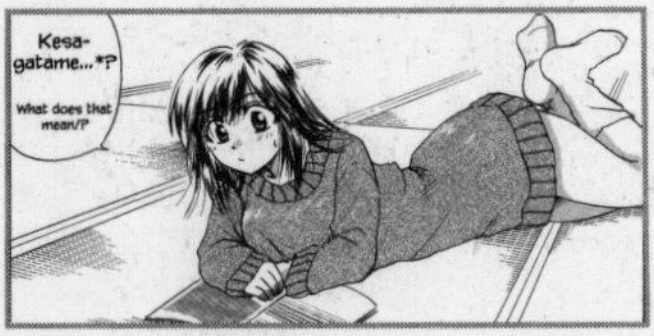
Kesa-gatame...*?
What does that mean/?

Page 33, *Kesa-gatame*

Kesa-gatame, the "scarf" hold, is a technique in Judo. It's a way of holding the opponent by the edge (the so-called scarf) of his jacket in an attempt to immobilize him.

Page 33, Judo

Judo (which literally means the way of gentleness) is a well-known Japanese sport, and was introduced in 1882 by Dr. Jigoro Kano, using principles of movement and balance. It is practiced as a sport or form of physical exercise. Judo is commonly taught in gym class at Japanese schools.

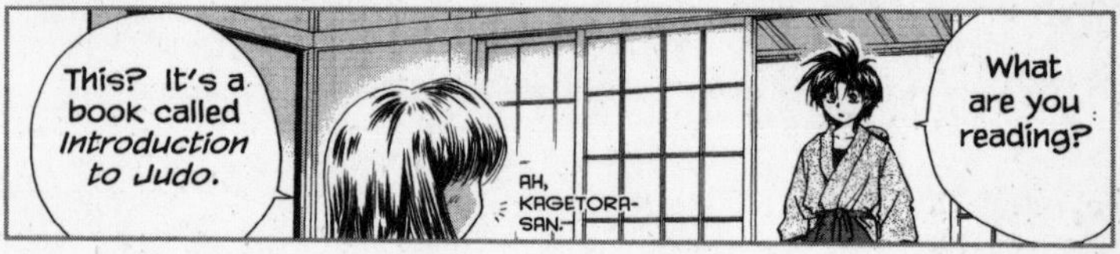
What are you reading?
AH, KAGETORA-SAN.
This? It's a book called *Introduction to Judo.*

Page 40, *Kendo*

Kendo, the way of the sword, is the art of Japanese swordsmanship. Its origin comes from Budo, the Martial way. *Kendo* is one of the most popular sports taught at Japanese schools, along with Judo.

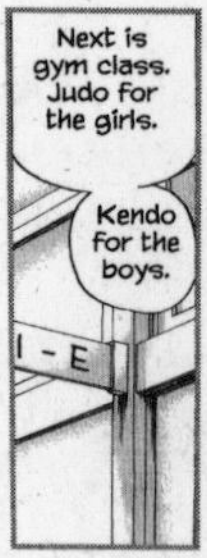
Next is gym class. Judo for the girls.
Kendo for the boys.
1-E

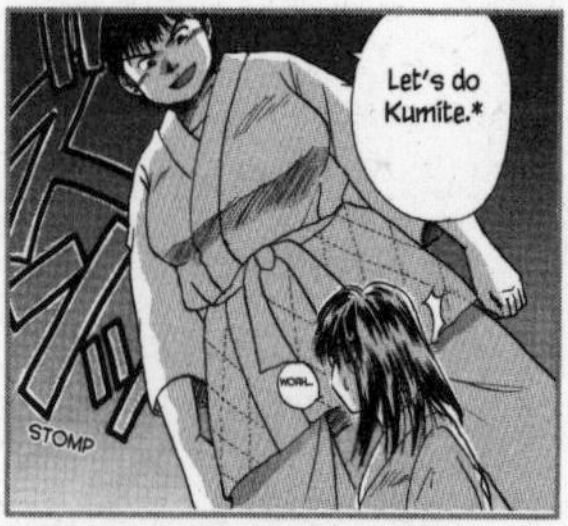
Let's do Kumite.*
STOMP

Page 42, *Kumite*

Kumite means Judo sparring.

Page 67, Journal, Day Duty

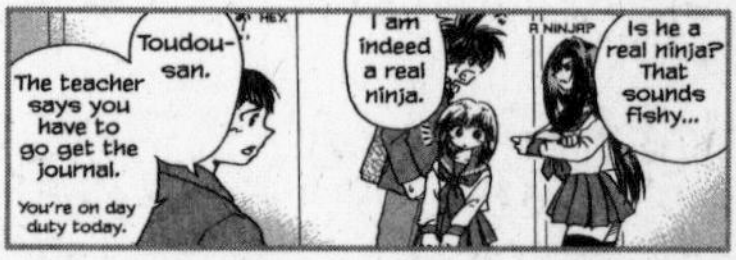
Is he a real ninja? That sounds fishy...
A NINJA?
I am indeed a real ninja.
HEY.
Toudou-san.
The teacher says you have to go get the journal.
You're on day duty today.

In Japanese classes, the journal is a daily record of the class activities. Day duty is a tradition in Japanese schools where students take turns assisting their teacher. The duties include picking up the class journal and keeping it for the day, as well as cleaning the blackboard and other such tasks.

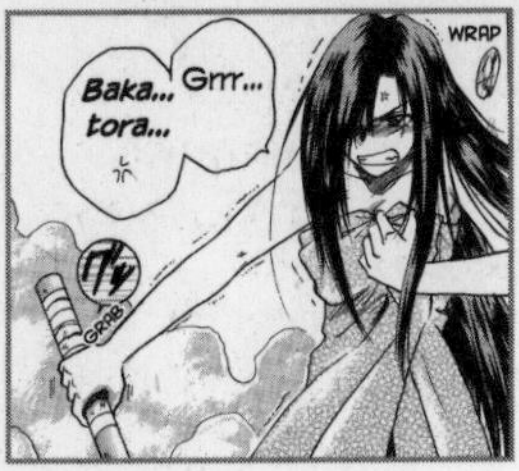
WRAP
Grrr...
Baka... tora...
GRAB

Page 79, *Bakatora*

Baka means "dumb" or "stupid."

Page 82, *Okayu*

Okayu is rice porridge. It is easy to digest and easy to eat. For this reason, in Japan it is common to eat *okayu* when you have a stomach ache or a cold. Depending on your appetite, scallops, eggs, boiled chicken, or shrimp are often added. In China, *okayu* is often served for breakfast.

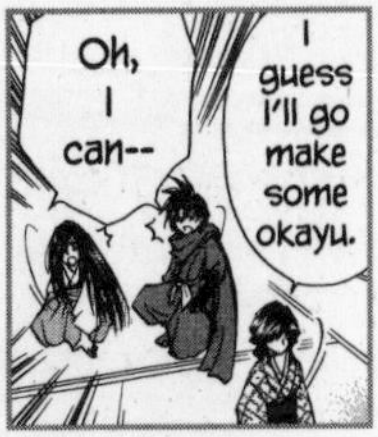
I guess I'll go make some okayu.
Oh, I can--

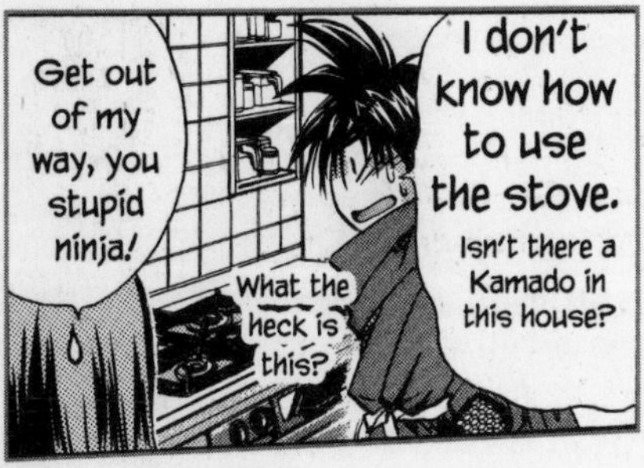
I don't know how to use the stove.
Isn't there a Kamado in this house?
What the heck is this?
Get out of my way, you stupid ninja!

Page 83, *Kamado*

A *Kamado* is a cooking range, constructed primarily of earth or clay. A *Kamado* was one of the two basic forms of domestic cooking appliances used in pre-modern Japan. Kagetora, being a ninja from the historical village Hoorai, is familiar with the *Kamado,* and doesn't know how to use a gas stove.

Page 131, *Hanare*

Hanare is a detached building, separate from the main building in classical Japanese homes. Usually farm machines and implements are kept inside the *Hanare.*

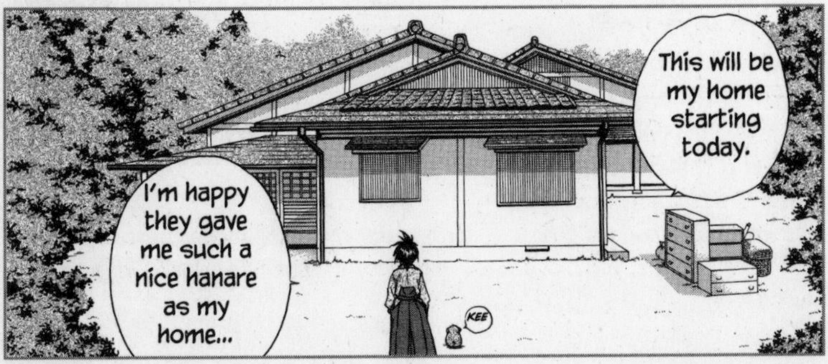
This will be my home starting today.
I'm happy they gave me such a nice hanare as my home...
KEE

Page 163, *mehn*

Men is a shout used in Kendo. This was the word in the Japanese version of this manga. However, since "men" is a word in English, the phonetic spelling, mehn, was used to distinguish the term.

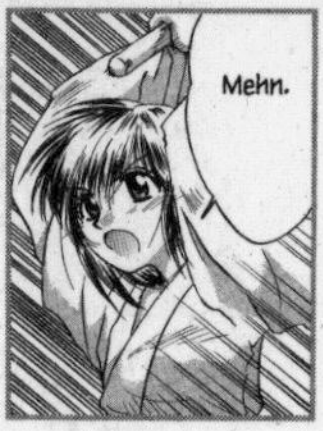
Mehn.

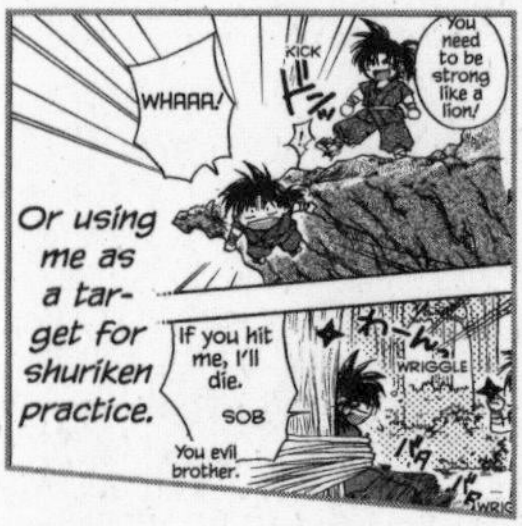
You need to be strong like a lion!
KICK
WHAAA!
Or using me as a target for shuriken practice.
WRIGGLE
If you hit me, I'll die.
SOB
You evil brother.

Page 171, *Shuriken*

A *Shuriken* is a throwing blade, often used by ninjas and sometimes by samurais. The most common are *hira shuriken,* throwing blades with multiple points, sometimes called Throwing Stars by Americans. Contrary to popular cultural representations in comic books and video games, *shuriken* were used as a distraction or tactical weapon, rather than as a primary weapon.

Page 178, *Kata*

Kata are styles of Karate.

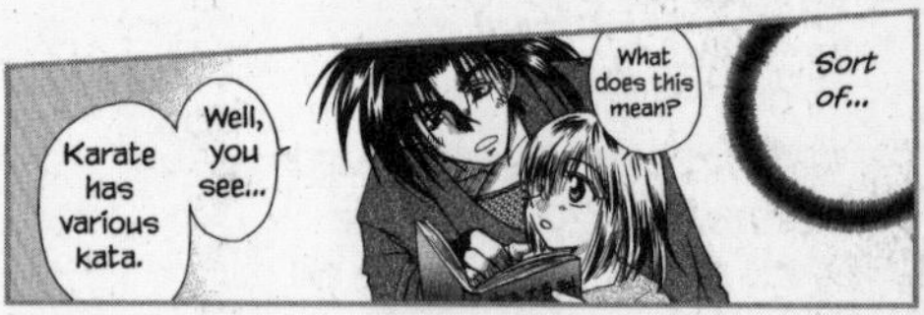
Sort of...
What does this mean?
Well, you see...
Karate has various kata.

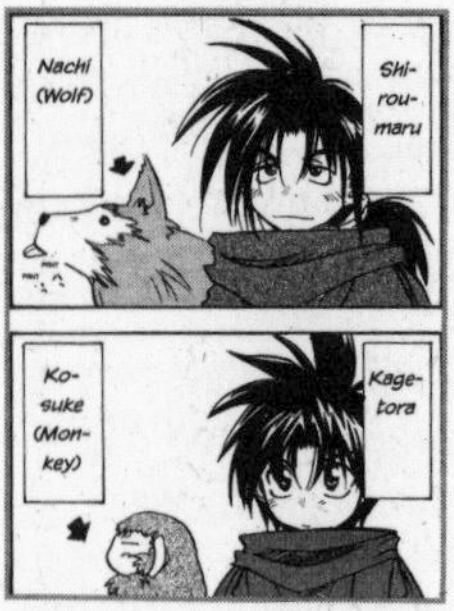
Shi-rou-maru
Nachi (Wolf)
Kage-tora
Ko-suke (Mon-key)

Page 195, Rou and Tora

The character *Rou* in the name Shirou means wolf. The character *Tora* in the name Kagetora means tiger. The joke is that Shirou, whose name includes wolf, has a wolf. But Kagetora, whose name includes tiger, has a monkey.

Page 195, Horse and Deer

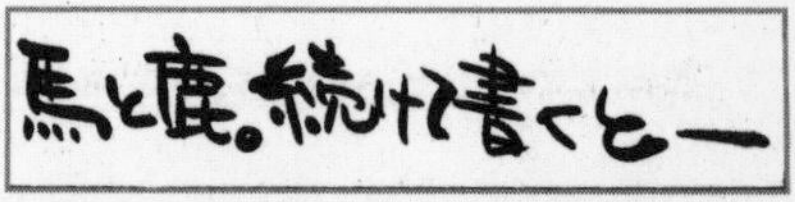
馬と鹿。続けて書くと一

The title of the interstitial is a *horse* and *deer* if you write both characters one after another. If you write the Japanese character for horse and the Japanese character for deer back to back, you make the word "idiot." So the title is just a long way of saying Idiot.